Autumn
on the farm

by Jillian Powell

WAYLAND

Titles in the series

Summer on the farm
Autumn on the farm
Winter on the farm
Spring on the farm

Picture Acknowledgements

The publishers would like to thank the following for allowing their photographs to be reproduced in this book: Agripicture: Peter Dean 19; Cephas Picture Library *title page* (Mick Rock), 7 top (Lance Smith), 12, 13 top (Frank B. Higham), 13 bottom (Nigel Blythe) 17 (Frank B Higham); Bruce Coleman Ltd 14 (Graham Jennings), 15 bottom, 16 bottom (Gordon Langsbury), 18 (Julie Fryer); Eye Ubiquitous 5 bottom (David Nunn); Farmers Weekly Picture Library 10 top, 19; Frank Lane Picture Agency 5 top (Ray F. Bird), 6 (D Dugan), 7 bottom (Silvestris), 9 (Peter Dean), 23 top (R.P. Lawrence), 27 top (P Reynolds), 27 bottom (D.T. Grewcock); The Hutchison Library 26 (Jeremy Hall); Natural History Photographic Agency 4 (G I Bernard), 10 bottom (Patrick Fagot), 12 (Brian Hawkes), 15 top (David Tomlinson), 16 top (Roger Tidman), 20 (David Woodfall), 22 (Manfred Danegger),23 bottom (David Tomlinson), 24 (William Paton), 25 top (E.A. Janes), 25 bottom (G I Bernard); Oxford Scientific Films Ltd 8 (G.A. Maclean), 15 top (Harold Taylor), 16 bottom (Tony Tilford), 17 (David Cayless); Tony Stone Worldwide *front cover* (Hugh Sitton), *back cover* (David Austen); Survival Anglia 11 top (Ton Nyssen); Wayland Picture Library 11 bottom, 16 top, 21 (both), 28, 29, 30 (both), 31 (both).

Series editor: Francesca Motisi
Book editor: Joan Walters
Series and book designer: Jean Wheeler

First published in 1996 by
Wayland (Publishers) Limited
61, Western Road, Hove
East Sussex, BN3 1JD England

© Copyright 1996 Wayland (Publishers) Limited

British Cataloguing in Publication Data
Powell, Jillian
Autumn on the farm. - (The farming year)
1. Agriculture - Juvenile literature 2. Autumn - Juvenile literature
I. Title II. Series
630

ISBN 0-7502-1733-2

Typeset by Jean Wheeler
Printed and bound by G. Canale and C.S.p.A., Turin, Italy

Contents

Introduction

Autumn is a season of changes.
Every day the sun rises a little later
and sets a little earlier, so the days
begin to get shorter.

Some days are warm and sunny.
Other days bring wind and rain.
At night it may be cold enough
for frost.

Heavy rain, wind and frost can spoil crops. The farmer must harvest and store the crops before the bad weather comes.

The farmer must also make sure there is plenty of food for the farm animals during the cold autumn and winter months, when the grass stops growing. Hay is stored for winter feed.

Harvesting root crops

By the autumn, potatoes and sugar beet have grown big enough to harvest. These are called root crops because we eat the roots of the plants.

The farmer uses a special machine called a root crop harvester. It lifts the plants out of the ground and shakes the earth off them.

The vegetables fall into a trailer and are taken back to the farm. The potatoes will be sold in supermarkets and other shops.

Sugar beet (right) will be taken to factories where machines take the sugar from the roots.

Harvesting the maize crop

Maize is ripe and ready to harvest in the autumn. It is grown for people and animals to eat. There are different types of maize. We eat it as cornflakes and popcorn.

Sweetcorn is a crop which is very like maize. Here, sweetcorn cobs are being harvested.

Another type of maize is made into a food
called silage, to feed to animals during the
winter months.

The farmer harvests maize for silage using
a machine called a forage harvester. It cuts
the plants and then chops up the leaves,
stems and cobs into small pieces. It is taken
back to the farmyard in a trailer to be stored.

The fruit harvest

Sunshine helps the fruit trees make sugar in the fruits, so they become sweet and ripe.

Fruits like apples (right), pears and plums (below) are ready to be picked in the autumn.

We can tell when a fruit is ripe because it changes colour.

Fruit has to be picked carefully. Some fruit farms have special fruit-picking machines which gently knock the fruit off the trees.

On small farms, farm workers pick the fruit by hand. The fruit is carried back to the farm in a trailer.

The fruit is sorted into sizes and stored in big trays. Any fruit which is not perfect is taken out and sent off to be made into fruit juice.

All the good fruit is stored in cold, dry sheds. This is so it will not go bad before it is taken by lorry to fruit and vegetable markets.

Harvesting hops

Hops are climbing plants which grow along posts and wires. The flowers from hops are used to give beer its special bitter taste and to help it keep longer.

At harvest time, the farmer cuts the strings holding the hop plants so that they fall into a trailer.

The hops are taken to a harvesting machine which picks the hops away from the stems and leaves.

The hops are taken to a special building called an oast house, where they are stored and left to dry.

Autumn ploughing

As soon as the harvest is over, the farmer starts thinking about the next crop. The first job is to prepare the fields using a tractor pulling a plough. This turns over the earth and buries all the stubbly straw left after the harvest. The straw stubble and weeds rot back into the earth and make more food for next year's crops.

The farmer then fixes a tool called a harrow to the tractor. A harrow has big teeth to break up the earth and make it ready for sowing new seeds.

Sometimes the farmer spreads animal manure over the fields before ploughing. It is full of goodness and food for plants.

Now the fields are ready for the farmer to sow wheat, barley or oats for harvest next summer.

15

Cutting hedges

Hedges grow between fields of different crops. They also stop farm animals from getting out of the fields.

Hedges give shade and shelter to animals all year, and protect crops from wind, rain and snow.

Hedges also provide a home for wild animals, birds and insects.

If the farmer waits until late autumn before cutting the hedges, there will be hedgerow fruits and seeds which birds and animals can eat.

This tractor carries a hedge cutter which has strong metal teeth to cut back the branches. Cutting hedges helps them grow thick and strong.

Making silage

In autumn the farmer must plan ahead so that the farm animals will have plenty to eat when there is no fresh grass. The grass will stop growing as the days get shorter and the weather gets colder.

The farmer cuts the grass to make a food for the winter called silage. The grass is cut and sucked up by a machine called a forage harvester.

The grass is gathered and wrapped tightly in black plastic so no light or air can get in. This keeps it soft and juicy. Some big farms have tall buildings for making silage called silos. You may see silage stored on a farm under black plastic with old car tyres on top.

Beef and dairy farming

Farmers who farm cattle for milk or beef keep their animals outdoors as long as possible in the autumn. The cattle feed on grass growing in the fields. This is called grazing.

As the autumn weather gets colder, the farmer may bring the animals into covered yards where they stay warm and dry for the winter months.

They are given straw to sleep on, and they are fed with grass which has been made into hay or silage.

Some calves are born in the autumn. On dairy farms they feed on their mother's milk for the first few days. Then they are fed on dried milk by the farmer. The cow can then be milked twice a day in the milking parlour.

Deer farming

Autumn is the time of year called 'the rut' when female deer, called hinds, are mated with the male deer, called stags. The stags make a roaring noise and become very excited.

The hinds are put in groups with a stag for mating.
Deer calves are born the following spring.

By autumn the calves no longer need
their mother's milk. The farmer takes
them indoors, checks that they are
healthy and weighs them. Then they
are let out to graze on their own.

They will stay outdoors until the
weather turns cold and wet.

The sheep farm

In the autumn, female sheep, called ewes, are ready to mate with the rams. The farmer checks to see that the ewes and the rams are healthy before they are put together to mate.

The farmer knows when the sheep have mated because a coloured crayon tied to the ram leaves a mark on the ewe. The ewes will give birth to their lambs in the spring.

In autumn, sheep must be dipped in a bath with special chemicals in the water. This will kill any insects living in the sheep's wool. The sheep are sent through the dip one at a time.

The fish farm

As the autumn brings chilly weather, the
water on the fish farm becomes colder.
Fish swim in the deeper water, which is
the warmest part. In cold water they grow
more slowly and need less food.

The fish farmer gives them fish meal, which contains everything they need to keep healthy. Fish swim to the surface of the water to feed.

This Scottish fish farmer is harvesting large salmon, which he will sell.

The harvest festival

Autumn is the time when farmers finish harvesting the crops which have been growing through the spring and summer months.

Harvest festivals are held in schools and churches, to give thanks for all the cereal crops, fruit and vegetables which have ripened ready for harvest.

People bring fruit and vegetables which
have been growing in their gardens.
Sometimes there is a sheaf of wheat, or a
special sheaf-shaped loaf of bread.

On the farm, everyone is happy when the
harvest is safely gathered in.

The farming year calendar

Spring

Sowing crops for summer
and autumn harvest
Harvesting vegetables
grown through the
winter
Fertilising and spraying
crops against weeds
and diseases
Lambing
Putting animals out
to graze
Silage making

Summer

Harvesting vegetables
and soft fruits
Watering crops
Haymaking
Silage making
Sheep shearing and
sheep dipping
Harvesting crops such as
wheat and barley

Autumn

Ploughing fields after
 harvest
Sowing winter wheat
 and barley
Harvesting fruits such as
 apples and pears
Harvesting potatoes and
 sugar beet
Autumn calving
Hedge trimming

Winter

Clearing and draining
 ditches
Pruning fruit trees
Housing animals
Early indoor lambing
Fertilising crops
Repairing farm
 buildings, fences
 and machinery

31

Glossary

Hay Grass that has been dried in the sun. It is used to feed farm animals in the winter.

Manure Animal waste, such as cow pats, mixed into the earth to help plants grow.

Mate When a male and female animal join together to produce babies.

Rams Male sheep.

Sheaf Cut wheat, tied up in a bundle.

Silage Grass or other crops harvested when green and kept juicy. It is fed to farm animals in winter.

Straw The stalks of grain crops, such as wheat, barley and oats.

Books to read

Farming Sue Hadden (Wayland, 1991)
Farming Ruth Thomson (Franklin Watts, 1994)
Let's Visit a Farm series S. Doughty & D. Bentley (Wayland, 1989-90)

Index

Hands-On Microsoft® Windows® Server 2003 Active Directory

Byron Hynes

Byron Wright

Michael Bell

THOMSON

COURSE TECHNOLOGY

Australia • Canada • Mexico • Singapore • Spain • United Kingdom • United States

THOMSON

COURSE TECHNOLOGY

Hands-On Microsoft® Windows® Server 2003 Active Directory

is published by Course Technology

Senior Editor:
William Pitkin III

Product Manager:
Charles G. Blum

Production Editor:
Elena Montillo

Manufacturing Coordinator:
Trevor Kallop

MQA Technical Leader:
Nicole Ashton/Marianne Snow

Product Marketing Manager:
Jason Sakos

Associate Product Manager:
Tim Gleeson

Associate Product Manager:
Nick Lombardi

Cover Design:
Julie Malone

Text Designer:
GEX Publishing Services

Compositor:
GEX Publishing Services

Disclaimer
Course Technology reserves the right to revise this publication and make changes from time to time in its content without notice.

ISBN 0-619-18610-0

▬
BRIEF
Contents

...PTER FIVE
...naging Directory Objects: Users, Groups, and Resources   **117**

Introduction

Welcome to *Hands-On Microsoft® Windows® Server 2003 Active Directory.* This book offers you real-world examples, interactive activities, and hundreds of hands-on projects that reinforce key concepts and help you prepare for a career in network management and administration, using Microsoft enterprise-level directory service, Active Directory. This book provides in-depth study of designing, planning, installing and administering Active Directory. Throughout the book, we provide pointed review questions to reinforce the concepts introduced in each chapter. In addition to the review questions, we provide detailed hands-on projects that let you experience firsthand the processes involved in working with the Microsoft Windows Server 2003 version of Active Directory. Finally, to put a real-world slant on the concepts introduced in each chapter, we provide case studies to prepare you for situations that must be managed in a live Active Directory environment.

INTENDED AUDIENCE

Hands-On Microsoft® Windows® Server 2003 Active Directory is intended for people who have some experience working with Active Directory (in either the Windows 2000 Server or Windows Server 2003), or with other directory services. To best understand the material in this book, you should have a background in basic computer concepts and have worked with the material presented in Course Technology's *Hands-On Microsoft® Windows® XP Professional* and *Hands-On Microsoft® Windows® Server 2003.*

CHAPTER DESCRIPTIONS

Chapter 1 "Active Directory: The Directory Service for Microsoft Networks" provides an overview of Active Directory and introduces the role of a directory service in a modern network, important Active Directory concepts, and the components or "building blocks" of Windows Server 2003 Active Directory.

Chapter 2 "Planning an Active Directory Installation" emphasizes the importance of planning an Active Directory installation before installation. It describes how the Domain Naming System (DNS) operates and how it is used by Active Directory. It also shows how to install Active Directory after gathering the required information.

Chapter 3 "An Active Directory Design Philosophy" outlines the importance of considering the "big picture" of how Active Directory will operate in your network. Various viewpoints or philosophies are described and information is provided about how Active Directory design decisions made early in the process can affect the life of your project.

Chapter 4 "Practical Active Directory Design Decisions" continues from the design issues raised in Chapter 3 to specific planning decisions, and explains how to choose a DNS name, how to design your forests and domains, and how you might choose to work with organizational units OUs.

Chapter 5 "Managing Directory Objects: Users, Contacts, Groups and Resources", focuses on creating and managing the objects commonly found in Active Directory, and their key properties. This chapter also teaches how to publish key resource objects in the directory. In addition, organizing objects in the directory is also explored.

Chapter 6 "Securing and Protecting the Network" describes security concepts in Active Directory, as well as how to control access to objects in the directory. It also focuses on how audit settings can be used to monitor access to objects, and how users are authenticated and authorized in a Windows Server 2003 network.

Chapter 7 "Active Directory Sites" outlines the way that Active Directory models your physical network with Site objects, and explains how information is replicated between sites. This chapter also outlines how you, as an administrator, can control which servers are used by clients and the manner in which Active Directory information moves between sites.

Chapter 8 "Active Directory Replication" explains the functions of replication within sites and between sites and how to configure the options available to you as an administrator. We also discuss the automatic choices made by the Inter-Site Topology Generator (ISTG) and the Knowledge Consistency Checker (KCC), and when you might wish to override them.

Chapter 9 "Active Directory Maintenance and Data Recovery" explains the purpose of Active Directory backups, as well as how the Active Directory files are structured, and how to manage those files if required. The chapter also takes a look at the utilities and methods that can be used to recover or restore Active Directory in the event of catastrophic failures or unintentional object deletion.

Chapter 10 "Using Active Directory as a Tool to Enforce Your Corporate Policy" outlines how to use Group Policy to enforce corporate settings in your network. It also discusses how to distribute software automatically, and how to troubleshoot Group Policy problems.

Chapter 11 "Interoperability between Active Directory and Other Directories" explains how to use different protocols to access the information contained in Active Directory. These protocols include LDAP and ADSI. It also examines how to use the connectors and applications, such as Microsoft Metadirectory Services to connect with other directories.

Chapter 12 "Upgrading a Windows NT or Windows 2000 domain" outlines the different functionality levels available in Windows 2003 Active Directory. It also discusses how to upgrade from older domain structures to the newest Active Directory.

FEATURES AND APPROACH

Hands-On Microsoft® Windows® Server 2003 Active Directory differs from other networking books in its unique hands-on approach and its orientation to real-world situations and problem solving. To help you comprehend how Microsoft Windows network management concepts and techniques are applied in real-world organizations, this book incorporates the following features:

- **Chapter Objectives** — Each chapter begins with a detailed list of the concepts to be mastered. This list gives you a quick reference to the chapter's contents and is a useful study aid.

- **Hands-On Activities** — Hands-on activities are incorporated throughout the text, giving you practice in setting up, managing, and troubleshooting a network system. The activities give you a strong foundation for carrying out network administration tasks in the real world. Because of the book's progressive nature, completing the hands-on activities in each chapter is essential before moving on to the end-of-chapter projects and subsequent chapters.

- **Chapter Summary** — Each chapter's text is followed by a summary of the concepts introduced in that chapter. These summaries provide a helpful way to recap and revisit the ideas covered in each chapter.

- **Key Terms** — All of the terms within the chapter that were introduced with boldfaced text are gathered together in the Key Terms list at the end of the chapter. This provides you with a method of checking your understanding of all the terms introduced.

- **Review Questions** — The end-of-chapter assessment begins with a set of review questions that reinforce the ideas introduced in each chapter. Answering these questions will ensure that you have mastered the important concepts.

- **Case Projects** — Finally, each chapter closes with a section that proposes certain situations. You are asked to evaluate the situations and decide upon the course of action to be taken to remedy the problems described. This valuable tool will help you sharpen your decision-making and troubleshooting skills, which are important aspects of network administration.

- **On the CD ROM** — On the CD-ROM you will find a free 180-day evaluation copy of Windows Server 2003 Enterprise Edition.

TEXT AND GRAPHIC CONVENTIONS

Additional information and exercises have been added to this book to help you better understand what's being discussed in the chapter. Icons throughout the text alert you to these additional materials. The icons used in this book are described below.

 Tips offer extra information on resources, how to attack problems, and time-saving shortcuts.

 Notes present additional helpful material related to the subject being discussed.

 The Caution icon identifies important information about potential mistakes or hazards.

 Each Hands-on Activity in this book is preceded by the hands-on icon.

 Case project icons mark the end-of-chapter case projects, which are scenario-based assignments that ask you to independently apply what you have learned in the chapter.

INSTRUCTOR'S RESOURCES

The following supplemental materials are available when this book is used in a classroom setting. All of the supplements available with this book are provided to the instructor on a single CD-ROM.

Electronic Instructor's Manual. The Instructor's Manual that accompanies this textbook includes Additional instructional material to assist in class preparation, including suggestions for classroom activities, discussion topics, and additional projects.

Solutions. Solutions to all end-of-chapter material, including the Review Questions, and where applicable, Hands-on Projects and Discovery Exercises.

Data files. Data files to be used in conjunction with Hands-on Projects.

ExamView®. This textbook is accompanied by ExamView, a powerful testing software package that allows instructors to create and administer printed, computer (LAN-based), and Internet exams. ExamView includes hundreds of questions that correspond to the topics covered in this text, enabling students to generate detailed study guides that include page references for further review. The computer-based and Internet testing components allow students to take exams at their computers and also save the instructor time by grading each exam automatically.

PowerPoint presentations. This book comes with Microsoft PowerPoint slides for each chapter. These are included as a teaching aid for classroom presentation, to make available to students on the network for chapter review, or to be printed for classroom distribution. Instructors, please feel at liberty to add your own slides for additional topics you introduce to the class.

Figure files. All of the figures and tables in the book are reproduced on the Instructor's Resource CD, in bitmap format. Similar to the PowerPoint presentations, these are included as a teaching aid for classroom presentation, to make available to students for review, or to be printed for classroom distribution.

Minimum Lab Requirements

- **Hardware:**

  Each student must have access to a computer capable of running Windows Server 2003 Standard or Enterprise Edition. All computers should meet the System requirements defined by Microsoft, listed at *http://www.microsoft.com/windowsserver2003/evaluation/sysreqs/default.mspx*. (As the Microsoft Web site is often reorganized, you can search the site for "Windows Server 2003 system requirements".) Also, download the latest Windows Server 2003 Service Pack, if available.

- **Set Up Instructions:**

  To successfully complete the lab exercises, set up classroom computers as listed below:

  1. All classroom computers, including the instructor's server, should have Windows Server 2003, Enterprise (or Standard) Edition pre-installed.

  2. The instructor's computer is assumed to be named **MNC-FRDC**, and to be a domain controller in a forest root domain called **ad.multinatcorp.com**. It should be running DNS and have this zone active.

  3. When installing the ad.multinatcorp.com, change the NETBIOS name from the default ("AD") to "MNC-DOMAIN".

  4. The administrator of the Administrator's computer should be named **administrator** and have a password of **domainpw**. Windows 2003 will flag this as a weak password, so acknowledge the warning and continue.

  5. Remove "Administrator" from the Enterprise Admins group. Create a user named **ea** with a password of "**Forestpw1**". Make **ea** a member of **Enterprise Admins** and **Schema Admins**.

  6. Optionally, one or more Windows XP Professional workstations could be used to demonstrate client concepts or extend the hands-on exercises when behaviors would differ on a server or DC from a workstation-class machine. This would be particularly useful for Chapter 10 when GPOs are studied.

  7. A useful option, although not described in the book, would be to install VMWare on each student computer and use it to create a client that they could use for testing. This, however, is an advanced setup that would likely require knowledge (on the part of the instructor) beyond that described in the book.

  8. All systems should be configured with static IP addresses, using an appropriate address range that doesn't interfere with other systems or classrooms.

  9. Internet access would be useful, but the author recommends using a NAT device or Proxy such as ISA, Linksys or RRAS to isolate the classroom while still providing Internet access.

10. Student computers are assumed to be named SERVER1 through SERVER24 (the numbers may end earlier or later depending on the class size). Students will work in pairs, so an odd-numbered machine and an even numbered machine should be in close physical proximity (i.e., SERVER1 and SERVER2; SERVER3 and SERVER4; etc.)

11. Student servers should initially be configured to use the instructor server as their DNS server. The initial password assigned to the administrator account on each student machine should simply be *password*. Again, Windows Server 2003 will flag this as a weak password, however the students will be changing passwords throughout the course. Alternatively, any password could be used as long as it is clearly communicated to the students when necessary.

12. On the instructor's computer create a folder called **c:\students** that will be used to hold a folder for each student. (It may be located on another drive if necessary.)

    ■ For each student:
    - Create a user account in the domain named studentXX (where XX is a number from one to the maximum number of students, normally 24). Accounts will be named student1, student2, and so on up to student24.
    - Set the password on each student's user account to be PasswordXX (where XX is the student number). Therefore, the user account student1 will have a password of "Password1", and the user account student24 will have a password of "Password24". (Note that the capital P and the numbers are used because the default Windows Server 2003 installation will not let you use a weak password.)
    - Create a folder under c:\students (which you created above). Each student's folder will have the same name as their user account. Therefore, the folders will be named c:\students\student1; c:\students\student2, and so on, up to c:\students\student24.
    - Create a sample text file in each student directory.
    - Share each student folder in the c:\students folder as \\mnc-frdc\student1, \\mmc-frdc\student2, etc.
    - For each student directory, set the NTFS permissions so that only the appropriate student and Domain Admins have permissions on it. This means that the folder c:\students\student1 should have the Apply: Full Control permission granted to Domain Admins and Apply: Change granted to student1. All other permissions should be removed. (Note: this step should be done last so that you do not receive errors creating the text file.)

13. Classroom computers should have hard drive partitions of at least 4 GB to avoid any space-related issues. All partitions must be formatted with the NTFS file system. It does not matter for the purposes of the course if that is one drive or two, or one partition or more, so long as each partition has sufficient space. Do not use partitions less than 4 GB.

14. The DNS zone for ad.multinatcorp.com must be configured to accept dynamic updates. Computer accounts for the student servers can either be pre-created in Active Directory in the ad.multinatcorp.com domain, or added to it as part of their installation process.

15. Active Directory should not be installed on the student computers.

16. A student account should be created in the domain for each student. The user name should be **student1** through **student24**, and the passwords set to **Password1** to **Password24**. Make each student's password different and match it to their user.

17. Because this course uses multiple domains in multiple sites, it is difficult to apply GPOs to all computers. Bear this in mind if you need to control the environment.

18. It may be necessary to access the files contained on the Windows Server 2003 CD-ROM, therefore it is recommended to create a share on the instructor's computer that holds the i386 directory from the CD.

19. It is recommended to use volume license editions of the software and Volume License Keys (VLKs), otherwise a plan regarding CD Keys and activation must be in place. The activities assume that the software is activated.

20. If a Windows Server 2003 service pack is available at the time of the course, the single full executable file should be copied to a shared folder on the instructor's machine.

21. The Activities make mention of a number of other computers. If possible, a VMWare image or physical machine should be configured to represent:

    a.   A Foreign Forest Domain Controller (preferably Windows Server 2003 for Chapter 4)

    b.   A Domain Controller for a Windows NT 4.0 domain (Chapter 4)

    c.   A Terminal Services/Remote Desktop Host named RDESK1 (Chapter 1)

22. The Heartland Hospital cases will work best if each pair of students has an additional domain controller to represent the hospital. If this is not feasible, they will simulate the Hospital domain as OUs in their domain. This is less effective.

23. The instructor computer should have a share called **Activity**. Files required for Hands-On activities will be placed in that share. Within the Activity share, create a folder called **Chap4**. From the Instructor Resources CD, copy the file **default.asp** into the Chap4 folder.

24. Students will be searching for a printer and creating printer objects in Active Directory (which require the shared printer path to be valid). If you have one connected to the domain controller (instructor's computer), share it. If not, create a "fake" printer on LPT1 for Active Directory searching. Ensure that you populate the Location and Comment fields with something interesting.

25. Once the installation process is complete, use Device Manager to ensure that all devices are functioning correctly. In some cases, it may be necessary to download and install additional drivers for devices listed with a yellow question mark icon.

26. Create a new folder named **ServicePack** on drive D of all classroom servers. Download and then copy the most recent Windows Server 2003 Service Pack file (not extracted) to this folder on all servers. If any post-service-pack hot fixes are available, consider downloading one or two of these to the instructor machine only to be used for illustration purposes during the class. No hot fixes are explicitly required by the classroom setup procedure.

ACTIVE DIRECTORY: THE DIRECTORY SERVICE FOR MICROSOFT WINDOWS NETWORKS

After reading this chapter and completing the exercises, you will be able to:

♦ Understand the uses of Active Directory, especially its role in a local area network built around Windows Server 2003

♦ Describe the structure and operations of two fictious organizations—Multinational Mega Corporation and Heartland Hospital—used in Hands-on Projects and Case Projects

♦ Understand the important elements that comprise Active Directory

As in Windows 2000, the Active Directory service is a central component of a local area network (LAN) based on current Microsoft Windows software. Active Directory now includes features that increase performance and scalability, making it easier to manage complicated network environments. It also offers greater flexibility in designing, deploying, and managing an organization's directory, which is increasingly significant as more directory-enabled applications are developed.

This chapter describes the role of **Active Directory (AD)**, Microsoft's directory service for Windows Server 2003. A **directory service (DS)** is a network service that allows users or computers to look up things, such as other users, e-mail addresses, the location of network **resources**, or the rights and security settings assigned to a user. First, you will learn how Active Directory provides essential information used to manage users and control resources in networks that use the Windows Server 2003 operating system (OS). Then, you will learn the fundamental components, or building blocks, that make up an Active Directory implementation.

INTRODUCING ACTIVE DIRECTORY

A directory service is an essential piece of any network operating system (NOS). Though "directory service" is a generic term, most NOS publishers have a name for the service used in their own networks. Microsoft chose the name Active Directory (AD) for the directory service that was introduced in the Windows 2000 Server family. Improvements to the directory service have been made for the release of the Windows Server 2003 family.

To further understand what a directory service is, think of the directory assistance service offered by most telephone companies. Even if you don't know the phone number of a person you want to contact, you probably know the name and perhaps some other identifying information, such as a street address or city. You can then call a special number, such as 411, and ask the directory operator to look up the person's number. You will probably get one of three replies: You receive the person's phone number; you are told it can't be found; or you are told that the number is unlisted, meaning you don't have the required permission to access the information. A directory service for a NOS is very similar. Its first function is to provide information about objects in the directory, including users and resources such as file shares, printers, or e-mail mailboxes.

In the following sections, you will learn the different facets of Active Directory. It is important to look at Active Directory from several different angles because it means different things to different people and can be used in so many ways. After examining three of the roles played by Active Directory, this section will end with a discussion of its power and usefulness in these roles.

Active Directory as the Directory Service for the Operating System

More important than a simple phone book, the information contained in Active Directory is crucial for the correct operation of the network. The security information stored in Active Directory protects information on the network and controls which users are authorized to use which resources.

In the following sections, you will learn about the objects stored in Active Directory that represent users and other security principals. You will also learn the general process used when someone logs on to the network, as well as how objects are stored, organized, and managed in the directory.

Security Principals

When it comes to accessing resources on a network, different users have different needs and different rights. Some are allowed to read or change any document stored on the computer, while others are permitted to read only a few files. By logging on, the user is identifying himself or herself to the local computer or network so that his or her permissions can be established properly. Users most commonly log on with a username and password combination.

 As you go through this chapter, remember that Active Directory stores information about users and other security principals, and that this information is essential to keeping your network secure and operational.

As a network administrator, you will control access to resources by setting permissions. You can assign permissions to one or more users, to groups of users, or even to computers. These three types of objects—users, security groups, and computers—are called **security principals**. By using Active Directory, the administrator can grant permissions to security principals.

 You will be focusing on the security principals maintained in Active Directory, however security principals can also be found in standalone Windows Server 2003 operating systems, Windows NT, Windows 2000, and Windows XP Professional.

Activity 1-1: Logging on and Changing Your Password

Time Required: 10 minutes

Objective: Explain and perform the log-on procedure and explain and perform a change of password.

Description: In the Windows Server 2003 family of operating systems, all users must log on to the computer (or to the domain) before executing any programs. The most common way of authenticating a user is with a username and password. To improve security, users should always keep their passwords secret and change them periodically. This is especially important with administrative accounts. When your computer was installed for the classroom, it's likely that a weak, easily guessed password was used. In this activity, you will log on to your computer as the computer's administrator and change the password.

1. Start your computer and ensure that all users are logged off.

2. When the computer first starts, the Welcome to Windows Screen opens. If you wish, you can click **Help** for more information about the Ctrl+Alt+Delete key sequence.

3. Press **Ctrl+Alt+Delete** to bring up the Log On to Windows dialog box.

4. Clicking the **Options** command button will toggle the display of all available options. Ensure that all options are displayed by clicking **Options**. Observe that the text characters on the Options button change slightly to indicate when the full set of options is shown, and when it is not.

> If a Windows Server 2003 family computer is a member of a domain, showing the options allows you to choose whether to log on to the local workstation or a domain in the computer's forest. The Shut Down button is grayed out because, by default, you must be logged on as an administrator to shut down a computer running Windows Server 2003 software.

5. Log on to the machine by typing **Administrator** for the username and **password** (all lower case) for the password, and then click **OK**. Notice that your password is not visible, but hidden as a series of dots, as shown in Figure 1-1.

6. Click **OK**.

Figure 1-1   The Log On to Windows screen

> To protect an administrative account from unauthorized access, you should change your password to one that only you know. A more secure password should consist of numbers, letters, and special characters. Windows passwords are case sensitive (meaning that the lowercase "a" is considered different from the uppercase "A").

> A common trick to building a strong password is to think of a phrase and use the first letter from each word. For example, the phrase "Darrian is the cutest baby in North America" could make it easy to remember the password "DitcbiNA", and is much harder to guess than using just your child's name. Another trick is to substitute symbols or numbers for letters that they resemble or sound like. For example, "h0mel@nd" is a more secure password than "homeland."

7. Once the desktop has loaded, the **Manage Your Server** window will appear by default. To prevent this window from opening each time you start your computer, check the **Don't display this page at logon** checkbox.

8. Close the **Manage Your Server** window.

9. Press **Ctrl+Alt+Delete** again to open the Windows Security dialog box.

10. In the Windows Security dialog box, click **Change Password**, to open the Change Password dialog box, as shown in Figure 1-2.

Figure 1-2   The Change Password dialog box

11. Type the current password (**password**) in the Old Password text box.

12. Type your new password in the New Password and Confirm New Password text boxes.

13. Click **OK**.

14. Click **OK** again to clear the Change Password confirmation dialog box.

15. Click **Log Off** to log off the computer.

16. Click **Log Off** (again) in the Log Off Windows confirmation dialog box.

17. Test your new password and your understanding of the process by logging back on to the computer.

18. Leave your computer logged off (at the Welcome to Windows screen) or shut down (turned off) when you have completed this activity.

Security Identifiers and Other Security Attributes

The system uses a special identifier, called the **security identifier (SID)**, to keep track of security principals. An object's SID is stored with the object in Active Directory as an attribute, and is generated automatically by Active Directory when you create a new user or other security principal.

When you manage permissions on a network resource, such as a file, a printer, or even an Active Directory object, a **discretionary access control list (DACL)** is assigned to the resource to record the permissions you granted and to whom. The DACL also uses SIDs to record the permissions. Chapter 6 covers this process in detail.

To log a user on to a domain, the computer needs to verify that the user knows the correct password. Active Directory is used to keep track of items such as a user's name and SID, his or her password (in an encrypted form), and the groups to which the user belongs.

Active Directory and Logging On

The log-on process described here is for a Windows domain with Active Directory. The process is different if you are using a Windows domain without Active Directory—for example, if you are logging on to an older Windows NT domain or logging on with a local account on a single machine. Those scenarios are outside the scope of this discussion.

A corporate user usually sits down at his or her computer to use applications and data stored locally and to access resources on the corporate network. Determining if a user can access a particular resource is known as **authorization**, as opposed to authentication. **Authentication** determines who the user is, while authorization determines what a previously authenticated user is allowed to access. From the user's point of view, authentication and authorization are seen as one step, known as **single sign on**, because the user only has to type his or her password once, no matter how many network resources are being accessed.

An overview of the log-on process using Active Directory is shown in Figure 1-3.

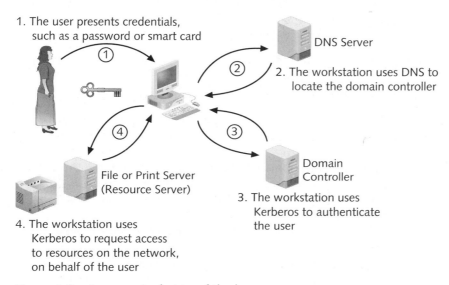

Figure 1-3   A conceptual view of the log-on process

First, the user supplies a username and a password, or in some cases, inserts a smart card into a reader. Second, the user's workstation has to find a **domain controller (DC)**, which is a computer that stores a copy of the Active Directory database. To locate a domain controller, the workstation queries a Domain Name System (DNS) server, which allows it to look up names and network addresses of computers offering specific services, including domain controllers. In this case, the request from the workstation to the DNS is to look up a service locator (SRV) record, which is a pointer to a domain controller. DNS is covered in detail in Chapter 2.

 SRV records were rarely used before the introduction of Windows 2000. With Windows 2000 and Windows Server 2003 they are essential. Your DNS system must be correctly configured so that all servers and client workstations can locate these SRV records. A misconfigured DNS system will cause network slowdowns and can even make it impossible for users to access the resources they need.

For the third step, the workstation uses the **Kerberos protocol** to authenticate the user, meaning the domain controller responds to the Kerberos request to verify whether the user is who he or she claims to be. If successfully authenticated, the user's computer receives a special response packet, called a Kerberos ticket, which can then be used for authorization.

The Kerberos protocol is used by Windows XP and the Windows Server 2003 family because it ensures that the user's password is never actually transmitted on the network. Kerberos also allows the workstation to verify the identity of the server at the same time that the server identifies the user (a two-way authentication), and it reduces exposure to many types of hacker attacks. In addition, Kerberos was designed to be efficient and flexible on local and wide area networks running the Transmission Control Protocol/Internet Protocol (TCP/IP) transport protocols.

In the fourth and final step, the Kerberos ticket is used to request access to a resource—the local workstation, the DC, or another server. The information exchanged during the Kerberos protocol logon is then used to generate other tickets that can be presented to the resource server. Based on the information contained in the Kerberos tickets received from the DC, the resource server decides whether to allow the user to access the resource.

 If the requested resource doesn't support Kerberos, the client reverts to older Windows-based protocols, such as NT LAN Manager (NTLM). The actual choice of an older protocol depends on a number of factors, including security policies and negotiation between the resource server and the requesting client. Kerberos is the default and preferred protocol.

The Kerberos and NTLM authentication processes are described in much more detail in Chapter 6.

Organizing and Finding Objects in Active Directory

Active Directory allows users to easily find objects such as users, groups, computers, and printers on the network. For example, if you need to print a document while visiting another building in your company's campus, Active Directory provides a search mechanism to help you find a nearby printer. Active Directory also allows objects to be grouped into a logical, hierarchical structure using containers and organizational units (OU). **Containers** are special objects that can contain other objects, similar to the way a folder contain files on a hard drive. An **organizational unit (OU)** is a special kind of container that can be used to control how Group Policy is applied. Although you can delegate administrative authority to manage objects in containers and OUs, most Active Directory designers use OUs as the preferred unit of delegation.

 There are many possible ways to organize your Active Dirctory structure. You will read about domain design in Chapters 3 and 4, and Group Policy is discussed in Chapter 10. The next section of this chapter will look more closely at containers and OUs.

Before Active Directory was released with Windows 2000, network objects in a Microsoft Windows network could only be grouped by domain. This often made network directory designs confusing and difficult to maintain, and there was no easy search method. With Active Directory, once your network designers and administrators agree on how to best organize the objects in your network, both users and administrators benefit from the ability to find objects quickly. Administrative rights can be assigned on a granular basis, and administrators can be given permissions for the appropriate parts of the network; it's not an "all-or-nothing" approach.

Active Directory for Central Management

Administrators use an administrative console called Active Directory Users and Computers to manipulate users and resources. The Active Directory Users and Computers console is a snap-in, or specialized console, for the Microsoft Management Console (MMC), the standard administrative interface of Windows 2000 and the Windows Server 2003 family. Active Directory Users and Computers is a central point of management and control for your network, large or small. Just as single sign on benefits users, the centralization of user management benefits administrators. An administrator does not have to separately manage the network security, database security, e-mail security, file share security, and every other application that requires authentication or authorization. Instead, an administrator can use Active Directory Users and Computers to centrally manage access to resources across the entire company.

With the release of the Windows Server 2003 family, Microsoft has made it easier than ever to manage a server without being physically present at the server's keyboard. You can use Active Directory Users and Computers to manage servers from a workstation running Windows XP Professional, or you can connect to the server using Remote Desktop.

Activity 1-2: Connecting to a Server with Remote Desktop

Time Required: 10 minutes

Objective: Understand and practice using Remote Desktop to make a connection to another server.

Description: The Windows Server 2003 family of operating systems supports the ability to make a remote connection to the server from another Windows Server 2003 computer, a Windows 2000 Server, Windows XP Professional, or Windows 2000 Professional using the Remote Desktop feature. (The Windows 2000 family uses Terminal Services, a predecessor of Remote Desktop.) A server in your classroom has been configured to allow you to connect to it. In the following steps, the server is named RDESK1. Your instructor will advise you if classroom constraints require you to use another server.

1. Log on to your computer as **Administrator**, using the steps you practiced in the earlier hands-on activity. If the **Manage Your Server** page opens, close it (and check **Don't display this page at logon**).

2. After the logon is complete, you will be shown the Windows Server 2003 desktop. Click **Start**.

3. Point to **Administrative Tools** and then click **Remote Desktops**. Remote Desktops is an MMC snap-in that allows convenient access to multiple remote computers. Its functionality is similar to the Remote Desktop application in Windows XP Professional.

4. In the tree-view pane (on the left), right-click the node **Remote Desktops** and click **Add new connection**.

5. Enter the name **RDESK1** in the **Server Name or IP address** text box.

6. Clear (uncheck) the **Connect to console** checkbox.

7. Click **OK**.

8. Expand the **Remote Desktops** node by clicking the plus sign beside the node.

9. Click the name **RDESK1** in the tree view.

10. After a few moments, you will be connected to a remote desktop of the RDESK1 server. Enter your student# and password# credentials to log on.

11. If you receive the message "The terminal server has exceeded the maximum number of allowed connections," click **OK**, then try to connect again (by right-clicking on the name of the server and clicking **Connect**) after some students have completed step 13.

12. Time permitting, use the **Start** menu to execute a program on the remote desktop.

13. In the remote desktop, close all windows and log off the remote desktop.

14. Close all windows on your computer and log off.

Active Directory as a Directory Service for Applications

Applications can make use of a directory service. Many applications make reference to users or other directory objects, either for security or to actually work with the attributes of the object, or both. The Active Directory schema, discussed later in this chapter, lists all of the objects and attributes stored in the directory. It is possible to extend the schema, adding new types of objects or additional attributes to the directory. Applications can take advantage of this extendibility.

Applications Using Active Directory for Authentication and Authorization

The best example of an application using Active Directory, is Microsoft Exchange Server 2000 or Exchange Server 2003. Exchange is a high-powered e-mail server solution. Prior to the release of Active Directory, the Exchange application installed its own directory service to keep track of e-mail users, their addresses, security information, and other attributes. Sound familiar? It is the same sort of information that is stored in Active Directory.

One of the classic issues plaguing network administration with Windows NT 4.0 and Exchange Server 5.5 is the constant need to keep the network directory (the domain) synchronized with the Exchange Directory. Rather than duplicate effort, Microsoft decided to leverage the power of Active Directory for Exchange 2000. Exchange 2000 no longer maintains its own directory information. Instead, it relies on the services of Active Directory and extends the schema, so that the e-mail system can use Active Directory to resolve names and addresses, locate mailboxes, and set security. In a Zen-like way, the user and the mailbox become one.

Any application developer can use the authentication and authorization services provided with Active Directory to write their applications as **Active Directory-aware**. This gives an application a rich set of functionality in security, organization, and management of users, groups, and resources. Many Microsoft applications—like Exchange and the Internet Security and Acceleration (ISA) server—make use of information stored in Active Directory. And, third-party applications that use Active Directory are becoming more common.

Later in this book you will see some examples of how to access Active Directory information through an application. It is not difficult, and many administrators have scripted day-to-day tasks for consistency and the automation of routine jobs. In-house programmers can also link to Active Directory. Since administrators control the access to Active Directory information, Active Directory can contain confidential information, and as a network administrator, you can control how your confidential directory is made available.

Applications Using Active Directory as a Data Store

Applications can also use Active Directory to store information that is proprietary to an application. The schema is extensible, which means applications can create new object classes in Active Directory or define new attributes for new or existing classes. An application can also choose to store its data in a dedicated section of the database, called an application partition, to control where the data is stored and how it is replicated.

Because Active Directory information is usually stored redundantly and backed up regularly, using Active Directory for critical application information ensures that the application's data is also highly available. In addition, Active Directory can be easily searched and manipulated through industry-standard interfaces like the Lightweight Directory Access Protocol (LDAP). Using Active Directory to store application data means that the data can also be manipulated.

For some types of information, the most logical place for storage is the Active Directory—particularly if it is additional information relating to objects already in the directory. For example, Exchange 2000 needs to have the default information that exists in Active Directory, but it needs more information as well. So, when you install Exchange 2000, it extends the schema, allowing you to see additional attributes that have been added to the user objects to track information for Exchange.

Another example of an application using Active Directory, is Microsoft Internet Security and Acceleration Server (ISA), which is Active Directory-aware and relies on Active Directory to determine if a user is authorized to send traffic through the firewall. The ISA Enterprise Edition also stores enterprise-wide firewall policies in Active Directory, and extends the schema to accommodate the storage of these policies. These firewall policies would not normally be used by any other application.

In fact, the success of Active Directory in storing application-related information has led Microsoft to release a specialized version that is *not* used by Windows, but is available for use by applications. This version, called Active Directory/Application Mode (AD/AM), is available with Windows Server 2003. AD/AM is outside the scope of this book, however, you can learn more about it by visiting *http://www.microsoft.com/windowsserver2003/techinfo/overview/adam.mspx*. (Note that the Microsoft Web site is often reorganized, so if the document is not present at this link, search the site for "Introduction to Active Directory in Application Mode.")

Changing what is stored in Active Directory affects the entire network, so only certain administrators should be authorized to make these changes. You must be a member of the Schema Admins Group in the forest root domain to extend the schema. Normally, the Schema Admins Group would include a very small number of people.

Active Directory Is an Application Itself

Active Directory is a very important part of your network, but it is also an application in its own right, though it is not a "user application" in the way that Microsoft Word is. Specifically, Active Directory is a highly optimized database application, implemented as Windows services running on domain controllers. The network absolutely depends on this application being available. The Active Directory application uses resources, such as disk space and processor time. It should be backed up, maintained, and monitored, as discussed in Chapter 9.

If you are familiar with the concepts of database design, you may be more familiar with Active Directory than you think, because of its roots as a database. Many features and design specifications of Active Directory came out of Microsoft's long history with the Exchange Directory service, while others stem from the Windows NT 4.0 (and earlier) domain model. Microsoft chose to use an improved version of the Joint Engine Technology (JET) database, called the Extensible Storage Engine (ESE), as the database engine for Active Directory.

As with most high-end databases, this engine uses **write-ahead log files** to help protect the database from corruption when changes are made to the information in the database. Active Directory first records any change to the database in the current log file, *edb.log*. This file is always 10 MB in size, but is only partially used. Rather than make the file larger when it becomes full, Active Directory starts a new log file and names it with a sequential number, like *Edb00001.log*. As time goes on, Active Directory writes the changes from the log file(s) to the database file and purges the oldest log entries once they have been written to the main database file.

A checkpoint file, called *Edb.chk,* is used to track which transactions from the log have been successfully written to the database. When the system starts up after a shutdown, ESE checks to see if the last record recorded indicated a clean or planned shutdown. If not, any transactions since the checkpoint are "replayed" from the log file and entered into the database. This system of write-ahead logging helps protect the Active Directory database from corruption.

When you install Active Directory, you can choose the location for the database file and the log files. Most administrators ensure that the log files are stored on a separate physical disk than the database file, or placed on a redundant array of inexpensive disks (RAID).

The Power of Active Directory

In addition to being the directory service, Active Directory is a fundamental technology that the Windows Server 2003 family, Microsoft Windows XP, and Windows 2000 build on to offer services that weren't previously available.

As an example of its importance, consider the following facts about Active Directory:

- It is required for Group Policy. **Group Policy** is the feature that lets you enforce company policies automatically across the network, as well as automatically deploy software.

- Active Directory provides greater control over which servers are authorized to act as DHCP servers. This cuts down on network problems caused by "rogue" DHCP servers—those DHCP servers installed (accidentally or otherwise) without an administrator's knowledge—which give out incorrect addressing information and disrupt the network.

- Active Directory provides control over Remote Installation Services (RIS), the feature that allows the entire operating system to be installed on a new computer or over the network with little or no manual intervention.

- Active Directory is easily scriptable and interacts with a variety of other software using industry-standard protocols and interfaces.

INTRODUCTION TO MULTINATIONAL MEGA CORPORATION AND HEARTLAND HOSPITAL

Throughout the chapters of this book, you will be introduced to case studies, mini-cases, and examples. These are intended to help you gain experience working with Active Directory concepts in the same way they would be used in a real enterprise. They will also help prepare you for certification exams from Microsoft. More and more, certification exams are requiring candidates to synthesize and analyze information presented in case-based scenarios, as well as traditional multiple-choice questions.

Multinational Mega Corporation is a fictitious enterprise with many holdings and interests in mining and fabrication. It is a large company with more than 17,000 employees who are geographically dispersed around North America, Africa, Australia, and Europe. MultiNatCorp, as it is commonly known, grew over many years from its beginnings as a single mine in the outback of Australia. Much of its growth came about through mergers and acquisitions, and although mining and minerals are still important to the company, it has expanded into a number of new markets, most notably fabrication and manufacturing of plastics and chemicals. It also has a large financial division, providing financial services to leverage its own extensive assets and fund-management needs. The corporation's head office is now in Montreal, Canada, but the financial center and most of the staff are located in New York. A significant number of people work in Toronto, Denver, and San Jose, with smaller pockets in Sydney, Vancouver, London, and Chicago.

In our imaginary world, you have joined MultiNatCorp's IT division. This division originally performed only in-house work, but about 5 years ago, the company saw an opportunity to resell its well-developed expertise to other firms. Your primary role is to assist clients based in mid-sized firms that do not have their own internal expertise. However, as your virtual career progresses, you will gain more and more exposure to the large networks at MultiNatCorp, both as a user and an administrator.

The first project to which you have been assigned is to support the networks at Heartland Hospital in Marieville, Illinois.

Heartland Hospital is a 200-bed facility with an active emergency department. The hospital is located on one piece of private land, although the maintenance, shipping/receiving, and supply services departments are located in a separate building. All patient-care areas are in one building, which has Category 5 (CAT5) cabling throughout. The maintenance building is connected with dedicated network lines.

THE BUILDING BLOCKS OF ACTIVE DIRECTORY

Active Directory is a highly specialized database and, as in any well-designed database, the structures are representing some *thing* (a physical object) or some concept found in the real world. For example, the sample database that is provided with Microsoft SQL Server and with Microsoft Access has tables defined as "customers," "orders," and "employees." Clearly, these database objects are representations of the people and paperwork that must be managed at the fictitious company made up by Microsoft. Regrettably, the real world is not often so kind, and database designers struggle to choose the best tables or constructs to represent complex business environments.

The Active Directory database is a logical representation of your network. The objects in Active Directory describe "things" like users or printers, as well as concepts like "domains." No wonder some find it confusing; Active Directory is a logical model of a logical model!

Throughout the rest of this chapter, you will examine how Active Directory represents the "virtual" or "logical" design of your network, because before you can install or manage Active Directory, there are concepts and terms that you must understand. This section outlines the building blocks of Active Directory and the role that each plays in your network design.

Windows Domains

In a Windows network, a **domain** is a group of computers, users, and resources using a joint security model. By **joint security model** we mean the security principals (users, security groups, and other computers) defined in the domain that can access resources hosted on all machines in the domain (subject to permissions controlled by Discretionary Access Control Lists). In addition, the account policy that governs issues like minimum password length will be the same for all users with domain accounts.

Generally speaking, all computers in a domain eventually fall under the same authority for management. In some companies this is very tightly controlled, and a central Information Technology (IT) group is responsible for every aspect of every computer. Users are forbidden and prevented from customizing anything. In other companies, the control is not so tight, and users can do what they want with the machine, but ultimately the computer and its data are an asset of the company.

Of course, most companies fall somewhere between the extremes, but whatever the corporate culture, each domain has a group of users defined who have administrative rights for the whole domain. Those users, the domain's Administrators Group, can gain control of any resource in the domain. By default, the global group called **Domain Admins** is also part of this Administrators Group and has the same powers.

In contrast to the joint security model, is the stand-alone machine. With a stand-alone machine, a local administrator controls all security settings for that machine. No other person can access or change anything, except if the local administrator specifically allows them to do so. If that stand-alone machine is sharing resources (such as files or a printer), users must authenticate individually with that machine, with no benefit of single sign on. It is not uncommon for corporations to have dozens or hundreds of servers making resources available to users. Without a domain model, administrators would have to maintain permissions separately on each of those machines, and users would have to keep track of passwords for each and every one of them. Imagine having to change your password on two dozen different file servers.

Activity 1-3: Accessing Resources Without a Domain

Time Required: 10 minutes

Objective: To access a corporate network without the benefits of Active Directory domain structure.

Description: Your instructor or coordinator should have configured an Active Directory domain, domain controller, domain users, and file shares according to the guidelines provided. In the following examples, the domain is named ad.multinatcorp.com, with a domain controller called MNC-FRDC (perhaps more easily remembered as "MultiNatCorp-ForestRoot-DomainController"). Student machines are named SERVER1 through SERVER24. Your instructor will advise you if different names are being used because of constraints in your classroom or lab environment.

1. Log on to your computer as **Administrator** using the steps you practiced in the last hands-on activity. If the Manage Your Server page opens, close it (and check **Don't display this page at logon**).

2. After the logon is complete, you will be shown the Windows Server 2003 desktop. Click **Start**.

3. Click **Windows Explorer**.

4. Click the **My Network Places** icon on the left side of the screen.

5. The My Network Places details appear on the right side of the screen (the area called the details pane). You may see several network shares in this window. Windows Server 2003 adds shares to this view when it learns that they have become available. (If your lab is isolated, you may not see any shares. If your lab is connected to your facility's network, you could see several shares.)

6. Double-click the **Entire Network** icon in the details pane.

7. Double-click the **Microsoft Windows Network** icon. The Microsoft Windows Network window will show all domains and workgroups that Windows has identified on your LAN.

8. Double-click the **MNC-DOMAIN** network icon.

When the window for the MNC-DOMAIN domain opens, a single computer named MNC-FRDC should appear. This is the domain controller for the ad.multinatcorp.com domain. You may also see other computers in the domain, such as RDESK1.

9. Double-click the MNC-FRDC icon to see the resources being advertised as available by MNC-FRDC. You are prompted to enter a name and password before seeing the list of resources. Each student has been assigned a username, consisting of the word "student" and a unique number; the password has been set in a similar way. For example, user student1 has a password of password1, user student2 has a password of password2, and so on. Enter your assigned username and password and click **OK**.

10. In the resulting display of resources, locate the file share that matches your username. Double-click that file share.

11. The file share contains one text file, also named to match your username. Double-click that file to open it in Notepad.

12. Once you have read the file, close Notepad.

13. Use the Up icon, or the backspace key, to travel back up the resource hierarchy.

14. Try to open the network share for another student.

15. On the Desktop, click **Start** and then click **Search**.

16. Once the Search Results window opens, click **Other search options**. Observe the choices that are available under "What do you want to search for."

17. Close all open windows.

18. If you are continuing to the next activity immediately, you do not need to log off. If you are taking a break, you should log off the machine, as it is unwise to leave a machine logged on to an administrative account. (To log off, click **Start**, click **Log Off**, and then click **Log Off** again in the Log Off Windows confirmation dialog box.)

When you install a client operating system that can participate in a domain—Windows NT, Windows 2000, Windows XP Professional, or the Windows Server 2003 family—in a corporate environment, you are asked if the new machine will participate in a domain. If the machine joins a domain, users will be able to authenticate with the domain through Active Directory when they log on. Or, to put it another way, security principals defined within the domain can be allowed access to this machine and its resources.

It also means that administrators of the domain have some control over this machine. Normally, the Domain Admins Group is a member of the local Administrators Group on each machine that is a member of the domain, and can, therefore, manage every machine on the domain. Even if they aren't members of the Administrators Group, they could still use Group Policy to place themselves into the Administrators Group and gain administrative access to the machine.

Although a domain is a virtual concept, it must exist somewhere. It has objects, such as users, defined in it. You can log on to it. Even though you can't point to it, you can find it. So where does a domain live? The Active Directory database is where the domain information is stored. Objects in Active Directory describe the entire structure of a domain. For example, when a computer joins a domain, a computer object representing that computer is created in Active Directory. When a user is created in a domain, an object representing that user is created in Active Directory, and so on.

Activity 1-4: Joining a Domain

Time Required: 10–15 minutes

Objective: To learn how to join a computer that is in a workgroup (sometimes referred to as a stand-alone computer) to a domain.

Description: In this activity, the student computers in the classroom will join the domain.

1. Ensure that you are logged on to your machine as Administrator. (If you are continuing directly from the last activity, it is not necessary to log off and on again.)

2. Click **Start**.

3. Right-click the **My Computer** icon, and then click **Properties**.

4. Click the **Computer Name** tab. On the Student Answer Sheet, record the existing settings.

5. Click the **Change** button to open the Computer Name Changes dialog box.

6. Click the **Domain** radio button in the Member of Option group.

7. Type **ad.multinatcorp.com** in the Domain text box.

8. You will be prompted to authenticate with the domain using credentials that represent someone with permission to let new computers join the domain. Type the username **Administrator** and the password **domainpw**.

 This "administrator" on the domain is not the same entity as the administrator on your machine, even though the name shown on the screen looks the same. They are different security principals, with different SIDs. To join a domain, you have to have administrative privileges on the machine trying to join and permissions on the domain to create new computer objects.

9. Click **OK** in the confirmation dialog box.

10. Click **OK** to acknowledge that a restart is required.

11. Click **OK** to close the System Properties dialog box.

12. Click **Yes** to restart your computer.

Activity 1-5: Accessing Resources Using a Domain

Time Required: 10–15 minutes

Objective: To demonstrate the effectiveness of single sign on and domain membership.

Description: In this activity, you will log on to a Windows Server 2003 computer using domain credentials and access shared resources on the domain using those same credentials via single sign on.

1. Log on to the machine by specifying your student username (studentx) and password (passwordx). Before clicking **OK**, make sure that Log On to Drop List is set to **MNC-DOMAIN**, not the local computer. (If you do not see a Log On to List box, click **Options**.)

2. After you log on to the computer, the Windows desktop will appear. Launch Windows Explorer using the same steps you practiced in Activity 1-3. Use Windows Explorer to open the Entire Network, then MNC-Domain, and MNC-FRDC to see the resources available on the MNC-FRDC computer.

3. Open your folder on MNC-FRDC and verify that you have access, then open your text file.

4. Use the Up icon, or the backspace key, to travel back up the resource hierarchy, and try to open the network share for another student.

5. Close all open windows.

6. Click **Start**, right-click **My Computer**, and click **Properties**. Click the **Computer Name** tab. Record the information on this tab on your Student Answer Sheet.

7. Close all open windows.

 If you are not continuing immediately to the next activity, you should log off your machine or lock its desktop, as it is unwise to leave a machine logged on. To lock the desktop, press Ctrl+Alt+Delete, then click **Lock Computer**, or use the keyboard shortcut: hold down the Windows key (to the left of the Alt key, on most newer keyboards), and press **L**.

When you create a domain, you must choose one or more computers that will hold the domain's Active Directory database. A computer that is running the Active Directory software (implemented as several Windows Services) and that has a copy of the Active Directory database is called a domain controller. Whenever we speak of interacting with "the domain," the actual exchange of information is between a computer and a domain controller. Whenever we require the services of a domain—like to log on—your computer will find a domain controller, usually through the DNS system. The domain controller is not the domain, but it manages the domain.

Activity 1-6: Loading Active Directory Management Tools on Another Computer

Time Required: 10–15 minutes

Objective: To practice the installation of server management tools.

Description: You do not need to be working at a domain controller to administer Active Directory with the Active Directory Users and Computers console. It can be installed on any Windows 2000, Windows XP Professional, or Windows Server 2003 server family computer.

1. Insert your Windows .NET server installation CD, or connect to the network share containing the installation files.

2. Locate and double-click the **\i386\adminpak.msi** file. Note that if you are accessing this file from a network share (not from a CD) you may be prompted to open or download the file. If this occurs, choose **Open**.

3. When the welcome page opens, click **Next**.

4. Wait for the Windows Installer to complete the installation of the administrative tools and consoles.

5. Click **Finish**.

Activity 1-7: Viewing the Objects in an Active Directory Domain Partition

Time Required: 5 minutes

Objective: To view the objects in a domain partition of an Active Directory database.

Description: Once the administrative tools and consoles have been installed, if your computer is a member of a domain and you have permission, you can connect to a domain controller and view or change Active Directory objects.

1. Your computer must be a member of a domain in the forest you wish to view.

2. You must be logged on to the computer using a domain user account from a domain in the forest. (For this example, you can use the domain "Administrator" account and the "domainpw" password.)

3. Click **Start**, point to **All Programs**, point to **Administrative Tools**, and click **Active Directory Users and Computers**.

4. Click on each of the nodes (domain, containers, and OUs) shown in the tree in the left pane. Review each of the objects shown in the details pane on the right side.

Forests and Trees

Since the release of Windows 2000, the needs of the majority of business enterprises can be met by using one Active Directory domain. However, sometimes a company requires more than one domain. If a company is widely dispersed, has autonomous units with its own management or its own public identity, or if different business units need different Account Policies, the company may need to create more than one domain. Examine the content of Figure 1-4.

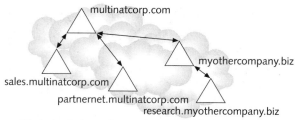

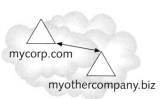

Figure 1-4   Domains, trees, and forests

Figure 1-4 demonstrates the following points:

- You can simply create two separate domains, as shown in Figure 1-4 (Part A), but those independent domains cannot transparently share resources. Multiple independent domains have the same kind of problems as multiple independent computers—it takes considerable administrative effort to manage them. Instead, we can create a "forest" of domains. A **forest** is a group of domains within the same enterprise that share the same configuration partition. Each domain in the forest can be managed independently, although there is an all-encompassing management function for forest-wide tasks.

- If the last part of two domain names is the same, such as multinatcorp.com and sales.multinatcorp.com, this is called a contiguous name space. Domains in a contiguous name space are called **trees**, as shown in Figure 1-4 (Part B), and the whole structure is called a forest. (The DNS system is discussed in Chapter 2, and choosing a DNS name for your domain is discussed in Chapter 4.)

- If the name space is discontiguous (such as mycorp.com and myothercompany.biz), then there are multiple trees. In Figure 1-4 (Part C), there are two trees, each with only one domain, but they still make a forest.

- You can have multiple trees in one forest. Figure 1-4 (Part D) shows multiple trees, each with a varying number of domains. However, if you have only one domain, then your forest has only one tree, and your tree has only one domain.

 The way information is shared between domains will be covered later in this chapter, when replication and naming contexts are discussed.

The Active Directory Schema

The **schema** is the set of specifications that determine what information is stored in Active Directory. The Active Directory schema provides the same sort of specification that a database schema or data dictionary does in a traditional business database. It sets out exactly what kind of data objects will be represented in Active Directory, what properties or attributes are required or optional for each data object, and even what types of values are acceptable for each attribute.

Active Directory Classes, Objects, and Attributes

Each item of data stored in Active Directory is called an **object**. The definition of each type of object is called a **class**. A class is like a template, or blueprint, from which objects are created. For example, the User class defines how a user object will be implemented.

Consider an analogy from architecture—a builder has a blueprint for a house, but he doesn't have a house. After the house is created, he still has the blueprint, and he also now has an existing house. He can then make another house from the same blueprint. If he needs to build a grocery store, he needs to have a blueprint for a grocery store before it can be built. A class is like the blueprint, and an object is like the house or store. You could also say that the schema as a whole, is like a bound set of all blueprints used to construct an entire subdivision. The important part of class definition is that it specifies the attributes that are stored for each object.

The schema contains a list of all possible attributes. From this list, a class is assigned both mandatory and optional attributes. An attribute can be used in more than one class definition. When an object is created from the class definition, all of the mandatory attributes are needed, but optional ones are, well, optional. It is also worth noting that security principals—users, computers and security groups—have properties that other objects do not.

For example, the user object has an optional attribute to hold a telephone number. Some users will have this attribute populated with a value, but the system will let you create a user object without a telephone number. However, the printer object does not have this attribute at all, since it wouldn't make sense to telephone a printer.

> Attributes are sometimes called "properties," but the term "attributes" is used when discussing Active Directory.

In a philosophical sense, an object is the sum of its attributes. Given enough of an object's attributes, you can define that object. If an acquaintance tells you that he has an object of the "vehicle" class in his driveway, the statement is not very unique or descriptive. But when he lists some of its attributes, you get a much clearer picture: color=red, make=Chevrolet, model year=1999, model name=Venture, interior state=constantly messy. As in Active Directory, there are additional attributes that can identify this person's vehicle. For example, if he specified an attribute for the license plate number, you would be able to uniquely identify his vehicle.

Activity 1-8: Using ADSI Edit to View Mandatory and Optional Attributes of a User Object in Active Directory

Time Required: 10 minutes

Objective: To understand and practice using ADSI Edit to view detailed information about objects in Active Directory.

Description: Microsoft provides a tool called ADSI Edit that uses a Dynamic Link Library (DLL) that follows the Component Object Model (COM) specification. The DLL contains code to implement the Active Directory Services Interface (ADSI). ADSI is used by applications, including ADSI Edit and Windows Scripting Host, to access Active Directory. This tool allows you to view or manipulate objects in the directory, including the schema definitions.

1. Your computer must be a member of a domain in the forest you wish to view.

2. You must be logged on to the computer using a domain user account from a domain in the forest. In order to install ADSI Edit, you must be an administrator on the computer. Therefore, log on to your computer as the Administrator from the domain, using the "domainpw" password. Consult your instructor if you have difficulty logging on as the domain administrator.

3. ADSI Edit is supplied on the distribution CD with your Windows Server 2003 Server product. Insert your Windows Server 2003 Server installation CD, or connect to the network share containing the installation files.

4. Locate and double-click the **\support\tools\suptools.msi** file.

5. When the Welcome page opens, click **Next**.

6. Click **I Agree** to accept the license terms, then click **Next**.

7. Enter your name and organization in the text boxes, and then click **Next**.

8. Click **Install Now**.

9. Wait for the Windows Installer to complete the installation of the support tools.

10. Click **Finish**.

11. Click **Start**, point to **All Programs**, point to **Windows Support Tools**, and then click **Command Prompt**.

12. When the Command Prompt window opens, type **adsiedit.msc** at the command prompt and press **Enter**. The ADSI Edit graphical interface will appear.

13. Expand the node labeled **Domain**, and expand the nodes under it until you can locate **CN=Users**.

14. Click the node labeled **CN=Users**.

15. In the details pane (on the right), right-click the item **CN=Administrator**, and click **Properties**.

16. Review the types of attributes (mandatory and optional) by clicking the **Show mandatory attributes** and **Show optional attributes** checkboxes.

 Do not click **Edit**. Do not change the values of any attributes or you may disrupt the correct operation of your computer or the domain.

17. Click **Cancel** to close the property sheet.

As time permits, examine properties of other objects in the domain-naming context or the other naming contexts present on the domain controller. However, *do not* change any value.

18. Close all open windows and log off your computer.

Using Active Directory Users and Computers, you can create computer objects, printer objects, file share objects, groups, contact objects, and OUs. Each of these objects are described individually in the following list:

- *Users* — The User class represents the users of your computer network. Users are security principals, so security information is included in the object's attributes. Although the User class defines several mandatory properties in order to create a user with Active Directory Users and Computers, you will need to specify a logon name and a display name. The Active Directory system will automatically assign other mandatory attributes, such as the SID and an object ID. The console fills in the others automatically. If you were creating users directly through code, you would need to specify any mandatory attributes that Active Directory doesn't create.

  Normally, you will want to set several of the optional attributes, including a password. Once a user object has been created and enabled, the new user can authenticate with the domain controllers. If you are using an Active Directory-aware mail system, such as Exchange 2000 or 2003, more user attributes will be added to the schema and may also need to be set at the time the object is created. You will work with user objects during the hands-on activities and labs included in this course. They are discussed in detail in Chapter 4.

- *Computers* — The Computer class represents computers that are members of the Active Directory domain. When a computer joins the domain, a computer object is created in Active Directory. A computer is a security principal, so it has security-related attributes. There are also general attributes that can hold a description, location, or the name of the operating system installed. If the computer is sharing published resources, such as printers, or is acting as a domain controller, additional properties are made available.

- *Printers* — Shared printers on the network are resources that can be published in Active Directory to provide a means of easily searching for printers across the enterprise. The Printer class specifies a number of attributes that provide Active Directory with a search mechanism for the printer.

- *File shares* — A file share is another resource that can be published in Active Directory, and like the Printer class, the File Share class specifies attributes allowing Active Directory to provide a search mechanism for finding file shares.

- *Groups* — Active Directory supports two types of groups: Distribution Groups and Security Groups. Distribution Groups are groups of users, contacts, and nested groups that can receive e-mail at once (like distribution lists in Exchange 5.5). Security Groups are security principals, and they are best described as a list of other security principals. Using Security Groups makes administration and assignment of access rights simpler. Groups are discussed in detail in Chapter 4.

- *Contacts* — The Contact class provides a way to make external addresses and contact information available in your directory. Having contacts in Active Directory is like using a personal address book (PAB) or a contacts folder in Outlook or Outlook Express, but on a larger scale—often for the whole organization. If you have contacts outside your organization, or even internal contacts that will never need to access resources, you can use a contact object to represent them in the directory. Contacts are not security principals and cannot be granted permissions on resources.

- *Containers and OUs* — In general terms, containers are objects that can contain other objects, in the same way that folders on a hard disk can contain files or even other folders. For our purposes, though, container refers to a specific class of Active Directory objects. Two containers that you will see in Active Directory are users and computers. (Note that there is a Computer class, and a computers container.) As you might suspect, the users container normally contains user objects, and the computers container usually contains computer objects. If Active Directory has been installed as an upgrade to an existing Windows NT domain, the upgraded objects are placed in these containers. The users container also contains the user accounts created by the system, such as the guest account and the administrator account. Other than providing a means of grouping objects to make them easier to find, a container does not add much functionality. You cannot create a container with the Active Directory Users and Computers console, but you can create OUs.

  OU objects are similar to container objects, in that they are both used to hold or group other Active Directory objects together. However, OUs have more attributes of their own and add more functionality. An OU is one of the levels at which you can apply policies using Group Policy; you cannot apply group policies to a container object.

- *New classes of objects* — You can decide to store new, additional classes of objects in Active Directory by defining them in the schema. This is called extending the schema. For example, installing Exchange 2000 as your e-mail server will extend the schema by adding new classes that define objects used only for Exchange. As mentioned earlier, to extend the schema, you must be a member of the Schema Admins Group. Members in the Schema Admins Group have the required rights to modify the default schema in an Active Directory forest.

There are many issues to consider before extending the schema. If not planned and tested properly, adding new classes to the schema can result in reduced performance for the entire network.

1

Replication and Partitions

A domain controller runs Active Directory, manages the domain, and has a copy of the Active Directory database. However, having only one domain controller in a domain has its disadvantages. Recovering from a system failure could take a long time—time during which your users cannot log on or access resources. If, for any reason, your backup can't be restored, or if it is out of date, significant data could be lost. And, it is not pleasant to spend a weekend (or longer) rebuilding an entire domain from scratch.

In any well-designed Active Directory network, you will have several domain controllers. You need to have more than one for fault tolerance and to share the workload in a busy domain. Because each domain controller has a copy of the Active Directory database for its domain, and there are multiple domain controllers, there will also be multiple copies of the database. In Active Directory, the term for a database copy is **replica**.

Keeping multiple copies of a database up to date is difficult, because you must either limit where changes can be made (in one place and only one place), or find a way to deal with the conflict that can arise if the same object is changed in different places at the same time. In all but a few circumstances, a client can write changes to any of the replicas of the Active Directory database. This means Active Directory is a **multiple-master** technology, whereas its predecessors in Windows NT had to make all changes at only one domain controller. The magic that makes this work, is called **replication**, and it has a conflict resolution mechanism. The Active Directory replication process ensures that information in the database is copied everywhere, and that all copies are synchronized and conflicts are resolved. Conflict resolution is discussed in Chapter 8, and replication across a wide area network with sites is discussed in Chapter 7 and with replication in Chapter 8.

To effectively manage the replication of Active Directory, the database is divided into groups called **partitions**, or **naming contexts**. Although all of the naming contexts are stored in one big file on the domain controller, each naming context is replicated independently of the others. This makes sense because some information changes more frequently than other information, and different partitions are replicated to different domain controllers. You should be aware of the following partitions: the schema partition, the domain partition, the configuration partition, and the application partition. Figure 1-5 shows how these partitions might be arranged in a typical forest.

Schema Partition

Active Directory stores the schema in its own partition, called the schema partition. This partition contains all of the definitions of all the classes and attributes in the entire forest. It is replicated to all domain controllers in the forest, and the content will be the same throughout the forest. Every domain controller has one of these partitions.

Although Active Directory is a multi-master technology, there are a few operations that must be guaranteed in order to complete (or abort) without the possibility of having to resolve a conflict. To ensure that this happens correctly, one domain controller is designated as an operations master for these less frequent operations (such as changing the schema). Operations masters are discussed in Chapter 8, but you should be aware that only the schema operations master can write changes to the schema partition.

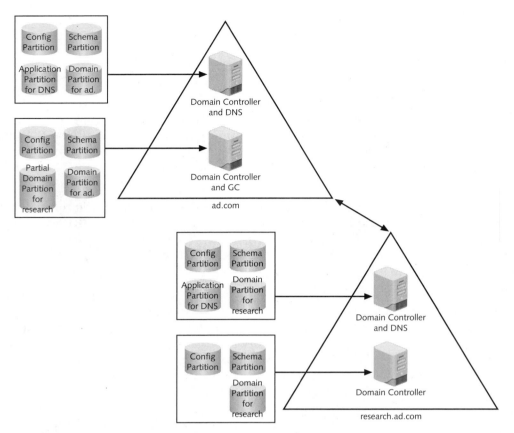

Figure 1-5   Domain controllers and partitions

Domain Partition

When people talk about objects in Active Directory, they are usually talking about objects contained in the domain partition. This is the naming context that contains the users, computers, groups, and OUs created in a Windows domain. This naming context is replicated to all domain controllers in the domain. It is often a large amount of data, and it is usually the partition that changes the most frequently as users are added, deleted, and modified. Each domain controller is—by definition—a member of a domain and will have a copy of this naming context for its own domain. You cannot choose to replicate only part of a domain between domain controllers in that domain. Every domain controller has a full copy of the domain partition for its own domain.

If a domain controller is a Global Catalog server, it will also have partial replicas of the domain partitions for all of the other domains in the forest. These partial replicas from other domains will contain only selected attributes of each object. Global Catalog servers are discussed later in this chapter.

Configuration Partition

The configuration partition stores information about the replication topology used in the forest. This replication topology information specifies how a domain controller determines which other specific partners it will replicate with. This partition also contains information about every other domain in the forest, the names and configuration of sites, and service-specific information, such as the information used by certificate servers if you are using a Public Key Infrastructure (PKI). This partition will also be found on all domain controllers and will be the same throughout the forest.

Application Partition

Application developers can create an application partition and control where it is replicated to. Application partitions cannot contain security principals (users, groups, or computers), but they can be replicated to many different domains in the forest without necessarily being included on all domain controllers. An application partition is used when the developer of an Active Directory-aware application wants to store information in Active Directory, but either wishes to control exactly where it is replicated, or needs to have it replicated beyond one domain.

For example, the Windows DNS server that shipped with Windows 2000 could store information in Active Directory, and have Active Directory replicate it between domain controllers. However, it was stored in the domain-naming context, so to make it available across domains, standard secondary zones had to be used. Also, the DNS information was stored on every domain controller, regardless of whether that domain controller was also a DNS server. The introduction of application partitions in Windows Server 2003 allows DNS information to be replicated to DNS servers running on domain controllers in any domain in the forest and not be replicated to domain controllers that are not DNS servers.

Searching and Global Catalog Servers

Early in this chapter, Active Directory was compared to a telephone company's directory information service. The comparison still applies when you need to look up something in a one-domain forest, or when you stay within a single domain of a multi-domain forest. You simply go out to DNS, find a domain controller, and send it the query. It is more complicated, however, when you need to search across the forest to a different domain.

Activity 1-9: Searching Active Directory

Time Required: 10 minutes

Objective: Practice searching Active Directory for users and printers.

Description: Active Directory provides a robust framework that can be accessed by a wide variety of search tools. Searching will be more meaningful if there are objects in the directory to be found. Your instructor can advise you of any specific objects available in your Active Directory structure, such as printers or published file shares.

1. Ensure that you are logged on to your machine as student*x* with a password of password*x*.

2. On the Desktop, click **Start** and then click **Search**.

3. Click **Other search options**. Record the choices that are available.

4. Click **Printers, computers or people**.

5. Click **A printer on the network**.

6. If you know information about a printer on your network, fill in the Name, Location, or Model text boxes. If not, leave them blank. Click **Find Now** to find all printers listed in the directory.

7. Experiment with selecting different choices on the Features and Advanced tabs to include and exclude various printers.

8. Close the **Find Printers** dialog box.

9. In the Search Companion, click **People in your address book**.

10. Record the locations that can be easily searched by selecting a choice from the Look in drop-down list.

11. Click **Active Directory** in the Look in drop-down box.

12. Type **student** in the Name text box, and click **Find Now**. Note the results that are returned.

13. As time permits, experiment with the options and conditions available for searching.

14. Close all open windows.

15. If you are not continuing immediately, you should log off the machine, as it is unwise to leave an unattended machine logged on.

To get information about an object in another domain, you would first need to know in which other domain to search. Then, you would need to locate a domain controller in that domain. The query and the response would need to travel all the way to that other domain and back, probably crossing over some slower, wide-area links. This kind of system could be problematic. Active Directory poses a better solution. Some domain controllers can be designated as Global Catalog (GC) servers, sometimes referred to as just Global Catalogs.

A GC server, like any other domain controller, has complete information about all of the objects in its own domain, which is stored in a domain partition. In addition, a GC also has a partial replica of the domain partition for all other domains in the forest. Each domain will replicate selected attributes of every object to the GC. You can control which attributes are replicated to the GC, but normally only attributes that are small but useful are replicated, such as the name of the object and where to find more information.

Sometimes the operating system on your workstation needs to query Active Directory on its own, whereas at other times, you (as a user) will wish to search the Active Directory, perhaps to find information on users, printers, or file shares. In either case, when a client workstation wants to search the directory, it needs only to connect to the closest GC for basic information about any object. By using the SRV records in the DNS system, a workstation can locate a GC server in the same site. If more detailed information is needed, the GC can always supply enough information so that the querying client can find the originating domain. A GC also plays a role in the log-on process in a multiple-domain forest, providing information about the user's membership in Universal Groups and finding the home domain of a user if the username is specified in the User Principal Name (UPN) format.

Activity 1-10: Reviewing the JR East Japan Information Systems Company Case Study (Internet access required)

Time Required: 10 minutes

Objective: To learn from published case studies how and why real companies have implemented Active Directory.

Description: Often, software publishers will solicit willing clients to describe their situations and then write case studies about how their products are deployed in the real world. Though written by the company that produces the software, these case studies help explain why a company chose to implement a particular product, and may provide interesting technical information. Some case studies also describe how a product, such as Active Directory, integrates with several related products, third-party tools, or custom in-house software. Case studies were written for the initial release of Active Directory with Windows 2000 and for pre-release and Beta versions of Windows Server 2003, as well as for the final version. Although some of them may be dated, they still provide a relevant overview of how businesses see the product.

1. Read the case study, currently located at *www.microsoft.com/resources/casestudies/CaseStudy.asp? CaseStudyID=13214*, and answer the following questions. Time permitting, visit the other sites listed in the article for more information.

2. Answer the following questions:

    a. Would you describe JEIS as a small, medium, or large business?

    b. What is its geographic presence? Is it LAN-based or WAN-based?

    c. What were the key business factors that drove the need for a change in the network?

    d. How did Active Directory specifically address those business drivers?

    e. What are the one or two specific Active Directory features highlighted most in this case study?

    f. Did Active Directory reduce costs? Did it improve performance?

Activity 1-11: Reviewing the Peoplesoft Case Study (Internet access required)

Time Required: 10 minutes

Objective: To learn from published case studies how and why real companies have implemented Active Directory.

Description: This case study is similar in format to the last activity, allowing you to make comparisons and draw contrasts between the two.

The Microsoft Web site is often reorganized, so if the document is not present at this link, search the site for "Active Directory case study."

1. Connect to *www.microsoft.com/resources/casestudies/CaseStudy.asp?CaseStudyID=12353*. Time permitting, visit the other sites listed in the article to obtain more information, or review additional Microsoft case studies on Active Directory or Windows Server 2003.

2. Answer the following questions:

    a. Would you describe PeopleSoft as a small, medium, or large business? What is its geographic presence? Is it LAN-based or WAN-based?

    b. Are there any immediate similarities as to how the companies in these two case studies view network infrastructures and the role of Active Directory? Are there differences?

    c. List some specific Active Directory features highlighted in this case study, which were not mentioned in the earlier case study.

CHAPTER SUMMARY

❑ A directory service provides a way to locate, manage, and control objects and resources on the network. Specifically, Active Directory is the directory service for networks running Windows Server 2003 or Windows 2000 network operating systems. It is a single point of management for the network, providing search mechanisms and enabling single sign on for users. Active Directory provides authentication and authorization for the operating system, and is a critical application for the proper and secure functioning of your network.

❑ Active Directory can also be used by applications and the operating system to centralize authentication and authorization functions.

❑ Other application developers can choose to add new objects and new attributes or associate additional attributes with an object class in the directory by extending the schema.

❑ Application developers can also create an application partition to store information in the directory for their own application's use.

❏ Whether information is to support the operating system or for an application, everything stored in Active Directory is secured and administrators can determine who can see which pieces of information.

❏ Active Directory is a database that represents your network. Windows networks are usually organized into domains, which are groupings of computers with common management and a joint security model. Domains are also grouped into trees and forests. The Active Directory schema defines everything that can be stored in Active Directory.

❏ A schema defines classes, which are like blueprints from which objects are created. Common objects include users, computers, printers, file shares, groups, contacts, and organizational units. Each class identifies the attributes associated with each object of that type. Security principals have attributes used in the security system. Users, computers, and security groups are security principals.

❏ Machines that run Active Directory and have a copy of the database are called domain controllers. The database is divided into partitions (or naming contexts) so that different parts of the database can be replicated to the domain controllers. Partial information from every object in every domain in the forest is replicated to designated Global Catalog servers to facilitate the search for objects across different domains in a forest.

KEY TERMS

Active Directory (AD) — Microsoft's directory service for Windows networks. Active Directory is a Microsoft trademark.

Active Directory-aware — A term used to describe application software that makes use of information stored in Active Directory.

attributes — The schema contains a list of all possible properties or attributes that can be included in class definitions. When speaking of a class, its attributes are a collection of information (or properties) about each object instantiated from the class, which is stored in Active Directory. Collectively, an object's attributes define the object.

authenticate — Determination of which security principal is attempting to log on or access a resource. Most often, proving that a user is who they claim to be through the use of a name and password combination.

authorization — Once the identity of a security principal has been determined (through authentication), it is necessary to determine whether that security principal is allowed to access a particular resource (authorization).

container — Generically speaking, a container is an object in the directory that can contain a collection of other objects. Specifically, a class of objects called "container" is available in Active Directory. Two default containers created in an Active Directory installation are called Computers and Users.

directory service (DS) — A network application or database, usually integrated as a core component of a network operating system, that provides information about users, computers, resources, and other network elements and a centralized location to manage security permissions and access to network resources.

discretionary access control list (DACL) — A list of SIDs used by the system to control which security principals can gain access to a resource.

domain — Computers, users, and resources using a joint security model, usually under common management.

Domain Admins — The group of users with complete administrative control over domain controllers, and by default, control over all machines in the domain.

domain controller (DC) — A Windows server, hosting the Active Directory database, which manages operations of a domain.

Global Catalog server — A designated domain controller that holds partial replica of every domain naming context in the forest as well as a complete copy of its own domain naming context. That is, it has key attributes of every object in the forest, available primarily for searching.

Group Policy — A technology, enabled by Active Directory that allows administrators to define policy and rely on Active Directory and the operating system to ensure that policies are enforced. Also used to automatically distribute software.

joint security model — A means of organizing a computer network so that security principals (such as a user) can access resources hosted on all machines participating in the model. All users and resources share a common authentication scheme. A Windows domain is a joint security model.

Kerberos protocol — A network protocol first developed at MIT to allow for a wide-area, distributed method of securely authenticating users before they are allowed to access network resources.

multiple-master — A database that has many copies of the same information; each copy is writeable.

naming context — A category or division of information within Active Directory. Each naming context is replicated separately.

object — This is an instance of a class. That is, one particular item created from a class definition, such as a user object created from the definition contained in the user class.

operating system (OS) — The software that runs the computer itself, such as Windows, Linux, or DOS.

organizational unit (OU) — An Active Directory object used to contain or group other objects. An OU is a point at which group policy can be applied or permissions delegated.

partition — *See* naming context.

replica — A copy of the Active Directory database stored on a domain controller.

replication — The process by which Active Directory information is copied to multiple domain controllers and conflicts are resolved.

resources — Any shared piece of equipment or information made available to users on the network, such as file shares, e-mail systems, printers, and the like.

schema — The list of object classes and attributes that describes what can be stored in the Active Directory database.

security identifier (SID) — A binary number that uniquely represents a security principal. For most security principals, the two key components are a domain identifier and a RID that are unique within the domain.

security principal — An object in the directory to which resource permissions can be granted. In Active Directory, security principals are users, computers, and security groups.

single sign on — The concept that a user only has to identify himself or herself once (with a password or other security token) to access all resources that he or she has been authorized to use throughout the enterprise's network.

tree — A group of one or more domains in a forest that have a contiguous namespace.

write-ahead log files — A database technology that ensures that any proposed changes to a database are written to a log file on disk before the transaction is confirmed to the originator, and before changes are actually made to the data. If the system fails, all confirmed transactions could be recreated from the log file(s).

REVIEW QUESTIONS

1. A(n) _____ provides organization, control, searching, or management of network objects.

2. What is special about objects that are "security principals?"

   a. They are the user objects representing network administrators.

   b. They can have other objects created beneath them in a hierarchical structure.

   c. They can be granted (or denied) permission to access specific network resources.

   d. They are used only in networks with more than one domain.

3. Which of the following objects are security principals? (Choose all that apply.)

   a. Users

   b. Distribution groups

   c. Security groups

   d. Published folders

   e. Organizational units

   f. Computers

4. The _____ stored in Active Directory, is also stored in Discretionary Access Control Lists to manage permissions.

5. What is special about a DC?

   a. It stores a copy of the Active Directory database.

   b. It is the server that always runs Microsoft Exchange.

   c. It must be running Windows Server 2003, Enterprise Edition or Windows Server 2003 Datacenter Edition.

   d. It stores some attributes for every object in the forest.

6. What is the advantage of single sign on?

   a. Users only have to authenticate once during their work session.

   b. It is more secure than using smart cards.

   c. It can be used without an Active Directory or Windows NT domain.

   d. Users don't need to use a password as long as they always use the same workstation.

7. The _____ protocol is used when a user of Windows 2000, Windows XP Professional, or Windows Server 2003 logs on to an Active Directory domain.

8. Where is the directory information for Microsoft Exchange Server 2000 or 2003 (an e-mail system) kept?

   a. In the Exchange Directory service

   b. In the Security Account Management (SAM) database

   c. In the domain partition

   d. In the mail server's registry

9. Active Directory uses a highly customized version of the _____, which was based on the joint engine technology for its database engine.

10. In an Active Directory domain, users need a different password for each domain controller. True or False?

11. How are domains, trees, and forests related?

12. How are objects, classes, and attributes related?

   a. An object has many classes and attributes.

   b. A class has many objects, but only one attribute.

   c. A list of attributes that are all equal is called a class.

   d. A class defines the attributes that make up an object.

13. Which kind of object *cannot* be created with the Active Directory Users and Computers MMC snap-in?

   a. User

   b. Organizational unit

   c. Distribution Group

   d. Container

14. For which attributes do you need to supply values when creating a user?

    a. Password and object ID

    b. Display Name and Password

    c. Security ID (SID) and Logon Name

    d. Logon Name and Display Name

15. Which of the following functions do OUs provide?

    a. OUs can each have their own password-length policies defined for domain user accounts.

    b. OUs can each have their own group policies applied.

    c. OUs are each stored in their own partition (naming context).

    d. OUs each have their own dedicated domain controllers.

16. In a default installation, which partition (naming context) is *not* automatically installed on every domain controller?

    a. Schema

    b. Domain

    c. Configuration

    d. Application

17. User passwords can be changed by updating the replica on any domain controller in the user's domain. True or False?

18. Administrators control how every _____ is replicated. It can be replicated to any or all of the domain controllers in a forest.

19. Only members of the _____ group are allowed to extend the Active Directory schema.

20. Which is a key difference between a user object and a contact object?

    a. Users can have e-mail addresses; contacts cannot.

    b. Users can be organized in OUs; contacts cannot.

    c. Contacts can have e-mail addresses; users cannot.

    d. Users can be granted permissions on resources; contacts cannot.

MNC/Heartland Hospital Case Projects

Case Project Background

Despite its size, the hospital doesn't have a dedicated IT staff, as this is seen as a luxury in a tightly funded healthcare environment. Instead, clerical and administrative staff handle most of the administration of the computers, relying as well on a variety of suppliers, consultants, and the children of secretaries. Your initial contact is Mary Firth, a competent office manager who, although self-taught with computers, does have a good grasp of the concepts. Three new support staff members were recently hired, and new computers have been installed for Bob Baker, Jane Julliard, and Pat Peters.

Mary calls you and asks you to come over and address a few issues that seem to be cropping up with some of the new computers.

Case Project 1-1: Setting a Local Password

Jane Julliard works in the medical records department. When her computer was delivered, the reseller told her that her password was left blank "so it would be easier for everyone to access her files." She has been logging on to the workstation as an administrator, and is uncomfortable with the possibility of confidential records being accessed. How would you address the problem? Refer to the steps you practiced in Activity 1-1 for guidelines on how to change a password.

Case Project 1-2: Peer-to-Peer Problems

Bob Baker is the new facilities manager working with the physical plant. His new computer is constantly asking him for a password and he sometimes has to use different passwords to access different file shares. He also reports a great deal of trouble printing. He would like to access the color printer and high-speed laser printer, but doesn't know which server they are connected to. When he shows you how he logs on, you notice that he is not able to select the hospital's domain on his log-on screen. What are some possible causes of this problem? How would you resolve the problem and make him part of his domain?

Case Project 1-3: Active Directory-Aware or Not?

Mary tells you that the hospital is considering purchasing some new database and e-mail software. Although they realize it's time to make a purchase, the board is concerned with cost and wants to maximize the use of funds. They are considering Exchange Server 2003 and SQL Server 2000 (an e-mail and database application, respectively), which are both Active Directory-aware and can participate fully in the domain security model. The other option is to purchase Windows Server 2003 to use for Active Directory, but use Microsoft Access for database projects and a Web-based e-mail provider (such as MSN Hotmail or Yahoo! Mail) for their e-mail. Assuming that both solutions provide the functionality required for database and communications, what advantages would be gained from using Active Directory-aware applications? In addition to cost, what other factors would you advise the client to consider when making her decision?

2

INSTALLING ACTIVE DIRECTORY

> **After reading this chapter and completing the exercises, you will be able to:**
> ◆ Describe the purpose and general functionality of the Domain Name System on the Internet and local networks
> ◆ Understand how Active Directory relies on the Domain Name System
> ◆ Use the Active Directory Installation Wizard to install Active Directory

In Chapter 1, you learned about the role of directory services—particularly Active Directory—in a modern computer network. You also learned the fundamental concepts and components of Active Directory and practiced using some of the tools and programs that work with Active Directory.

This chapter introduces the Domain Name System (DNS) that is used on the public Internet and explores how DNS provides crucial support to Active Directory. You will learn how to install and configure the Microsoft DNS Server components on a server, and how to configure DNS services to support Active Directory.

This chapter will also teach you how to install Active Directory in a variety of situations. It is important to note an essential difference between a classroom and a production business environment. In a classroom or testing lab, it doesn't really matter if a system is not online constantly or if it is not running in the most efficient way possible. Because you are learning and testing, errors and problems are possible, and they are tolerated. You can "play with" a system in a non-production environment, and try out different options, just to see what they do. This wouldn't be acceptable on a live network, often called a production environment, on which an enterprise is depending. In a production environment, it is crucial to the success of an Active Directory deployment that you design, plan, and test before leaping into installation. Design and planning issues are discussed in Chapters 3 and 4.

Understanding the Domain Name System

The **Domain Name System (DNS)** is the network service that allows us to connect to a server on the Internet by name, rather than by its network address. This process, called name resolution, translates a host name (such as *www.microsoft.com* or *mailserver1.northamerica.corporate.multinatcorp.com*) into an Internet Protocol (IP) address (such as *207.46.230.229* or *192.168.71.8*). For most people, names are much easier to remember than numbers and tend to remain relatively constant, while IP numbers change from time to time. DNS is similar to a telephone directory in its ability to give you a number from a name.

When a network connection is made between computers on the Internet, the computers can then pass information back and forth using their IP numbers. DNS can also be used to provide **reverse lookup** services, which is the ability to identify a host's name by knowing its IP number. This is useful for logging and reporting, analysis, and configuring certain types of security.

 DNS can provide name services for private networks; however, it is most commonly known for its role in the operation of the public Internet. DNS works well on the Internet because it is a distributed system that scales well (it currently holds millions of names and IP addresses).

Like all Internet standards, the operation of DNS is defined by a set of documents collected by the Internet Engineering Task Force (IETF). No one person or company invented DNS, but all properly working DNS software follows the same set of basic rules. It is beyond the scope of this book to discuss in detail the standards development process, but if you are interested in learning more, you can visit the IETF at *www.ietf.org* or download the DNS standard from *ftp://ftp.isi.edu/in-notes/rfc1034.txt*.

All network administrators need to have some knowledge of the DNS system. We will begin our discussion with DNS structure.

DNS Structure

When you wish to organize a pile of papers into files, you first have to find a logical way to divide them. Perhaps you will put all of your personal files in the top drawer of the file cabinet, and all work-related documents in the bottom drawer. You can then choose to divide them by year and, within each year, alphabetically. While many different filing approaches can be used, anyone who knows your chosen method should be able to find a document quickly.

A similar sorting of DNS names makes it possible to find a desired IP number quickly using the DNS system. For example, consider a mail server located at our sample company, Multinational Mega Corporation. A machine operating on the Internet is called a host. Its full DNS address is called a **fully qualified domain name (FQDN)**. The FQDN for our mail server is *mailserver1.northamerica.corporate.multinatcorp.com* and its IP address is *192.168.71.8*.

DNS Names

All possible DNS names are contained in what is sometimes called the **DNS namespace**. Figure 2-1 shows a simplified view of this namespace concept. The namespace is divided into domains. There is a **root domain** that represents the entire namespace and is represented by a single period ("."). The next level of categorization is a **top-level domain (TLD)**, which is the rightmost part of a host's name. In this example, the mail server is in the *.com* TLD, which is the most widely known of all TLDs. There are many other TLDs, which are divided into two categories: **country code TLDs (ccTLD)** and **generic TLDs (gTLD)**. The next two sections will look at each of these top-level domains.

 A DNS domain and a Windows domain are not the same thing, although they may share the same namespace. To avoid confusion, we will use the term "domain," if used alone, to refer to a Windows domain, and the terms "top-level domain," "TLD," or "subdomain" to refer to a DNS domain.

TLD by Country

Each country has been assigned a two-letter TLD, such as *.ca* for Canada and *.uk* for the United Kingdom of Great Britain and Northern Ireland. These are called country code TLDs (ccTLDs). Each national government defines the rules for its own ccTLD. Some, like Tuvalu (.tv) and Micronesia (.fm) have sold rights to their ccTLD namespace to corporate entities to gain much needed capital. Other countries may do the same. Although not as commonly used, there is a *.us* ccTLD.

The ccTLD abbreviation for each country is assigned by the Internet Assigned Numbers Authority (IANA), and is based on the list of country codes maintained by the International Standards Organization (ISO). Ranging from *.ac* for Ascension Island to *.zw* for Zimbabwe, the complete list of ccTLDs and policies concerning their assignment can be found at *www.iana.org/cctld/cctld.htm*.

Generic TLD

Generic TLDs are termed as such because they are not tied to any one particular country, and they can include very common TLDs, such as .com, .net, and .org.

New gTLDs are being created everyday. Some of the newer ones include *.info, .biz*, and even *.museum*. Each of these TLDs has specific criteria governing who can register names within it. For example, only U.S. military entities exist in *.mil*. The most exclusive TLD is probably *.int*, which allows only entities created by multinational treaty to register. Current examples include *worldbank.int* and *nato.int*. Although there are a number of proposals for new gTLDs, as of this writing, the current list is as follows: *.aero, .biz, .com, .coop, .edu, .gov, .info, .int, .mil, .museum, .name, .net, .org*, and *.pro*. You can read more about gTLDs at *www.iana.org/gtld/gtld.htm*.

There is one additional TLD, known as the *.arpa* domain, which is used to provide reverse lookup services. IANA calls it an "infrastructure TLD," and states that the abbreviation means "address and routing parameter area." It is worth noting, however, that the Defense Advanced Research Projects Agency (DARPA) developed the first networks that became the Internet, and was commonly called ARPA. The forerunner of the Internet, in the late 1960s, was known as the ARPANET.

Figure 2-1 shows how the many gTLDs and ccTLDs fit within the root namespace.

 Because an address can be assigned at any level of the DNS hierarchy, some TLD operators have a Web site on a host directly in a TLD, such as *www.lk* (a host called *www* in the *lk* TLD). In theory, an IP address could even be assigned directly to a TLD, and in the past there have been Web sites like *http://cc* or *http://tv*. In practice, however, a fully qualified domain name has at least two parts.

The Role of Subdomains

Each TLD is further subdivided into smaller portions, called **subdomains**. There is really no difference between a subdomain and any other DNS domain, except that a subdomain is always contained within a TLD or another subdomain. Subdomains are usually registered to organizations or individuals. For example, *microsoft.com* is a subdomain in the *.com* gTLD, and has been registered to Microsoft Corporation. The government of Canada has registered *gc.ca*, a subdomain in the .ca ccTLD.

A subdomain can be divided into even more subdomains, particularly if your DNS domain encompasses a large network or needs to be divided for organizational reasons. As discussed later in this chapter, an Active Directory domain also needs its own DNS subdomain. The example mail server *mailserver1. northamerica.corporate.multinatcorp.com* is in a subdomain called *northamerica*. The *northamerica* subdomain is, in turn, a subdomain of *corporate*; *corporate* is a subdomain of *multinatcorp*; and *multinatcorp* is a subdomain of the gTLD *.com*. Knowing that there can be multiple subdomains is useful because DNS is hierarchical, not flat. In a flat namespace, no two computers could have the same name—only one server could be named *www*! Multiple subdomains make management easier, searching more efficient, and names of computers only have to be unique within their subdomain. So, *www.mycorp.com*, *www.yourcorp.com*, and *www.sales.mycorp.com* are all separate machines.

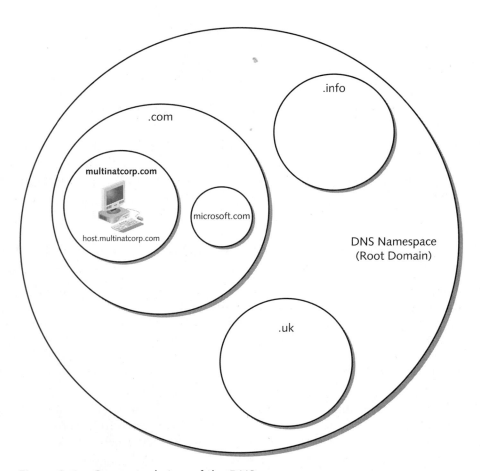

Figure 2-1   Conceptual view of the DNS namespace

Activity 2-1 Examining the Registration of a Subdomain

Time Required: 5 minutes

Objective: To practice looking up the registration information of a DNS subdomain that has been publicly registered.

Description: Before creating a new Active Directory domain (*research.multinatcorp.com*) that will be part of an existing DNS subdomain (*multinatcorp.com*), be sure that you know how the subdomain is registered on the Internet and that authority is properly delegated for your new subdomain.

1. If necessary, start your computer and log on.

2. Start **Internet Explorer** or a Web browser of your choice, and connect to the Internet.

3. Go to **www.internic.net**.

4. Click **Whois** from the menu near the top of the page.

5. Type **multinatcorp.com**, which is the name of the DNS subdomain in the text box on the Whois search form. Then click **Submit**.

6. The basic information will be shown in the result page, including the names of registered DNS name servers for the subdomain. Because there are now multiple registrars, you may also see a line labeled Referral URL.

7. If desired, browse to the Referral URL and search for more detailed information.

2

The Internet is dynamic, and each registrar is responsible for its own Web site. You may have to explore a bit to find the detailed information.

Each computer's FQDN has a name for the host itself. In the example mail server *mailserver1.northamerica. corporate.multinatcorp.com*, the machine's hostname is *mailserver1.* The hostname, by itself, is not unique. There could be another *mailserver1* out there, perhaps in the *southamerica* subdomain. An FQDN, however, is unique in a properly configured network. There can be only one TLD called *.com*; only one *multinatcorp* in *.com*; only one *corporate* in *multinatcorp.com*; only one *northamerica* in *corporate.multinatcorp.com*; and only one host called *mailserver1* in *northamerica.corporate.multinatcorp.com*.

Registrars Operate TLDs

Each TLD is operated by a registrar who collects and manages information from those who register in it, usually for a fee. If a network operator were to set up a DNS Server and establish his own *microsoft.com* subdomain without regard to the registration process, the DNS system would be unable to function properly within that network. The rest of the world would carry on operations, but users of that DNS Server would not be able to reach the Microsoft Web site.

In most cases, this is not desirable. However, it is one way to deliberately block access to certain sites (but only by name, not by IP number). It is also a way to create a private DNS structure that will not be exposed to any user or service outside a private network. For this reason, some DNS Servers have information about fictitious TLDs or subdomains, such as *.local* or *.private*. However, all subdomains within a public TLD should be registered with that TLD's registrar. In other words, a private DNS structure under *.net*, such as *mycorp.net* should be registered with *.net*. If not, problems could arise later if someone else registers your fictitious subdomain.

The IANA pages mentioned for gTLD and ccTLD information also include the name and contact information for the registrars or operators of each TLD.

DNS Servers

With an understanding of how the DNS is organized, you can examine how a computer actually finds an address for a given FQDN. Just as certain computers keep a copy of the Active Directory database and are known as domain controllers, certain computers store parts of the DNS database and are called DNS Servers. Often, domain controllers are also DNS Servers, but DNS Servers also commonly run on Unix/Linux platforms or dedicated Windows servers. The purpose of a DNS Server is to answer queries presented by clients or other DNS Servers about hosts and related addressing information.

Each piece of DNS information, such as the address for a particular host, is called a Resource Record (RR). There are several types of RRs in the DNS system. The most common is an **address (A)** record that records the IP address of a host. Other important RR types include the **mail exchanger (MX)** record that directs e-mail to the correct server, the **name server (NS)** record, and **start-of-authority (SOA)** records.

RRs are kept in either a text file or a database and are collected or grouped into DNS zones. A zone normally includes all the RRs for a subdomain, but a single zone could include a subdomain and all subdomains contained within it. For example, the RRs for *mydomain.com* and *subdivision.mydomain.com* could be kept in one zone or divided into two zones. **Zones** are administrative divisions that allow you to manage how DNS information is replicated between DNS Servers, and allow you to control which DNS Servers provide information about which DNS subdomains. To put it another way, a zone contains all the information about a DNS domain, except for any parts of that DNS domain that are delegated elsewhere (such as another level of subdomain).

Zones are sometimes referred to as zone files because in most non-Windows implementations, the RRs are stored in text files. The most common DNS Server software used on the Internet is called BIND. BIND is an acronym for Berkeley Internet Name Domain. (It is no longer developed at Berkeley, and it used to be called a "Naming Daemon," but its acronym has now become its name in almost all common uses.) Originally designed for UNIX, versions of BIND are also available for Windows. BIND uses zone files and because of its popularity, BIND terminology permeates the industry. Zone or zone data are better terms than zone file, because DNS Servers can use databases, Active Directory, or even the Windows registry to store RRs.

No one DNS Server could possibly hold all of the RRs used on the Internet. Rather, when a DNS Server is configured, its administrators decide which DNS subdomains that particular server will provide answers about. The administrators then make sure that the server has copies of the zone information for those DNS subdomains. For example, a host called *nameserver1.mydomain.com* could be the DNS Server for the *mydomain.com* subdomain. *Nameserver1* would then be configured to store all of the RRs relating to *mydomain.com* in a zone. A second server, *nameserver2*, could also be created to share the workload and to keep a redundant copy of the zone in case something were to happen to *nameserver1*.

Authoritative Servers

When a DNS Server has a zone containing a particular subdomain, it is said to be authoritative for that subdomain. In other words, a DNS Server that knows all there is to know about that subdomain without asking any other name server is an "authority" on the subject. A DNS Server will *never* ask another server about a subdomain for which it is authoritative. This means that if a DNS Server has a zone file for a particular subdomain, it will never ask any other DNS Server about that zone. When troubleshooting a DNS or name resolution problem, it is important to remember that the request does not go to any other servers after it has been processed by an authoritative server. If a given record is in one server but not another, this is almost always an error (except in the special case called "split DNS," discussed in Chapter 4) and can be difficult to troubleshoot.

When a subdomain is registered in a TLD, the registrar collects information about the person or organization registering the subdomain. From a technical standpoint, the most important information gathered includes the names and IP addresses of at least two authoritative DNS Servers that will answer queries about the new subdomain. The registrar enters NS records into the TLD zone so that the TLD DNS Servers can refer queries to the subdomain's name servers. This is called delegation. For example, the *.com* TLD has delegated the authority for *learning.com* to the server *ns011.intelonline.com*. The root domain has delegated authority for a TLD to a DNS Server operated by the TLD. The TLD usually delegates authority for each subdomain to DNS Servers in that subdomain.

As you will see in the next section, this process of delegation that begins at the root domain and follows down through all subdomain levels is fundamental to the operation of the DNS system.

Most DNS Servers for the root domain and for TLDs refer queries only to other DNS Servers that provide more specific answers—that is, most TLD DNS Servers do not provide answers themselves (unless there are hosts in the TLD itself). This is because the root and TLD servers must answer hundreds of millions of queries in the fastest possible time. As of this writing, the root DNS name server in London, England (k.root-servers.net), averages three million queries a day, and there are 12 other root-server sites.

 The word "authoritative" is sometimes used to describe the servers listed with NS records in the TLD or in the subdomain's own zone. This is not necessarily incorrect, because a registered DNS Server should always be an authoritative DNS Server. Regrettably, it is not always so. Avoid confusion by using the term "registered DNS Server" for servers registered with a public registrar and "authoritative DNS Server" for servers that have zone information for the subdomain. The term "delegated DNS Server" can be used to refer to a server listed with an NS in a higher-level subdomain.

Prior to the advent of Active Directory, changes to RRs in a zone could only be made at one DNS Server. This DNS Server with a read-write copy of the zone is called a **primary name server**. Any other DNS Servers with read-only copies of the zone are called **secondary name servers** (see Figure 2-2). In our example, *nameserver1* is our primary name server, and *nameserver2* is our secondary name server. In a properly configured environment, the secondary name servers receive updated information and new RRs from the primary name server. A common misconfiguration occurs when you accidentally create two (or more) primary servers for the same zone, which results in changes not being propagated to all of the authoritative servers.

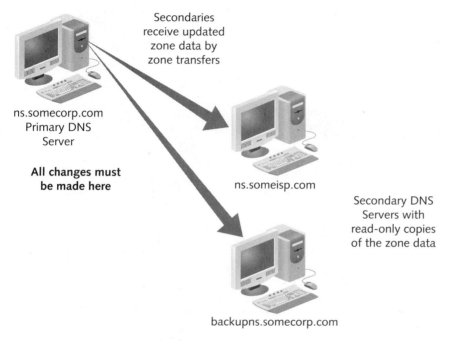

Figure 2-2   Primary and secondary name servers

Using the Microsoft DNS Server that is shipped with all versions of the Windows Server 2003 family simplifies the process and can eliminate the need for primary and secondary servers. The Microsoft DNS Server can be configured to store zone information in Active Directory, where it is automatically replicated as an updateable copy between domain controllers.

Transferring Information

Zone information is transferred from a primary DNS Server to a secondary DNS Server using a process called **zone transfer**, which is shown in Figure 2-2. Traditional DNS Servers copied the entire zone whenever a change was made, no matter how small the change.

To make the process of updating secondary DNS Servers more efficient, modern DNS Servers, including Microsoft DNS, support incremental zone transfer. **Incremental zone transfers** are more efficient because they send only new or changed information across the network, which decreases traffic. Traditionally, a secondary DNS Server had to poll its primary DNS Server to check for changes. Newer servers, including Microsoft DNS, can be configured so that the primary DNS Server will notify the secondary DNS Servers as soon as a change occurs. This reduces the time it takes for all authoritative servers to receive the correct information. Information about the current version of the zone is stored in the SOA resource record and is kept in all copies of the zone.

Primary Does Not Mean Authoritative

Many people mix and match DNS terms incorrectly. It may be confusing at first, but a primary DNS Server and an authoritative DNS Server are not the same. Many organizations publicly register only secondary servers, because their primary server is behind a firewall. An example of this arrangement is pictured in Figure 2-3. In this case, the TLD and other hosts on the Internet know that the secondary DNS Servers are authoritative, but know nothing about the primary server. Inside the organization, however, the primary server is still an authoritative server because it has a copy of the zone.

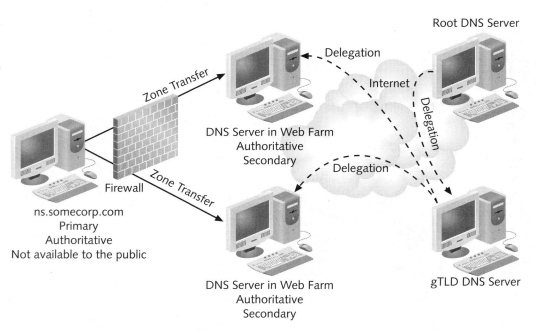

Figure 2-3   A typical DNS scenario

The DNS Name Resolution Process

A computer workstation that accesses the Internet uses an IP number to indicate its preferred DNS Server. If the workstation has been configured manually, an administrator has entered the DNS Server's IP number. If the workstation is configured automatically with Dynamic Host Configuration Protocol (DHCP), then a DNS Server's IP address is usually provided by the DHCP Server. When the workstation needs to look up an IP address, perhaps because the user wishes to browse a Web site, the workstation will use the IP address for its DNS Server to send a query to the DNS Server.

There are two kinds of queries that can be issued to a DNS Server: recursive and iterative (or nonrecursive). Recursive queries are the default and indicate that the client wants the address resolved if at all possible, or an error if it cannot be resolved. The client does not want to ask any other DNS Server, but wishes the DNS Server to find an address, even if it has to ask another DNS Server. Conversely, an iterative (or nonrecursive) query indicates that the client wants the DNS Server to respond only with information from that particular DNS Server. It expects a resolved address, an error, or a referral to another server.

It is this ability to issue referrals that makes the DNS system both highly scaleable and geographically dispersed. This is very useful if *nameserver1* doesn't have zone information about the *nt.scouts.ca* subdomain, but knows where to find it.

Figure 2-4 illustrates the resolution of a DNS query.

A client workstation *mydesk.corp.multinatcorp.com* needs to resolve an IP address for *www.nt.scouts.ca* so that the user can browse the photo album of her child's last scouting trip. The workstation has been configured by DHCP to use *192.168.71.7* (the host *nameserver1.corp.multinatcorp.com*) as its DNS name server, so the workstation issues a recursive request to the name server.

The name server looks at its cache of recently retrieved records. Because the name server has not looked up this entry before, it finds no match. The DNS Server also checks its own zones. It quickly determines that it is not authoritative for *nt.scouts.ca*. If it did have a copy of the *nt.scouts.ca* zone, it would immediately return the entry for *www*, or an error if it did not exist.

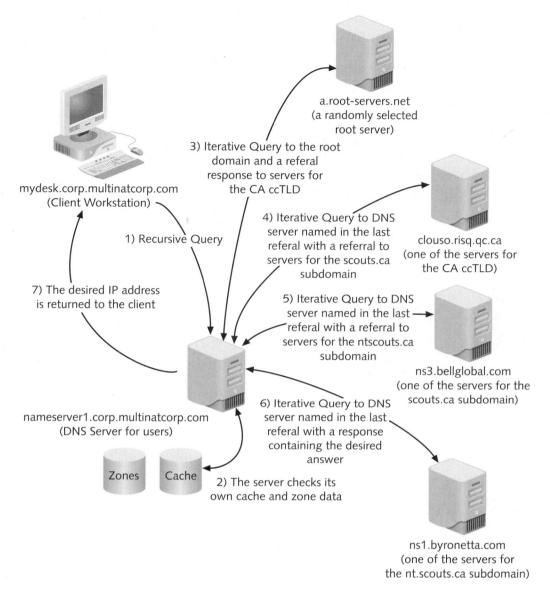

Figure 2-4   Resolving a DNS query

Nameserver1 has no information about the desired host, but it knows where to look. Name servers that perform recursion have entries in their databases that point to the servers for the root DNS domain. These entries are called root hints, and are shown in Figure 2-5. The name server picks one of the root servers and sends it an iterative (nonrecursive) query for the desired record. The root name server, *a.root-servers.net* in this example, checks its own zones and cache.

 For some interesting statistics and information about root servers, visit the Root Servers Technical Operations Association at *www.root-servers.org*.

Because *www.nt.scouts.ca* is not in the root DNS domain, the root name server checks to see if it has NS records delegating authority for the gTLD or ccTLD (in this case a ccTLD). Because *.ca* is a common ccTLD, it finds several records pointing to authoritative servers for *.ca* and sends these NS records back to the requesting server. *Nameserver1* now knows something about the *.ca* domain. To avoid the need to resolve the IP address for the next name server, the records returned include the IP numbers for the delegated name servers. The name server that sent the query (*nameserver1*) will cache this information for future use, so a new query for any host in any .*ca* subdomain will not need to go to the root server, and will skip this step in the future. See Figure 2-5.

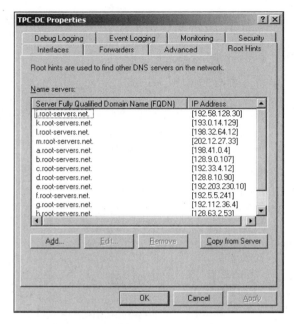

Figure 2-5   Root hints in Microsoft DNS Server

 In production environments, the root servers are rarely queried as the TLD referrals are cached, usually for 48 hours or longer.

The process repeats again, this time by sending an iterative query to one of the name servers included in the records returned from the root. Name server referrals are usually returned in a round-robin order to divide up the work. The next name server up in the batting order for .*ca* happens to be *clouso.risq.qc.ca*, in Montreal. Like the root name servers, TLD name servers are usually operated by larger organizations that are geographically dispersed. RISQ is the scientific and post-secondary education network for the Province of Québec. The TLD server *clouso* checks its zone information and its cache, but does not have a record for the requested host. It does, however, have NS records delegating authority for the subdomain *scouts.ca*, and returns the names and IP addresses of those authoritative servers.

Nameserver1 now caches the information for future use and will keep it for the length of time specified in the NS record. The name server submits the query to *ns3.bellglobal.com*. The ISP for the National Office of Scouts Canada operates this machine, which checks its own zone and cache and finds no record for the desired host. As in the last two cases, there are records delegating the authority for the next level of subdomain (*nt.scouts.ca*) to a different set of DNS Servers.

The requesting server caches the new information and then presents the query to *ns1.byronetta.com*, a name server operated by a small company that provides Web hosting for this particular site. This name server *ns1* checks its cache and zone information and finds that it is authoritative for *nt.scouts.ca*, and that it does have an A record for the desired host. It returns the IP address to the requesting name server.

Finally, *nameserver1* has collected all of the required information, cached it for future use, and can now send the answer back to the client's workstation, complete with an IP address. The user's browser can now retrieve the Web pages, allowing her to view the photographs of her child.

2

Written out, this seems like a lengthy process, but it is very efficient. This process uses the User Datagram Protocol (UDP), not the Transmission Control Protocol (TCP), in order to avoid the overhead required to set up and tear down TCP connections. Caching the results improves performance and eliminates all but a few trips to the root server (and many trips to the gTLD servers). You can work through these steps manually using the nslookup included with Windows, but one of the BIND tools—DIG—will show these details automatically, making it worth the effort to download the BIND tools. A sample DIG output is shown in Figure 2-6.

Figure 2-6   Sample DIG output

Activity 2-2 Tracing DNS Name Resolution

Time Required: 15 minutes

Objective: To trace DNS name resolution and referrals from the root servers to the destination.

Description: Although you thought all DNS authorities were properly delegated, you are experiencing occasional DNS name resolution problems. You suspect that perhaps one host has been registered incorrectly or a delegation record might have the wrong IP address. You know that one domain controller is named *dc1.ad.multinatcorp.com*. You want to quickly view all relevant information in as few steps as possible.

1. If necessary, start your computer and log on to **Windows**.

2. Use your Internet browser or an FTP client to visit the Internet Software Consortium so that you can download a free copy of the BIND name server and tools, precompiled for the Windows platform. Begin at the location: **ftp://ftp.isc.org/isc/bind/**. Note that BIND is usually distributed as source code to be compiled by the user; however, precompiled versions for Windows are in the contrib folder (short for *contributed*).

3. Open the **contrib** folder (in Internet Explorer and most FTP clients, double-click to open a folder).

4. Click the most recent version folder that starts with **ntbind**. Ensure that it is a version greater than 9.1. (We wrote and tested this activity using version 9.2.2.)

5. Download the .zip file from this folder. To do so, follow these steps:

   a. Double-click the zip file. As of this writing, the file is named **BIND9.2.2.zip**.

   b. When the Internet Explorer security warning appears, click **Add**.

   c. In the Trusted Sites dialog box, click **Add**.

   d. In the Trusted Sites dialog box, click **Close**.

    e. Click **OK**.

    f. In the newly opened Internet Explorer window titled "No page to display", click the refresh icon (the 4th icon from the left on the standard toolbar).

    g. In the File Download dialog box, click **Save**. Specify a suitable location, such as your **My Documents** folder.

    h. When the download is complete, click **Open Folder**.

6. Open the downloaded .zip file, by double-clicking it. (*Note*: If your client workstation is running an OS earlier than Windows XP or Windows Server 2003, you will need a tool such as Winzip, which can be found at *www.winzip.com*.)

7. Extract the files **dig.exe**, **dig.html**, **libdns.dll**, **libeay32.dll**, and **libisc.dll** to a suitable directory on your hard disk, such as c:\dig.

8. To start a command prompt, click **Start**, click **Run**, and then type **cmd** and press **Enter**.

9. When the command prompt window opens, change the default directory to the one used in Step 7, where you just placed the DIG files. To do this, type **cd c:\dig** and press **Enter**.

10. Determine the IP address of your DNS Server. You may know this already. If not, look at the properties of the network connection. To get the information from a command prompt, type **ipconfig /all** and press **Enter**. The IP number of the current DNS Server is presented near the bottom of the list. In the example below, it is *199.247.2.1*.

 You must substitute your own values for the DNS Server. If your classroom is not connected to the public Internet, your instructor may give you a different target host.

11. Run the DIG command in trace mode by typing **dig @199.247.2.1 mnc-frdc.ad.multinatcorp. com +trace** and press **Enter**. The format of this command is *dig @<name server> <target host or domain> +trace*. Details of the DIG command are found in the dig.html file.

12. Review the output of the DIG command and note how each level of DNS referral is reported.

Common Errors and Misconceptions About DNS

The DNS system is complex, and as a result, configuration errors can occur, particularly in large networks. Most errors occur in one of three areas:

- *Resource record errors*—Resource record errors are greatly reduced by using modern software and graphical tools. Manual editing of resource records is an advanced skill and is not usually necessary.

- *Delegation errors*—To avoid delegation errors, plan carefully and document the configuration of all servers involved. Make sure that any contractors used, such as ISPs and domain registrars, are well versed in DNS and understand how NS and SOA records are used.

- *Weak authorities*—Weak authority is a general term used to describe a situation in which a machine that is supposed to be authoritative isn't, or a machine that isn't supposed to be authoritative thinks it is. Imagine that you have your public DNS hosted at your ISP, and your ISP suddenly ceases operations. All of the root and gTLD name servers will delegate authority for your domain to servers that no longer exist. You quickly arrange to have new DNS service provisioned elsewhere, but it takes longer than expected to get the delegation changed through your registrar. During this time, your new DNS services do not have the delegated authority that they need for the public to access your networks.

  Conversely, imagine that someone chooses to set up a zone for microsoft.com on a DNS Server on his own network. All of the workstations on this network use this DNS Server for lookups. None of these clients will receive correct DNS information from Microsoft's servers. This could be some sort of deliberate attack or blockade against Microsoft (although not very effective unless done on the servers of a large ISP), but more likely, a misinformed administrator thought this would improve caching performance, which is simply incorrect. You can avoid weak authority situations by planning, documenting, and ensuring that adequate redundancy exists for your critical services.

Most client software, including Windows 2000 and Window XP, can be set so that more than one DNS Server is able to resolve names. For example, *nameserver1* and *nameserver2* could both be available to all clients on the LAN. However, the client applications only send queries to the second server if the first server is not available. A common misconception is that if the first server doesn't find a record, the query will be tried on the second. This is not the case. If the first server replies but cannot find the record, the second server is not queried.

Remember that a server that is authoritative for a subdomain will never recurse or otherwise ask another name server for entries in that subdomain (except for delegations). If a zone for a DNS subdomain exists on a DNS name server, only records from that file will be returned in answer to queries. In rare cases, this can be a good thing, especially if you are trying to keep certain resource records private. More often, someone has made a mistake when configuring the DNS Servers involved.

Using DNS with Active Directory

Active Directory requires a much deeper understanding of DNS issues than do older Windows server products. With Windows NT networks, all that was required was the ability for a client to find a working name server to surf the Web, and perhaps an A or MX record for inbound mail or Web services. In many cases, these services were provided by the company's ISP and were rarely changed.

The release of Windows 2000 and Active Directory altered the picture considerably. A solid DNS is an essential foundation for a proper Active Directory deployment. Windows 2000 and Windows XP clients rely on DNS for name resolution within the LAN as well as on the Internet. These clients also dynamically update their own resource records in the DNS system. This book is about Active Directory, and focuses on how DNS supports domain controllers and Active Directory, not on how client functions are implemented.

There are three essential functions of DNS that affect Active Directory:

- Defining the namespace
- Locating services
- Resolving names to IP addresses

After covering these functions, we will discuss Microsoft DNS Server installation in Windows Server 2003.

Defining the Namespace

Active Directory domains use the same namespace as the DNS. This does not mean that an Active Directory domain and a DNS domain are equal, but it does mean that they use the same hierarchical system. There is a one-to-one relationship between Active Directory domains and DNS domains.

Locating Services

The netlogon service running on a domain controller is responsible for registering a number of records in DNS, as long as the DNS Servers support dynamic updates. If the DNS Server does not support Dynamic DNS (DDNS), then an administrator must make the entries manually. Each domain controller registers an A record for the name of the domain. This allows a client to resolve the name of the domain (for example *mydomain.mycorp.com*) to an IP address, making that IP address the address of a DC. Usually, an A record links a host or machine to a specific IP number, but in this case it allows the domain to be resolved without a hostname. Because a domain normally has several DCs, the name of the domain will resolve to several IP addresses, each representing a DC.

In addition to this A record, Active Directory clients make extensive use of a comparatively new type of RR called a **service locator (SRV)** record. An SRV record allows a client to send a DNS query specifying the type of service that it is looking for, and the DNS Server will return the name of a computer providing that service. SRV records are created to allow clients to locate a domain controller in a particular domain, a domain controller in a particular site in a particular domain, the domain controller acting as the PDC Emulator for a particular domain, a Global Catalog server for a forest, or a particular domain controller based on its own unique identifier.

SRV records are also created to assist clients in the Kerberos authentication process, the Kerberos password-changing process, and general Lightweight Directory Access Protocol (LDAP) lookups. (Kerberos is discussed in detail in Chapter 6, and LDAP is discussed in Chapter 11.) Although DNS would support these records as they point to any hosts, in practice, it is rare that they point to anything other than a Windows Active Directory domain controller. When a server is acting as a Windows Active Directory domain controller, its netlogon service will create numerous SRV records, and some A records.

When a client computer running Windows 2000, Windows Server 2003, or Windows XP software needs to use one of these services, perhaps during the log-on process or to search the global catalog, the system first tries to locate the desired resource using a DNS query. The client issues a DNS query for the appropriate SRV record. For example, to find a GC in the default site of the *multinatcorp.com* domain, a query is issued for an SRV record matching *_gc._tcp.Default-First-Site-Name._sites.multinatcorp.com*. After looking up the SRV record, the client could look up the address record for the host named in the SRV record, but to avoid another round-trip, the DNS Server usually returns the IP address as well, though only the name is stored in the SRV record.

To support pre-Windows 2000 configurations, these clients can try other name resolution methods, but if your DNS configuration is wrong, Active Directory will not function properly and a host of problems may become evident.

Resolving Names to IP Addresses

As with any host on the Internet, clients participating in an Active Directory domain will use DNS to resolve host names to IP addresses. In addition to traditional Internet use, the process extends to hosts on the internal LAN as well as hosts on extranets or intranets. This name resolution follows the process discussed in the last section, although it is often the case that the first name server queried will have information about the target subdomains without having to go back to the root servers.

Installing Microsoft DNS Server in Windows Server 2003

Any DNS Server software that supports the functions required by Active Directory can be used. It is sometimes believed that only Microsoft DNS can be used with Microsoft Active Directory, but this is not the case. You can use recent versions of BIND under UNIX or Windows, as well as other third-party servers. If you choose to use a different DNS Server, it must support SRV records, and it is recommended that you use a server that supports incremental zone transfers and dynamic updates. In the BIND product, for example, version 4.9.7 is the oldest tested and supported version; however, version 8.2.1 or newer is recommended.

The Microsoft DNS Server that ships with all versions of the Windows Server 2003 family was specifically designed to support the needs of Active Directory. It can handle a large workload and is much easier to administer than most third-party software, including BIND. The advantage to using the Microsoft DNS Server is its ability to store zone data in Active Directory. Under Windows 2000, DNS information was stored in the domain data partition, but with the Windows Server 2003 family, zone data is stored in an application partition, allowing more flexibility regarding which DCs can be DNS name servers for which zones. Zones stored in Active Directory are called **Active Directory integrated zones**, not primary or secondary zones. The Microsoft DNS Server can run on any Windows Server 2003 family system, but only DNS Servers running on domain controllers can use Active Directory integrated zones.

Storing zone data in Active Directory ensures that the DNS Servers can handle zone transfers effectively. The Active Directory replication process makes a copy of the zone data available to all DCs running DNS. The zone data can be changed by sending a DDNS update to any DNS Server or by using the DNS administrative tool for any of the DNS Servers, and it will be automatically updated in the others.

During the installation of Active Directory (discussed later in this chapter), the installation wizard examines the computer's DNS settings and contacts the DNS Servers. If it does not find an existing DNS Server that supports SRV records, DDNS, and incremental transfers, it will allow the installation of the DNS Server components as part of the Active Directory domain controller creation, or allow the administrator to research and correct the error. The DNS Server components can also be installed separately, either before or after promoting a machine to a domain controller, or on a machine that will not be a DC. To install DNS Server components, start the Add Windows Components Wizard by clicking Control Panel and then clicking Add/Remove Programs.

Activity 2-3 Renaming Your Windows Server 2003 Computer

Time Required: 20 minutes

Objective: To rename your Windows Server 2003 to support the delegation of authority for a new DNS zone.

Description: At Multinational Mega Corporation, you have been promoted to the position of team leader for all junior network technicians. As part of your expanded responsibilities, you have been asked to create a new Active Directory domain to test Active Directory more fully before it is deployed. In some of the following steps, you will work with a partner. To avoid confusion in the classroom, each student has been assigned a role, as shown in the Table 2-1.

Table 2-1   FQDNs and roles for student computers

Your Server Name	Your Domain Name	Your DC Role
SERVER1	oneandtwo.ad.multinatcorp.com	First Domain Controller
SERVER2	oneandtwo.ad.multinatcorp.com	Additional Domain Controller
SERVER3	threeandfour.ad.multinatcorp.com	First Domain Controller
SERVER4	threeandfour.ad.multinatcorp.com	Additional Domain Controller
SERVER5	fiveandsix.ad.multinatcorp.com	First Domain Controller
SERVER6	fiveandsix.ad.multinatcorp.com	Additional Domain Controller
SERVER7	sevenandeight.ad.multinatcorp.com	First Domain Controller
SERVER8	sevenandeight.ad.multinatcorp.com	Additional Domain Controller
SERVER9	nineandten.ad.multinatcorp.com	First Domain Controller
SERVER10	nineandten.ad.multinatcorp.com	Additional Domain Controller
SERVER11	elevenandtwelve.ad.multinatcorp.com	First Domain Controller
SERVER12	elevenandtwelve.ad.multinatcorp.com	Additional Domain Controller

If there are more than 12 servers in the lab, the pattern continues. Your instructor may advise you of local variations in naming or numbering. You will also need to know the name and IP address of your partner's computer. At this stage, it is expected that your computer is a member server in the ad.multinatcorp.com domain, with a domain controller called MNC-FRDC. To avoid having incorrect names in resource records in DNS after this computer is eventually promoted to a DC, you will change the FQDN of this computer to match what it will be after the promotion has been completed.

1. If necessary, turn on your computer and log on using the local administrator account (not the domain account), using the skills you learned in Chapter 1.

2. Click **Start**, right-click **My Computer**, and click **Properties**.

3. Click the **Computer Name** tab.

4. Click **Change**.

5. Click **More**.

6. Change the primary DNS suffix of this computer to match the new domain name in Table 2-1. For example, *server1* will be changed from *ad.multinatcorp.com* to *oneandtwo.ad.multinatcorp.com*.

7. Click **OK**, then click **OK** again.

8. Click **OK** to acknowledge that this change will require a reboot.

9. Click **OK** to close the properties sheet.

10. Click **Yes** to restart the machine.

11. Once the restart has completed, it will be ready for the next hands-on activity.

Activity 2-4 Installing the Microsoft DNS Server Service

Time Required: 10 minutes

Objective: To install the Microsoft DNS Server service on your Windows Server 2003 computer.

Description: The Microsoft DNS Server service provides a full-featured DNS Server for use on Windows-based platforms, including the Windows Server 2003 family. You will now install the service on your computer so that it can function as a DNS Server on the network. You could use third-party software, such as BIND, but the Microsoft service included with Windows is simpler to operate and integrates with Active Directory.

1. If necessary, turn on your computer. Log on as the local administrator (not a domain account) using the skills you learned in Chapter 1.

2. Once the log-on process is complete, click **Start**, click **Control Panel**, then click **Add or Remove Programs**.

3. Click **Add/Remove Windows Components** to start the Windows Components Wizard.

4. Click **Networking Services** in the list in the scroll box. (Do not click the checkbox; click the words themselves.)

5. Click **Details**.

6. Click the **Domain Name System (DNS)** checkbox.

7. Click **OK**.

8. Click **Next**.

9. Wait for the Windows Components Wizard to copy files and configure the system. If your classroom has been configured dynamically with DHCP, you will receive a warning and be given the opportunity to change the IP address. If this occurs, please consult your instructor.

10. Click **Finish**.

11. Click **Close**.

12. Click **Start**, click **Administrative Tools**, and then click **DNS**.

13. Verify that the server opens in the DNS tree in the left pane.

14. Expand the server's node by clicking the **+** sign next to its name.

15. Click the **Forward Lookup Zone** and **Reverse Lookup Zone**. Note which zones, if any, appear.

16. Close the DNS management MMC and log off your computer.

Activity 2-5 Configuring the DNS Server and Creating Zones

Time Required: 20 minutes

Objective: To configure the DNS Server and a forward lookup zone.

Description: Active Directory makes use of specific zones in the DNS system. Now that the DNS Server service is installed, you will configure it and create the zones that will soon hold the resource records for your Active Directory installation. After Active Directory is installed, you will see the records it has created.

1. If necessary, turn on your computer and log on using the domain administrator account from the *ad.multinatcorp.com* domain (not a local account). Consult Chapter 1 if you need to review the steps involved. In our examples, the user name is *administrator* and the password is *domainpw*. Your instructor will advise you if it is different in your classroom lab.

This is a different logon than the one used in Hands-on Activity 2-4. Ensure that you are using the domain account.

2. To start the DNS Administration console, click **Start**, click **Administrative Tools**, and then click **DNS**.

3. Click on the name of your server in the tree pane on the left side of the console. If the DNS Server has not been configured previously, the details pane will show a page titled Configure a DNS Server with a brief explanation.

4. On the menu bar, click **Action**, then click **Configure a DNS Server**.

5. The Configure a DNS Server Wizard starts. Time permitting, click **Help** and review the information provided, then close the Help window. You can also click **DNS Checklists** for additional background on DNS setup tasks.

6. In the Configure a DNS Server Wizard, click **Next**.

7. Click **Create forward and reverse lookup zones (recommended for large networks)** and click **Next**.

8. Click **No, don't create a forward lookup zone now**, and then click **Next**.

9. Click **Yes, it should forward queries to DNS servers with the following IP addresses** and enter the IP number for *mnc-frdc.ad.multinatcorp.com* on your LAN. You can find this number by typing the **ping mnc-frdc.ad.multinatcorp.com** command from a command prompt, or by asking your instructor. Setting this option will make this DNS Server send any unresolved queries to the *mnc-frdc* DNS Server, not to a root server.

10. Click **Next**.

11. Click **Finish**, then click **OK** to acknowledge that root hints will not be configured.

12. Click on the name of your server in the tree pane on the left. Expand the node for your server by clicking on the plus sign to the left of its name. Make sure that your server's name is still selected (highlighted).

13. Click **Action**, then click **New zone**.

14. When the New Zone Wizard welcome screen opens, click **Next**.

15. If your role will be First Domain Controller (or, if your server name ends in an odd number), then:

   a. Click **Primary zone**, then click **Next**.

   b. Click **Forward lookup zone**, then click **Next**.

   c. Type the name of your new domain/zone from Table 2-1, including the punctuation, then click **Next**.

   d. Click **Create a new file with this name** and accept the default name, then click **Next**.

   e. Click **Allow Any Dynamic Updates**, select "Allow both nonsecure and secure dynamic updates", and then click **Next**.

   f. Click **Finish**.

   g. Double-click **Forward Lookup Zones**.

   h. Right-click on the name of your new zone, then click **Properties**.

   i. Click the **Zone Transfers** tab.

   j. Make sure that **Allow zone transfers** is checked.

   k. Click **To any server**.

   l. Click **OK**.

16. If your role will be Additional Domain Controller (or, if your server name ends with an even number), then:

    a. Click **Secondary zone**, then click **Next**.

    b. Click **Forward lookup zone**, then click **Next**.

    c. Type the name of your new domain/zone from Table 2-1, including the punctuation, then click **Next**.

    d. Type your partner's IP number in the box, then click **Add**. This step configures your DNS Server to act as a secondary DNS Server and will request zone data from your partner's computer, which will be a primary DNS Server.

    e. Click **Next**.

    f. Wait for your partner to complete Step 14.

    g. Click **Finish**.

17. Expand the **Forward Lookup Zones** node.

18. Click the name of your new zone to see the records that have been created or transferred.

Activity 2-6 Delegating DNS Authority for a Subdomain

Time Required: 10 minutes

Objective: To delegate the authority from the classroom DNS Server to a student server for the subdomain that will be used by you and your partner.

Description: When a query is received at the DNS Server that is authoritative for the *ad.multinatcorp.com* subdomain, it must be able to provide a referral to the correct servers handling each of the student subdomains. Because your student computers will be handling those subdomains, you will now need to create the proper delegations.

1. Work with your partner and decide which of you will complete this procedure. The procedure should only be completed once, but both partners should be aware of the process.

2. If necessary, turn on your computer and log on using the domain administrator account from the *ad.multinatcorp.com* domain (not a local account). Consult Chapter 1 if you need to review the steps involved. In our examples, the user name is *administrator* and the password is *domainpw*. Your instructor will advise you if it is different in your classroom lab.

3. To start the DNS Administration console, click **Start**, click **Administrative Tools**, and then click **DNS**.

4. Click on **DNS**, the top node in the tree.

5. Click **Action**, then click **Connect to DNS Server**.

6. In the resulting dialog box, click **The following computer**, type the name **mnc-frdc.ad. multinatcorp.com** in the text box, then click **OK**. This step causes your DNS administrative console to connect to and manage another DNS Server.

Remember that you are now managing the DNS Server for the entire lab. Exercise caution to avoid misconfigurations that could cause your labs, or those of other students, to fail.

7. Expand nodes under the *mnc-frdc.ad.multinatcorp.com* server node (as necessary) to be able to double-click the name of the *ad.multinatcorp.com* domain. Many records and subdomains should be visible.

8. Locate the folder for your DNS subdomain, as indicated in Table 2-1.

9. Right-click your subdomain folder, and then click **Delete**, since it will be replaced by a delegation. Click **Yes** to confirm.

10. The *ad.multinatcorp.com* node should be highlighted. Click **Action**, then click **New Delegation**.

11. When the New Delegation Wizard welcome page opens, click **Next**.

12. In the Delegated domain text box, type the first part of your DNS subdomain, as indicated in Table 2-1 (for example, *oneandtwo*). Notice that as you type, the full name appears in the box below but is grayed out.

Stop typing the name before the first period. (No periods should appear in the white text box.) Occasionally, someone will accidentally type the full name, resulting in an incorrect record (like *subdomain.mydomain.com.mydomain.com*). This is an easy error to make, but also easy to correct.

13. Click **Next**.

14. Click **Add** to specify which name servers will handle requests for the new subdomain.

15. Enter the name of your computer, as specified in Table 2-1 (for example, *Server1.oneandtwo.ad.multinatcorp.com*) and, enter your IP address, and click **OK**.

16. Click **Add** again to add your partner's server to the delegation.

17. Click **Add** again to enter a new IP number, then enter your partner's server, as specified in Table 2-1 (for example, *Server2.oneandtwo.ad.multinatcorp.com*), enter its IP address, and click **OK**.

18. Click **Next**, and then click **Finished**.

19. If desired, your partner can complete Steps 1 through 8 to see the effects of adding a delegation.

20. Close the **dnsmgmt** console.

Activity 2-7 Configuring Your Computer to Resolve DNS Itself

Time Required: 5 minutes

Objective: To configure your computer to use its own DNS Server service to resolve DNS queries.

Description: Now that your computer has an installed, working, and configured DNS Server service running, there is no need for queries from your own server to first go to another DNS Server. This procedure will set your server to use its own DNS Server service to resolve DNS queries.

1. If necessary, turn on your computer and log on as an administrator (either a local or domain administrator).

2. Click **Start**, click **Control Panel**, and then click **Network Connections**.

3. Right-click the name of your primary network connection, usually called **Local Area Connection**, although in some classroom labs it may have been renamed.

4. Click **Properties**.

5. Click **Internet Protocol (TCP/IP)**, then click **Properties**.

6. Replace the existing Preferred DNS Server entry with your own IP address.

7. Click **OK**, then click **Close**.

8. Close all open windows.

9. Restart your computer to ensure that all DNS registrations are refreshed. To do this, click **Start**, click **Shutdown**, choose **Restart** from the drop-down list, and click **OK**. (*Note:* Depending on the configuration of your server, you may be asked to specify a reason for shutting down the computer. This information is collected by Windows Server 2003 family products to help administrators track the amount of time their servers are available. It does not affect the operation of the computer; it is for information only.)

INSTALLING ACTIVE DIRECTORY

If you have followed the recommended approach for building and testing functional specifications, the installation of Active Directory is simple. Microsoft has provided the Active Directory Installation Wizard, which takes the administrator, step-by-step, through the process of installing Active Directory and creating a domain controller.

In a production environment, you should know exactly which choice you will be making for each of the steps in the wizard. The process described in Chapters 3 and 4 will help you build a solid plan. Hopefully, you will have completed this book and have an understanding of the issues presented in the remaining chapters before being called on to design and implement an Active Directory installation on your own.

In the next few sections, you will explore some of the available options—without making any changes—and then gather the information required for the installation. You will then use the Active Directory Installation Wizard to install Active Directory on your computer.

Exploring Available Options in the Active Directory Installation Wizard

The Active Directory Installation Wizard is more commonly called **dcpromo**, after the name of the executable that runs the wizard. The wizard installs the Active Directory database and domain controller features on a server running the Standard, Enterprise, or Datacenter editions of Windows Server 2003.

Activity 2-8 Exploring the Active Directory Installation Wizard

Time Required: 5 to 10 minutes

Objective: To explore the options available in the Active Directory Installation Wizard.

Description: To fully understand the Active Directory Installation Wizard, we will explore the available options. Do not perform this activity on a production domain controller or production server! Use this activity for testing only.

1. Click **Start**, then click **Run**.
2. Type **dcpromo** and press **Enter**.
3. Choose different settings and compare the options that are shown after each choice.
4. Click the **Back** and **Next** command buttons to navigate through the wizard.
5. At the Summary page, *do not* click **Next** and no changes will be made.
6. If you accidentally click **Next** on the Summary page, click **Cancel**.
7. If changes are made, reboot the machine after the wizard finishes and run the wizard again to remove Active Directory.

Gathering the Required Information

Before using the Active Directory Installation Wizard you will need to have some information on hand, preferably from your planning documents. You will need to decide on a secure password for administrative access to the recovery console. (The recovery console is used when the server is off-line to fix a serious problem or to restore from a backup. The recovery console is discussed in Chapter 9.)

You will also need some essential information about how this domain controller (DC) will interact with the rest of the Active Directory forest. First, will this be an additional DC in an existing Active Directory domain, or the first controller in a new domain? If a new domain is being created, will this be a domain in an existing tree or forest, or will you be creating a new tree, or even a new forest? We discuss these issues in the following sections.

If an Additional Domain Controller Is Joining a Domain

In the simplest case—adding a DC to an existing domain—you will need to know the name of the existing domain. You will also need a set of credentials—a name and password combination—for a security principal from the existing domain that has the authority to join a new domain controller to the domain. You will also need to have a password for recovery purposes if this DC needs to be restored from a backup.

If You Are Creating a New Domain in an Existing Forest

If a new domain is being created, you will need to know the DNS name for the new domain. If it is not the first domain in a tree, the existing tree will determine the last part of the DNS name. If a new tree is being created, you will need to know the full DNS name of the new domain, which will be the root of the tree. In either case, you will need to know the name of the existing domain or forest and have credentials that will allow you to create a new domain. By default, only users in the Enterprise Admins Group can do this.

If You Are Creating a New Forest

If this is the first DC in your enterprise, then you will be creating a new domain, in a new tree, in a new forest, and you must have a DNS name chosen for this new domain that will become the forest root domain. Choosing a name for a new forest root domain is important, because it is very difficult to rename the forest root at a later date. (Changing the forest root name is a large task because it involves re-creating every object in the forest to reflect the change in forest structure. This cannot be done unless all DCs are running the most recent version of Active Directory, and will usually have a noticeable impact on users' ability to work during the process. In a large forest, it can be a lengthy process.) Choosing your forest root domain name is discussed in more detail in Chapter 4.

Activity 2-9 Gathering the Information Required for a New Domain

Time Required: 10 minutes

Objective: To practice the steps required for gathering information before running the Active Directory Installation Wizard.

Description: Work with your partner to gather the information required before installing Active Directory. Consult resources such as this book, tools on your computer, and your instructor. If desired, this can also be done as a full-class or large-group activity.

1. Refer to Table 2-1 to determine your domain name and your server's role in the new domain. Students with odd-numbered servers will create the first domain controller in a new domain. Students with even-numbered servers will create additional domain controllers in the same domain as their partners.

2. Determine the username and password of an administrator on your computer and your partner's computer. Both local administrators and domain administrators should be considered.

3. Be aware that an Enterprise Administrator account exists in the *ad.multinatcorp.com* domain, with a login of *EA* and a password of *Forestpw1*, and consider how this will be used during the installation process.

4. Examine the hardware setup of your server. Consider the best placement for database files, log files, and shared system volume files. Discuss with your partner or instructor how a production domain controller might differ from your lab equipment.

5. Consider the information you gathered when creating your DNS Server and determine where Active Directory resource records will be created.

Running the Active Directory Installation Wizard

To use the Active Directory Installation Wizard, more commonly called dcpromo, use the following steps:

1. Click **Start**, click **Run**, and type **dcpromo** in the text box, as shown in Figure 2-7.

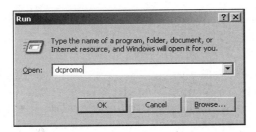

Figure 2-7 Launching the Active Directory Installation Wizard

2. Click **OK**.

3. A welcome screen opens, similar to Figure 2-8.

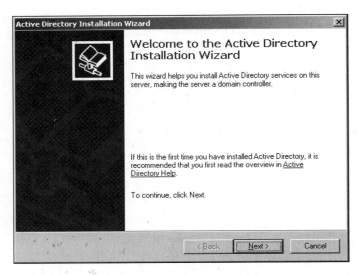

Figure 2-8 The Active Directory Installation Wizard welcome screen

4. Completing the wizard is a matter of answering the questions presented, which appear after you click **Next**, and click **Next** again.

The first choice the wizard asks you to make is whether this new DC will be joining an existing domain or creating a new domain (see Figure 2-9). The next few screens will vary depending on your choices. Joining an existing domain is the simplest operation and is described in the next section.

Joining an Existing Domain

In the Active Directory Installation Wizard, on the Domain Controller Type screen, choose **Additional domain controller for an existing domain** and click **Next**. The prompt for credentials will then open, as shown in Figure 2-10. You must provide a name and password that is valid on the domain this computer is joining, not credentials from the local machine. Domain Admins have permission to add a domain controller to a domain and this permission can be assigned to others. Enter the network credentials and click **Next**.

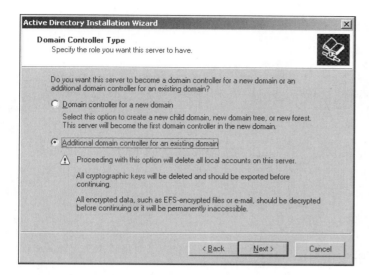

Figure 2-9   Choosing the DC type

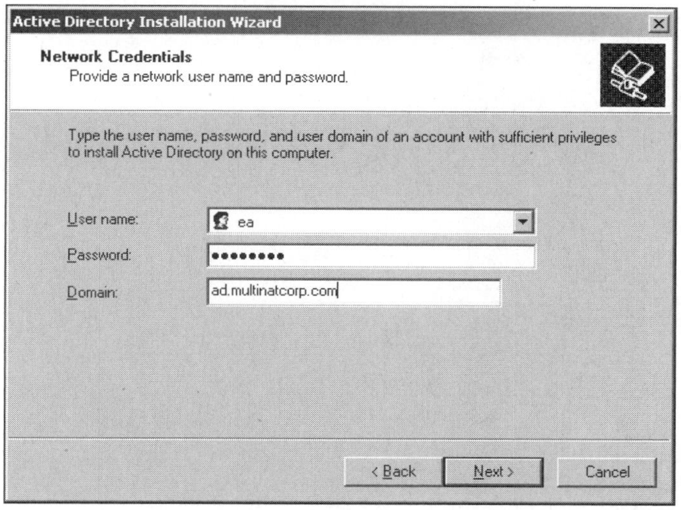

Figure 2-10   Entering network credentials

The next screen in the wizard will prompt you for the name of the existing domain to join, as shown in Figure 2-11. You can click the Browse button or type the DNS name of the domain. This is one operation that will often fail if DNS is configured incorrectly. Once you have supplied the name of the domain to join, click **Next**.

The next screen in the wizard, shown in Figure 2-12, allows you to specify locations for the directory database storage and the write-ahead log files. While the default is often adequate, you may wish to place the logs on a separate physical disk for optimum performance, which will increase the probability of recovering from a main hard disk failure. You may wish to select a location that is hosted on a redundant array of inexpensive disks (RAID) subsystem. The location must be a locally attached device; you cannot use network paths. Enter your locations (or leave the default), and click **Next**.

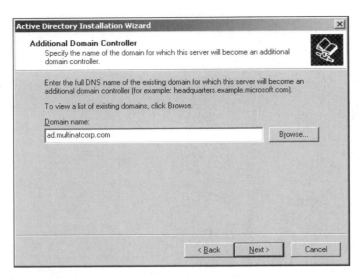

Figure 2-11   Specifying the domain to be joined

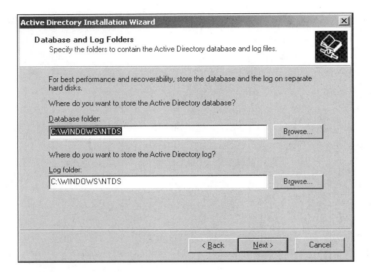

Figure 2-12   Specifying file locations

On the next screen you will select the physical location of the Shared System Volume folder. As indicated in the wizard (and shown in Figure 2-13), this volume contains publicly accessible information that is replicated to all DCs in the domain. This includes Group Policy information and the contents of the netlogon share. This replication of the system volume is automatic, and easier to implement than previous import/export configurations in Windows NT. Choose a new location or accept the default, and click **Next**.

The next page in the wizard will prompt you for a Directory Services Restore Mode Administrator Password, as shown in Figure 2-14. As discussed previously, this password is used when the DC is running in the Directory Restore Mode. Normally, a DC does not have any local accounts, but during a Directory Restore, the computer cannot access the Active Directory information. This password protects against unauthorized database restoration, tampering, or information theft. Choose a strong password that uses a combination of letters, numbers, and special characters, and store the documentation of this password in a secure, locked environment. Enter the password twice to ensure accuracy, then click **Next**.

A summary screen will open, as shown in Figure 2-15. Review all of the information, and if you are satisfied that it is correct, click **Next** to commit to the operation. The wizard will then begin installing Active Directory on the new DC. The process is automatic from this point, although it can take a considerable amount of time.

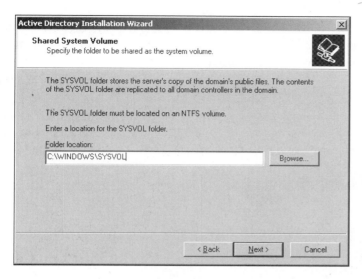

Figure 2-13   Location of the Shared System Volume folder

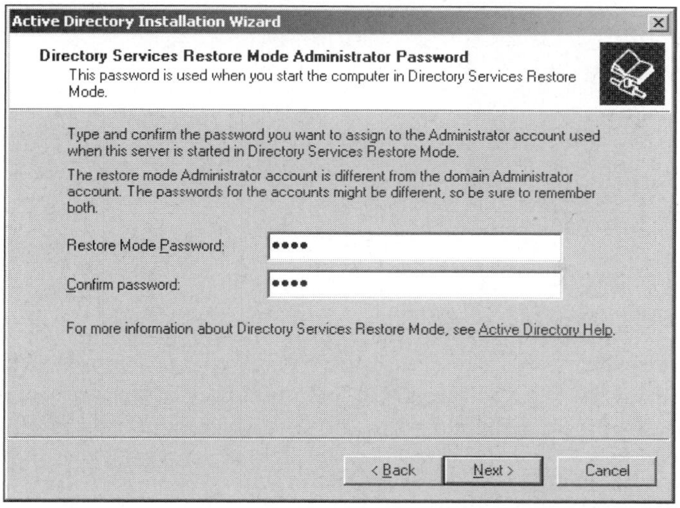

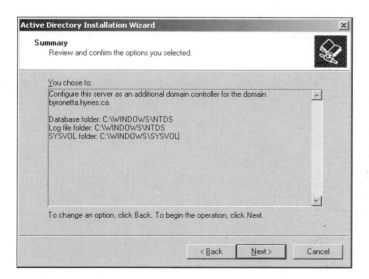

Figure 2-14   Specifying the Directory Services Restore Mode Administrator Password

Figure 2-15   The Active Directory Installation Wizard summary screen

Creating a New Domain

Creating a new domain in Active Directory is essentially the same as joining an existing domain, although some of the screens presented by the wizard will request different information. To create a new domain, click **Domain controller for a new domain** in the Domain Controller Type screen of the Active Directory Installation Wizard (shown in Figure 2-9).

A screen presenting three new choices will open, as shown in Figure 2-16. Are you creating a new forest, a new domain in an existing tree (such as *sales.multinatcorp.com* in the *multinatcorp.com* existing tree), or a new tree in an existing forest (as in *superwidgets.com* as part of the *multinatcorp.com* forest)? Click the appropriate option.

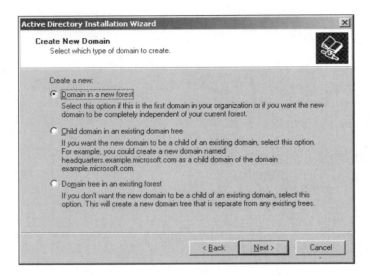

Figure 2-16   Specifying where the new domain will be created

If the new domain will be in an existing forest (either as a new tree or in an existing tree), you will be asked for credentials valid in the forest, as shown in Figure 2-17. The user you specify must have permission to add a new domain to the forest, which means the user will normally be a member of the Enterprise Admins Group. (If you are creating a new forest, this page is skipped.) Enter the valid credentials and click **Next**.

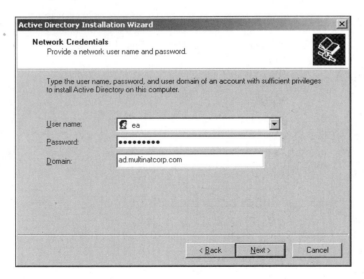

Figure 2-17   Specifying the network credentials

The next two screens in the wizard will ask you for the name of the new domain. The DNS name (Figure 2-18) must fit within the DNS namespace, although it can be a private DNS name. Windows 2000 servers and clients, Windows 2003 servers, and Windows XP clients will use the DNS name to locate the domain and its resources. However, for older clients (sometimes called **down–level clients**) the domain is also given a NetBIOS name (Figure 2-19). It is a good idea to use the first part of the DNS name as the NetBIOS name, unless that conflicts with an existing NetBIOS name. Provide both names, and click **Next** on each screen.

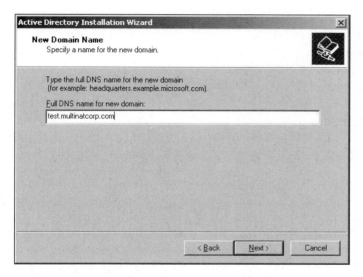

Figure 2-18   Specifying the DNS name for the new domain

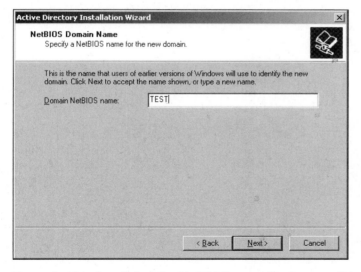

Figure 2-19   Specifying the NetBIOS name for the new domain

The next two screens in the wizard are Database and Log Folders and Shared System Volume. They both allow you to specify the desired location of the files used by Active Directory. Change the locations or accept the defaults, then click **Next** on each screen.

Before beginning the actions required to install Active Directory, the Installation Wizard performs some diagnostics on the DNS configuration. If any problems with the DNS structure are detected, a warning window will open (similar to the one shown in Figure 2-20). This is a new feature to the Windows Server 2003 family version of Active Directory, and it helps avoid many of the DNS configuration errors that can cause problems with Active Directory. Scroll down to see the text under Details to view the cause of the error, as shown in Figure 2-21.

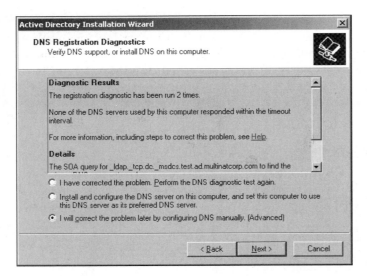

Figure 2-20   A DNS diagnostics problem

The problem shown in Figure 2-21 is common. The user is trying to create a new domain (in a new forest) called *test.multinatcorp.com*. The Installation Wizard has found the primary DNS name server that will handle this DNS subdomain. Because *multinatcorp.com* is registered with an Internet authority, the root name servers and gTLD name servers have delegated this subdomain to its registered name server: *ns1.domainpeople.com*. However, this name server is outside the direct control of the administrators creating the new Active Directory domain. The Active Directory administrators may not even know what operating system it is running, or if it supports DDNS or SRV records. In many companies with an established Internet presence, the administrators of the DNS Servers used for the Internet presence do not wish to allow Windows-based machines to make updates to the DNS records.

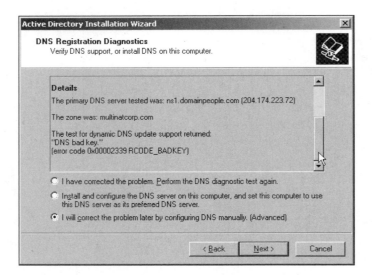

Figure 2-21   Details of the DNS diagnostics problem

This diagnostic information is very helpful, but the Installation Wizard also provides some common solutions. The administrator can resolve the existing problem or choose to have the Active Directory Installation Wizard automatically install and configure a DNS Server on the first domain controller in the new tree. In most cases this is the preferred solution. A simple delegation from the main name servers for the company is all that is required to find the Active Directory DNS records, and there is no need to worry that the Internet presence name servers will be misconfigured or overloaded by internal Windows clients.

If your DNS configuration is correct, and the DNS Servers for the new domain support DDNS, you will see a slightly different DNS Registration Diagnostics screen indicating that the DNS Servers have been successfully verified. This is shown in Figure 2-22.

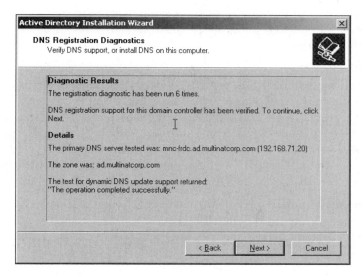

Figure 2-22   DNS diagnostics success

As Figure 2-23 shows, you will have the opportunity to choose the security level on the new domain. To ensure optimum security, it is best to choose that permissions are compatible with only the Windows 2000 or Windows Server 2003 operating system, unless you have a particular need for lower security. In versions of Windows released before 2000, any machine on the network could read certain types of information without first authenticating. Because most machines are now participating in wide area networks (WAN) or the Internet, this can create a significant security threat. Unfortunately, some legitimate software relies on this functionality and does not work with tighter security. Once you have made a choice, click **Next**.

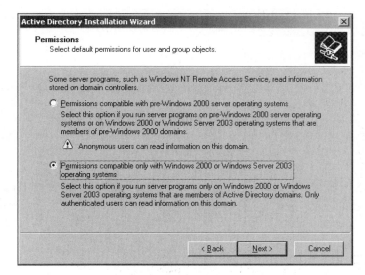

Figure 2-23   Choosing the permissions level

You will now need to supply a Directory Services Restore Mode Administrator Password. You can leave this password blank, although this is not recommended. Click **Next** to proceed to the summary screen where all of your choices can be reviewed. If they are correct, click **Next** again and the Installation Wizard will begin the process of promoting the computer to a domain controller in the new domain.

Explaining the Installation Process

The installation process will take several minutes, regardless of the options you selected. Whether creating a new domain or joining an existing one, the basic process is the same. The wizard will first adjust the machine's domain membership, leaving or "disjoining" any other domain. Then the netlogon service is stopped and the initial, empty database files are copied to the specified location. A number of configuration changes and registry entries are made to make the machine ready to host the Active Directory service. Local users and groups will be removed, as a domain controller cannot have local users and groups.

If you are joining an existing forest, the wizard will replicate the Active Directory schema to the new database file. If you are joining an existing domain, the wizard will replicate all existing objects after the schema is updated or allow you to provide off-line media (such as a CD-ROM), which contains the existing data to be loaded. Using off-line media is convenient when the domain controller is connected to the rest of the domain over a slower wide area network (WAN) link. This replication of content can also be deferred until after the system is rebooted and online. Finally, the wizard configures a number of security settings and places DACLs on various files, folders, and registry entries.

After the configuration is complete, you are prompted to restart the machine. Though you can delay restarting the machine, many functions will not be available until after the reboot. When the system starts up, the netlogon service will register the new SRV, A, and CNAME records in DNS, and the system will be operating as a domain controller.

Canceling or Interrupting the Installation

You can click **Cancel** to stop the installation of Active Directory whenever the Cancel button is present. Doing so will return the computer, if possible, to the state it was in before the wizard was started. This is the only safe way to stop the installation. If the process is complete or nearly complete, a dialog box similar to the one pictured in Figure 2-24 will appear. As it instructs, running dcpromo again will remove Active Directory from the computer.

Figure 2-24   The wizard completed before being canceled

You should not interrupt the installation process by restarting, resetting, or turning off the machine. If possible, you should ensure that the machine will not be vulnerable to power failures during the installation process. Although the wizard does a good job of leaving the machine in a consistent state, a power failure or interruption at an inopportune moment can result in a partially installed domain controller and require complicated manual steps to return the computer and Active Directory to normal operation.

Activity 2-10 Using the Active Directory Installation Wizard to Promote a Computer to a Domain Controller

Time Required: 30 minutes

Objective: To practice the installation of Active Directory.

Description: Both you and your partner will be involved in this exercise. The lower-numbered server will become the first domain controller in a new domain. The higher-numbered server will then join that domain. The second domain controller cannot join the domain until the domain is created. Therefore, you may prefer to work together, first promoting one server and then the next.

Perform the following steps on each of the two servers, beginning with the lower-numbered one.

1. If necessary, turn on your computer and log on as an administrator.

2. Click **Start**, then click **Run**.

3. Type **dcpromo** and press **Enter**.

4. Once the Active Directory Installation Wizard welcome screen opens, click **Next**.

5. Complete each page of the wizard, using the information you previously collected, and referring to Table 2-1. If you are unsure of the correct settings, consult your instructor. After each page, click **Next** until you reach the Summary page.

6. At the Summary page, carefully review the options you have selected. Click **Back** to correct any errors. Once you are satisfied that the Summary page is correct, click **Next**.

7. After the wizard completes the upgrade, click **Finish**.

8. Click **Restart Now**.

Verifying the Installation of Active Directory

To determine that an Active Directory domain controller promotion has been successful, verify the following:

- The database files have been created in the location specified in the Active Directory Installation Wizard.

- The shared system volume files have been created in the location specified in the wizard.

- Menu items have been created including Active Directory Users and Computers, and they open a Microsoft Management Console (MMC) to manage Active Directory.

- In Active Directory Users and Computers, the default containers Built-in, Computers, and Users have been created, as well as the default domain controller's OU.

- If this is the first DC in a new forest, a default site called Default-First-Site-Name has been created, the new domain is the forest root domain, and because it is the first DC in a forest, the machine is now a Global Catalog server.

- SRV, A, and CNAME records have been created in DNS (unless these are maintained manually). In particular, a unique CNAME record has been created in the _msdcs.<domainname> DNS subdomain, where <domainname> represents the DNS name of the domain.

The best indicator of a successful completion is that the computer starts up without error pop-ups or errors in the Event Log. However, any errors or error events will contain useful troubleshooting information.

The administrator password for a newly created domain is the same as the password for the local administrator account that existed on the machine before it was promoted to a domain controller. You are not prompted to enter the new domain's administrator password during the Active Directory Installation Wizard.

Activity 2-11 Verifying the Installation of Active Directory by Checking SRV Records

Time Required: 10 minutes

Objective: To verify the successful completion of the Active Directory Installation Wizard.

Description: To verify that Active Directory has been installed and your server is a domain controller, you will need to check the existence of a number of service locator (SRV) resource records in the DNS zone. Verifying this information is useful because it ensures that client computers will be able to use Kerberos for security and find Global Catalog servers correctly.

To verify the creation of SRV records using the DNS administrative console, complete the following steps:

1. Log on to your computer as the Administrator of your newly created domain, as specified in Table 2-1 (for example, *oneandtwo*). Remember that this "Administrator" is not the same security principal as the "Administrator" from the ad.multinatcorp.com domain, or the one that previously existed on your local computer. During the installation of Active Directory, however, the Wizard configured this administrator account with the same password as existed for the previous local Administrator (you set this password in Activity 1-1).

2. Click **Start**, click **Administrative Tools**, and then click **DNS**.

3. Expand the node for any DNS Server that is authoritative for the zone containing the RRs for the domain.

4. Expand each DNS subdomain under the Active Directory domain name.

5. Verify that a number of SRV records and A records were created.

To verify the creation of SRV records using nslookup, complete the following steps:

1. Click **Start**, then click **Run**.

2. Type **nslookup** in the Open text box and click **Enter**.

3. Type **server** followed by the IP number of a DNS Server that is authoritative for the domain, as in *server 192.168.0.1*. Press **Enter**. Depending on the configuration of your network, you may receive a warning if a reverse DNS lookup is not available for your server's IP address.

4. Type **ls -t SRV** *domain* where *domain* is the name of the domain you are investigating. For example, *ls -t SRV oneandtwo.ad.multinatcorp.com*.

5. Review the resulting output.

6. Type **exit** to quit nslookup.

Automating the Active Directory Installation Wizard

The Active Directory Installation Wizard can be run without user intervention by being scripted. You can include all settings required by the Active Directory Installation Wizard in an answer file—either the same answer file used to script a Windows Server 2003 installation or its own answer file.

An answer file is a simple text file that is read during the setup process. It contains answers to questions needed for the installation, so they do not have to be supplied by a user sitting at the computer. An answer file is divided into sections and uses the same format as the Windows 3.x-style INI files where each section has a name enclosed in square brackets.

The settings for the wizard are contained in the [DCInstall] section of the answer file. If you want the wizard to be invoked immediately after the OS is installed, use [GUIRunOnce] to invoke the dcpromo command. The [GUIUnattended] entries Autologon and AutoLogonCount will force the wizard to run without human intervention by automatically logging on an administrator. Many administrators prefer to install domain controllers manually, but if you have to manage a large number of DCs or if they are remotely located, an answer file is a valuable aid.

 You can find more information regarding automated installation in the Help and Support information supplied with Windows Server 2003 products, or by searching the Microsoft support Web site (*http://support.microsoft.com*) using the term "224390" for an article on the subject.

Upgrading a Domain

It is also possible to upgrade an existing Windows NT or Windows 2000 domain to a Windows Server 2003 Active Directory domain using the Active Directory Installation Wizard. This is discussed separately in Chapter 10.

CHAPTER SUMMARY

- ❏ In a real-world environment, develop a complete plan before starting the installation.

- ❏ The Domain Name System (DNS) is a distributed, scalable, hierarchical system that provides name resolution services (lookup of IP numbers from names, or vice versa) for the Internet and private networks.

- ❏ DNS is defined by multivendor standards coordinated by the IETF.

- ❏ The DNS namespace is organized into divisions called domains and subdomains. The namespace hierarchy begins at a root domain, represented by a single period. The next level, containing top-level domains, consists of generic top-level domains and country-code top-level domains.

- ❏ TLDs are further divided into subdomains. Most subdomains are registered to companies, individuals, or organizations, and authority for those subdomains is delegated to servers maintained and operated by the registrants or their ISPs.

- ❏ Subdomains can be divided into more subdomains.

- ❏ DNS data is organized into resource records. Important RR types include address (A), name server (NS), statement of authority (SOA), mail exchanger (MX), and service locator (SRV) records.

- ❏ RRs are grouped into zones. Zones include all of the information for a domain or subdomain that is not delegated to another name server. Zone data can be stored in text files, databases, the Windows registry, or Active Directory depending on the DNS Server software used.

- ❏ A common implementation of DNS Server software is called BIND, which has become a de facto industry standard. With all operating systems in the Windows Server 2003 family, Microsoft supplies a DNS Server that is well suited to general use and to supporting Active Directory.

- ❏ A DNS name server that has zone data for a given subdomain is authoritative for that subdomain.

- ❏ Authority can be delegated from a TLD or subdomain to another name server.

- ❏ Names are resolved to IP addresses using either iterative or recursive queries. With a recursive query, the DNS Server will return the best result it can find. With an iterative query, the DNS Server will only return records for which it itself is authoritative, a referral to another name server, or a "not found" message.

- ❏ Configuration errors can occur in the DNS structure. This will often prevent Active Directory from working properly.

- ❏ Active Directory uses DNS to define the namespace, to locate resources with SRV records, and to look up IP numbers from host names.

- ❏ A large number of SRV records are registered dynamically in the DNS system by the netlogon service on domain controllers. These SRV records are used by clients or other servers to locate particular domain resources.

- ❏ The Microsoft DNS Server can be installed from Windows 2003 server setup, from the control panel, or automatically during Active Directory installation.

- ❏ Active Directory is installed by running the Active Directory Installation Wizard, usually called "dcpromo." This process is also referred to as the promotion of a server to a domain controller.

- ❏ The wizard collects information from an administrator—such as where the domain controller will be placed in the forest and the required credentials and file locations—and then performs the installation. The wizard can also be scripted.

KEY TERMS

A record — An address (A) resource record maps a hostname to an IP address.

Active Directory integrated zone — A DNS zone in which data is stored as objects in Active Directory. Available only on Microsoft DNS servers running on domain controllers.

country code TLD (ccTLD) — A top-level domain assigned by ISO country codes on a geo-political basis, such as *.ca* for Canada.

dcpromo — The program that initiates the Active Directory Installation Wizard.

DNS namespace — The entire map of valid names in the domain name system.

Domain Name System (DNS) — A highly available, scalable, and dispersed system that provides name resolution on the Internet or private networks.

down-level clients — Clients older than the current operating system that lack some functionality. Usually refers to Windows products released prior to 2000.

forest root domain — The first domain in a forest that is the root for one tree in the forest, and for the forest itself.

fully qualified domain name (FQDN) — A host name that includes all parts necessary to resolve a name to an IP address from the host name to the root domain, including any subdomains or TLDs, such as *myhost.mysubdomain.mycompany.com*.

generic TLD (gTLD) — A top-level DNS domain that is not assigned to a specific country, and is directly delegated by the root servers .aero, .biz, .com, .coop, .edu, .gov, .info, .int, .mil, .museum, .name, .net, .org, and .pro.

incremental zone transfer — A process whereby a secondary DNS Server can request changes made only to zone data, not the entire zone.

MX record — A mail exchanger (MX) resource record specifies the host that can receive SMTP mail for the subdomain.

NS record — A name server (NS) resource record is used to delegate authority for a subdomain to another zone or server.

primary name server — The DNS Server where changes can be made to zone data.

reverse lookup — The process of looking up a host's FQDN using its IP address, which is the reverse of the normal process.

root domain (".") — The top of the DNS hierarchy, which delegates authority for all TLDs.

secondary name server — An authoritative DNS Server that has a read-only copy of zone data that has been transferred from a primary name server.

SOA record — A statement of authority (SOA) resource record provides information about the zone data.

SRV record — The service locator (SRV) resource record provides a method to locate servers offering specific services in specific sites by using the DNS system.

subdomain — A subdivision of a DNS.

top-level domain (TLD) — A division of the DNS namespace that is divided directly off the root domain. It includes ccTLDs and gTLDs.

zone — A file or database containing DNS records for a subdomain.

zone transfer — The process by which a primary DNS Server sends copies of the zone data to secondary DNS Servers.

REVIEW QUESTIONS

1. Active Directory is installed by running _____.

2. _____ greatly increases the chance of a successful deployment of Active Directory.

2

3. More than one host can have the same fully qualified domain name. True or False?

4. Which statement is most accurate?

   a. Active Directory only works with Microsoft DNS Servers.

   b. Active Directory only works with BIND DNS Servers.

   c. Active Directory will not work with BIND servers before version 4.9.

   d. Active Directory will use NetBIOS broadcasts if no DNS Server is configured.

5. The root domain of the DNS system is _____.

   a. .local

   b. .root

   c. .com

   d. a period (".")

6. Which statement concerning ccTLDs is most accurate?

   a. A ccTLD can only be used by a host in a particular country.

   b. A ccTLD cannot be divided into subdomains.

   c. Policies regarding ccTLDs are set by the country concerned, and therefore vary.

   d. ccTLDs will not be used once all of the new gTLDs are established.

7. Anyone can register a subdomain in any TLD if they are willing to pay the prescribed fee. True or False?

8. A Windows domain and a DNS domain are exactly equal and synonymous. True or False?

9. A host called *server1* belongs to Microsoft Corporation and is a member of the Windows domain referred to as Redmond. If we know that Redmond is a subdomain (or child domain) of *ds.microsoft.com*, then this machine's fully qualified domain name is most likely _____.

   a. *redmond.microsoft.com*

   b. *server1.microsoft.com*

   c. *server1.redmond.ds.microsoft.com*

   d. *server1.ds.microsoft.com*

10. Microsoft DNS Server offers several choices for how store zone data is stored, including the registry, zone files, or a(n) _____ partition.

11. If an authoritative server for a particular zone cannot find any entries for a particular host in that zone, it will:

    a. return a result indicating failure

    b. send a recursive query to its own secondary servers

    c. return a random IP number

    d. send a recursive query to the root domain

12. It is not necessary to register your subdomain name with a public registrar when:

    a. it is a subdomain of a TLD, such as *.com* or *.uk*

    b. you have a public Web site in that subdomain

    c. it is a subdomain of a private TLD, such as *.private* or *.local*

    d. your DNS Server is behind a firewall

13. _____ reduces network traffic by transferring only changes to the zone data, not the entire zone.

14. A(n) _____ is the one DNS Server in which changes are made for a particular zone and then propagated to other DNS Servers.

15. A DNS Server can be primary for one zone and secondary for another. True or False?

16. The default type of query issued by a client workstation locating a Web site is_____.

17. Most DNS Servers for TLDs accept recursive queries. True or False?

18. Every DNS lookup involves a trip to the root servers. True or False?

19. DNS referrals from the _____ are usually cached for a fairly long period of time.

20. Active Directory creates a great number of _____ resource records in DNS to allow clients to locate domain controllers.

21. You can only install Active Directory on a DNS Server. True or False?

22. By default, any _____ is allowed to add a new DC to an existing domain.

23. On a production system, it is a good idea to store the _____ on a separate drive from the database files, or to use a RAID.

24. You can use the Directory Services Restore Mode Administrator Password at any time to log onto the local console if you don't have a domain account. True or False?

25. While the Active Directory Installation Wizard is running, _____.

    a. all services on that computer remain fully available

    b. any existing Active Directory objects are replicated to the new DC

    c. no new objects can be created in the forest

    d. you should simply turn off the computer if you change your mind

MULTINATIONAL MEGA CORPORATION CASE PROJECTS

Multinational Mega Corporation, the vast organization with a multinational presence introduced in Chapter 1, is your fictitious employer. You began working on smaller projects, but are beginning to build on your successes. In the cases that follow, you will be assigned to various short-term projects in which the specific knowledge you have gained in this course will be of great use. In the last case project, you will return to your principal client, Heartland Hospital, to find and fix network issues.

Case Project 2-1: Gathering Pre-Installation Information

You have been asked to work on an in-house project at Multinational Mega Corporation. The U.S.-based Research and Development (R&D) team wants to establish a Windows domain using Active Directory, and you have been assigned to the deployment. Specifically, you have been asked to gather all of the information required for the deployment.

Although R&D is creating its own domain, it will remain part of the corporate forest and be a subset of the existing domain tree. The R&D team operates some older equipment and software that may stop working if anonymous network sessions are denied all access to the DCs. Also, some existing software requires a connection to the domain using the NetBIOS named *RANDD*.

R&D purchased two new servers that will become domain controllers. They have been assembled, the hardware has been configured, and Windows Enterprise Server 2003 has been installed. The TCP stack is operational on the servers and they have been named *DC-A* and *DC-B*. They are not currently in a domain.

What pieces of information do you need to gather, and from where?

Case Project 2-2: The Case of the User Who Didn't Understand

A question from one of the help desk staff at Multinational Mega Corporation has been passed to you. The caller decided that a particular server should be promoted to a domain controller and ran the Active Directory Installation Wizard (by typing *dcpromo* at a command prompt). After the promotion, however, he could no longer log on with his local user account, even though his domain account still works. What needs to be done to allow this user to log on to the newly promoted domain controller with a local (machine-based) account, not his domain account?

Case Project 2-3: Dilemma Down Under

 Consider completing this project as a group discussion.

After your success in Case Project 2-1, another company division has tagged you for assistance in an Active Directory deployment. This department offers a variety of financial services to the public in Australia.

You now understand the importance of a correct DNS configuration to support Active Directory, and your role is to specify the DNS configuration to support Active Directory. It has already been determined that your Active Directory domain will be called *directory.finance.oceania.multinatcorp.com*. Two high-end servers have been purchased, and they will be known as *dc1* and *dc2* once they are installed and configured. Therefore, the FQDN of *dc1* will be *dc1.directory.finance.oceania.multinatcorp.com*.

Your company already has a strong Internet presence, selling approximately $37 million worth of products annually through a busy e-commerce system (*saleshost.getrichnow.com*) and providing several hundred related pages of documentation through a support Web site that is open to the public (*dochost.oz-money.com*).

All Web configurations are currently run on UNIX hosts, including the DNS Servers. The Web DNS Servers (*ns1.oceania.multinatcorp.com* and *ns2.oceania.multinatcorp.com*) run BIND 9.1.3, which supports SRV, DDNS, and IXFR. The UNIX administrators are willing to assist, but they are adamant that any software involving their machines must be thoroughly tested and adhere to strict guidelines. Changes can take weeks to be approved, but there is no animosity. Executive management is supportive of this approach and recognizes the importance of maintaining the Web site revenue stream and good customer service, both of which would suffer with any loss of online availability.

In meetings with the UNIX/Web site team, you learn that public queries are not directed to *ns1* or *ns2* but rather to two off-site DNS name servers hosted by two separate ISPs. Everyone seemed surprised to realize this because internal clients use your ISP's name servers. Even internal requests for the company's own Web sites are resolved by these external name servers. (That is, the company's internal clients are not set to use *ns1* or *ns2* for name resolution.)

Where would you host the zones required for your Active Directory domain? Which DNS Servers would you set for your internal clients to use for name resolution? What are the advantages and drawbacks of your solution?

Case Project 2-4: Heartland Headache

Meanwhile, back at Heartland Hospital, a problem has come to light. Most of the LAN clients use Windows 2000 Professional or Windows XP Professional, but about 10 percent use a variety of other operating systems. Recently, all DNS Servers have been migrated from UNIX to Microsoft DNS which run on three machines, each using Windows Enterprise server for their operating system. These machines are not DCs.

Although there are three DNS Server machines, statistics show that almost all traffic is going to the host called *DNS1*, while *DNS2* and *DNS3* are practically idle. All three DNS Servers have copies of the zone data. Everyone would like to see the load split more evenly among these three machines.

Why do you think this load is being handled by just one machine? What can you do to even it out?

3

AN ACTIVE DIRECTORY DESIGN PHILOSOPHY

After reading this chapter and completing the exercises, you will be able to:

♦ Choose an appropriate design philosophy
♦ Describe the roles of service owners and data owners
♦ Determine which individuals should be given access to Active Directory
♦ Make the proper Active Directory design decisions
♦ Understand the importance of a shared vision for an Active Directory design project

You may be surprised to find the term "philosophy" in a technical book, as many network administrators focus on the hands-on, practical work that pervades day-to-day operations. In this chapter, however, you will examine the bigger picture—how to approach a large-scale Active Directory project.

The approach taken by a design team or an individual designer is based on their design philosophy. As with most areas of work, individual viewpoints, team dynamics, and corporate attitudes all play a role in shaping the philosophy and thus the end result. This chapter discusses some of the elements of design philosophy and presents some issues that should be considered when choosing how to approach the project.

INTRODUCING DESIGN PHILOSOPHY

Active Directory has many roles to play as the directory service in a wide area network. As discussed in Chapter 1, Active Directory is the primary directory service for the operating system (OS), supporting security and routine network operations for large and small networks. Networking has evolved over the past few years, especially as more and more computers are connected to the Internet, wide area networks (WANs), and multiple local area networks (LANs). All of this interconnectivity leads to increased demands for all sorts of directory structures and directory services. Some of the roles for which organizations are deploying Active Directory include the following:

- The directory service for the operating system
- An enterprise-wide directory (of both people and resources)
- An e-mail directory (of internal users or external contacts)
- A "white pages" directory (external users looking up internal addresses)
- An e-commerce authentication system

The particular roles that Active Directory will be deployed to perform will affect the design of that Active Directory structure. However, all deployments need to follow some sound Active Directory design principles.

Activity 3-1 Identifying Roles for Active Directory

Time Required: 10 minutes

Objective: Identify ways that Active Directory can be used in an organization.

Description: In this activity, you will begin pulling together information from some of the case studies to see how each potential Active Directory deployment might differ. Also, Mary from Heartland Hospital has set up an appointment to discuss the potential uses of Active Directory in the hospital. You may choose to complete this project individually, with a partner, or as a class group.

1. Prepare for your meeting by reviewing the information in the client's file (represented by the seven Case Projects in Chapters 1 and 2).

2. From the list of the roles preceding this activity, record the ones that would be well-suited to an Active Directory deployment at Heartland Hospital.

3. List any additional directory service functions or roles you believe the hospital will require.

Note that Active Directory is an infrastructure for a business enterprise, just like roads and bridges are for a transportation system, or water and pipes are for a city sewage system. Because of its nature as an essential infrastructure, Active Directory is involved in issues that cross many boundaries.

First, an Active Directory deployment will cross the boundary between technology and business. A good Active Directory deployment is unlikely to happen in an enterprise where the technical leadership (technicians, engineers, programmers, or analysts) can't speak the same language as the business management and executives.

Second, Active Directory will also cross boundaries between departments and divisions within an enterprise. If the decision is made to operate separate Active Directory forests in a properly designed, planned, and deployed environment, that decision should be made after consultation. A successful Active Directory design process will require conversations, consultations, and consensus between and among many parties in an enterprise. You will first want to determine the key roles that departments, groups, or staff will play in the new Active Directory installation.

OWNERSHIP ROLES

Because of the way Active Directory crosses boundaries within the organization, it is often necessary to determine or define owners for parts of the directory. While every object in Active Directory has an **object owner**, a design team must also consider ownership on a much broader scale—including the sense of responsibility and accountability for the operation of the **directory service** and for the data that it contains. Microsoft documentation uses two terms to describe different types of ownership: **data owner** and **service owner**.

Data owners, also called object owners, are responsible for the contents of the directory. They create, modify, delete, and manage objects in the directory, such as users. The data owner may also be responsible for defining policies for the network they control. Active Directory supports this through the application of **Group Policy**. You will learn about Group Policy and its application in Chapter 10, but for now you should be aware that data owners are often well-positioned in their organization in order to determine how Group Policy should be applied to the objects they manage or own.

Service owners, sometimes called directory owners or directory administrators, are responsible for the operation of the directory service itself. This role includes creating or removing domains, implementing changes to the schema, installing and managing domain controllers, creating the site topology, and monitoring the health of the domain controllers.

As an example of how these roles might be played out in real life, consider a human resources (HR) department that is the data owner for part or all of the Active Directory structure. In this role, HR staff members have been given permissions that allow them to create, delete, and modify the attributes of users. In other words, they are responsible for the contents—the information—in the directory. However, they are not the service owner. They do not have the ability to create new domains to back up the directory or to determine the location of domain controllers (these functions are performed by the staff of a central IT group).

Activity 3-2 Identifying Data Owners

Time Required: 10 minutes

Objective: To identify potential data owners for the Heartland Hospital Active Directory system.

Description: Mary from Heartland Hospital has faxed over an organizational chart of the hospital. She noted that it is a bit dated, and that she heard significant growth is soon expected. In this activity, you will review this corporate information and consider possible role assignments. You may choose to complete this project individually, with a partner, or as a class group.

Examine the organizational chart in Figure 3-1. Think about who in the organization will be responsible for creating or deleting users, who will decide which resources a user is allowed to access, who will need to act immediately if an employee is terminated for cause, and who has the most vested interests in the people and resources represented by objects in Active Directory. Your instructor may play the role of the client, if you wish to clarify roles shown on the chart.

Remember that although users are probably the most common object, resources, groups, contacts, or other objects may need to be managed as well.

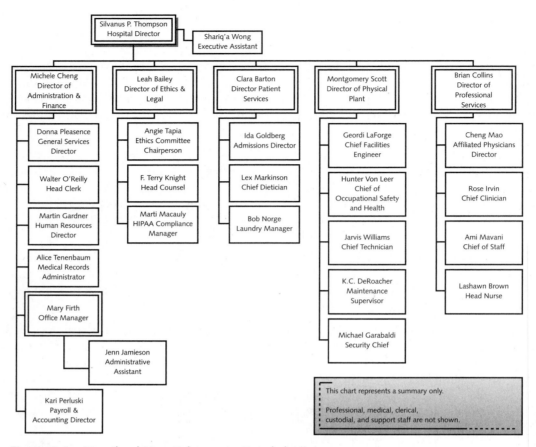

Figure 3-1   Heartland Hospital organizational chart

1. List any questions you might ask Mary to help determine potential data owners.

2. Identify and list prospective data owners.

Activity 3-3 Identifying Service Owners

Time Required: 10 minutes

Objective: To identify potential service owners for the Heartland Hospital Active Directory system.

Description: Mary also faxed a block diagram of the Heartland Hospital network. In this activity, you will review corporate information about the computers and networks at the hospital and consider possible role assignments. You may choose to complete this project individually, with a partner, or as a class group.

1. Examine the block diagram of the Heartland Hospital network, as shown in Figure 3-2.

2. Review the diagrams and the other information you have about the hospital.

3. List any additional questions you might ask Mary to help determine potential service owners.

4. Identify and list prospective service owners.

3

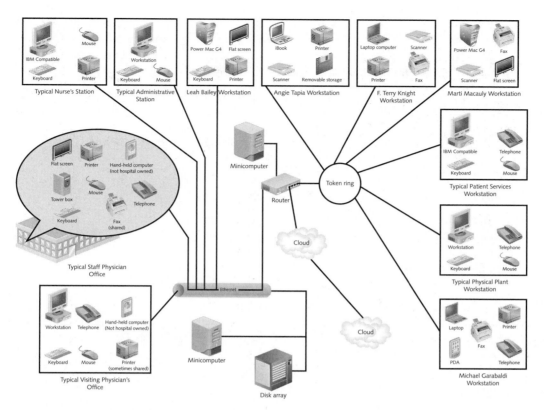

Figure 3-2   Heartland Hospital computer systems

This division of ownership between those who own the data and those who own the infrastructure is a key concept in the forest and domain design in a Microsoft Active Directory network. Microsoft promotes the use of this **split administration model**, which leverages granular security settings in Active Directory to allow people to do their jobs without giving them more authority than they need. It can also help you avoid arguments and allow the design team to come to a consensus quicker, since data owners don't need to give up ownership and control of "their" data. It also allows more flexibility than the Windows NT domain model, in which being an administrator was much more of an all-or-nothing proposition.

A QUESTION OF TRUST

In today's world, the security of a company's computers and the information they contain is crucial. Administrators are constantly receiving updates and newsletters filled with descriptions of denial-of-service attacks, virus outbreaks, malicious actions by users, and security breaches resulting from security gaps that should have been closed. It is very important that all of your design decisions—from the first idea through to final implementation—give consideration to security.

Throughout any discussion of Active Directory design, the word "trust" appears in its normal definition as well as in the context of how credentials from one domain or forest can be used in another (**trusts** are discussed in Chapter 4). When you set up a technical trust, you should also trust the person or organization in the traditional sense. It is good practice to allow computers and networks to trust each when the people involved also trust each other.

Any administrator of a domain controller or anyone who is given membership to the administrative groups of a domain or a forest is being explicitly trusted with very valuable assets of the enterprise. A domain controller often stores information from other domains (in the configuration partition or in the global catalog), and it might be possible for an unscrupulous, but highly skilled, administrator to misuse this information or to attack the network from within the organization.

Microsoft wrote about one such possibility in its *Knowledge Base* article *289243*, which stated: "Exploiting this vulnerability would be a challenge. At a minimum, an attacker would need administrative privileges on the trusted domain, and the technical wherewithal to modify low-level operating system functions and data structures." In other words, unlikely and difficult, but possible.

Finally, remember that anyone who can gain physical control of a domain controller can eventually compromise it. Part of your Active Directory planning should include proper physical security of DCs. When considering physical security, don't neglect servers, especially DCs in remote sites where building security may not be as obvious and the servers may not be in a dedicated computer room.

MAKING ACTIVE DIRECTORY DESIGN DECISIONS

A joke circulating among trainers who teach Active Directory courses states that no matter what the question, the only correct answer to any Active Directory design question is "it depends." There is so much variation between one Active Directory deployment and the next that it is sometimes a formidable task to even get started. With so many variables, options, and possibilities, how can a stable and reliable Active Directory structure ever emerge?

Active Directory design is the process of creating a structure around the objects to be stored in the Active Directory database. Your first step is to realize that it is a process, not a one-size-fits-all answer. Because each organization is different, each Active Directory deployment will also be different, and each design team must consider the following issues.

Design to Support the Organization's Goals

First and foremost, the design of an enterprise's directory service needs to support the goals of the organization. What does the organization want to accomplish by using Active Directory (or, for that matter, any other directory service)? A for-profit company, by definition, has the ultimate goal of making money. But each business will choose its own way of being profitable and its own way of doing business. In most large companies, business goals are already defined; however, in small businesses they may need to be discussed or documented before planning the Active Directory structure.

When Active Directory is used in government, military, educational, or nonprofit settings, the goals may not always be as clear, and they may be very different than those pursued by a for-profit organization. In either case, it is essential to determine the organization's business goals so that the directory can support them, not hinder them. Any large organization will have many people and many departments or divisions, some of which will have conflicting goals. As the design team works to achieve a common vision, trade-offs will be likely, even if the goals are defined. If the goals have never been defined, complete chaos can easily ensue.

Gaining Executive Sponsorship with Documented Value

Early on in the project, and throughout its life, executive management should be involved. This ensures that business goals are well represented and avoids a waste of resources by making sure that the power exists to see that the resulting design is implemented. To gain executive sponsorship and justify the costs that will be incurred for planning, testing, and employment, you must be able to identify the value of Active Directory to the executives within your organization. To reach a consensus, you may need to show the value of the design in concrete terms.

Activity 3-4: Identifying Executives Who Can Sponsor the Project

Time Required: 10 minutes

Objective: To stress the importance of gaining the support of senior management within the organization.

Description: In this activity, you will review the organizational chart for Heartland Hospital and consider which executives will need to sponsor the project to ensure its success. You may choose to complete this project individually, with a partner, or as a class group.

1. Refer back to Figure 3-1 to identify the key members of the executive and management levels.

2. Identify and list some of the potential managers and executives who will need to be involved in the Active Directory deployment project.

3. Prepare a brief explanation for each of your choices, including any assumptions you made.

Designing for the Future and the Present

An Active Directory design should have long-term value and validity. The right choices for DNS names, the number of forests and domains, and the OU structure (each discussed in Chapter 4) are driven by the organization's current needs, as well as what its future needs might be. For example, is your organization expected to grow by acquisition? Does your company work intimately with a partner agency on a project basis that changes from month to month? Are your company's organizational charts redrawn as a quarterly exercise? Is the number of staff expected to change significantly? Consider these kinds of questions as you design your Active Directory deployment.

Activity 3-5: Considering Corporate Change

Time Required: 10 minutes

Objective: To understand the need to include the known and predictable future in your design plans.

Description: Mary just called to tell you that Heartland Hospital will be merging with another hospital and several clinics in the area, creating a much larger organization. She does not yet have all the details, but felt that it might affect the Active Directory plans. In this activity, you will act on information provided by Heartland Hospital and consider the impact of future plans on your design vision. You may choose to complete this project individually, with a partner, or as a class group.

1. Consider this new information and list or state how the amalgamation might affect the recommendations made during earlier activities.

2. State whether you believe this would be a reason to put the project on hold.

3. If the project will not be put on hold, identify any added elements or constraints created by this new information.

Designing to Support the Delegation of Authority

One of the strengths of Active Directory is its ability to delegate authority and permissions on a granular basis. When combined with the ability to separate ownership of data from ownership of service, it becomes very powerful.

You should make design choices that support the ability to delegate authority. This means that services and service owners should most often be grouped together, while resources owned (or managed) by the same people should probably be placed in the same OU or domain in Active Directory. Delegation of authority and permissions are discussed in Chapter 6.

Designing to Support the Application of Group Policy

Group Policy allows an organization to define rules or policies and allows the system to enforce them automatically. Group Policy can also be used to distribute software or lock down systems. A good Active Directory design will group objects that will be subject to the same policies in the same OU. For example, if all of the desktops in the finance department must use a secure, smart-card logon, it makes sense to locate the computer objects representing the finance computers in one OU. An Active Directory design that doesn't consider Group Policy makes administration more complex, requires the needless duplication of Group Policy objects (GPOs), and may result in longer log-on times as inefficient policies are processed.

Parts of your organization with similar policy needs should be grouped together in your Active Directory design. Why? Because doing so allows you to administer one (or a few) GPOs that apply to one OU, rather than managing several GPOs scattered throughout the forest.

The application of Group Policy becomes particularly relevant as choices regarding OUs are made, since Group Policy can only be applied to a domain, a site, or an OU.

 In Chapter 10, the role of Group Policy is examined in detail.

Justifying the Design

Every forest, every domain, and every OU in a proposed design should serve a particular purpose. Do not create these structures just for the sake of doing so. Do not even create them to fill in the organizational chart. Some designs are based on geography (continents, regions, even cities); some designs are based on the administrative organization of an enterprise (departments, divisions); and others are based on a functional model (what people do in their jobs, regardless of which part of the organization they work in). None of these models are wrong, but none of them are necessarily right either. What makes them correct is that the design team has considered the issues and is able to justify why the choice was made in terms of value, business goals, and business requirements.

STARTING A DESIGN PROJECT

Sometimes the terminology surrounding a project or deployment can be confusing. Different schools of thought will also use different terms that mean essentially the same thing. Many companies have established processes or frameworks that they use consistently. This is more likely to be the case in large organizations with well-established, central IT departments. Other companies, especially small ones, may not have any guidelines. Regardless of the size of the company for which you are working, resist the urge to just jump in and start changing configurations and installing software. Instead, rely on a disciplined, logical approach to apply a consistent design philosophy.

Over the past few years, Microsoft has examined the long-standing processes used by successful IT firms to manage change or projects. Microsoft combined this wisdom and documented it in models—or frameworks—that its customers can use to increase their success rate while lowering costs. Other companies publish similar frameworks, and your company may already use one of them. Some adventurous companies have established their own framework through years of developing policy and procedures.

Two of the most common frameworks are the **Microsoft Solutions Framework (MSF)** and the **Microsoft Operations Framework (MOF)**. MSF is suited to the creation of new software or a new computer infrastructure. MOF is suited to the day-to-day operations of complex computer systems. The larger the organization, the more value is brought by using these formally defined processes.

Microsoft Solutions Framework (MSF)

MSF is ideally suited to the business of creating and publishing software. A project managed with the philosophy of MSF will go through a number of stages leading to a product's release. The common MSF stages are envisioning, planning, developing, stabilizing, and deploying. Older versions of the MSF model may combine stabilizing and deploying. These five stages can also be applied to an Active Directory project. Here's how:

Envisioning Phase

To begin, the project needs a vision and scope. This is the stage in which a project team is assembled and definition of common goals based on business objectives is achieved. Risks and specific requirements should also be identified. You will learn more about the envisioning phase in the next section of this chapter.

Planning Phase

Next, you will need to create a detailed plan of exactly what the resulting Active Directory structure will look like, starting with the vision. While the vision has broad goals, now is the time to generate specifics. The planning phase ends with the creation of a document called the **functional specification**, which contains detailed, low-level specifications and a project schedule.

In Chapter 4, you will learn about some of the Active Directory design decisions to be considered during the planning phase, as well as when schedules, costs estimates, and job assignments are developed.

Developing Phase

The developing phase takes the results of planning—the functional specification—and creates the components required to make it a reality. In a software project, this is where the coders do a great deal of work. However in a project like an Active Directory deployment, the code is already written. Despite this, domain controllers will probably need to be purchased and configured, and depending on the complexity of the installation, some customization or third-party add-ons may need to be developed or purchased. Testing is usually extensive during the developing phase, although "proof-of-concept" tests may be done as part of the planning stage (or even earlier), and testing may also continue into the stabilizing phase, especially if pilot projects are used.

Stabilizing Phase

While testing may continue into this phase, the key difference between developing and stabilizing is that the features of the product (in the case of software) or the details of the design (in the case of a project like Active Directory) are complete. For example, in the case of an Active Directory project, any changes to be made to the schema are known and finalized. At the end of this phase, the project is deemed ready for use, and control of the new project moves from the designers and builders to those who will operate and support it.

Deploying Phase

At long last you are ready to deploy the system. Your project goes into full production status, and the organization starts reaping the benefits. There may be some overlap between phases, particularly if you already have a live network and are migrating to a new Active Directory environment.

 Active Directory does not always fit precisely into the MSF process, but many organizations are familiar with MSF and choose to use it—perhaps modified slightly—to lend the needed structure and discipline to creating their Active Directory deployment. MSF is designed to be flexible, allowing organizations to use the parts of the model that assist them.

Activity 3-6: Locating Additional MSF Information

Time Required: 10 minutes (plus additional research time if desired)

Objective: To learn how to access additional information on MSF.

Description: In this activity you will visit the Microsoft Web site and research additional information on MSF. MSF is not a part of Active Directory, and is not tested by Microsoft on Active Directory examinations. However the model is used in large organizations, and being familiar with it (at least in general terms) will be valuable as you begin to work with large projects, such as an enterprise-wide Active Directory deployment.

1. Go to *http://www.microsoft.com/technet/treeview/default.asp?url=/technet/itsolutions/tandp/innsol/ msfrl/default.asp*.

2. Follow the links and download or read the document titled, *Microsoft Solutions Framework Process Model*.

3. Review additional MSF information as desired.

The Microsoft Web site is frequently updated. If the URL is no longer accurate, search *www.microsoft.com* for *MSF Process Model*.

Microsoft Operations Framework (MOF)

While MSF is designed around the creation of software, MOF is designed around the operation of the IT infrastructure. MOF consists of a series of guidelines, **best practices**, and how-to guides that maximize the availability and performance of a network and its components. In short, MSF deals with the creation of new software and new systems, while MOF deals with the effective management of existing systems, particularly core Microsoft enterprise offerings.

Activity 3-7: Locating Additional MOF Information

Time Required: 10 minutes (plus additional research time if desired)

Objective: To learn how to access additional information on MOF.

Description: In this activity, you will visit the Microsoft Web site and research additional information on MOF. Unlike MSF, which deals with new projects, MOF helps organizations run the infrastructure they have established. Once a large Active Directory deployment goes into production, it is crucial that Active Directory runs without disruption to users. Following a formal procedure like MOF helps achieve that goal, and is therefore something that you should know about, at least in general terms.

1. Go to *http://www.microsoft.com/technet/treeview/default.asp?url=/technet/ittasks/plan/ sysplan/mofovrv.asp*.

2. Follow the links and download or read the document titled, *MOF Executive Overview*.

3. Review additional MOF information as desired.

The Microsoft Web site is frequently updated. If the URL is no longer accurate, search *www.microsoft.com* for *MOF Executive Overview*.

A detailed analysis of MOF and MSF is outside the scope of this book, and outside the published exam objectives of the Microsoft Certification Exams on Active Directory. However, it will benefit you to be familiar with some of their terms and concepts.

THE NEED FOR A VISION

Chapter 4 deals with activities that would occur in the planning phase of an MSF-managed project. The rest of this book focuses mainly on operational issues—the day-to-day things in a small organization that might be managed under MOF in a larger institution.

Before leaving the topic of design philosophy, consider some of the specifics of what should occur in the envisioning stage. The choices made early in a project—that is, those that are largely governed by the design philosophy—have lasting impact throughout the deployment process and the life of the directory service.

At the beginning of an Active Directory project, the designer and other project team members should gain a shared vision of the end result. It is important that all key stakeholders have the same goals for the big picture. Who are the key stakeholders? How are they represented? That will, of course, depend on the organization. Some stakeholders can include:

- Executive management, owners, or shareholders

- Functional management, especially those responsible for the people and budget being used to implement the project

- Employees (including managers), especially those whose jobs will change as a result of the project

- The IT department, especially if it will be the service owner and responsible for making sure the system runs reliably

- Customers or the public, especially in government projects or in projects that involve systems interacting directly with customers

The relative importance of each of these stakeholders can only be considered along with the business goals of the organization. The ideal is for your Active Directory system to help an organization reach its business goals.

Business goals are as varied as the organizations that use computers. A business is ultimately concerned with profit—creating value for owners and shareholders. Therefore, most for-profit organizations have business goals centered on lowering costs, increasing profits, and serving customers in faster or better ways. The stakeholders will want to see a return on investment (ROI) for the project, including the time spent planning and testing.

Even nonprofit organizations have business goals. Most organizations of this type have a burning desire to make a difference. Their stakeholders might be any number of groups from the disadvantaged to the alumni of a prestigious college. Instead of owners, stakeholders may worry about donors, and making sure that the money given to them is not wasted. Planning and testing is not wasting money.

In the government sector, stakeholders might include politicians and the public that elects them. The pressure for accountability and to stretch every dollar to its furthest is no less in government than in business.

In addition to identifying the stakeholders as a broad group, at the beginning of a project, the owners of the project must also be identified. In other words, everyone involved must know who is responsible for the project. Rarely will a project be completed by only one or two people; there will usually be a project team. The best teams include representation from all of the relevant stakeholders. Outside help, such as contractors or consultants, may also be part of an Active Directory project team. As the team is being put together, it is important to ensure the following:

- Business goals have been defined and communicated to the design team.

- Everyone on the design team has an awareness of the "big picture" and the design philosophy, even if they will only be working on a small part of the project.

- The design team understands the ownership roles of both services and data, and key data owners are either members of the design team or are regularly involved in conversations.

- The role of Active Directory as infrastructure is understood by the design team and key contacts.

- Executive management is either actively represented on the team, or is supportive, involved, and sponsoring the project.

Activity 3-8: Building the Team

Time Required: 10 minutes

Objective: To identify project team members and practice assembling a project team.

Description: In this activity, you will review the Heartland Hospital information and consider who should be included on a project team. You will need to look back at the information provided in Figures 3-1 and 3-2, and consider your earlier decisions. You may be instructed to complete this project individually, with a partner, or as a class group.

1. Refer back to Figures 3-1 and 3-2 and the earlier Heartland Hospital activities.

2. Identify and list potential project team members, keeping in mind the following:
   - Who did you identify as data owners, and should they be included on the project team?
   - Who did you identify as service owners, and should they be included on the project team?
   - Who did you identify as potential executive sponsors? What would you expect their involvement to be?
   - Are there other key stakeholders? Should they be represented on the team?
   - Does the hospital have internal staff with adequate experience to successfully complete a project like this? If so, who do you see filling the role of project owner? If not, how could you address the situation?

3. Prepare a list of your team and a brief explanation of its composition. Be prepared to present your team's makeup to your partner and your instructor, and to discuss your choices.

CHAPTER SUMMARY

- ❑ Active Directory can play many different roles in modern networks. The type of role that is chosen will affect the design, but all design projects should follow sound principles.

- ❑ Active Directory is an infrastructure, and because of its importance to the entire organization, design issues will cut across political and departmental boundaries. The design team should be broadly based and seek consensus by collaboration and conversation with all key stakeholders.

- ❑ Active Directory allows networks to be managed with a split administrative style that divides data ownership from service ownership.

- ❑ Data owners are responsible for the contents of the directory. They create, modify, delete, and manage objects in the directory, such as users.

- ❑ Service owners are responsible for the operation of the directory service itself, including domain controllers.

- ❑ When you set up a trust relationship between forests (or to a Windows NT domain), you are also trusting a person or an organization and letting them into parts of your network. Therefore, careful consideration should always be given so that this trust is not misplaced.

- ❑ Any administrator in a domain or forest is being trusted with the valuable assets of the enterprise. The enterprise should have full confidence in the trustworthiness of its network administrators.

- ❑ Domain controllers should always be physically secured.

❐ Active Directory design is the process of creating a structure around the objects to be stored in the Active Directory database. It is a process, not a one-size-fits-all answer.

❐ Active Directory design decisions should be based on defined business goals or requirements.

❐ Executive management should be involved with and sponsoring the Active Directory design project. This may require documentation of the value of Active Directory to the company.

❐ A good Active Directory design will allow for growth and reasonable amounts of change in the business.

❐ A good Active Directory design will support delegation of control to data owners and the application of Group Policy in a logical, consistent way.

❐ The design team or architect should be able to justify design decisions and tradeoffs in terms of value, business goals, and business requirements.

❐ Documenting the value of Active Directory in business terms will be helpful in gaining executive support.

❐ Microsoft recommends following a philosophy called the Microsoft Solutions Framework for project management during development of new software or network infrastructure. A project using MSF has five stages: envisioning, planning, developing, stabilizing, and deploying.

❐ Microsoft also publishes a framework called the Microsoft Operations Framework to promote high-availability operations of network infrastructure.

❐ During the envisioning stage, a project team is created and a common vision is built around business goals and the needs of stakeholders.

KEY TERMS

best practice — A preferred way of doing something, defined either by an authority or by common practice in well-run companies.

data owner — A person or team responsible for managing the content of a part of the directory, not maintaining the directory service itself. Data owners will usually create objects and edit their attributes.

directory owner — *See* service owner.

directory service — A central database that stores information about network-based objects such as computers, printers, users, and groups. Active Directory is a directory service.

functional specification — The document created at the end of the planning stage that describes the Active Directory design.

Group Policy — A technology enabled by Active Directory that allows administrators to define policy and rely on Active Directory and the operating system to ensure that policies are enforced. Group Policy is also used to automatically distribute software.

Microsoft Operations Framework (MOF) — A set of documents, guidelines, and models developed by Microsoft to help companies increase reliability, availability, and ease of management and support. MOF provides guidance for the operation of systems, particularly Microsoft infrastructure systems in large enterprises. Visit *http://www.microsoft.com/mof*.

Microsoft Solutions Framework (MSF) — A set of documents, guidelines, and models developed by Microsoft to help companies improve the effectiveness of software or infrastructure development projects. Visit *http://www.microsoft.com/msf*.

object owner — Specifically, each object in the directory has an identified owner. More generically, sometimes used to mean data owner.

service owner — A person or team responsible for maintaining and operating the directory service as a whole. The service owner will manage domain controllers and the site structure.

     split administration model — The concept that service ownership and data ownership can be divided.

     trust relationship (trust) — A link between two domains that allows security principals from one domain to be recognized by the other.

REVIEW QUESTIONS

1. The _____ owner is responsible for the proper operation of the directory service system.

2. The _____ owner is responsible for the content of the directory, such as creating new users.

3. Active Directory can be used as a public e-mail directory to allow your clients to find staff e-mail addresses on a Web page. True or False?

4. In which of the following roles can Active Directory be found? (Choose all that apply.)

    a. Enterprise-wide directory (of people and resources)

    b. E-mail directory (of internal users or external contacts)

    c. White pages directory (external users looking up internal addresses)

    d. E-commerce authentication and authorization

5. No matter what role Active Directory is used in, all Active Directory designs use the same domain structures. True or False?

6. The deployment of Active Directory is a technological issue only of concern to technologists, such as the IT department. True or False?

7. Active Directory is part of your company's network _____, just like water and pipes are part of a city's sewer system.

8. Put the following in the order they would occur under the Microsoft Solutions Framework philosophy of deployment.

    a. _____ The functional specification is complete.

    b. _____ The first domain controller running Active Directory is installed on the live production network.

    c. _____ The envisioning phase begins.

    d. _____ The planning stage begins.

9. Documenting the value of Active Directory in _____ terms will be helpful in gaining executive support.

10. Each object in the Active Directory database has an object _____.

11. An Active Directory design should be forward-thinking enough to allow for _____ in the enterprise or business environment.

12. The division between service owners and data owners is called the _____.

13. Which person or team would install and configure a new domain controller?

    a. Service owner

    b. Data owner

    c. Either

    d. Neither

14. You should always plan to create trusts between your forest and those in all subsidiaries or other departments of your company. True or False?

15. Which statement is most correct?

    a. Executive management should become involved as soon as the functional specification is complete.

    b. Documenting the value of Active Directory in business terms will be helpful in gaining executive support.

    c. Executive management does not need to be involved in the planning process.

    d. Executive management is the best choice for the service owner role.

16. How does projected future growth in your company affect the Active Directory design process? Choose the best response:

    a. Designs should be reevaluated every six months.

    b. Additional forests should be created if the company grows by more than 10 percent.

    c. The designs should be forward-thinking enough to allow for predictable change.

    d. It is impossible to predict the future, so designs reflect the current needs only.

17. Should every department or division shown on the organizational chart have its own OU in Active Directory?

    a. Always

    b. Never

    c. Only when doing so is warranted by data ownership roles

    d. Only if the department or division is a service owner

18. Nonprofit agencies and for-profit businesses may both use Active Directory to help accomplish their unique business or organizational goals. True or False?

19. Delegation of _____ means that data owners can be given permissions to manage their own objects in the directory.

20. The Active Directory design team should be prepared to _____ their design decisions and trade-offs.

21. A good design will support the logical application of _____ to enforce rules or policies defined by the organization.

22. MSF is used to manage projects that develop new software or new infrastructure, while following the procedures in _____ may help maximize the availability of your infrastructure.

23. Within Active Directory, don't leave the issue of _____ to be considered only at the time you deploy the equipment. It should be considered from the beginning of the envisioning phase to the final deployment and operation.

24. The _____ owner is responsible for the contents of the directory service (or part of it).

25. The _____ owner is responsible for the operation of the directory service.

CASE PROJECTS

For the following case projects, you will be in the role of a consultant working for Multinational Mega Corporation, the fictitious company introduced in Chapter 1. As your knowledge of Active Directory grows, your employer is calling on you to provide input into Active Directory situations arising with customers.

Case Project 3-1: Identifying Service and Data Owners

Consider a company that has about 1,000 staff members, with qualified and competent people working in both the human resources (HR) and information technology (IT) departments. Currently, IT maintains an Active Directory forest for the company. The IT staff creates and deletes users in the directory on receipt of written instructions (by memo) from the HR department. The instructions from HR are not reviewed or questioned. The company would like to find a way to reduce the delay sometimes caused by this process.

Describe how the roles of data owner and service owner might apply in this situation.

Case Project: 3-2: Negotiating on Cross-Departmental Issues

You have been asked to coordinate a design team working on a new Active Directory forest plan for a legal services firm. In early meetings, there is resistance from the HR division and the Commercial Litigation division, neither of which have participated in a central directory service before. HR is concerned that it will have to spend a lot of time and effort chasing down information and coordinating with the IT department when people are hired and fired. The Commercial Litigation lawyers do not want to put their file server in the forest, because they do not want the "busybodies in the Real Estate division nosing about" in their confidential files.

What roles and concerns do you see being played out here? What are some possible solutions?

Case Project: 3-3: Working with a Customer

You have been asked to install a domain controller for a new client, a mid-size hotel in the same city as your office. When you arrive on site, they show you the domain controller computer and tell you that they would like to have their new domain working by the end of the day. With a quick, "We'll leave you to it, then!" they leave you alone in the equipment room. What stage of the design project do you think this firm is currently in? How would you proceed?

4

PRACTICAL ACTIVE DIRECTORY
DESIGN DECISIONS

**After reading this chapter and completing the exercises,
you will be able to:**

♦ Choose the best DNS name for a domain
♦ Make Active Directory forest design decisions
♦ Understand the roles and describe the characteristics of trusts
♦ Describe the characteristics of domains
♦ Describe the role and characteristics of organizational units

Chapter 1 defined the basics of Active Directory; Chapter 2 looked at planning and conducting Active Directory installations. In Chapter 3 you learned about the "big picture" of Active Directory, including how your design philosophy might affect the choices you make. Chapter 3 also introduced you to MSF, a multi-stage approach to managing software or infrastructure creation.

During the second phase of an MSF project—the planning phase—you translated the goals and visions created in the envisioning phase into specific, actionable plans. You then tested your design to ensure it worked as intended. While the design philosophy guides the overall approach to designing and configuring Active Directory, the design team must also make specific implementation decisions for each Active Directory installation. You will learn about those kinds of decisions in this chapter.

We will begin by looking at how the Active Directory namespace interacts with DNS, and present some of the choices regarding DNS and Active Directory. You will then learn about the situations that might require the creation of more than one forest in an organization. You will also learn how a forest or domain can interact with other forests and domains through the use of a trust relationship. Then you will learn how to select from different possible configurations of domains within a forest, as well as how to select from choices for arranging the OUs within the domain.

CHOOSING A DNS NAME

As you already learned, DNS defines the namespace used by Active Directory. Choosing the DNS name of a domain is not a decision to take lightly or to put off until the last minute. It is used extensively throughout the domain and affects every member of the domain. Changing the domain name after the domain has been created can be complicated, time consuming, and expensive. If a DNS name is widely circulated, a company may be reluctant to change it once people have started using it.

For example, in the 1990s, a large, international nonprofit organization began deploying networks in its enterprise. This was before the days of Active Directory, but DNS was already in common use. Someone in the organization's Canadian office registered a domain name. The name they picked was cute and colloquial and was based on a common nickname of the organization. It was registered within the .ca subdomain and then deployed. At the time, e-mail was mostly internal and only a few people—primarily in the IT department—ever saw the domain name. But then members of the public learned that staff could be reached via e-mail, and started asking for staff members' e-mail addresses. Shortly after, the public relations department wanted to launch a Web site. Although the domain name wasn't offensive or obscure, it wasn't professional or representative of the organization either. In addition, no thought had been given to how international offices would fit into a global naming structure.

By the time these issues became paramount, no suitable .com or .org names were left. At that time, rules in the .ca TLD only allowed an organization to register one .ca subdomain, so it was not easy to switch to a new one. Eventually, management of the .ca ccTLD relaxed the rules, allowing the organization to establish a worldwide scheme for formatting its DNS name and register a new, more suitable name. This change, however, came only after a great deal of time and expense was wasted on renaming servers and updating references that contained the old name.

What Makes a Good DNS Name?

Avoid unnecessary expense and trouble by choosing a good DNS name for your domain at the beginning of the process. A good DNS name for your Active Directory domain will be meaningful and scalable—that is, it will represent your entire business and support current and future plans. You also need to consider the difference between a DNS name used for a public Internet presence and one used just to support Active Directory.

Making the Name Meaningful and Scalable

The DNS name chosen for the first domain created in a tree will be a part of the DNS names for all the **child domains** in that tree, the same way that *ad.multinatcorp.com* is contained in *northamerica.ad.multinatcorp.com*. Because a domain name can be difficult, impractical, or even impossible to change, your DNS name should be both meaningful and scalable. It needs to represent the whole of the enterprise not just part of it, and allow for future growth. The issue of domain renaming is discussed in more detail later in this chapter.

Take the fictitious case of Billy Bob's Seafood Restaurant—a small, but growing chain of specialty dining establishments. Rushing in to an Active Directory deployment, it chose *bbseafood.com* as the DNS name for its domain. However, the IT department didn't consider its wholly owned subsidiary, JoJo's Fine Coffees, the arm of the business that procures coffee for its own restaurants and also resells it to other establishments. The DNS name it selected does not represent its entire enterprise; therefore, it is not a good, long-term choice.

Two Common Uses for DNS: Internet Presence and Active Directory

Most companies using Active Directory will have two uses for DNS. The first (and of most consequence to this book) is to define the namespace used by Active Directory and thus how resources are located within the network. The second is to provide a way for the rest of the world to contact the enterprise—via e-mail, the company Web site, or an e-commerce initiative. This role—a company's public address on the Internet—is sometimes called its **Internet presence**. For example, Microsoft Corporation uses *microsoft.com* for its corporate Internet presence. Its main Web site is *www.microsoft.com*, and e-mail is addressed as follows: *webmaster@microsoft.com*. However, *microsoft.com* is not the namespace used by its corporate Active Directory implementation.

Activity 4-1: Listing DNS Entries for an Internet Presence Zone

Time Required: 5 minutes

Objective: To develop familiarity with the DNS system and identify characteristics of a DNS zone used only for Internet presence.

Description: In this activity, you will examine the resource records (RRs) returned from a public DNS server for a zone used only to provide an Internet presence. You will see that a DNS zone used for a public Internet presence usually has only a few RRs, normally the ones required to facilitate delivery of e-mail and inbound Web access. (*Note*: depending on your classroom configuration, your instructor may specify a different domain name or server.)

1. If necessary, turn on your computer and log in as the administrator from your own domain.

2. Click **Start**, then click **Run**.

3. When the Run dialog box appears, type **nslookup** in the Open combo box, and then click **OK**.

4. At the prompt ("<"), type **server ns1.domainpeople.com** and press **Enter** to specify that queries should be directed to that server.

5. When the prompt returns, type **ls −d multinatcorp.com** and press **Enter** to request a list of RRs for the *multinatcorp.com* domain.

6. Notice that only a few records were returned, and they do not disclose information about the internal network at Multinational Mega Corporation, or information about computers designated to receive contact from outside the network.

7. At the prompt, type **exit** and press **Enter**. If you are not continuing directly to the next activity, log off your machine.

Activity 4-2: Listing DNS Entries for an Active Directory Zone

Time Required: 5 minutes

Objective: To develop familiarity with the DNS system and identify characteristics of a DNS zone used only for Active Directory.

Description: In this activity, you will examine the resource records returned from a public DNS server for a zone used to support Active Directory. In contrast to the zone used in Activity 4-1, much more information will be provided in this case. The response from this server will include more records, including several SRV records. This is the kind of information that a malicious hacker could use to help him attack the network.

1. If necessary, turn on your computer and log in as the administrator from your own domain.

2. Click **Start**, then click **Run**.

3. When the Run dialog box appears, type **nslookup** in the Open combo box, then click **OK**.

4. At the prompt (">"), type **ls –d** *yourdomain*.**ad.multinatcorp.com** and press **Enter**, where *yourdomain* is the name of your assigned domain as installed in Chapter 2. Notice that many records are returned, more than in the last activity. Notice in particular that the list includes SRV records describing the location of domain controllers and the services available on the network. This sort of information detailing crucial resources describes the internal structure of the classroom network, and in a business would usually be considered confidential enough to keep within the company.

5. At the prompt, type **exit** and press **Enter**.

6. Log off your machine.

Choosing How DNS Names for Internet and Active Directory Will Be Related

The relationship between a DNS name used for an Internet presence—such as e-mail and a Web site—and the DNS name used for an Active Directory domain can be complicated. You have several choices:

- Use the same DNS name for both.
- Use completely different names altogether.
- Delegate a subdomain from your Internet name for Active Directory.

The next few sections will examine each of these possibilities.

Using the Same DNS Name for Active Directory and Internet Presence

The problem with using the same name for both Active Directory and the Internet presence is that it requires complicated steps to prevent confidential data from being made available publicly, and is therefore not recommended. Crackers and hackers love to discover the details of systems implementation within a company. Every bit of knowledge they gain adds to their ability to attack the network or socially engineer additional information from unsuspecting employees. Even learning the names and IP numbers of important hosts on your network, such as the DCs, increases their probability for success. For these reasons, it is not recommended that your SRV records or unnecessary hostnames be publicized.

When you use the same name on the Internet as used internally, all of your RRs are publicly available (which is not desirable), unless you use a technique called split DNS. Split DNS, as seen in Figure 4-1, gives internal DNS Servers complete zone data, including all SRV records, and gives external DNS Servers only the public records for that same zone. That public zone data has to be maintained manually, and care must always be taken to ensure that internal clients connect only to internal servers (because the external ones won't be able to handle their requests) and that external clients only connect to the external servers.

Using split DNS is even more complicated if internal users start connecting from the outside, perhaps over a virtual private network (VPN). There is nothing inherently wrong with this approach, but it is complex to administer. The more complex something is, the greater the chance for error. It also requires additional hardware, as the internal and external zones cannot be hosted on the same DNS Servers. There is no particular benefit to this arrangement that offsets the great amount of work required to maintain it, so it is rarely recommended.

Split DNS structure, using the same DNS subdomain
for Internet presence and Active Directory

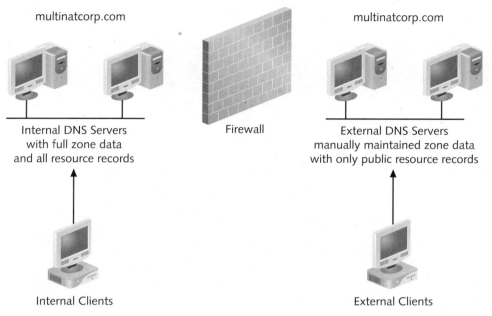

multinatcorp.com

Internal DNS Servers
with full zone data
and all resource records

Firewall

multinatcorp.com

External DNS Servers
manually maintained zone data
with only public resource records

Internal Clients

External Clients

Figure 4-1   Split DNS

Using Completely Different Names for Active Directory and Internet Presence

In a scenario where the Active Directory DNS name is completely removed from the Internet presence DNS name, there is no possibility of conflict between them. Management of the names and hosts for the Internet is completely separate from Active Directory. The Active Directory DNS name may be completely private, such as a name ending with *.local* or *.private*. As an example, consider *multinatcorp.private* used for Active Directory and *multinatcorp.com* used for the Internet presence, as shown in Figure 4-2. Of course, a variation on the same approach would be to have the Active Directory DNS name registered separately with a TLD registrar, such as *multinatcorp.net* for Active Directory and *mulitnatcorp.com* for the Internet.

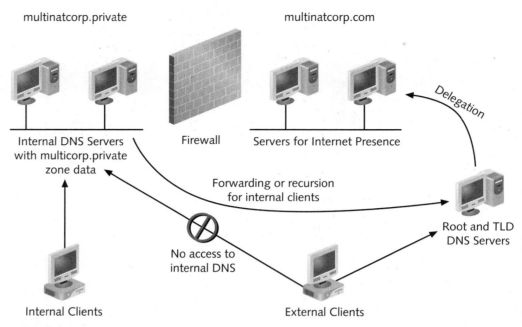

Figure 4-2   Separate DNS structure

In the type of design shown in Figure 4-2, the designers must ensure that internal clients can resolve both internal names to support Active Directory, and external names to access Internet resources. To accomplish this, clients can query the internal servers using a forwarder or recursion to resolve external names. The potential downfall of this design is that if an internal client is not correctly set to use an internal name server, it will not receive a referral unless the internal subdomain name is also within a public TLD and registered with the TLD's registrar. In small organizations, the private and public zones could be hosted on the same DNS Servers, but in most cases they are separated. Public DNS Servers are often located with the Web servers, while the internal DNS usually runs on the DCs.

Activity 4-3: Creating a Simple Web Site

Time Required: 15 minutes

Objective: To create a simple Web site used to demonstrate how to connect to a company Web site that uses separate DNS names for its Internet presence and its Active Directory domain.

Description: In this activity, you will create a simple Web site that can be used to test DNS configurations. The Web site will provide the current date and time, as well as other interesting information. You will access the Web site, as well as your partner's (optional), by IP number. We will use this Web site again after configuring DNS.

1. If necessary, turn on your computer and log in as the administrator from your own domain.

2. Click **Start**, click **Administrative Tools**, and then click **Internet Information Services (IIS) Manager**.

If your computer was not installed with Internet Information Server (IIS), you can add IIS from the Manage Your Server application found on the Start menu.

3. In the left pane, expand the node for your computer, and then expand the **Web Sites** node.

4. Right-click **Default Web Site**, then click **Properties**.

5. When the Default Web Site Properties dialog box appears, click the **Home Directory** tab. Note the location of the **Local path** setting, where files for this Web site are stored. The default is *c:\inetpub\wwwroot*.

6. Click the **Documents** tab.

7. Check that **Enable default content page** is checked. Ensure that *Default.asp* appears in the list of default pages and that it is listed above the entry for *iisstart.htm*. (If the *Default.asp* entry is missing, create a new entry at the top of the list for *Default.asp*. Consult your instructor if you need assistance with this step.)

8. Click **OK**.

9. In the left pane, click the **Web Service Extensions** node.

10. Verify that **Active Server Pages** is marked **Allowed**. If it is not:

    a. In the details pane, under Web Services Extensions, click **Active Server Pages**.

    b. Click the **Allow** button.

11. Close the Internet Information Services (IIS) Manager MMC window.

12. Copy the file *default.asp* from the MNC-FRDC computer to your Web directory. You can do so by copying and pasting the file.

13. Close any open windows.

14. Start Internet Explorer.

15. In the Internet Explorer address bar, type **http://127.0.0.1** and press **Enter**.

16. Verify that a sample Web page is returned from your computer. If not, consult your instructor for assistance.

17. If time permits, wait until your partner has completed Steps 1–16, then enter your partner's server name or IP number in the Internet Explorer address bar. Compare the results from your computer with your partner's.

18. Close Internet Explorer.

Activity 4-4: Simulating an Internet Presence Zone

Time Required: 10 minutes

Objective: To create a zone that will be used only for resolving Web site information.

Description: In this activity, you will create a DNS zone used only to connect to the Web page created in the previous activity. You will observe that a Web server can remain a member of an Active Directory domain using private records and still respond to Web requests made to a public DNS name.

1. If necessary, turn on your computer and log in as the administrator from your own domain.

2. Start the **DNS Management console** as in previous activities.

3. In the tree pane, right-click **Forward Lookup Zones**.

4. Click **New Zone**.

5. When the New Zone Wizard window appears, click **Next**.

6. Click **Primary zone**, and click **Next**.

7. Click **Next** again.

8. In the Zone name text box, type the name of any zone you would like to use for your Web site. You could use your name, such as **byronphynes.com**, or a catchy phrase, such as **MCSEs-R-us.net**. You and your partner should choose different names. After choosing and typing a name, click **Next**.

9. Click **Next**.

10. Click **Finish**.

11. Click the name of your new zone in the tree in the left pane. Notice in the right pane that SOA and NS records have been created.

12. Right-click the name of your zone. Then, click **New Host (A)**.

13. In the Name (uses parent domain name if blank) text box, type **www**.

14. In the IP address box, type the IP address of your computer.

15. Click **Add Host**.

16. Click **OK**.

17. Click **Done**.

18. Close the **DNS console**.

19. Run Internet Explorer and enter the hostname you just created in the Address bar. When you press **Enter**, the default page is returned from your own server, even though you did not use its Active Directory name. (If you do not see the same page, review the steps above to check for errors, or consult your instructor for assistance.)

20. Time permitting, try browsing to your partner's computer using the name he or she created. Try browsing to other names created by other class members. Observe that if everyone completed the steps exactly, you can connect only to your own computer and your partner's using these fake names. Discuss this issue with others or with your instructor until you are confident that you understand why some names could resolve and others could not.

21. Close all open windows on your computer. If you are not proceeding directly to another activity, log off your computer.

Delegating a Subdomain from the Internet Presence Subdomain for Active Directory

This solution also uses separate zones to keep Active Directory and the Internet presence apart, but rather than creating a new name, a subdomain is delegated from the existing Internet presence name. For example, *ad.multinatcorp.com* is a delegated subdomain of *multinatcorp.com*. This design is simple to administer and is extremely palatable to organizations with a large existing investment in DNS infrastructure, or existing DNS Servers running BIND or other UNIX software.

Setting up the **delegation** is a simple matter of the existing DNS administrators entering the delegation records to point all queries related to Active Directory to the correct servers. It is not necessary to reconfigure clients, as any client that can find a working DNS Server can find the address for the DNS Servers providing resolution for the Active Directory subdomain. (Usually, most external clients would still be blocked by a firewall from making a connection.) This example is shown in Figure 4-3.

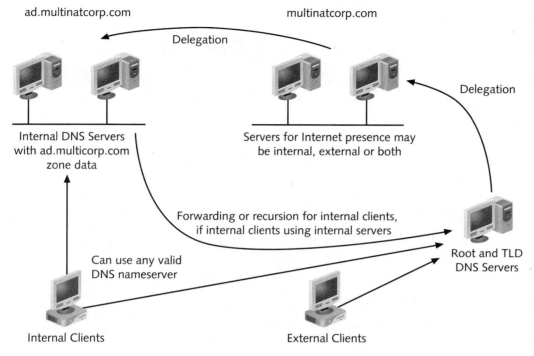

Delegated DNS structure, using a delegated subdomain for Active Directory

Figure 4-3   Delegated DNS subdomain

   Recall that you learned the skills to delegate a subdomain in Chapter 2.

Best Practices for Choosing a DNS Name

Microsoft recommends a delegated subdomain as a best practice for DNS design with Active Directory in organizations that already have an existing DNS structure. Even in organizations without existing DNS implementations, Microsoft recommends the creation of a new registered DNS name with a delegation to a zone dedicated to Active Directory.

Microsoft also recommends that all DCs run the DNS Server software with the zones for Active Directory configured as Active Directory integrated zones. In multiple-domain forests, it is often necessary to locate the services provided by DCs in the forest root domain. If your DNS servers are running on Windows 2000 or non-Microsoft operating systems (OSs), it is also recommended that the forest root domain's _msdcs zone be replicated to all other domains as a standard secondary zone. If your DNS Servers are all running on Windows 2003 Server, then you should replicate the forest root zone to all DCs running DNS by using an application partition. (The replication of application partitions is discussed in Chapter 8).

As network designers gain experience and encounter more unique situations, they will occasionally have good reason to deviate from the recommended configuration or best practice. However, doing something contrary to best practices should be a rare exception, not a rule, and the designer should always be able to justify the decision.

Activity 4-5: Restricting Access to DNS Zone Data

Time Required: 5 minutes

Objective: To learn how to prevent the listing of all RRs in a DNS zone.

Description: In this activity, you will prevent DNS clients from listing all of the records in a zone by preventing zone transfers. Clients will still be able to look up individual records, but are not able to request the whole file. This is a common practice that prevents the release of confidential DNS information, except to authorized secondary DNS Servers.

1. If necessary, turn on your computer and log in as the administrator from your own domain.

2. Start the DNS Management console as in previous activities.

3. In the tree pane, click **Forward Lookup Zones**.

4. In the details pane, right-click the name of your Active Directory domain (such as *oneandtwo.ad.multinatcorp.com*), and then click **Properties**.

5. Click the **Zone Transfers** tab.

6. Uncheck the **Allow zone transfers** checkbox.

7. Click **OK**.

8. Close the **DNS Management console**.

9. Click **Start**, then click **Run**.

10. When the Run dialog box appears, type **nslookup** in the Open combo box, and then click **OK**.

11. At the prompt ("**>**"), type **ls –d** *yourdomain***.ad.multinatcorp.com** and press **Enter**, where *yourdomain* is the name of your assigned domain as installed in Chapter 2.

12. Notice that unlike Activity 4-2, no records are returned.

13. At the prompt, type the name of your server and press **Enter**. Note that individual records can still be looked up.

14. At the prompt, type **exit**, and press **Enter**.

15. Close all open windows on your computer. If you are not continuing directly to another activity, log off your computer.

DESIGNING A FOREST

When designing Active Directory, start with the forest and work down to domains. This logical approach of working from the big to the small ensures that you tackle the most important issues first and keeps you from letting small, operational decisions dictate the answers to large, enterprise-wide issues.

This section will begin by examining the characteristics of a forest and then discusses why many forests are required.

Characteristics of a Forest

A forest has some fundamental characteristics. First, it is the implementation of Active Directory. That is, one single forest really represents one single Active Directory installation. Each and every time you have an Active Directory structure, you have a forest. If you have two forests, you have two separate Active Directory structures. If you have multiple configurations of Active Directory, you have multiple forests.

As well as being an "instance" of Active Directory, a forest can also be viewed as a collection of domains, and a domain can be considered a partition (or section or division) of a forest.

Keep in mind that the data for each domain is stored in a domain partition. All domain partitions, combined with the configuration partition, the schema partition, and any defined application partitions, make up the forest. Even though partitions will be stored on separate DCs in a multiple-domain forest, the forest is not complete without its domains, and a domain cannot stand alone without its forest.

A forest is also a security and administrative boundary. Security information is not propagated between forests. Within the boundary of a forest, some information is common. All domains in a forest share these items:

- A centrally controlled schema, stored in a schema partition that is replicated to all domain controllers in the forest.

- A common configuration, stored in the configuration partition that is replicated to all domain controllers in the forest. This configuration information includes infrastructure and topology elements such as domains, sites, and site links. Sites and site links are discussed in Chapter 7.

- A single Global Catalog, stored on designated Global Catalog servers to allow for quick searches for any object in the forest. (Global Catalog servers have copies of the domain partition for their own domain, plus partial copies of the domain partitions from any other domains in the forest.)

- Complete trust relationships, in that Active Directory automatically creates transitive two-way trusts between all domains in a forest. Trusts are discussed more fully in the next section, but within a forest, any security principal from any domain in the forest can be granted access to any resource in any domain in the forest.

How Many Forests?

There is not usually a need to create more than one forest for an organization—even in a very large organization. A single forest can contain millions of objects and provide excellent performance. It is necessary to create multiple forests only when one of the items shared within a forest must not be shared without violating a business objective. Here are some examples of situations that justify multiple forests:

- If two parts of an organization must have different schemas, they must have different forests. For example, a division might require that Active Directory be populated with objects from new classes, or a subsidiary that runs custom software requiring a schema incompatible with the rest of the organization.

- If two parts of an organization must have complete separation of administration, they must have different forests. This is most commonly seen in multinational organizations, where specific national laws impose restrictions on where data is kept and how it is managed.

- If one part of a company cannot participate in a complete trust model, then separate forests are justified. One example of this situation includes high-security areas, such as military or classified projects. Another situation where a second forest is justified is to support a large Web farm or Internet presence. If the computers serving the public need maximum isolation from the corporate network, but still require the services of Active Directory, it may be a good idea to have a second forest.

So when the business requirements dictate a high degree of separation between entities, creating separate forests may be necessary. Keep in mind, though, that making more forests adds work for administrators, and forfeits the benefit of a single Global Catalog. Additional costs are incurred for hardware, software, and labor.

Creating a new forest means creating a new implementation of Active Directory, and each forest must also have a clearly defined service owner. Create more than one forest only when it is necessary to meet a defined business requirement.

UNDERSTANDING AND IMPLEMENTING TRUST RELATIONSHIPS

A **trust relationship** is what gives the ability for a security principal in one domain to access a resource in another without needing separate credentials for each domain. Recall that joining a domain lets a security principal access resources on more than one server in the domain. In a similar way, trust relationships extend that ability across multiple domains, and possibly across multiple forests.

To help with terminology, remember that the *trusting* domain trusts the *trusted* domain to authenticate a user. The security principal exists in the *trusted* domain; the resource is in the *trusting* domain. Think of one domain as trusting another to vouch for one of the trusted domain's users. In Figure 4-4, the arrow points from the trusting domain to the trusted domain.

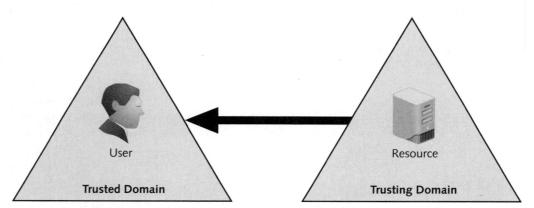

Figure 4-4   Typical trust diagram

Two-Way, Transitive Trusts

Two-way, transitive trusts are best explained by breaking the term into its components. The term "two-way" means that domain *A* trusts domain *B*, and domain *B* trusts domain *A*. The term "transitive" means that if *A* trusts *B*, and *B* trusts *C*, then *A* also trusts *C*. These are important characteristics, especially when compared to trusts that are made between other forests or Windows NT domains that may be **one-way** and **nontransitive**.

Trusts are established on a domain-to-domain level. Even though all domains in a single forest automatically participate in a complete trust model, the complete trust is built on a series of individual two-way, transitive trusts between particular domains in the forest. Take, for example, the forest pictured in Figure 4-5. There are six domains in this large forest. The domain named *ad.multinatcorp.com* was the first domain created and is the forest root domain. Two other domains form part of its tree, while a second tree beginning with *ad.superwidgets.com*, is also part of the forest.

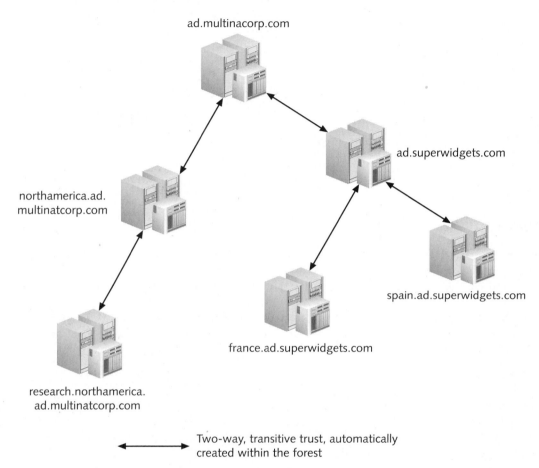

ad.multinacorp.com

ad.superwidgets.com

northamerica.ad.
multinatcorp.com

spain.ad.superwidgets.com

france.ad.superwidgets.com

research.northamerica.
ad.multinatcorp.com

Two-way, transitive trust, automatically
created within the forest

Figure 4-5   Two-way, transitive trusts within a forest

If a domain is a child domain of another domain in a tree, there is a trust relationship formed between the parent domain and the child domain. If the domain is at the top of a tree, but is not the forest root domain, a trust is formed between it and the forest root domain. Each is a two-way, transitive trust.

Activity 4-6: Viewing Intra-Forest Trust Relationships

Time Required: 5 minutes

Objective: To view the trusts created automatically in a forest.

Description: In this activity, you will use Active Directory tools to view the two-way, transitive trusts that are automatically created for a domain in a forest. This will help you understand the roles that trusts play in the forest, and see the trusts that have been automatically created.

1. If necessary, turn on your computer and log in as the administrator from your own domain.

2. Click **Start**, click **Administrative Tools**, and then click **Active Directory Domains and Trusts**.

3. In Active Directory Domains and Trusts, expand the node for the forest root domain (*ad.multinatcorp.com*).

4. Right-click the name of the forest root domain and click **Properties**.

5. Click the tab labeled **Trusts** and review the trusts that have been created for the forest root domain.

 Remember, you are not logged in as an administrator in the forest root domain. Although you can view the existing trusts, you would need to supply different credentials to reconfigure the trusts on the forest root domain.

6. Click **Cancel** to close the properties sheet.

7. Click the name of your assigned child domain to select it.

8. Right-click the name of your assigned child domain and click **Properties**.

9. Click the tab labeled **Trusts** and review the trusts that have been created in your assigned child domain.

10. Close all open windows on your computer. If you are not continuing directly to another activity, log off your computer.

Shortcut Trusts

The effect of two-way transitive trusts within a forest is that a trust path can always be found from one domain to any other in the forest. This is sometimes called "walking the tree," as several domains may have to be traversed along the way. For example, take the domains shown in Figure 4-5. A user in *research.northamerica.ad.multinatcorp.com* can be given permissions to resources in *france.ad.superwidgets.com*, but in order to be authenticated, the DCs in *france.ad.superwidgets.com*, *ad.superwidgets.com*, *ad.multinatcorp.com*, *northamerica.ad.multinatcorp.com*, and *research.northamerica.ad.multinatcorp.com* would all need to be involved in the process. Although the trusts are transitive, authentications must follow a trust path.

To cut down on the number of steps involved, administrators can define **shortcut trusts** that allow quicker authentication of security credentials by pointing one domain directly to another, without intervening steps. In this case, *france* can trust *research* directly. Shortcut trusts reduce the number of DCs that must be involved in a cross-domain authentication, thereby increasing efficiency and reducing the number of possible points of failure. In the kind of cases demonstrated in the example, a shortcut trust would be a good idea. The addition of a shortcut trust is shown in Figure 4-6.

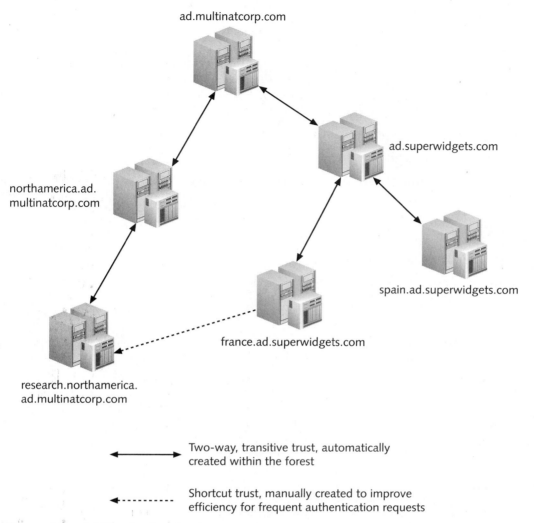

ad.multinatcorp.com

ad.superwidgets.com

northamerica.ad.
multinatcorp.com

spain.ad.superwidgets.com

france.ad.superwidgets.com

research.northamerica.
ad.multinatcorp.com

⟷   Two-way, transitive trust, automatically
created within the forest

◄-------   Shortcut trust, manually created to improve
efficiency for frequent authentication requests

Figure 4-6   Adding shortcut trusts

Activity 4-7: Creating a Shortcut Trust

Time Required: 10 minutes

Objective: To create a shortcut trust between domains in the forest.

Description: In this activity, you will gain experience creating trust relationships by using the Active Directory Domains and Trusts console to configure additional trusts within the forest. You and your partner will work together.

1. Choose one computer (yours or your partner's) on which to perform the following steps.

2. If necessary, turn on your computer and log in as the administrator from your own domain.

3. Click **Start**, click **Administrative Tools**, and then click **Active Directory Domains and Trusts**.

4. In Active Directory Domains and Trusts, expand the node for the forest root domain.

5. Right-click the name of your assigned child domain and click **Properties**.

6. Click the tab labeled **Trusts** and review the trusts that have been created. You will see trusts to the parent domain in the tree.

7. Click **New Trust**.

8. Click **Next** to begin the New Trust Wizard.

9. Type the name of the next domain to yours, working in pairs of domains. For example, *oneandtwo.ad.multinatcorp.com* will work with *threeandfour.ad.multinatcorp.com* and so on. (Your instructor will advise you of the domain to trust if the classroom is configured differently. If you are working independently, you may choose any domain in your test forest.)

10. After typing the name of the domain you are working with, click **Next**.

11. Choose **Two-way** and click **Next**.

12. Choose **This domain only** and click **Next**. (The team next to you will be creating the trust for the other domain.)

13. Type your password in both the Trust password and Confirm trust password text boxes, then click **Next**.

14. Click **Next** to create the trust.

15. Observe the results presented in the box labeled Status of Changes. If the creation was not successful, consult your instructor.

16. Click **Next**.

17. Wait until the other team has created the corresponding trust in their domain. Click **Yes**, confirm the outgoing trust, then click **Next**.

18. Click **No, do not confirm the incoming trust** and click **Next**.

19. Review the information presented in the Completing the New Trust Wizard page. If the status does not indicate a successful confirmation of the trust, consult your instructor.

20. Click **Finish**.

21. Note the addition of the new trust in the list.

22. Click **OK**.

23. Close all open windows on your computer. If you are not continuing directly to another activity, log off your computer.

Explicit Inter-Forest Trusts

Administrators can also create an explicit inter-forest trust to another forest, to an existing Windows NT domain, or to a UNIX Kerberos realm, if that realm is compatible with Active Directory trusts. Explicit inter-forest trusts must be manually created. If a design contains many explicit inter-forest trusts, especially to other domains, you should probably revisit the design, as it might be better if these domains were merged into one forest. Explicit trusts have been added to the forest shown in Figure 4-7.

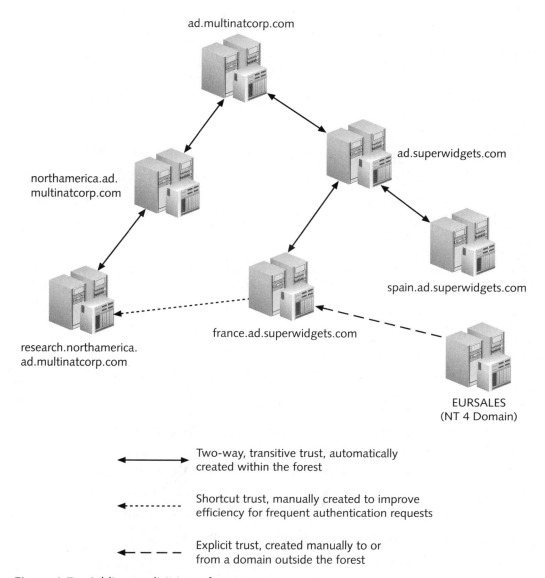

ad.multinatcorp.com

northamerica.ad.
multinatcorp.com

ad.superwidgets.com

spain.ad.superwidgets.com

research.northamerica.
ad.multinatcorp.com

france.ad.superwidgets.com

EURSALES
(NT 4 Domain)

Two-way, transitive trust, automatically
created within the forest

Shortcut trust, manually created to improve
efficiency for frequent authentication requests

Explicit trust, created manually to or
from a domain outside the forest

Figure 4-7   Adding explicit inter-forest trusts

The ability to have two-way, transitive trusts between separate forests is a big step forward in the Windows 2003 Server family. In Windows 2000 Active Directory, external trusts were not transitive, and with Windows NT, there were no forests, so there was no such concept.

The term "inter-forest" means between two different forests, between a forest and a Windows NT domain, or between a forest and a Kerberos realm found in certain UNIX implementations. Not all realms are compatible with Active Directory trusts. An intra-forest trust is a trust between two domains in one forest, either an automatic trust or a shortcut trust.

Activity 4-8: Creating a Trust to Another Forest

Time Required: 10 minutes

Objective: To create a two-way trust to an external forest.

Description: In this activity, you will gain experience creating trust relationships by using the Active Directory Domains and Trusts MMC to configure additional trusts outside the forest. You will set up a two-way trust with an independent forest.

1. Choose one computer (yours or your partner's) on which to perform the following steps.

2. If necessary, turn on your computer and log in as the administrator from your own domain.

3. Click **Start**, click **Administrative Tools**, and then click **Active Directory Domains and Trusts**.

4. In Active Directory Domains and Trusts, expand the node for the forest root domain.

5. Right-click the name of your assigned child domain and click **Properties**.

6. Click the tab labeled **Trusts** and review the trusts that have been created. You will see trusts to the parent domain in the tree, as well as any shortcut trusts that you added in previous activities.

7. Click **New Trust**.

8. Click **Next** to begin the New Trust Wizard.

9. Type the name of a domain from outside your own forest and click **Next**. (The example domain is *FOREIGN*. Your instructor will advise you if another domain is to be used, or if no external forest is available.)

10. Click **Two-way**, then click **Next**.

11. Choose **Both this domain and the specified domain** and click **Next**.

12. Type a username and password that is valid as an administrator on the external domain. (The example is *foreign-admin*, with a password of Password1.) Then click **Next**.

13. Review the summary information, then click **Next** to create the trust.

14. After the Trust Creation Complete page appears, review the result messages and click **Next** again.

15. Click **Yes, confirm the outgoing trust** and click **Next**.

16. Choose **No, do not confirm the incoming trust** and click **Next**.

17. Review the information presented in the Completing the New Trust Wizard page, then click **Finish**.

18. Note the addition of the new trust in the list.

19. Click **OK**.

20. Close all open windows on your computer. If you are not continuing directly to another activity, log off your computer.

Activity 4-9: Creating a Trust to a Windows NT 4.0 Domain

Time Required: 10 minutes

Objective: To create a two-way trust to an external down-level domain.

Description: In this activity, you will gain experience creating trust relationships by using the Active Directory Domains and Trusts MMC to configure additional trusts outside the forest. You will set up a one-way trust with an independent Windows NT 4.0 domain, which allows users from that domain to be added to DACLs in your domain.

1. Choose one computer (yours or your partner's) on which to perform the following steps.

2. If necessary, turn on your computer and log in as the administrator from your own domain.

3. Click **Start**, click **Administrative Tools**, and then click **Active Directory Domains and Trusts**.

4. In Active Directory Domains and Trusts, expand the node for the forest root domain.

5. Right-click the name of your assigned child domain and click **Properties**.

6. Click the tab labeled **Trusts** and review the trusts that have been created. You will see trusts to the parent domain in the tree, as well as any shortcut or external trusts that you added in previous activities.

7. Click **New Trust**.

8. Click **Next** to begin the New Trust Wizard.

9. Type the name of an NT domain from outside your own forest and click **Next**. (The example domain is *NT4DOM*. Your instructor will advise you if another domain is to be used, or if no external forest is available.)

10. Click **Two-way** and click **Next**.

11. Choose **Both this domain and the specified domain** and click **Next**.

12. Type a username and password that is valid as an administrator on the external domain. (The example is *nt4dom-admin*, with a password of *password*.) Click **Next**.

13. Review the summary information, then click **Next** to create the trust.

14. After the Trust Creation Complete page appears, review the result messages and click **Next** again.

15. Click **Yes, confirm the outgoing trust** and click **Next**.

16. Review the information presented in the Completing the New Trust Wizard page, then click **Finish**.

17. Note the addition of the new trust in the list.

18. Click **OK**.

19. Close all open windows on your computer. If you are not continuing directly to another activity, log off your computer.

DESIGNING DOMAINS

An important part of planning an Active Directory deployment is determining the number of domains that are needed. There are a few reasons for creating more than one domain. Some are organizational or administrative, and some are technical. In the sections that follow, we will first review the major functions of a domain, in particular the special role of the forest root domain. We will then discuss the limitations of considering a domain as a security boundary. Next we will look at the advantages of a single domain and the advantages of using multiple domains, and end with a discussion of Microsoft's recommendation of a dedicated forest root domain.

Functions of a Domain

A domain is a partition—or division—of a forest. The most important characteristic of a domain is **replication boundary**. As discussed in Chapter 1, every DC in a domain has a complete copy of that domain's partition in its Active Directory database. This means that the objects in a domain are replicated fully to all replicas in the domain, and except for the specific attributes replicated to GC servers, the domain data is not replicated at all outside the domain. The main purpose of configuring domains is to control where data is replicated in the network.

Limiting the replication of Active Directory data allows an Active Directory forest to be scaled out to a very wide area network, even over slow or heavily congested networks. A domain also provides some important and useful functions for a Windows network. The main functions of a domain include:

- *Authentication*—A domain stores objects representing users, groups, and computers—security principals—that can be granted or denied access to resources anywhere in the forest. However, the actual authentication involves a domain controller located in the same domain as the security principal object.

- *Policy-based administration*—Group policy is easily applied at the domain level.

- *Setting account policies for user accounts in the domain*—Account policies, such as password length and complexity requirements, affect the entire domain.

- *A directory for publishing shared resources*—Objects in the domain represent printers, file shares, and other resources, making them easier to find.

A domain also functions as an administrative boundary. Each domain can be administered separately and have both service owners and data owners that are separate and distinct from those of other domains. Administrative rights assigned in one domain do not propagate to others. For example, if a forest has a domain called *northamerica.ad.multinatcorp.com* and a child domain called *chicago.northamerica.ad. multinatcorp.com*, the Domain Admins Group in *northamerica* is not a member of the Domain Admins Group in *chicago*. There is a common misconception that permissions and rights assigned in a parent domain are inherited to child domains in the tree, which is not the case.

 Administrators of the forest root domain are, by default, given special privileges throughout the forest. During installation, the administrator of the forest root domain is placed in the Enterprise Admins Group as well as in the Domain Admins Group. The Enterprise Admins Group can, by default, manage any domain controller in the forest.

Activity 4-10: Examining the Enterprise Administrators' Group Memberships and Permissions

Time Required: 5 minutes

Objective: To understand the effective permissions assigned to the Enterprise Admins Group.

Description: In this activity, you will examine the Enterprise Admins Group, a special security group created in the forest root domain. By default, the administrator of the forest root domain is a member of this group. Anyone in this group can manage any domain controller in the forest, unless the default permissions are changed.

1. If necessary, turn on your computer and log in as the administrator from your own domain.

2. Click **Start**, click **Administrative Tools**, and then click **Active Directory Users and Computers**.

3. Expand the nodes in the tree pane until you can click the **Users** container in your own domain and view the objects in the container in the details pane.

4. Double-click the **Domain Admins** security group.

5. Click the **Members** tab.

6. Note that the default membership of Domain Admins contains only the administrator of the local domain. This Domain Admins Group is, by default, added to the local administrators group on computers that are members of the domain. Click **OK**.

7. Click the **Builtin** container in the tree pane.

8. Double-click the **Administrators** security group.

9. Click the **Members** tab.

10. Note that the administrator and the Domain Admins Group are added to this group. However, notice as well that the Enterprise Admins Group from the forest root domain is also added. Members of the Builtin\Administrators Group have full administrative capability on domain controllers in the domain. Thus, an Enterprise Admin can manage domain controllers on any domain in the forest. Double-click the **Enterprise Admins** entry.

11. Click the **Members** tab. Notice that in the setup of the lab, the forest root domain's administrator account was removed from the Enterprise Admins Group, and a dedicated account called Forest (Enterprise) Admin was created to be the enterprise-wide administrator. The Add and Remove buttons are grayed out because you do not have permission to change the membership of Enterprise Admins.

12. Click **Cancel**.

13. Click **OK**.

14. Close all open windows on your computer. If you are not continuing directly to another activity, log off your computer.

In the role as an administrative boundary, a domain can implement unique policies. Group policy can be applied at the domain level, and certain specific settings related to user accounts in the domain cannot be applied at any other level. These domain-level settings include the password policy, the account lockout policy, and the Kerberos ticket policy.

The Forest Root Domain

The first domain created in an Active Directory forest is called the forest root domain. This domain has a few special characteristics not shared by other domains:

- It is the domain that holds the security principals that can manage the forest, such as the Enterprise Admins Group and the Schema Admins Group.

- It is a central point for trust relationships. Each tree in the forest will have a trust relationship with the forest root domain.

- It is difficult to rename the forest root domain, and it cannot be deleted without deleting the entire Active Directory structure or using a complicated migration tool.

Is It a Security Boundary?

A great deal of discussion has taken place since the release of Windows 2000 about whether a domain can be considered a security boundary. On the one hand, a user is authenticated only by his or her own domain; group policy is often applied at the domain level; and account policies for domain users can only be set at the domain level. On the other hand, a domain is only part of a forest, sharing several partitions and sending information about security principals and other objects outside the domain. It is best, therefore, not to depend on a domain as a security boundary. If you need complete and secure isolation of a part of your directory, you should consider making it into a separate forest.

Which Works Better: Single or Multiple Domains?

Prior to the release of Active Directory, many large companies required multiple domains because of limitations in the Windows NT domain structure, primarily because an NT domain cannot practically scale beyond 40,000 objects, give or take. Active Directory has removed those limitations, and can support millions of objects in a single domain.

There are advantages to working with only a single domain and advantages to working with multiple domains.

Advantages of a Single Domain

A single domain is easier to manage. It is easier to delegate authority and apply group policy by OU, rather than across domains. It requires fewer hardware resources, such as domain controllers, and requires fewer domain administrators or less work for the current staff.

Advantages of Multiple Domains

By creating multiple domains, each can have a distinct set of administrators, policies, and data owners. This can provide tighter administrative control or support a decentralized administrative structure. For example, if two departments require different domain user account password policies, they can either come to some mutually acceptable agreement on policy, or two domains must be created. Another cause for multiple domains is the need to integrate external partner agencies into your directory, but keep them at a bit of a distance.

There may be organizational reasons to have separate domains. For example, if two divisions of an organization both have strong cases to be service owners and data owners of their own directory service, and neither is willing to "submit" to the administration of the other, then perhaps the easiest solution is to create two domains. To determine whether multiple domains are justified for organizational (or political) reasons, the designer must look at the vision and the business goals developed earlier in the process.

The most compelling technical reason for multiple domains is to control replication. For example, a multinational company may not wish to replicate the full database of all objects across slow and expensive wide-area links between continents.

Using a Dedicated Forest Root

Microsoft recommends that the forest root domain be completely dedicated to managing the infrastructure of the forest. That is, no regular users or even regular domain administrators should be created in the forest root domain. Rather, a single child domain is created under the forest root to handle all user and resource objects. Microsoft has found that dedicating a forest root domain allows the greatest flexibility for the future and minimizes the chance of a complete Active Directory redeployment to support growth or change. Microsoft also states that in this structure, fewer administrators are allowed to make forest-wide changes; the forest root domain is easily replicated for redundancy; it never becomes obsolete; and it can have its ownership transferred fairly easily.

Beyond this dedicated forest root, Microsoft recommends that an organization use one domain, unless business needs dictate otherwise. If multiple domains are required, Microsoft's general recommendation is to create domains based on geography, since geography is stable (unlike politics or organization charts). For example, a company may have a dedicated root domain, a domain for Europe, another for the Americas, and another for Africa, the Middle East, and Asia.

This is one of a series of recommendations, sometimes called "best practices," made by Microsoft. A **best practice** represents the opinion of consultants and developers in the industry, and is usually based on the real-life operations at companies using the product or technology in production.

Bear in mind, however, that Microsoft tends to view Active Directory, and Active Directory best practices in particular, from the point-of-view of large corporations. The dedicated forest root is an excellent idea in large, global corporations such as Microsoft and its largest clients. It is not a practical recommendation for small businesses, even though small businesses use Active Directory (provided in Word format).

DESIGNING ORGANIZATIONAL UNITS

An OU is used to group objects within a domain into a hierarchical structure. Having a hierarchical structure of OUs allows objects to be grouped for categorization, as well as for management.

Although an OU is not an administrative or replication boundary—like a domain—it is a division within the directory structure that allows for delegation of administration and controls the scope of policy application. Take, as an example, a mid-sized organization with about 1,000 employees. A competent IT department is the service owner for all of Active Directory. The HR department is the data owner for user objects, creating and managing users in the directory as people join and leave the company. The research division is the data owner for a number of resources in a highly dynamic environment, and administration, sales, and marketing all depend on stable access to fixed resources. These other divisions have staff with fewer technical skills than those in IT or research. Prior to the release of Active Directory, designers may have been tempted to create multiple Windows NT domains to meet the needs of different user groups, and to allow various data owners control over objects without giving them more authority than necessary.

However, with Active Directory, this scenario fits easily within one domain with several OUs. The IT department will delegate control over an OU containing user objects to the HR department. Separating the resources used by research into their own OU will allow different policies than those used by the rest of the company to be applied to those resources. One possible OU structure for this situation is shown in Figure 4-8.

Figure 4-8 Sample OU configuration

Activity 4-11: Creating an Organizational Unit

Time Required: 10 minutes

Objective: To create an OU.

Description: In this activity, you will create a new organizational unit (OU) in your domain. This is a very common job-related task for Active Directory administrators, and you can easily become proficient at it. Because OUs are the most common and important way to organize objects in the directory, you will use the OUs you create now to hold objects in later activities.

1. If necessary, turn on your computer and log in as the administrator from your own domain.

2. Click **Start**, click **Administrative Tools**, and then click **Active Directory Users and Computers**.

3. In Active Directory Users and Computers, expand the node for your domain.

4. Click the name of your domain.

5. On the Action menu, click **New**, and then point to **Organizational Unit**.

6. In the New Object dialog box, type **ouX** where *X* is the number of your server, and then click **OK**.

7. If desired, examine the properties of the OU by right-clicking the name of the OU and then clicking **Properties**. Click **Cancel** when done.

8. Close all open windows on your computer. If you are not continuing directly to another activity, log off your computer.

BEST PRACTICES FOR DESIGNING OUS

Although it is always a good idea to plan out your full structure before deploying Active Directory, the good news is that OUs are comparatively easy to restructure. They can be created, deleted, or renamed with little difficulty, and objects—such as users—can be easily moved between OUs. Using OUs to organize one (or a few) domains is much more flexible than creating multiple domains.

OUs are a better choice than a separate domain when a division, department, or organization within the enterprise wants ownership of its directory data. There is no need to create separate domains when delegation of control will allow that business unit to be a data owner without being a service owner. Since true autonomy can only be achieved with a new forest (not just a new domain), there is little value in needlessly creating domains. Instead, use OUs to organize and delegate a separate forest for those rare occasions when complete isolation is required.

Every OU that you create should serve a purpose. It is not necessary for every box on a company's organizational chart to have a corresponding OU in the directory. Unless a purpose is served (easier location, separate policies, separate administrative delegations, etc.), there is no reason to make extra OUs, as it results in an expenditure of time and resources without any return benefit.

OUs can be nested within one another. Technologically, there is no practical limit to how many levels of nesting can be supported in Active Directory, but Microsoft recommends that nesting not be more than 10 levels deep. Nesting OUs more than 10 levels deep introduces more complexity and confusion for administration, and could start to slow down the processing of Group Policy objects (GPOs) at logon.

Activity 4-12: Creating a Nested OU

Time Required: 5 minutes

Objective: To create an OU nested within another OU.

Description: In this activity, you will create another new OU in your domain to practice and build your skills. This time, the OU will be nested inside the one you recently created. In later activities you will change your OU structure by working with this OU object.

1. If necessary, turn on your computer and log in as the administrator from your own domain.

2. Click **Start**, click **Administrative Tools**, and then click **Active Directory Users and Computers**.

3. In Active Directory Users and Computers, expand the node for your domain.

4. Click the name of the OU created in the last activity.

5. On the Action menu, click **New**, then point to **Organizational Unit**.

6. In the New Object dialog box, type your own first name, and then click **OK**. Notice your new OU is created inside the container that was selected when you issued the New Organizational Unit command.

7. Practice creating additional OUs in other places in the structure.

8. Delete all except the first OU created in this activity by right-clicking the OU name and then clicking **Delete**. Click **Yes** to confirm deletion, but take care not to delete any containers that contain objects or were not created by you during this activity.

9. Close all open windows on your computer. If you are not proceeding directly to another activity, log off your computer.

Activity 4-13: Moving an OU within the Domain

Time Required: 5 minutes

Objective: To move an OU to another location within the domain.

Description: It is common to find that as companies change and evolve, the organization of objects in the directory must sometimes change as well. In this activity, you will move one of your OUs to a new location within the hierarchy, which is a task you may be called upon to do from time to time. You may also discover that a structure isn't working as well as intended, and this activity demonstrates the flexibility you have to change it. You will see that it is fairly easy to move objects between OUs.

1. If necessary, turn on your computer and log in as the administrator from your own domain.

2. Click **Start**, click **Administrative Tools**, and then click **Active Directory Users and Computers**.

3. In Active Directory Users and Computers, expand the node for your domain.

4. Click the name of the OU created in Activity 4-12 (the one named with your first name).

5. On the **Action** menu, click **Move**.

6. In the Move dialog box, expand nodes as required to see the structure of your domain.

7. Click the name of your domain (the top level).

8. Click **OK**.

9. Notice your new OU has been moved. Practice creating, moving, and deleting OUs in the structure, as desired and as time permits. Do not delete any pre-existing OUs or containers.

10. Close all open windows on your computer and log off.

CHAPTER SUMMARY

❏ DNS defines the namespace used by Active Directory, and you should carefully choose the best DNS name for your Active Directory domains and forests early in the planning process.

❏ A DNS name should be meaningful and represent your entire operation. It should be able to represent the organization across divisions and through expected growth.

❏ Most companies have two different uses for a DNS name: defining a public Internet presence for the company, and defining a namespace for Active Directory.

❏ The SRV resource records and other related records in DNS describe your network's internal operations, therefore most organizations would treat them as confidential information.

❏ When choosing DNS names for both an Internet presence and the Active Directory domain, there are three common choices: using the same DNS name for both, using completely different names altogether, or using a subdomain delegated from your Internet domain for your Active Directory domain.

❏ Using the same DNS name for both Internet presence and Active Directory requires complex administration to prevent the release of confidential information to the public networks. Therefore, it is not recommended.

❏ Microsoft recommends running DNS services on all DCs.

❏ A forest is an "instance" of Active Directory; if you have different forests, you have different Active Directory installations.

❏ Trust relationships are automatically created in a forest to allow security principals from any domain to be recognized anywhere in the forest.

❏ Trusts are established between domains on a one-to-one basis, but they are transitive, so they can be followed up and down tree structures in the forest.

❏ A shortcut trust allows a direct route for authentication between one domain and another to which it is not directly connected by an automatic trust.

❏ Explicit trusts can be manually created between different Active Directory forests, between an Active Directory forest and a Windows NT domain, or between an Active Directory forest and a Kerberos Realm (usually found in UNIX environments, and the Realm must support Kerberos version 5). These explicit, external trusts can be transitive or nontransitive.

❏ A domain is a partition, or division, of a forest. Domain partitions, along with the schema partition, configuration partition, and any application partitions make up the forest.

❏ A domain is a replication and administrative boundary. A domain is not a security boundary, although some security administration is managed by domain.

❏ Domains provide authentication and a directory in which to publish shared resources. They provide the basis for policy-based administration and setting domain user account policies.

❏ The first domain created in a forest is the forest root domain. The forest root domain is a central point for trust relationships. It cannot be deleted without deleting the entire Active Directory structure.

❏ Managing a multiple-domain forest is more complex and requires more resources than a single-domain forest, but it provides the ability to better support a decentralized structure with tighter administrative controls.

❏ Microsoft recommends creating a forest root domain dedicated to infrastructure functions (managing the forest).

❏ Besides the dedicated forest root domain, Microsoft recommends using only one domain for all directory objects, unless a business goal or defined requirement necessitates additional domains.

❐ If additional domains are required, Microsoft recommends using geography, rather than organization boundaries.

❐ OUs are used to group objects within a domain into a hierarchical structure for categorization and delegation of control to data owners.

❐ OUs can be nested without any practical limit, however more than 10 levels of nesting is not recommended.

❐ OUs are comparatively easy to restructure, while domains and forests are more difficult to restructure. In many cases, a forest cannot be renamed or significantly restructured without extensive disruption to the network.

4

KEY TERMS

child domain — A domain that is connected to another domain (its parent) in an Active Directory tree. The child domain uses a subdomain of the parent domain's DNS name in a contiguous DNS namespace. *Child.parent.company.com* is a child domain of *parent.company.com*. Parent and child domains are connected with a two-way, transitive trust.

delegation — The process of distributing and decentralizing the administration of Active Directory by granting permissions to data owners.

domain — A collection of objects that share the same user account database and security policy.

forest — A forest is the implementation of Active Directory. That is, one single forest really represents one single Active Directory installation. A forest consists of one or more domain partitions, a common schema partition, a configuration partition, and optional application partitions.

forest root domain — The first domain created in a forest. The forest root domain contains the security principals that can manage the forest.

group policy — A technology enabled by Active Directory that allows administrators to define policy and rely on Active Directory and the operating system to ensure these policies are enforced. Group policy is also used to automatically distribute software.

group policy object (GPO) — Specific group policy settings applied in Active Directory.

Internet presence — In the context of DNS, the Internet presence refers to the DNS subdomain name used by the public to reach an organization's e-mail or Web servers. The term can also be used generically, as in "our company needs an Internet presence."

nontransitive trust — A trust between two domains, realms, or forests that cannot be extended or used by other domains in the forest. *See* two-way transitive trust.

one-way trust — A trust relationship where security principals in the trusted domain can use resources in the trusting domain, but not vice versa. Two one-way trusts are equivalent to a two-way trust.

organizational unit (OU) — A grouping of common objects, such as users and groups, that share the same departmental and security policies.

parent domain — The domain *parent.company.com* is a parent domain of *child.parent.company.com*. *See* child domain.

replication boundary — A set of data which is replicated to only specific replicas, or a barrier (physical or logical) that prevents replication. In the case of Active Directory, it is used to describe the fact that domain information is not replicated to other domains (except for attributes sent to the GCs).

shortcut trust — A manually created trust that improves the efficiency of interdomain authentications within a forest.

trust relationship (trust) — A link between two domains that allows security principals from one domain to be recognized by the other.

two-way, transitive trust — A trust relationship between two domains that can also be used by any other domain trusted by either of the domains. For example if *A* trusts *B*, and *B* trusts *C*, then *A* also trusts *C*.

REVIEW QUESTIONS

1. In the context of Active Directory, the surest way to achieve complete separation, autonomy, and security control for a business unit is to place it in its own _____.

2. Split DNS is a complex configuration used to _____.

   a. Improve the efficiency of DNS

   b. Allow Active Directory to work with UNIX-based DNS Servers

   c. Prevent DNS designs from becoming obsolete

3. A domain is a partition, or division, of a _____.

4. Which option does Microsoft recommend as a best practice?

   a. Using a delegated zone for a dedicated subdomain of your Internet name for your Active Directory DNS name

   b. Using the same DNS name for your Internet presence as for your Active Directory implementation

   c. Using a private or fictitious DNS name for your Active Directory domains

   d. Ensuring that SRV records are replicated to your ISP's domain name servers

5. Which of the following are common across an entire forest, in all cases? (Choose all that apply.)

   a. Configuration partition

   b. Schema partition

   c. Domain partition

   d. Global catalog

6. A global catalog contains complete information about its own domain, and selected attributes from every object in every other _____ in the forest.

7. Any _____ defined in any domain in a forest can be granted access to any resource in any domain anywhere in the forest.

8. A(n) _____ trust is manually created and used within a forest.

9. A(n) _____ is a security boundary.

10. A(n) _____ is a replication boundary.

11. Business units that require a different or unique schema from other business units must be placed in different _____.

12. Managing a multiple-domain forest is more complex and requires more resources than a single-domain forest, but it provides the ability to better support a decentralized structure with tighter administrative controls. True or false?

13. Business units that require a unique account policy (such as password length or Kerberos ticket settings) for domain users' accounts must be placed in separate _____.

14. Explain the relationship between a forest and a domain.

15. You are a domain administrator (a member of the Domain Admins Group) in a domain called *parent.ad.multinatcorp.com*. It is not the forest root domain. In the same forest is a child domain called *child.parent.ad.multinatcorp.com*. Assuming only the default permissions are in place and you are not a member of any other groups, what permissions do you have in the child domain?

16. It is easier to move an object between _____ than to another domain.

17. Should every department or division shown on the organizational chart have its own OU in Active Directory?

    a. Always

    b. Never

    c. When warranted by data ownership roles

    d. Only if they are a service owner

18. Nesting OUs beyond _____ levels deep is not recommended.

19. In a forest with many domains, the security principals that can manage the forest are in the _____ domain.

20. When business units require that a different team of people create and manage user objects, which is the smallest or least divisive structure that will allow control to be delegated to a data owner?

    a. Forest

    b. Domain

    c. OU

    d. Site

21. Which of the following statements about the forest root domain is most accurate?

    a. The forest root domain can be created or deleted at any time.

    b. The forest root domain can be easily renamed.

    c. The forest root domain must have the same DNS suffix as all other domains.

    d. The forest root domain contains the user principal accounts that can manage the forest.

22. You must manually create all trusts in a forest. True or False?

23. Which of the following statements best describes Microsoft's recommended best practice?

    a. Create a dedicated forest root domain for managing the forest infrastructure, and create one additional domain for all other directory objects.

    b. Create a dedicated forest root domain, and use it for all directory objects.

    c. Create a dedicated forest root domain and additional domains for each office location in your enterprise.

    d. Do not create a forest root domain unless you have more than three other domains to manage.

24. Business units that require a unique schema from other business units must be placed in their own _____.

    a. Forest

    b. Domain

    c. OU

    d. Site

25. Business units that require a unique account policy (such as password length or Kerberos ticket settings) for domain user accounts must be placed in their own _____.

    a. Forest

    b. Domain

    c. OU

    d. Site

HEARTLAND HOSPITAL CASE PROJECTS

Heartland Hospital has decided to proceed with an Active Directory implementation. Management considered delaying the project until details of the proposed merger and expansion were known, but decided that it was in the best interest of the organization to proceed immediately. They feel that a solid infrastructure and well-designed network will bring benefits in the short term, and would also reduce confusion during any future reorganization. However, you should keep in mind as you design their network directory services that some change is to be expected, so avoid decisions that would needlessly narrow their options.

The design team met with a number of key personnel at the hospital and summarized their viewpoints as follows:

- **Mary Firth, Office Manager:** Mary fills many of the roles of a Chief Information Officer (CIO), although she is not considered executive management. She is concerned that the Active Directory structure be built correctly. She wants to retain control over hardware and other computing resources. She is prepared to request reasonable amounts of money for new equipment, but doesn't want to waste money needlessly. Additionally, since this is a hospital, she must document every decision and be prepared to justify them to the Regional Board of Hospital Quality Assurance. Security for the infrastructure is also an important concern.

- **Human Resources Director:** This person is concerned that information often contains errors because of the number of times it is handled. He is frequently frustrated in the amount of time it can take to have a user account configured after a new employee has been hired (in a few situations, this has resulted in "password sharing" so that a new employee could use a computer before being assigned an account).

- **HIPAA Compliance Manager:** This person is responsible for compliance with the newly formulated HIPAA (Health Insurance Portability and Accountability Act of 1996) standards set forth by Congress. She and her team manage the information about patients, policies, rates, and risks in several SQL databases. The biggest concern is controlling access to the data without causing unnecessary roadblocks for people trying to get their jobs done.

- **Jenn Jamieson, Office Computer Whiz:** One of Mary Firth's staff members who has become an unofficial "help desk," as users often approach her for help with computer problems. Because the hospital lacks a true IT department, the staff appreciates her efforts, but she feels she is overworked. Additionally, because she is self-trained, the hospital network was implemented in a piecemeal fashion that grew as her skill-set grew. While the network is functioning, many inefficiencies and incorrect settings exist. There is also a tendency (driven by the hospital director) to implement the "latest-and-greatest" technologies without supporting them appropriately or maintaining the older technologies. Her supervisors are concerned that her day-to-day duties sometimes fall by the wayside as she is often busy with new projects. It sometimes takes a while for her to respond to user requests—for example, if they forget their passwords.

The following information has also been provided about Heartland Hospital:

1. The hospital currently has 217 employees, divided into the following departments:

- Patient Services
    - Dietary
    - Laundry
- Professional Services
    - Staff Physicians
    - Affiliated Physicians
    - Full-time Nursing Staff
    - Professional Medical Staff

4

- ❑ Administration & Finance
  - ▪ Office Management and General Services
  - ▪ Human Resources
    - \- Full-time Employee Specialists
    - \- Temporary and Contracted Employee Specialists
    - \- Recruiters
  - ▪ Clerical
  - ▪ Payroll & Accounting
- ❑ Ethics & Legal
  - ▪ Legal Issues
    - \- Litigation Specialists
    - \- Legal Research Specialists
  - ▪ Ethics Committee
  - ▪ HIPAA Compliance
- ❑ Physical Plant
  - ▪ Plant/Building Engineering & Maintenance
  - ▪ Medical Equipment Technicians
  - ▪ Janitorial
  - ▪ Security
  - ▪ Occupational Health and Safety

2. Each department has its own computer files and printers, although users will often print to the closest physical printer, even if another department owns it.

3. Some users have blank passwords. This is not encouraged.

4. Management would like to introduce standard IT policies (such as required passwords) across the organization.

5. Payroll is considering a new service that gathers employee information directly from Active Directory. The payroll staff isn't exactly sure what proposed vendors mean when they say, "Just make sure that our salesperson is an Enterprise Admin, and he'll make all the schema changes when he drops off the software. No worries."

Case Project 4-1: Choosing a DNS Name

As one of the first steps in planning the new Active Directory structure, your team will recommend a DNS name to the client. In the first meetings with the client, the following information has been gathered:

- ❑ Up until now, the hospital has only used stand-alone file servers with no domain structure. All DNS operations have been managed by their ISP, and it is not known which DNS Servers each client computer is configured to use.

- ❑ Mary Firth, the de-facto CIO, would prefer not to have to change the configuration on each client computer, since she feels this would involve visiting each computer in the system and manually effecting the required changes. Mary views this as an unacceptable process because she is a salaried employee and is not eligible for overtime.

- ❑ As part of its Internet connection package, the ISP used by Heartland Hospital hosts a Web page containing basic contact information for the hospital. The address used is *www.heartlandhospital.org*. The hospital director likes this name and wishes to continue using it.

◻ The director is also concerned about meeting the new HIPAA guidelines, which require that no confidential patient information be made public, and has some worries about hackers being able to access these confidential records using a connection to the public Internet.

◻ The hospital director and Mary want the configuration of the hospital computers to be as simple as possible.

◻ The hospital does not want to deal with additional name registrations with ICANN and the .com registrars.

The following suggestions have been made for a DNS name for the forest root domain:

◻ heartlandhospital.org

◻ heartland-hospital.com

◻ heartlandhospital.life

◻ home.heartlandhospital.org

Discuss with the following issues in a small group or with your partner. Present your instructor with a summary of your answers.

1. Which of the choices would you recommend and why?

2. Where would you place DNS Servers for zones hosting the Active Directory subdomain?

3. How does your solution avoid having to configure individual workstations?

4. Would your recommendation change if the hospital did not have an existing Web page?

5. In the future, the hospital hopes to allow its patients and employees to retrieve information and submit forms for processing online. Will changes to your recommendations be required to support this?

Case Project 4-2: Choosing a Forest and Domain Structure

Review the background information provided above. How many forests are required? How many domains are required? List potential service owners and data owners within the company. Present your answers to your partner, your class, or your instructor either verbally or in writing, as indicated by your instructor.

Case Project 4-3: Documenting the Design Decisions

Draw your proposed design, showing forest(s), domains(s) and up to two levels of OUs. You may use pen and paper, or a drawing software (such as Microsoft Visio or Microsoft Paint). Be prepared to present and justify your design to your instructor or to the class.

Case Project 4-4: Establishing a Trust Relationship

The hospital uses the services of Medical Magic, Ltd., a company that provides editing and transcription services for the medical community. To streamline the process, Mary would like the staff at Medical Magic to save completed documents (in Microsoft Word format) directly to a designated share on one of the file severs. One of the ways to accomplish this is to build a trust relationship with the Windows NT domain at Medical Magic, called *MEDMAGDOM*, and allow any member of the global group *MEDMAGDOM\ Transcribers* appropriate permissions for the share.

What type of trust would need to be created (internal, external, one-way, two-way)? Who would be responsible for deciding whether a specific individual can access the files? What concerns do you think this would raise? Add this domain and a trust arrow to your proposed design diagram. Be prepared to present your revised diagram and conclusions to your instructor or a small group.

Case Project 4-5: Implementing the Design

If you have the equipment available (or access to emulation software such as VMWare), then implement the design developed in the Heartland Hospital project by completing the following steps:

1. If necessary, install Windows 2003 Server.

2. If necessary, install DNS services, or have access to a properly configured DNS Server.

3. Create the required DNS subdomains to support your structure, including any delegations that are required.

4. Create a Domain Controller in a new forest by using dcpromo.

5. If you have designed a solution with more than one domain, and you have the equipment available, repeat the previous steps to create additional domain controllers for the other domains.

6. Use Active Directory Users and Computers to create the OU structure described in your solution.

4

5

MANAGING DIRECTORY OBJECTS: USERS, GROUPS, AND RESOURCES

After reading this chapter and completing the exercises, you will be able to:

♦ Create user objects in Active Directory and set values for the attributes of a user object

♦ Create and manipulate groups in Activity Directory, and understand the effects of different group scopes

♦ Create objects for other resources, such as shared folders and printers

♦ Organize objects in Active Directory by leveraging the use of OUs

Although it is essential to understand the basics of Active Directory design and structure, most administrators don't spend much time redesigning or migrating their networks. Instead, they spend the majority of their time managing the network. Whether the network is a new Active Directory deployment or one that has existed since the time of the first release of Active Directory, there are many day-to-day tasks that need to be performed. This chapter looks at some of those tasks, including working with common objects.

CREATING AND MANAGING USER OBJECTS

Although an Active Directory design is fairly static, the contents of the directory can be very dynamic, and the most frequently changed objects are usually **user objects**, which are the objects in the directory that represent real people using your computer network.

Most changes made to the data in a network directory have to do with users. When a new employee is hired, someone creates a user object. When a user changes his or her password, changes are made to an attribute of a user object. When a user is assigned to a different security group, more changes are made to the directory. Although other types of objects are also modified, managing users and the objects that represent them is usually the most frequent task for network administrators.

User Classes, Properties, and Schema

Recall from Chapter 1, that the Active Directory schema defines the attributes that make up a class of objects. The user class defines a number of required and optional attributes that will be used with a user object. Specifically, every user object must have some value assigned to each mandatory attribute. Active Directory automatically manages several of the user object attributes for you, while other attributes hold values assigned by you (the object's creator) at the time the object is created. The following are the mandatory attributes for a user object:

- *cn* — This attribute uniquely identifies the object.

- *InstanceType, objectCategory* and *objectClass* — These attributes contain fixed values that are automatically assigned. Because these attributes represent the class of which an object is an instance, they are the same for all user objects, because all user objects are built from the same class definition (or blueprint).

- *ObjectSID* — This attribute holds the user's Security Identifier (SID), which is assigned automatically by the system, but is always unique.

- *sAMAccountName* — This attribute is a version of the username that can be used by older clients who don't expect to talk to Active Directory. For example, a Windows NT 4.0 workstation user would have to use this version of the username to log on.

 You can review the definitions of terms like schema, class, object, and attribute in the "The Building Blocks of Active Directory" section of Chapter 1.

The default schema provides more than 200 optional attributes for a user object, however administrators rarely have to deal with the majority of these attributes. An average user object is likely to have values assigned to around 40 or 50 of these attributes. It would be rare to find a company that populates all 200 attributes for every user, but it is possible, at least in theory.

Creating Users with Active Directory Users and Computers

To create a user with the Active Directory Users and Computers console, you must be working at a DC or have the administrative tools installed at your workstation. (Review Activity 1-6 if you do not have the full set of administrative tools installed on the computer you are using.) To start the console, click **Start**, point to **Administrative Tools**, and then click **Active Directory Users and Computers**. The console appears, as shown in Figure 5-1.

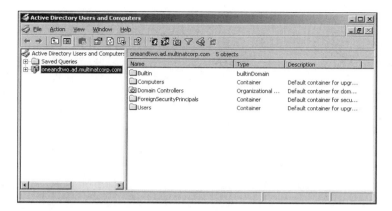

Figure 5-1   The Active Directory Users and Computers console

Before creating the object, choose the correct container that will hold the object. In most cases, this will be an OU, but you can create a user in the domain itself or in one of the container objects (such as Users). Expand the nodes in the tree pane on the left side of the console until the desired OU is visible. Click the name of the folder in the tree, then click the **Action** menu, click **New**, and then click **User**. The New Object–User dialog box will appear, as shown in Figure 5-2.

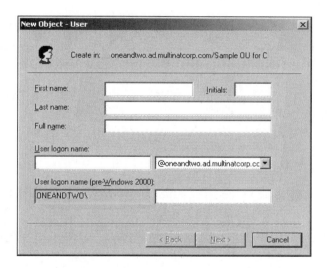

Figure 5-2   The New Object dialog box for a user and object

 Just because you *can* do something, doesn't mean you *should*. This is an important maxim for administration in networks, servers, and Active Directory installations. You *can* create users in the domain without using OUs. You *can* create users in the Domain Controllers OU. But that doesn't mean you *should*.

The New User Dialog Box

By looking at this dialog box, you will see that creating a new user object isn't very intimidating. Instead of being presented with hundreds of attributes, there are only a few text boxes to fill in. The top portion of the dialog box allows the administrator to specify the name attributes of the new object. As you type text in the First name, Initials, or Last name text boxes, the console automatically builds the full name for you, even adding a period after the initials. The specific components of the name are available for the basis of searches (like finding all the users with a first name of John) but the full name is displayed in most cases. If your organization requires names in a unique format, or if the user account is for a service, not a person, then you might want to override the automatically generated Full name, and type it in directly.

The Names of a User

Each user has two different names that can be used to log on to the domain. Names in Active Directory are stored in attributes called **sAMAccountName** and **userPrincipalName (UPN)**. However, the Active Directory Users and Computers console refers to the UPN as **user logon name** and the sAMAccountName as **user logon name (pre-Windows 2000)**. In Active Directory, only the sAMAccountName is a mandatory attribute, but the New Object-User wizard requires both.

You can use code or scripts to create a user that does not have a UPN, but this is not normally desirable. If a UPN is required but does not have a value set, Windows will try to combine the user name and the DNS name of the domain to create it.

A user with a **down-level client** such as Windows 98, Windows 95, or Windows NT must use the older format of the user name—the sAMAccountName—to log on, manually specifying the name of the domain or choosing it from a drop-down list. This pre-Windows 2000 logon name is made up of two parts—the domain's NetBIOS name and the user's logon name, separated by a backslash, for example: *MYDOMAIN\SomeUser*. The domain's NetBIOS name is set when the domain is created, and is not easily changed. When a user logs on with the sAMAccountName, the workstation must locate a DC from the user's domain using NetBIOS name resolution methods, such as WINS or broadcasts.

The preferred method of logging on to a domain using Windows 2000, Windows XP Professional, or Windows Server 2003 family workstations, is to use the UPN. The UPN is also composed of two parts—the username and a UPN suffix, joined by an @ symbol. This format resembles an e-mail address, and in some organizations a user's UPN is set to match his or her e-mail address, but this is not a necessity.

By default, the UPN suffix is the DNS name of the user's domain, but a different suffix can be chosen from the drop-down list in the second combo box. (The choice of suffixes can be controlled in the Active Directory Sites and Services console.) For example, if your corporation has many domains, you can still choose to have all UPNs end with the same suffix. For example, instead of *UserName@childdomain.somecorp.tld*, a user's UPN could be *UserName@somecorp.tld*, even if their account was created in the *childdomain* domain.

The Users and Computers console automatically fills in the same information from the User logon name text box to the User logon name (pre-Windows 2000) text box, as normally the username part of both is the same. However, if you have a need to do so, you can make them different. You could have a user known as *SUBDOMAIN\Bob* and *Bill@domain*.com. In addition to the potential confusion, this could cause other problems, particularly if the GC is offline or unreachable. So you should avoid making the username parts of the UPN and sAMAccountName different.

When a user logs on using a UPN, the operating system will issue a query to the closest GC to determine which domain can authenticate the user. Thus, the DNS system and the GC must be operational for this to function properly. (There are a few specific cases in which this query to the GC is skipped. If there is only one domain in the forest, the domain is in mixed mode, or if the user is the administrator, then the query is skipped.)

After supplying the logon name and information, click **Next**. Before creating the new user object, Windows will issue a query to the GC to verify that the UPN is unique within the forest. If a GC cannot be located, an error will occur, as shown in Figure 5-3. As the message states, you can still create the user object, but the account will not be active until it has been checked against a GC.

Figure 5-3   No GC available during user creation

Initial Security Settings

The next page of the wizard, as shown in Figure 5-4, is where essential security attributes can be set.

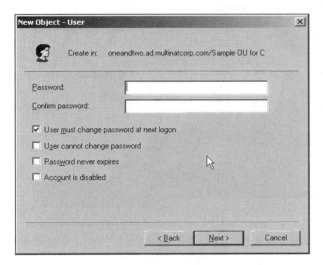

Figure 5-4 Password and security attributes

Two text boxes are supplied to enter and confirm a password. A password is not required by Active Directory—that is, it is not a mandatory attribute of the User class. However, since it is not a good idea to have a blank password, Group Policy can be used to enforce the password requirement and to require certain levels of complexity for the password.

The User must change password at next logon checkbox is provided so that a new user is forced to immediately change his or her password, as even an administrator should not know the user's password. In some organizations, however, passwords are centrally controlled, so clicking User cannot change password prevents this user from changing his or her password. This checkbox is useful for service accounts or accounts used, say, at a kiosk-type workstation. Clicking Password never expires overrides the password expiration policy set on the domain, and Account is disabled prevents the account from being used.

After supplying a password, choosing the desired options, and clicking **Next**, the summary page will appear, as shown in Figure 5-5. Review the summary to avoid errors, and then click **Finish**, which will actually create the user object in Active Directory, as shown in Figure 5-6.

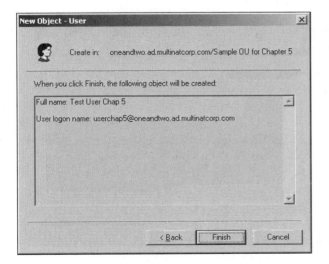

Figure 5-5 Summary page for new user objects

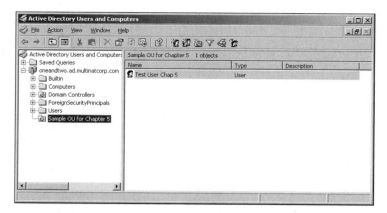

Figure 5-6   Newly created user

Activity 5-1: Create a New User Object

Time Required: 5 minutes

Objective: To practice creating new user objects.

Description: In this activity you will create three user objects. These users will be used throughout the chapter. Knowing how to create user objects is an essential skill because it is one of the fundamental tasks required to operate or administer a computer network.

1. If necessary, turn on your computer and log on as the administrator from your own domain.

2. In the last chapter, you created an OU with your first name. If this OU was deleted, you will need to create another OU to use in this chapter. You can use your name or your student number to name the OU. The name of your OU must be unique in your domain.

3. Click **Start**, point to **Administrative Tools**, and then click **Active Directory Users and Computers**.

4. Expand the nodes in the tree pane until your domain and your own OU are both visible.

5. Click the name of your own OU in the tree pane.

6. Click the **Action** menu.

7. Point to **New**.

8. Click **User**.

9. In the Full name text box, type **User1A** (where *1* represents your student/computer number).

10. In the User Logon Name text box, type **user1a** with no spaces (where *1* represents your student/computer number).

11. Click **Next**.

12. Clear all checkboxes.

13. In the Password and Confirm Password text boxes, type **p@ssw0rdA**. This represents a more secure password than the typical blank or "password" password. It is good practice to develop a habit of using reasonably secure passwords.

14. Click **Next**.

15. Click **Finish**.

16. Repeat Steps 5–15 to create a user named **User1B** (where *1* represents your student/computer number), with a password of **p@ssw0rdB**.

17. Repeat Steps 5 through 15 to create a user named **User1C** (where *1* represents your student/computer number), with a password of **p@ssw0rdC**.

18. Confirm that you now have three users in your OU.

19. If you are not proceeding immediately to the next activity, log off your computer.

How the Console Interacts with Active Directory

It is important to remember that Active Directory Users and Computers is not a direct interface to the Active Directory database. It is a program that uses the Lightweight Directory Access Protocol (LDAP) to send queries and commands to the DCs. This is sometimes described as a level of abstraction; administrators are not working directly with the database—they are working with a tool that works with the database. You will notice that it chooses defaults for you and saves typing. For example, what you see in the New Object-User wizard is not exactly the same as what you would see in the Active Directory database itself.

From the few entries made in the wizard, about 40 Active Directory attributes have been populated with values. Some of these, like the new user's SID, were created by Active Directory automatically. Others, such as the canonicalName attribute, were populated by the Active Directory Users and Computers console. The name and cn attributes are both set with the value that is displayed as the Full name in the wizard. GivenName and sn are set to the first and last names, respectively, and the middle initials are placed in the attribute called initials. The sAMAccountName is set to the username portion of the pre-Windows 2000 logon (the domain name is not included), whereas the UPN is set to the full value of the name and suffix.

The objectSID is the user's Security Identifier (SID), and it is created automatically as a unique number consisting of a portion that represents the domain and a unique value assigned in sequence by the DC (called a relative identifier or RID). The other mandatory attributes—instanceType, objectCategory, and objectClass—are the same value for all user objects and are set by Active Directory.

Setting Additonal Attributes

There remain dozens—potentially hundreds—of other attributes that can be set for each user. Some of these attributes are only used internally. Others can only be managed programmatically with code, script, or a tool like ADSI Edit. However, many of the attributes are exposed through property pages in the Active Directory Users and Computers console. To open the property pages for a user object, simply right-click the object in Active Directory Users and Computers and choose **Properties**. The window shown in Figure 5-7 will appear. You can open the same window by double-clicking the user object or choosing **Properties** from the Action menu.

The number of tabs and the tab headings that appear in this chapter may differ from what you see on your system. Because Active Directory is extensible (that is, the schema can be extended with new attributes and new classes), Active Directory-Aware applications may add tabs to the property pages of the Active Directory objects. A good example of this would be Exchange 2000, which adds three new tabs to the user property page.

When describing a value stored in the Active Directory database, or describing a class or object defined in the schema, the term *attribute* is usually used. The term *property* is generally used when describing the same piece of information exposed in a graphical user interface. You can consider these words to be synonyms, although attribute is a more precise and technical term, and a property may be used to create or manipulate more than one attribute.

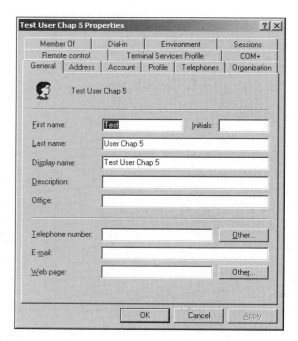

Figure 5-7   User object properties

The properties for each object are shown on several tabs in the Properties dialog box, and they can be categorized as follows:

- *General and Business Information* — General, Address, Telephones, and Organization tabs

- *Account and Profile Settings* — Account, Member Of, Profile, and COM+ tabs

- *Terminal Services Settings* — Environment, Sessions, Remote Control, and Terminal Services Profile tabs

- *Dial-in Settings* — Dial-in tab

- *Advanced Properties* — Object, Published Certificates, and Security tabs (shown only if View Advanced features is turned on). (*Note:* These additional tabs are shown in Figure 5-8, and can be enabled using the View menu at the top of the console.)

General and Business Information

The General, Address, Telephones, and Organization tabs show properties that relate to general attributes of the user and the user's role in the enterprise. The General tab (see Figure 5-8) contains the same name information as the New Object-User wizard, along with a general description. The office attribute is used to hold a room number or other location information. You can also specify an e-mail address, telephone number, and Web page URL on this tab. The telephone number and Web page attributes each have an Other button to allow for entry of more numbers.

The information contained in the telephone number attribute of the General tab is not as useful as might be expected. Any string can be entered, and issues with formatting will always arise, such as how to handle international numbers or whether to include area codes. More importantly, though, there is no consistent way to discern between different types of telephone numbers, such as home, office, and mobile.

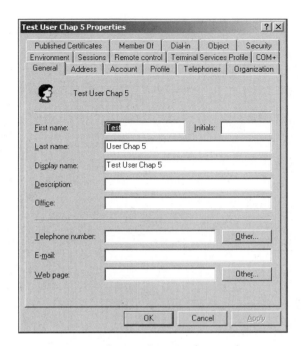

Figure 5-8   Advanced view of user object properties

The Telephones tab, shown in Figure 5-9, allows for some classification and general notes. However, it is important to realize that the telephone number(s) entered on the General tab do not appear on the Telephones tab. The first telephone number on the General tab is stored in the telephoneNumber attribute. Those entered by clicking Other are stored in the otherTelephone attribute, which is a multivalued attribute. The numbers from the Telephones tab are stored in specific attributes, such as the homePhone and otherHomePhone attributes, or the mobile and otherMobile attributes. Figure 5-10 shows how the properties from Active Directory Users and Computers are stored as attributes in the Active Directory database.

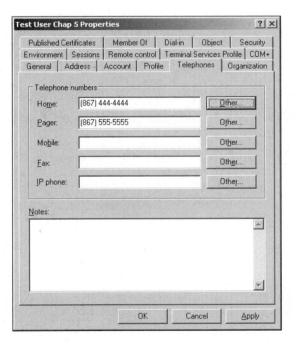

Figure 5-9   The Telephones tab

Figure 5-10   Telephone attributes as seen in ADSI Edit

If an organization is going to use the attributes to store this sort of information (which would be very useful), its design should specify which locations will be used, or a process should be in place to ensure that the relevant data is stored in both locations. Otherwise, the ability to retrieve the expected data or perform expected searches will be compromised.

Activity 5-2: Adding Telephone Number Information

Time Required: 5 minutes

Objective: To practice adding additional attributes to a user object.

Description: In this activity you will enter telephone numbers for the user objects that you just created. Knowing how to modify attributes is useful because you will need to update information in the directory as changes occur. Since the directory represents things in the real world, the directory will need to be updated as things in the real world change.

1. If necessary, turn on your computer and log on as the administrator from your own domain.

2. Click **Start**, point to **Administrative Tools**, and then click **Active Directory Users and Computers**.

3. Expand the nodes in the tree pane until your domain and your own OU are both visible.

4. Click the name of your own OU in the tree pane.

5. Click the **A** user that you created in the last activity.

6. Click the **Action** menu, and then click **Properties**.

7. In the Telephone number text box, type **(212) 555–0101**.

8. Click the **Telephones** tab.

9. In the Home text box, type **(250) 555–1001**.

10. Click **OK**.

11. Repeat Steps 5–10 for the B user, assigning a telephone number of **(212) 555-0102** and a home telephone of **(250) 555-1002**.

12. Repeat Steps 5–10 for the C user, assigning a telephone number of **(212) 555-0103** and a home telephone of **(250) 555-1003**.

13. If you are not proceeding immediately to the next activity, log off your computer.

Figure 5-11 shows the Address tab, which provides a way to record mailing address information. Active Directory is somewhat limited for this purpose, because there is no way to record multiple mailing addresses (e.g., home, work, summer, alternate) or to link many users to one address. (In database terms, Active Directory is not "well normalized.") For this reason, many organizations do not make full use of Active Directory's address attributes, or chose to populate them automatically from other databases.

5

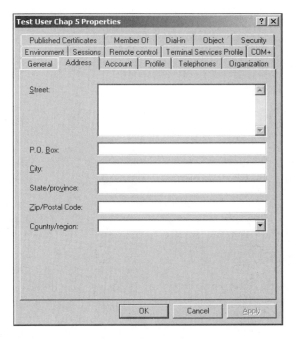

Figure 5-11 The Address tab

The Organization tab, as shown in Figure 5-12, is used to capture or display information about a user's role in the organization. The Title, Department, and Company attributes are used to describe the user's job. The Manager and Direct reports sections can be used to show how a user relates to other users in the company. The names shown in these areas will also be objects in Active Directory. To create a list of Direct reports, set the Manager value on the user objects of those subordinate employees.

 It is likely to take a few minutes for these changes to be updated throughout the directory.

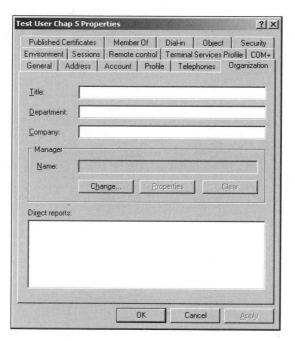

Figure 5-12   The Organization tab

Activity 5-3: Add Reporting Information

Time Required: 5 minutes

Objective: To practice entering management reporting information to user objects in Active Directory.

Description: In this activity you will enter reporting relationships for your three users. Users B and C will be direct reports of user A. While many companies do not record reporting relationships in Active Directory, doing so is a useful way to describe how the chain of command is set up in a company. Having the reporting relationships in the directory is particularly useful if your company has Active Directory-aware applications that can use the information, or if your company has a convenient means to search the directory, such as an intranet Web page. You should know how the values in these attributes are changed.

1. If necessary, turn on your computer and log on as the administrator from your own domain.

2. Click **Start**, point to **Administrative Tools**, and then click **Active Directory Users and Computers**.

3. Expand the nodes in the tree pane until your domain and your own OU are both visible.

4. Click the name of your own OU in the tree pane.

5. Click the **B** user that you created in Activity 5-1.

6. Click the **Action** menu, and then click **Properties**.

7. Click the **Organization** tab.

8. In the Manager panel, click the **Change** button.

9. In the Enter the object name to select text box, type **user1a** (where 1 represents your student/computer number), and then click **Check Names**.

10. If your user *1a* is not found, check for errors and retry Step 9, or search for the user object using the **Advanced** button.

11. Click **OK**.

12. Click **OK** again.

13. Repeat Steps 5 through 12 for user *1c*, who will also report to user *1a*.

14. Click your **user1a** object.

15. Click the **Action** menu, and then click **Properties**.

16. Click the **Organization** tab.

17. Verify that user *1b* and user *1c* appear in the Direct reports area. If not, consult with your instructor for assistance.

18. Click **OK**.

19. If you are not proceeding immediately to the next activity, close all open windows and log off your computer.

Account and Profile Settings

The Account tab, shown in Figure 5-13, is used to control most security-related account settings. The User logon name and User logon name (pre-Windows 2000) were described previously. Click the **Logon Hours** button to open a schedule, which controls the times and days this user account can be accessed. Click the **Log On To** button to restrict this user account to certain computers. (This is an excellent idea for service accounts, such as those used by SQL or Exchange.)

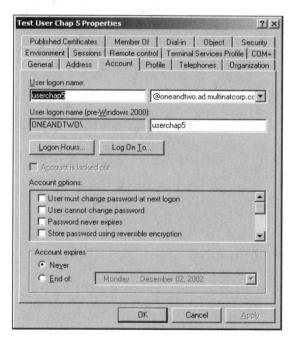

Figure 5-13   The Account tab

Activity 5-4: Add Account Restrictions

Time Required: 5 minutes

Objective: To practice adding account restrictions to Active Directory user objects.

Description: Your user 1c is a junior employee working with sensitive information. To reduce the risk of a confidentiality breech, company policy states that all such employees are restricted from logging on after hours. You will now add account information that prohibits the user from logging on outside of an 8 a.m. to 6 p.m. time frame.

1. If necessary, turn on your computer and log on as the administrator from your own domain.

2. Click **Start**, point to **Administrative Tools**, and then click **Active Directory Users and Computers**.

3. Expand the nodes in the tree pane until your domain and your own OU are both visible.

4. Click the name of your own OU in the tree pane.

5. In the details pane, click **user1c** (where *1* represents your student/computer number).

6. Click the **Action** menu, and then click **Properties**.

7. Click the **Account** tab.

8. Click the **Logon Hours** button.

9. Use the schedule grid to select all hours outside of the 8 a.m. to 6 p.m., Monday to Friday range, and then click **Logon Denied** to exclude them. (You may do this in several steps. If you accidentally select too many sections of the schedule, use the **Logon Permitted** button to reactivate them. You can also select an entire column or row with the buttons at the top left of the schedule grid.)

10. Click **OK**.

11. Click **OK** again.

12. If you are not proceeding immediately to the next activity, close all open windows and log off your computer.

You can also set a number of options, including the use of smart cards, how Kerberos is used with the account, and an expiration date. Be aware, however, that some of these settings can be overridden by the application of Group Policies.

Accounts can also be **disabled** or **locked out**. The effect of these two states is similar—an account cannot be used when disabled or locked out—but the implementation of each differs slightly. Enabling and disabling an account is an action usually performed by an administrator, although it can be automated. Disabling an account sets an option described as Account is disabled. An account can be disabled from the property pages, or by clicking on the Action menu in Active Directory Users and Computers.

On the other hand, an account cannot be locked out manually. Only the system can lock out accounts after too many consecutive bad password attempts. If this occurs, the Account is locked out checkbox will be checked on this property page. An administrator can reset the locked-out status by clearing this checkbox, or the system can be configured to automatically reset the lockout after a specified period of time.

The Profile tab, shown in Figure 5-14, controls some of the user's experience as he or she logs on to a Windows workstation. The profile path allows the user's settings (such as the desktop, menus, and favorites) to be stored centrally, rather than on the local workstation. This setting also allows administrators to set a mandatory profile that cannot be changed by the individual user. The logon script name specifies a batch file or script that runs every time the user logs on. The home folder settings allow you to specify a particular path to a local or network drive that will be available to the user. (Group Policies can also set logon scripts and control the elements found in the profile.)

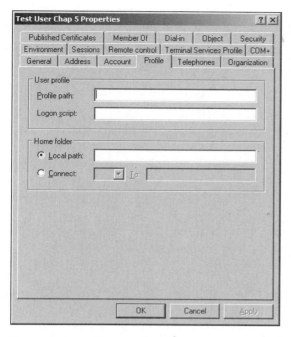

Figure 5-14   The Profile tab

The Member Of tab, shown in Figure 5-15, lists the groups to which the user belongs. Groups are used to manage permissions in the network for multiple users, rather than for each user individually. They are discussed in detail later in this chapter. A user can be added to or removed from groups using this property page, or from the property pages of the group object.

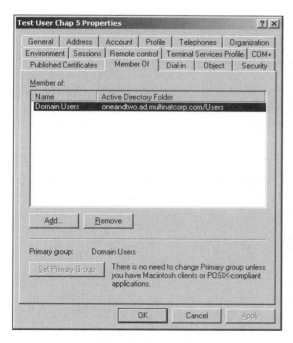

Figure 5-15   The Member Of tab

The COM+ tab, shown in Figure 5-16, configures how a user interacts with COM+ partition sets. A new feature of COM+ is the ability to concurrently load multiple versions of COM+ objects on one computer. In such an instance, COM+ partitions are used to manage which versions of which objects are used when. This tab allows the matching of users to particular COM+ partitions. (COM+ partitions are not related to Active Directory partitions or naming contexts.) This feature is used mostly with service accounts—accounts being used only to run server applications.

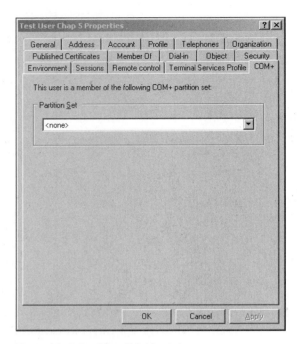

Figure 5-16   The COM+ tab

Terminal Services Settings

Beginning with the release of Windows 2000, Microsoft has promoted the use of Terminal Services (TS). Using TS, users connect to a server using thin clients, such as the Remote Desktop client that is included with Windows XP Professional. The programs that the user needs actually run on the server, and only keystrokes, mouse movements, and screen updates travel across the network (or dial-up connection). Several of the user attributes in Active Directory are designed to support the use of TS. The Environment tab, shown in Figure 5-17, allows administrators to override the default behavior of TS for a user and have TS automatically start a particular application. The properties on this tab also control the connection of client disk drives and printers.

The properties in the Sessions tab, shown in Figure 5-18, control how idle and disconnected TS sessions are managed by the server. A session is active when a client is connected and activity is occurring. It is idle if it remains connected but no activity occurs, and it is disconnected if a client is not connected. In the disconnected state, a user can still be logged on, and programs can still be executing. By configuring the settings on this tab, an administrator can choose whether to allow idle or disconnected sessions to consume resources on the server, or to end those sessions, freeing server resources.

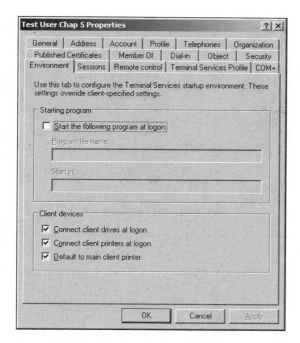

Figure 5-17   The Environment tab

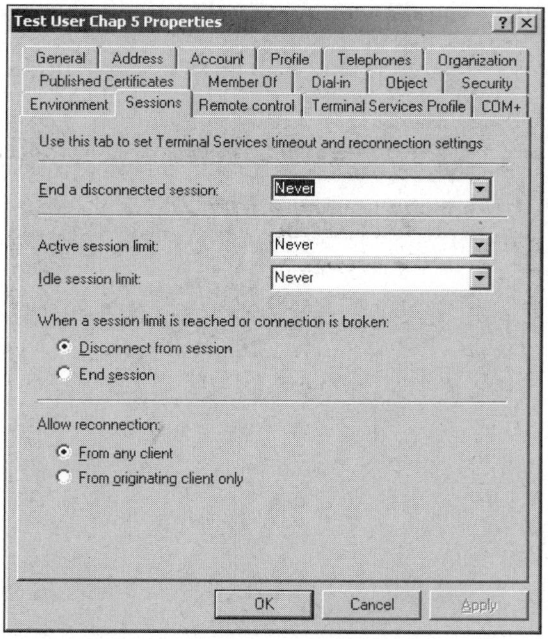

Figure 5-18   The Sessions tab

The Remote control tab, shown in Figure 5-19, controls whether a user's TS sessions can be remotely controlled by another TS client, such as an administrator or help desk support technician. These remote control settings apply *only* to TS sessions, not to interactive logons made at a workstation. Also, they do not govern remote assistance for Windows XP clients.

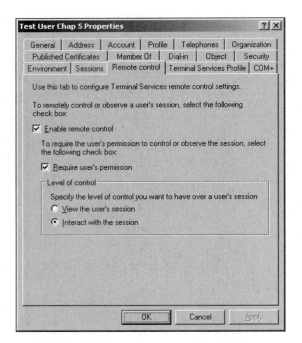

Figure 5-19   The Remote control tab

The properties on the Terminal Services Profile tab, shown in Figure 5-20, override the same properties shown on the Profile tab when the user is connected to a TS session. This allows you to have separate profiles for TS sessions and workstation sessions. The main benefit of this is to limit profile items that would consume large amounts of TS resources or network bandwidth. One of the most important properties—the checkbox labeled Allow logon to terminal server—is barely noticeable at the bottom of this property page. It controls whether the user is allowed to log on to any TS server that is a member of the domain. (*Note*: Clearing this checkbox does not prevent administrators from accessing servers running TS in administrative mode.)

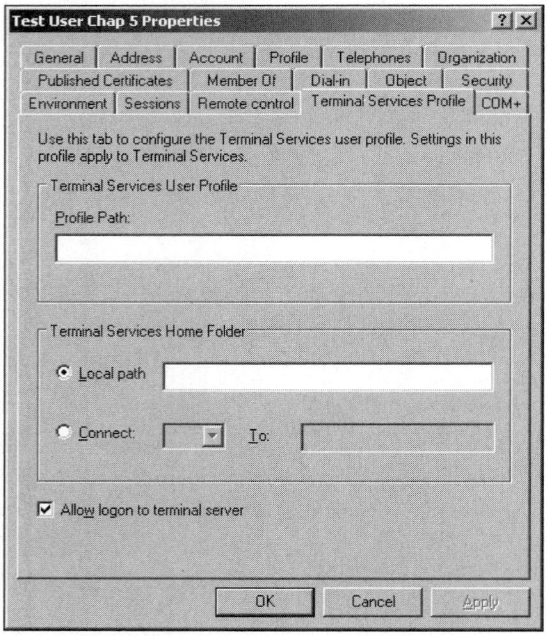

Figure 5-20   The Terminal Services Profile tab

Dial-in Settings

The Dial-in tab, shown in Figure 5-21, is used to control whether a user can access the dial-in services of servers running Routing and Remote Access Services (RRAS) in the forest. Several of these options are only available if the domain is operating in **native mode**. Native mode, for a domain, simply means that there are no pre-Windows 2000 DCs (such as Windows NT or Microsoft LAN Manager DCs) in the domain, and that an administrator has configured Active Directory to recognize this. (Native mode is further explained later in this chapter.) If the domain is not in native mode, it is said to be in **mixed mode**.

In native mode, you can require a user to dial in from one specific number (verified by caller-ID services), and assign static IP addressing and routing information. You can also use Remote Access Policy to control dial-in access on a granular level, using group memberships, time of day, and other parameters. For more information about Remote Access Policies, see *Hands-on Microsoft Windows Server 2003 Networking*. In a mixed-mode domain, the unavailable options are grayed out.

In either native or mixed mode, you can set a mandatory or optional call-back number to increase security or control long-distance charges. In Figure 5-22, the domain is in mixed mode.

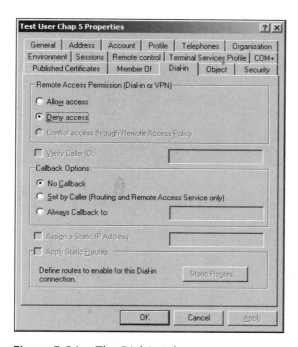

Figure 5-21   The Dial-in tab

Activity 5-5: Allowing Dial-in Access for a User

Time Required: 5 minutes

Objective: To practice allowing dial-in connections.

Description: User1b travels extensively for business and needs to access the network by dial-in modem and virtual private network (VPN). In this activity, you will enable his account for dial-in access. Knowing how to do so quickly and efficiency is an important part of a network administrator's job.

1. If necessary, turn on your computer and log on as the administrator from your own domain.

2. Click **Start**, point to **Administrative Tools**, and then click **Active Directory Users and Computers**.

3. Expand the nodes in the tree pane until your domain and your own OU are both visible.

4. Click the name of your own OU in the tree pane.

5. Click **user1b**.

6. Click the **Action** menu, and then click **Properties**.

7. Click the **Dial-in** tab.

8. Click the **Allow access** button.

9. Click **OK**.

10. If you are not proceeding immediately to the next activity, close all open windows and log off your computer.

Advanced Properties Tabs

Three tabs are visible only if you have activated the viewing of advanced features. The Security tab, shown in Figure 5-22, allows you to control access to the user object in Active Directory. Although it is recommended that you apply security settings to OUs or containers, it is possible to apply them on an object-by-object basis. Security settings in Active Directory are covered in Chapter 6.

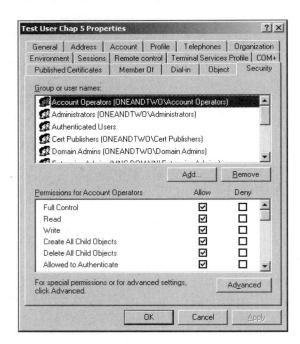

Figure 5-22   The Security tab

The Object tab, shown in Figure 5-23, contains information that may be of interest if you are troubleshooting an Active Directory problem, or require specific detail about the object itself. It would not be used for daily operations.

The Published Certificates tab, shown in Figure 5-24, displays information about Public Key Infrastructure (PKI) certificates that are stored and published in Active Directory. The full details of a PKI implementation are beyond the scope of this book, but some general PKI information is discussed in Chapter 6. If your enterprise uses PKI and stores certificates in Active Directory, this tab will allow you to see which certificates are published for a particular user, as well as add additional certificates.

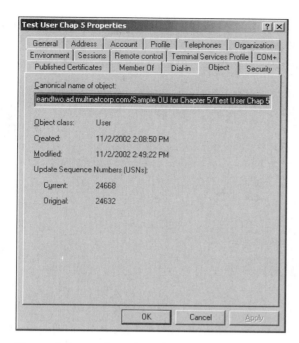

Figure 5-23   The Object tab

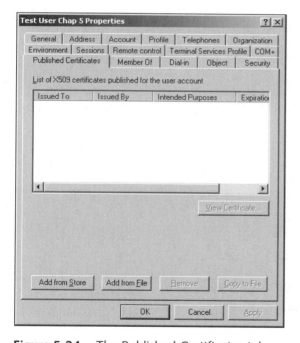

Figure 5-24   The Published Certificates tab

Resetting Passwords

When creating a new user, you are prompted for a password for that user; however, that password does not appear anywhere in the property pages. This is because the password attribute is write-only, meaning that once it has been set, a user (even an administrator) cannot read the value again. With Windows NT, the password field appeared in the property page of the user, but was masked with asterisks. The user's password is stored in an encrypted form, which the operating system can access to validate a user. The original or plain-text version of the password cannot normally be recreated from the encrypted version, although there are hacking tools that use a brute-force method to try millions of possible combinations, if the hacker has administrative access to the computer.

If a user forgets his or her password, an administrator cannot retrieve it for them. Instead, the password must be reset. Right-clicking on the name of the user in the Users and Computers console and clicking Reset Password (see Figure 5-25), brings up the simple dialog box shown in Figure 5-26. You can access the same command from the Action menu.

 Resetting a user's password in this way should only be done if no other options are available. When a password is reset in this way, access to encrypted files may be lost, as the system will not allow access to parts of the user's private certificate store after a password reset.

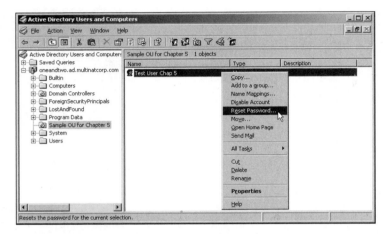

Figure 5-25   Invoking the Reset Password command

Figure 5-26   The Reset Password dialog box

Activity 5-6: Reset a Password

Time Required: 5 minutes

Objective: To practice resetting a user's password.

Description: User1a has just returned from a six-week vacation and has forgotten his password. In this activity, you will reset it to a known value. Such resetting is a common task for network administrators.

1. If necessary, turn on your computer and log on as the administrator from your own domain.

2. Click **Start**, point to **Administrative Tools**, and then click **Active Directory Users and Computers**.

3. Expand the nodes in the tree pane until your domain and your own OU are both visible.

4. Click the name of your own OU in the tree pane.

5. In the details pane, click your **A** user.

6. Click the **Action** menu, and then click **Reset Password**.

7. Type **newpass1** in the New Password text box.

8. Type **newpass1** in the Confirm Password text box.

9. Click **User must change password at next logon** so that it is checked.

10. Click **OK**.

11. Click **OK** again.

12. If you are not proceeding immediately to the next activity, close all open windows and log off your computer.

Creating Users Programmatically

Because Active Directory supports a number of open standards and interfaces, there are many ways to create a user, besides the Users and Computers console. Users can be created by scripts or programs, or automatically by a variety of tools. Some of these methods are examined in Chapter 11. It is fairly common to create users from a script, program, or enterprise-wide tool such as Microsoft Metadirectory Services (MMS). (MMS is a product allowing Active Directory to participate with other directory services and databases, such as Novell NDS or SQL server, by synchronizing data between them. MMS can also synchronize information between separate forests.)

WORKING WITH GROUPS

Administrators may be responsible for thousands of user accounts and hundreds of resources. Trying to manage each individual account is not very efficient. If you had five printers, 10 file shares, two SQL database servers, and 150 users in your company, that would be more than 2,500 sets of permissions to manage—at a minimum. On the other hand, if those 150 users all required the same level of access, then assigning permissions to a group—which could encompass all of those users with the same access needs—would take only a few minutes.

Group Types

There are two different types of groups in Active Directory: **distribution groups** and **security groups**. Distribution groups are used to allow Active Directory-aware e-mail systems to send e-mail to a group list. For example, you might use an "all employees" distribution group to send important e-mail announcements to everyone in the company, even though everyone in the company does not have the same security privileges on the network. The only function of these groups is the distribution of e-mail, so they often contain contacts as well as users. Distribution groups can also contain computers, but there is no real benefit to this, as most people don't send e-mail to a computer.

 Distribution groups cannot be used to control access to resources.

Conversely, security groups are named as such because they are used to enforce resource access. They have two main functions. First, they can be used to control access or audit access to resources, because a security group's SID can be included in an access control entry (ACE) in a Discretionary Access Control List (DACL) for access control, or a System Access Control List (SACL) for auditing. Second, security groups are used to filter the application of Group Policy. Special DACLs on Group Policy objects can prevent them from being applied to users who would otherwise be affected. (Group policy is examined in Chapter 10.) A security group can also be used in then same way that a distribution group is used—for sending e-mail to groups. They can also contain other groups, contacts, users, and computers.

Group Scopes

The **scope** of a group determines where that group can be used in the forest and which objects it can contain. In other words, the scope determines when a group can be nested in other groups, and when it can be referenced in DACLs and SACLs. In the Windows Server 2003 family and Active Directory, there are four possible scopes that a group can have:

- Local scope
- Domain local scope
- Global scope
- Universal scope

Technically speaking, a group is described as "a group with global scope." However, most people simply call it a global group. Likewise, the terms universal group and domain local group are also commonly used.

Before discussing the specifics of each type of scope, it is important to consider the mode setting of the domain, as the mode of the Active Directory domain also affects the scope of groups.

Domain Modes

Active Directory can interact with older Windows NT-based domains. A domain can have some DCs running Active Directory, although others are running earlier Windows versions, such as Windows NT 4. This situation is described as "mixed mode," because the DCs are a mix of Active Directory and non-Active Directory DCs.

Certain functions supported by Active Directory are not supported by DCs running the older versions, and are therefore not allowed in mixed-mode domains. When Active Directory is installed, it defaults to mixed mode.

When all DCs are running Windows 2000 or Windows Server 2003, you can upgrade the domain to native mode. The term native mode simply means the absence of any pre-Windows 2000 DCs. Because all DCs are running Active Directory, all of the Active Directory group types and scopes can be supported.

 Once you raise the Functionality level of a domain, it cannot be returned to mixed mode. It is a one-way process.

Local Scope

A **local group** (or, a group with local scope) is a group that is used only within the context of a specific machine. For this reason, they are often called **machine local groups** to make clear the distinction between machine local groups and **domain local groups**. Because the scope of a machine local group is the one machine only, you can only make reference to that machine local group on that local machine. For example, you could create a machine local group called "Color Printer Users" on a print server named PrnSrv01, which is running Windows Server 2003. You could assign permissions controlling the access to printers served by PrnSrv01 and include grant or deny permissions for this group to use the printer. However, the machine FileSrv01 would know nothing about this group (because it is local to PrnSrv01), and you could not assign permissions to access FileSrv01 using it.

Machines that are members of the domain (servers and professional-level workstations) can also have machine local groups. Machine local groups are not stored in Active Directory, but in the local accounts database on each local machine.

Local groups do not exist on DCs. A DC has a special type of group called "BUILTIN," which includes the default administrator and guest accounts. The only machine local group on DCs is the BUILTIN group, and you cannot change the members.

 A machine local group can contain members from anywhere in the forest or any other trusted forest or down-level domain.

Domain Local Scope

Domain local groups, like machine local groups, can contain security principals from anywhere in the forest, from any trusted forest, or any trusted down-level domain. The difference between a local (or machine local) group and a domain local group is where it can be used. A machine local group can only be used to assign permission on one machine, but a domain local group can be used at any machine in the domain.

For example, suppose there are five machines in a domain, as illustrated in Figure 5-27. These are two domain controllers, DC1 and DC2; two member servers SERVER3 and SERVER4; and one workstation, HOST5. A machine local group created on SERVER3 can be used in DACLs only on SERVER3. A machine local group created on HOST5 can be used in DACLs only on HOST5. A machine local group created on DC1 could be used in DACLs on DC1 and DC2, but only because DCs all share the same local account database. (You could conceive of this being two separate machine local groups, one on DC1 and one on DC2, but that are always kept synchronized.) A machine local group from DC1 cannot be used in a DACL on SERVER3, SERVER4, or HOST5.

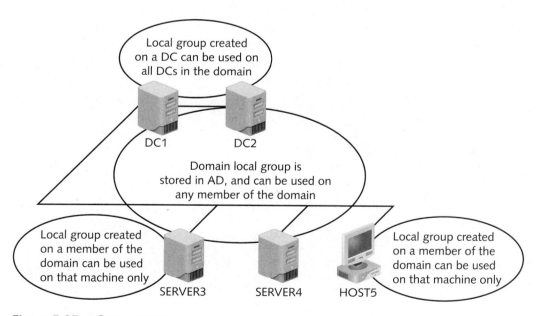

Figure 5-27   Group scopes

In contrast to a local group, a domain local group created in this domain could be used in DACLs on any of the machines in the domain. Domain local groups can only be created in a native-mode domain. This is because the NT4 and earlier DCs wouldn't know how to handle them. If you must keep your domain in mixed mode, careful application of machine local groups is the best way to come close to the benefits of domain local groups.

Activity 5-7: Create a Domain Local Group

Time Required: 5 minutes

Objective: To practice creating a domain local group.

Description: In this activity, you will create a group that can be used to assign permissions to resources within your own domain. It is common, especially in large forests, to use domain local groups to control access to resources.

1. If necessary, turn on your computer and log on as the administrator from your own domain.

2. Click **Start**, point to **Administrative Tools**, and then click **Active Directory Users and Computers**.

3. Expand the nodes in the tree pane until your domain and your own OU are both visible.

4. Click the name of your own OU in the tree pane.

5. Point to the **Action** menu, point to **New**, and then point to **Group**.

6. In the Group Name text box, type **Student *1* Domain Local Group** (where *1* is your student/computer number).

7. Click the **Domain local** radio button.

8. Click **OK**.

9. If you are not proceeding immediately to the next activity, log off your computer.

Global Scope

A **global group** can be created in both mixed-mode and native-mode domains. For members, it can contain any security principal from the same domain in which it was created. That is, unlike both types of local groups, all of the members in a global group will always be from the same domain. This concept is similar to the Global Group in Windows NT 4.0.

However, also unlike machine local and domain local groups, the global groups can be used in DACLs and SACLs anywhere in the forest, or anywhere that the domain is trusted. In particular, as is discussed in the next section, global groups are often made members of machine local or domain local groups in other domains.

Activity 5-8: Create a Global Group

Time Required: 5 minutes

Objective: To practice creating a global group.

Description: In this activity you will create a group that can be used to assign permissions to resources anywhere in the forest. You will need to know this in order to effectively manage access to resources.

1. If necessary, turn on your computer and log on as the administrator from your own domain.

2. Click **Start**, point to **Administrative Tools**, and then click **Active Directory Users and Computers**.

3. Expand the nodes in the tree pane until your domain and your own OU are both visible.

4. Click the name of your own OU in the tree pane.

5. Click the **Action** menu, point to **New**, and then click **Group**.

6. In the **Group Name** text box, type **Student *1* Global Group** (where 1 is your student/computer number).

7. Click the **Global** radio button.

8. Click **OK**.

9. If you are not proceeding immediately to the next activity, log off your computer.

Universal Scope

Universal groups were introduced with Windows 2000 and the first release of Active Directory. They can only be used in a native-mode domain (that is, one with a functionality level of Windows 2000 native or Windows Server 2003). In many ways they represent the best features of both local and global groups, but the impact of using universal groups in a large forest must be carefully considered.

Like a machine local group or domain local group, a universal group can contain security principals from any domain in the forest (including its own), or any trusted domain. However, like a global group, a universal group can be used in a SACL or DACL anywhere in the forest, or in any other forest or domain that trusts the universal group's domain.

 Including security principals from mixed-mode domains in a universal group is not recommended, but it is not prevented. Access problems could result because users authenticated by an NT4 DC won't have the universal group SIDs in their access tokens. This would also be difficult to troubleshoot.

Many new administrators wonder why they should even bother with domain local or global groups…why not just use universal groups exclusively? In fact, in small organizations—or any organization with only one domain—this could be a very good decision. However, it is impractical in large forests because of one key feature of universal groups: All universal groups, including the details of their membership, are recorded in the GC. Groups that are large in size, if created as universal groups, generate large amounts of data to be stored in the GC. Even more crucially than that, however, is that changes to the membership of a universal group must be replicated to all GC servers in the forest, as well as to all DCs in its own domain. This replication traffic could be extensive.

Activity 5-9: Convert the Domain to Native Mode

Time Required: 5 minutes

Objective: To practice converting a domain to native mode.

Description: You may have noticed in the last two activities that the universal scope option has not been available. To use native-mode features, you will now need to set your domain to operate in native mode. This is possible because there have never been any pre-Windows 2000 DCs in this domain. Because this is done by domain, either you or your partner should complete this activity, but not both.

1. Choose which partner will complete these steps.

2. If necessary, turn on your computer and log on as the administrator from your own domain.

3. Click **Start**, point to **Administrative Tools**, and then click **Active Directory Domains and Trusts**.

4. Expand the nodes in the tree pane until your domain is visible.

5. Right-click the name of your domain and then click **Raise Domain Functional Level**.

6. Click the drop-down list and change the selection to **Windows 2000 native**.

7. Click **Raise**.

8. Read the warning message, and then click **OK**.

9. Read the result message, and then click **OK**.

10. Close the Active Directory Domains and Trusts console.

11. It could take up to 15 minutes for this change to take effect on all DCs.

12. If you are not proceeding immediately to the next activity, log off your computer.

Activity 5-10: Creating a Universal Group

Time Required: 5 minutes

Objective: To practice creating a universal group.

Description: In this activity you will create a group that can be used to assign permissions to resources anywhere in the forest and that can contain security principals from any domain in the forest.

1. If necessary, turn on your computer and log on as the administrator from your own domain.

2. Click **Start**, point to **Administrative Tools**, and then click **Active Directory Users and Computers**.

3. Expand the nodes in the tree pane until your domain and your own OU are both visible.

4. Click the name of your own OU in the tree pane.

5. Click the **Action** menu, point to **New**, and then click **Group**.

6. In the Group Name text box, type **Student *1* Universal Group** (where 1 is your student/computer number).

7. Click the **Universal** option button. (*Note*: If this button is disabled, replication from Activity 5-9 has not been completed. Log off, wait a few minutes, and try again, or ask your instructor for assistance.)

8. Click **OK**.

9. If you are not proceeding immediately to the next activity, log off your computer.

The existence of domain local groups and global groups is also recorded in the GC, but their detailed membership is not. Therefore, groups that frequently change should not be universal in scope. Note that in a well-designed forest, the membership of universal groups is almost always made up of other groups, as discussed in the next section.

If your forest has only one domain and no external trusts, the effect of domain local, global, and universal groups will be the same. However, following good practices and understanding the differences will result in much easier expansion and future growth.

Groups as Members of Other Groups

Certain groups can contain other groups as members. This helps reduce network traffic, control the size of Active Directory updates, give flexibility in domain planning, and manage permissions in an effective and scalable way. These benefits will be examined later in this chapter.

Group Nesting in Mixed-Mode domains

In a mixed-mode domain, only local groups (specifically machine local groups, because mixed-mode domains have no domain local groups) can contain other groups, and they can contain only global groups and user objects. In addition, they can contain global groups from anywhere in the forest or other trusted domains.

Group Nesting in Native-Mode Domains

If the domain is in native mode, groups can be nested in more ways than if the domain is in mixed mode. These native-mode options are much more diverse:

- Domain local groups can contain universal groups and global groups from anywhere in the forest or any trusted domain, in addition to containing users.

- Global groups can contain other global groups from the same domain, in addition to containing users. For example, a domain might have a global group called "boys" and one called "girls." Both could be included in a global group called "children." In this case, adding a user to "boys" automatically includes him in "children." In a mixed-mode domain, you could still create the three global groups, but would have to add the new user to both "boys" and "children," which is not as easy to manage.

- Universal groups can contain user accounts, computer accounts, global groups, and other universal groups from anywhere in the forest or in any trusted domain. Universal groups do not exist in mixed-mode domains.

Creating Groups

Like many processes in Active Directory, planning the correct use of groups can be complicated, especially in a large network. However, actually creating a group is very straightforward. Simply right-click the container or OU that will hold the group and click **New**, then choose **Group**, as shown in Figure 5-28.

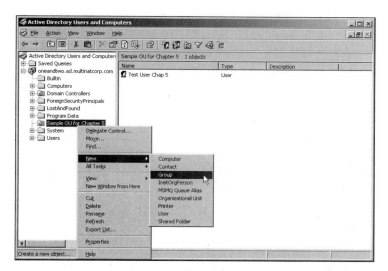

Figure 5-28   Invoking the New Group command

Figure 5-29 shows the single dialog box that is used to actually create the group. Like a user, a group has a cn attribute that is its name in Active Directory, as well as a NetBIOS-style name for use with older clients. This dialog box also allows you to specify the group type and scope. By clicking OK, the group is created and will be listed with other objects in Active Directory. (In the example pictured, the universal scope option is grayed out because the domain is still in mixed mode.)

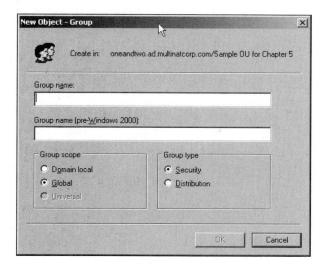

Figure 5-29   New Object dialog box for a group object

Changing Groups

There are three types of changes that you may be called on to make to a group. The most common is a change of membership—that is, to add or remove members of the group. Again, since your directory objects represent the real world, changes in the real world will result in changes in your directory.

Though it is less common, you may be called on to change the type of a group from distribution to security, or vice-versa. The most common example occurs when a distribution group is established for e-mail purposes, and after some time it is realized that the same people in the distribution group have common requirements to access a resource, such as a shared folder or a Web site. Rather than creating a new group and duplicating the content, it is a better idea to change the group's type.

It is also possible to change the scope of a group, though this is often an indication that planning was not as thorough as could have been. However, in the real world (unlike our ideal, imaginary world where planning is perfect), we sometimes just do what needs to be done.

Changing the Members of a Group

For a group to be of much use, it has to have members. There are two common ways to add members, such as users, to a group. Deciding which method is easier depends on whether you are working with a group or with an individual account.

To work with the group as a whole, view members, add members, or remove members, open the group's properties by double-clicking the group or right-clicking it and choosing Properties. A tabbed dialog box will appear, similar to the one shown in Figure 5-30. Select the Members tab, and use the Add and Remove buttons as necessary to change the membership of the group.

Figure 5-30   Properties of a group object

Most objects in Active Directory also have a tab in their property sheets called Member Of. This tab allows you to work with the individual objects and put them into groups, rather than work from the group perspective. Both methods have the same effect—as soon as you add a user to a group using the group's Member tab, that group will appear in the user's Member Of tab. This is shown in Figure 5-31.

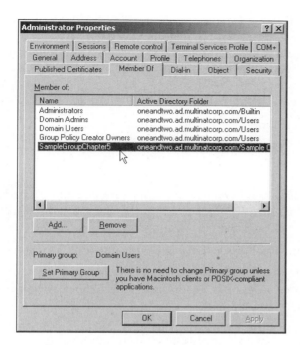

Figure 5-31   Member Of tab for Administrator

Activity 5-11: Add Members to a Group

Time Required: 5 minutes

Objective: To practice managing group memberships.

Description: In this activity you will make your three users members of your global group. All ACTIVE DIRECTORY network administrators need to know how to manage the memberships of groups.

1. If necessary, turn on your computer and log on as the administrator from your own domain.

2. Click **Start**, point to **Administrative Tools**, and then click **Active Directory Users and Computers**.

3. Expand the nodes in the tree pane until your domain and your own OU are both visible.

4. Click the name of your own OU in the tree pane.

5. Click the name of your global group in the details pane.

6. Click the **Action** menu, and then choose **Properties**.

7. Click the **Members** tab.

8. Click **Add**.

9. Click **Advanced**.

10. In the common queries area, type **user** after the "starts with" option.

11. Click **Find Now**.

12. Select your three users by clicking them while holding the Ctrl key.

13. Click **OK**.

14. Click **OK** again.

15. Click **OK** yet again.

16. If you are not proceeding immediately to the next activity, close all windows and log off your computer.

Changing a Group's Type

If you discover that you have created a security group that you don't need for permissions, but would like to use as a distribution group, you can change its type if the domain is in native mode. You can also change a distribution group (such as an e-mail list) into a security group, if you wish to include it in DACLs for permissions. Again, this conversion can only be made if the domain is in native mode.

If the domain is in mixed mode, the group's type cannot be changed. In native mode, a group's type can be changed between security group and distribution group without restriction.

Changing a Group's Scope

If an administrator decides that a group should have a different scope, it may be possible (in certain circumstances) to change the scope in a native-mode domain. In a mixed-mode domain, a group's scope cannot be changed. In a native-mode domain, two scope changes are commonly allowed:

- A global group can be promoted to a universal group, as long as it is not itself a member of another global group.

- A domain local group can be promoted to a universal group, as long as it does not have any other domain local groups nested as members in it.

You can also "demote" a universal group to a global group, although it is not encouraged by Microsoft. This is allowed by Active Directory as long as none of the rules are broken. In other words, if the members of a universal group can't be members of a global group because they are from more than one domain, then the conversion is not allowed. This means that in some circumstances you could turn a domain local group into a global group by first converting it to a universal group, and then back to a global group. Most of the time it would be easier to make a new group with the correct scope.

Activity 5-12: Change a Group Scope

Time Required: 10 minutes

Objective: To practice and observe the effects of changing a group scope.

Description: In this activity you will change the scope of your global group to universal and then back. While this would rarely happen in most networks, it is important that you understand the process and be able to do so, if needed.

1. If necessary, turn on your computer and log on as the administrator from your own domain.

2. Click **Start**, point to **Administrative Tools**, and then click **Active Directory Users and Computers**.

3. Expand the nodes in the tree pane until your domain and your own OU are both visible.

4. Click the name of your own OU in the tree pane.

5. Double-click the name of your global group to open its properties.

6. Notice that the Domain local scope button is disabled.

7. Click **Universal**.

8. Click **OK**.

9. The scope has changed in the type column in the details pane.

10. Double-click the name of your global group to open its properties.

11. The Domain local scope button is now available.

12. Click **Global**.

13. Click **OK**.

14. The scope has changed in the type column in the details pane.

15. If you are not proceeding immediately to the next activity, close all open windows and log off your computer.

CREATING RESOURCE OBJECTS

Recall that Active Directory, in addition to organizing security principals (such as users), also organizes resources on your network. An object in the directory represents a resource. Each object is created the same way, by choosing New (either from the context menu presented when a container is right-clicked, or from the Action menu), then choosing the correct object.

Don't be confused, however, between creating the directory object to represent the resource, and creating the resource itself. For example, creating a shared folder object in ACTIVE DIRECTORY does not create the file share on the file server; that must be done separately. Think of it this way: Creating a printer object obviously does not create a physical print device—someone still has to manufacture, deliver, configure, and connect the printer.

Shared Folder

Creating an object to represent a file share involves simply completing the dialog box shown in Figure 5-32. A **shared folder** object provides only a representation of the actual share in order to help network users locate resources. Active Directory does not even check to see if the server or the share exists.

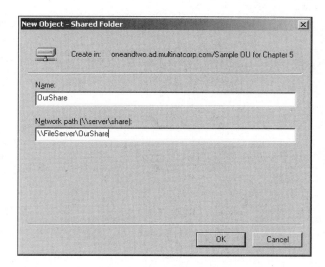

Figure 5-32   Creating a shared folder object

Activity 5-13: Create a Shared Folder Object

Time Required: 5 minutes

Objective: To practice creating a shared folder object.

Description: In this activity you will publish a shared folder in Active Directory, which will help you find resources on your network.

1. If necessary, turn on your computer and log on as the administrator from your own domain.

2. Click **Start**, point to **Administrative Tools**, and then click **Active Directory Users and Computers**.

3. Expand the nodes in the tree pane until your domain and your own OU are both visible.

4. Click the name of your own OU in the tree pane.

5. Click the **Action** menu, point to **New**, and then click **Shared Folder**.

6. In the Name text box, type **Student *1* Shared Folder** (where *1* is your assigned student/computer number).

7. In the Network Path text box, type **\\someserver\someshare**.

8. Click **OK**.

9. If you are not proceeding immediately to the next activity, log off your computer.

Printers

The process for creating a **printer** object in the directory is more robust than for shared folders. The dialog box requests the network path to the printer, as shown in Figure 5-33. When a printer is set up on a print server in Windows 2000 or Windows Server 2003, an option is presented that will automatically include an object to represent it in Active Directory. The reasons for placing printer objects in Active Directory are covered later in this chapter.

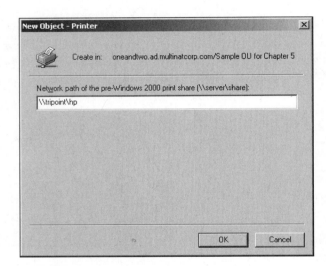

Figure 5-33   Creating a printer object

Unlike objects representing shared folders, Active Directory does check for the existence of a printer at the address specified. If the printer does not exist, the error shown in Figure 5-34 will appear.

Figure 5-34   Trying to create a printer object for a nonexistent printer

Other Resources

As more Active Directory-aware and Active Directory-enabled applications are released, administrators will have the ability to locate more and more information in the Active Directory database. Some of these applications will use existing classes, although others will want to extend the schema.

By way of example, Microsoft included objects in the default Active Directory schema to work with its flag-ship database product, SQL Server 2000. One role of the SQL Server is publishing database information for replication to other databases. SQL Servers and their publications can be represented by objects in Active Directory, allowing them to be more easily located by those needing to connect to the services offered.

You may have noticed the option to create a MSMQ queue alias. MSMQ is the Microsoft Message Queuing architecture used to facilitate interprocess communications with distributed applications. Active Directory provides a way to publish names for these queues, making it easier to set up the distributed applications. Each type of application or resource will have its own requirements, however the specifics are beyond the scope of this book.

 Wait a minute! What about this **InetOrgPerson object**? What's that all about? In the first version of Active Directory, Microsoft called a user a user, plain and simple. Unfortunately, many other directories, including Novell's Novell Directory Services (NDS), call a user an InetOrgPerson. To allow greater interoperability between Active Directory and other directory services, Active Directory now supports the use of this class. Unless you are working in a multiplatform environment, you can consider an InetOrgPerson and a user to be functionally equivalent, once the domain is set to use the Windows Server 2003 functionality level.

ORGANIZING OBJECTS IN THE DIRECTORY

Many network administrators, especially when starting out, work with networks that are fairly small, like the networks featured in most training courses and lab exercises. If a network has only a dozen users, there isn't much need for organization; finding an object such as a user or a network resource is straightforward and the lists are short. A large network, though, must be well organized. Before Active Directory, the Windows domain model was flat—it had no organization or structure. One of the major advantages of Active Directory is that information can be organized in a logical way.

Organizing and Controlling with OUs

You can organize an Active Directory structure by using OUs. Chapters 3 and 4 looked at some design criteria for OUs within a forest and a domain. This chapter will look specifically at how to create and use OUs for separating data ownership, facilitating directory browsing, and supporting the application of Group Policy. (Group Policy is discussed in detail in Chapter 10.)

Using OUs to Separate Service Ownership and Data Ownership

Chapter 3 introduced the concept of data ownership and service ownership in a directory service. The service owner is responsible for the operation of the directory as whole, and for maintaining the infrastructure and ensuring that the directory is available when it is needed. A data owner is responsible for the actual contents of the directory—that is, for the actual values stored in each object. In practical terms, a data owner will create or delete objects, will grant or deny access to resources, and will modify object attributes as the information that it represents changes. An organization may have many data owners, each responsible for a different part of the directory.

OUs provide a way to separate the objects belonging to one data owner from another. Each data owner can have their own OU or group of OUs. The Active Directory Users and Computers console provides a Delegation of Control wizard that allows the service owner to easily assign the correct permissions that enable each data owner to manage the objects in their own OU, without giving more permissions than are necessary.

To launch the **Delegation of Control wizard**, simply click the OU to be controlled, and then click **Delegate Control** on the Action menu (or from the pop-up menu that appears when you right-click the OU). In the wizard, specify which users should be given control over the OU, and what permissions they are to have.

The wizard doesn't do anything magical—it only sets permissions on the OU by making entries in the DACL, but it does make it easy to implement. (The details of managing directory permissions are discussed later in the chapter.)

> There is no "undelegate" wizard. To undo the effects of the Delegation of Control wizard, you must manually change the permissions on the OU. Therefore, it is always good to plan your delegations before using the wizard and to clearly document what permissions were delegated.

Using OUs to Facilitate Browsing the Directory

Sometimes you will know exactly what you are looking for when you search a directory. For example, if you are looking for a person and you know his or her last name, that is a specific piece of information and is a good basis from which to begin a search. However, there may be times when you don't have a specific piece of information to use, or you may simply want to browse the network.

Let's imagine a mobile user with a laptop who is attending a meeting in another office of his company. A large company could have hundreds or even thousands of printers. He connects his laptop to the network—perhaps wirelessly, or at a "hot desk" network jack—and logs on without trouble. He needs to print a document and doesn't want to retrieve it at his own desk, which is at his office across town. Which would be easier to find, a nearby printer from a list of hundreds of printers, or a nearby printer from a structure similar to the one shown in Figure 5-35?

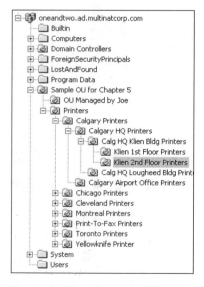

Figure 5-35 One possible browsing structure

Of course, it is possible to get carried away. In addition to the recommended maximum of 10 levels of OU nesting, it is also possible to create too many OUs. In the fictitious example, notice an OU created for the Yellowknife Printer. Is it reasonable to have an OU for just one resource? In most cases, it isn't.

Using OUs to Support the Application of Group Policy

Group Policy, which is discussed in Chapter 10, is used to apply security settings, scripts, administrative registry settings, and to install software to client computers. One of the easiest places to apply Group Policy is at the OU level. Therefore, it makes sense to group objects (mostly users and computers) that will have the same settings in the same OU.

Imagine a company that offers classroom training and seminars. It has a staff that uses computers to accomplish its work. It also has an Internet café set up at each site, allowing its customers a place to browse the Internet or check their e-mail during breaks. This company uses Group Policy to control how these computers are configured. For them, a structure like the one shown in Figure 5-36 might make good sense.

Figure 5-36   Possible OU structure to support Group Policy

Moving Objects between OUs

It may seem complicated to find the right balance between supporting data ownership, browsing, and applying Group Policy. It can be difficult to determine how much organization is needed without over-organizing, which can be just as hard to manage. Thankfully, it is fairly simple to move objects from one OU to another, so an error in your OU structure is rarely fatal.

In Chapter 4, you practiced moving OUs around the domain structure. Moving objects between OUs is done in the same way. Simply click the object you wish to move and choose Move from the Action menu, or right-click the object and select Move from the pop-up menu that appears.

Moving Objects between Domains

Unlike moving between OUs, moving objects between domains is not nearly as simple. A security principal's SID is made up, in part, of an identifier from its domain. Because it is changing domains, this part of the SID must also change. But the system also wants to keep track and recognize the security principal as the same object. There are two tools that are used to move objects (such as users), depending on whether the destination domain is in the same forest.

Movetree: Move Objects within the Forest

Movetree is a utility supplied with Windows Server 2003. It is one of the Windows support tools included on the CD. It's a good idea to install the support tools along with the operating system. Movetree also helps an administrator move an object or an entire OU from one domain to another. You can find the details of the Movetree syntax by clicking **Start** and then clicking **Help and Support** and searching for the term "Active Directory Support Tools."

ADMT: Move Objects to Another Forest

If a user is moved from one forest to another, a new user object is created. and the old one is deleted. These two user objects have different SIDs, so it is hard to say whether that user is really the same user. He or she is the same person, but how does Active Directory and Windows know that? The Active Directory Migration Tool (ADMT) provides a mechanism to move a user between forests. The main use for ADMT is to migrate users from an older structure (like a Windows NT domain) to a new Active Directory implementation, however, the same process can be used to move from one Active Directory forest to another.

If you only have a need to move one object, or even a few objects, it might be simpler to manually create the new object(s) and delete the old ones. However, if you are faced with moving a large number of objects and want to retain their identities, then ADMT or a third-party tool may be useful. For details on ADMT, click **Start**, then click **Help and Support**, and search for "How to Use Active Directory Migration Tool Version 2."

ADMT is also discussed in the context of upgrading a domain in Chapter 12.

CHAPTER SUMMARY

❐ Although an Active Directory design is fairly static, there are usually frequent changes to the objects contained in the directory, especially user objects.

❐ A user object has six mandatory attributes, but four of them are automatically assigned by the Active Directory system. There are more than 200 optional attributes for user objects.

❐ Active Directory Users and Computers is a snap-in for the Microsoft Management Console (MMC) used to manage user objects, computer objects, groups, and resource objects.

❐ To create a user object in Active Directory Users and Computers, you only need to supply a display name, a UPN, and a sAMAccountName. After the user object is created, you can manage properties in Active Directory Users and Computers on up to 16 property pages.

❐ Groups are used to work with a number of objects at once. There are two types of groups: distribution groups and security groups. There are four possible scopes of groups: machine local, domain local, global, and universal.

❐ Security groups can be included in SACLs and DACLs on resources to control access and auditing by group, rather than by individual users. Security groups can also be used to send e-mail to groups of users and contacts. Distribution groups are used to send e-mail to groups of users and contacts, but cannot be included in SACLs or DACLs.

❐ As objects are created, they should be organized in a logical way by the proper use of OUs. Objects can be easily moved between OUs.

❐ Objects can be moved between domains, but it is more complicated. Movetree is a utility that can move objects between domains in the same forest. ADMT is used to move objects between forests, including migrating objects from older domains.

KEY TERMS

Active Directory Migration Tool (ADMT) — A tool used to move objects between forests, such as during a migration to Active Directory.

Active Directory Users and Computers — A Microsoft Management Console (MMC) snap-in for managing common Active Directory objects, including users, computers, groups, and some resources.

Delegation of Control wizard — A wizard tool that facilities granting permissions on OUs to allow nonadministrators to perform certain functions.

disabled — An account is disabled or enabled by an administrator. Disabled accounts cannot be used. *See also* locked out.

distribution group — A group that can be used to send e-mail to a group of users and contacts. It cannot be used to control security.

domain local group — A group that can be used within its own domain, but can include security principals from other trusted domains as members.

down-level client — A client that was not designed to work seamlessly with Active Directory, including Windows 3.1 and earlier, Windows 95, Windows 98, Windows Millennium Edition (Me), and Windows NT 4.0 and earlier.

global group — A group that can contain only security principals from its own domain, but it can be used in other trusted domains.

InetOrgPerson object — A class of objects that is functionally equivalent to the user class. The InetOrgPerson object is provided for compatibility with other directory products, such as NDS.

local group — A group that can be used only in the context of one computer, such as a workstation or member server. Sometimes called a **machine local group**. Local groups do not exist on domain controllers; DCs use a similar type of group called BUILTIN.

locked out — An account can be locked out automatically by the system after too many failed log-on attempts. A locked-out account cannot be used. *See also* disabled.

machine local group — *See* local group.

mixed mode — A domain is operating in mixed mode if it contains domain controllers running Windows NT 4.0 or earlier. Several options are not available in mixed mode. See also native mode.

Movetree — A tool to move objects from one domain to another within the same forest.

native mode — A domain can be set to operate in native mode if it has no domain controllers that are running Windows NT 4.0 or earlier. *See also* mixed mode.

printer — An object in Active Directory that represents a print queue (which in Windows NT, 2000, and 2003 is also referred to a "printer").

sAMAccountName — A unique attribute of a user object that specifies the username used to log on to the domain. Active Directory domains can use the sAMAccountName or the userPrincipalName.

scope (group scope) — Groups can have the following scopes: machine local, domain local, global, or universal. A group's scope determines where it can be used in the forest.

security group — A group that can be used as a distribution group and can also be included in SACLs and DACLs to control access and auditing.

shared folder — An object in Active Directory that represents a shared folder (a share folder) on the network.

type (group type) — Groups can be either security groups or distribution groups. Distribution groups cannot be included in SACLs or DACLs.

universal group — A group that contains security principals from any trusted domain and can be used in any trusted domain.

user (user object) — An object in Active Directory that represents a user in your domain. A user is a security principal and may be a person or a network service.

user logon name — The Active Directory Users and Computers property that maps to the sAMAccountName attribute.

user logon name (pre-Windows 2000) — The Active Directory Users and Computers property that maps to the userPrincipalName attribute.

userPrincipalName (UPN) — A unique attribute of a user object that specifies the username that can be used to log on to the domain from clients that support Active Directory.

REVIEW QUESTIONS

1. A user object must have a cn attribute, which is also known as the Full Name property. True or False?

2. You must set all available user properties before the user can log on to the system. True or False?

3. Which of the following tools is used to reset a user's password in a native-mode Active Directory domain?

    a. User Manager for Domains

    b. Active Directory Migration Tool

    c. Active Directory Users and Computers

    d. Active Directory Sites and Services

4. Which is the most accurate statement?

    a. All Windows Server 2003 domains are native-mode domains.

    b. A domain with one Windows NT 4 domain controller can be set to operate in native mode.

    c. An administrator must set the domain to operate in native mode.

    d. Active Directory automatically controls when a domain is in native mode and when it is in mixed mode.

5. Which is the best choice for a location to create a new user object?

   a. In an OU called employees

   b. In the Domain Controllers OU

   c. In the root container of the domain

   d. Anywhere except in the Users container

6. Active Directory Users and Computers automatically creates the _____ property from other information that you supply, but it can be changed.

7. Which statement is the most accurate?

   a. Windows NT Workstation clients normally use the userPrincipalName to log on to an Active Directory domain.

   b. Windows XP clients can use the userPrincipalName or the sAMAccountName to log on to an Active Directory domain.

   c. You cannot use the userPrincipalName to log on to a domain that is in native mode.

   d. You cannot use the userPrincipalName unless the domain is in native mode.

8. When creating a new user object, Active Directory Users and Computers issues a query to the _____ to make sure the userPrincipalName is unique in the forest.

9. All user objects must have a password because the password attribute is a mandatory attribute. True or False?

10. Active Directory Users and Computers uses _____ to communicate with the Active Directory domain controllers, even if it is running on the same machine.

11. Every attribute of a user object can be accessed by using Active Directory Users and Computers, unless the schema has been extended. True or False?

12. In what circumstances is a user account locked out?

   a. When it is first created, but has not yet been used.

   b. When it is locked out by an administrator, perhaps because an employee is fired.

   c. When Active Directory detects too many failed logon attempts.

   d. When the password is not complex enough to meet domain policy.

13. In addition to the Member tab of a group object's properties, where else can information about group memberships be seen in Active Directory Users and Computers?

14. A user has forgotten her password. What can be done?

   a. Delete the user object for her account and create a new object with the same name.

   b. Use the Active Directory Users and Computers console to reset her password.

   c. Use the Movetree utility to reset her password.

   d. Log on to her workstation as an administrator and run the newpass command.

15. The _____ scope for groups is available only if the domain is in native mode.

16. A(n) _____ group is only used to send e-mail to multiple recipients.

17. You can change the type of a group in a native-mode domain. True or False?

18. You can change the type or scope of a group in a mixed-mode domain. True or False?

19. A good OU structure will support which of the following?

   a. A logical browsing structure

   b. Delegation of control and permissions

   c. Logical application of Group Policy

   d. All of the above

20. Objects can be easily moved between _____ using an Active Directory Users and Computers placeholder.

HEARTLAND HOSPITAL CASE PROJECTS

In Case Project 4–5 in Chapter 4, you were given the opportunity to implement the structure that you had designed for Heartland Hospital, if you had the equipment available to do so. One alternative to additional equipment is virtual machine software, such as VMware (*www.vmware.com*). If you do not have equipment available to create a separate Active Directory implementation for the Heartland Hospital case projects, then set up an OU in your own domain to represent the Heartland Hospital forest.

The remaining cases will assume that the forest name chosen was *home.heartlandhospital.org*. To create an OU representing this in your own domain, preface it with your student number to avoid conflicts with your partner. For example, if you are Student 1 in the oneandtwo domain, you would create an OU named *01.home.HeartlandHospital.org* and your partner would create one named *02.home.heartlandhospital.org*. This situation is shown in Figure 5-37. Also, if you and other students (including your partner) are both creating objects in the same forest, you must make sure that the usernames are unique. The easiest way to do this is to include your assigned student/computer number at the beginning or the end, such as maryfirth01 rather than just maryfirth.

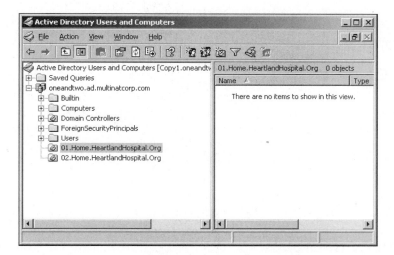

Figure 5-37   Using an OU to represent the Heartland Hospital structure

Your basic design of Active Directory is complete and you've created an empty, pristine Active Directory environment. You now need to begin populating your forest with everyone and everything that Heartland Hospital needs to place in its Active Directory structure. In the following projects, you will create the users, contacts, groups, and resources that Active Directory was designed to encompass.

Case Project 5-1: Creating Users

Using the Heartland Hospital organization chart from Chapter 3 (Figure 3-1), you can begin the process of creating your user accounts in Active Directory. Create user objects for S. Thompson, C. Barton, B. Collins, M. Cheng, and L. Bailey. For now, set their passwords to "p@ssw0rd" but set their accounts so the password must be changed at their next logon. Choose at least three more users from the organizational chart and create objects for them as well. If you wish, you may create user accounts for other users shown on the chart.

Case Project 5-2: Managing Users

After creating the Heartland Hospital users, you will now need to manage these users by configuring additional settings in Active Directory. Use Table 5-1 to enter job, department, and telephone information for the users shown in the table. Use the organizational chart to enter job and department information for the other users you created. If you wish, you may enter sample telephone numbers for them as well.

Review the organizational chart and other hospital sample documents and choose any other attributes that you think should be included. Make sure each user object has sufficient detail. Be prepared to explain your decisions in terms of the hospital business model and needs.

Table 5-1   Hospital user information

Name	Title	Department	Telephone
Silvanus P. Thompson	Hospital Director	Office of the Director	x5551
Clara Barton	Director of Patient Services	Patient Services	x5552
Brian Collins	Director of Professional Services	Professional Services	x5553
Michele Cheng	Director of Administration & Finance	Administration & Finance	x5554
Leah Bailey	Director of Ethics & Legal	Ethics & Legal	x5555

Case Project 5-3: Using Contacts

During a recent staff meeting, Ida Goldberg made the suggestion to use the Heartland Hospital Active Directory as a repository for patient account information, such as name, address, and room number. Based on your knowledge of Active Directory, prepare a response to this suggestion. Is this a good idea in this environment? Either on your own, with your partner, or in a small group, examine or discuss both the positive and negative aspects of doing so. Which attributes could be used to store this information? Be prepared to present your findings to the class and instructor.

Create at least three contacts that represent patients. Include imaginary names, e-mail addresses, and telephone numbers. (Remember to use your student number to keep each contact name unique in the forest.)

Case Project 5-4: Working with Groups

Users and contacts need to be in groups to ease the management of your domain. Create a security group for each department. Populate each group with the user objects created from that department. (Remember to use your student number to keep each group name unique in the forest.)

Case Project 5-5: Creating Other Resource Objects

To enhance the Active Directory experience for your Heartland Hospital users, you can now begin adding other resources to Active Directory. In an organization the size of Heartland Hospital, many additional objects exist that can be migrated into the Active Directory design. Examine the hospital network diagram to discover the various resources distributed throughout Heartland Hospital and determine which resource objects can be added to the Active Directory.

Choose at least three resources and create objects to represent them in Active Directory. Because printer objects can only be created if the printer is available, ask your instructor which printer path you should use to represent printers. (Remember to include your student number to make sure each object's name is unique in the forest.)

Case Project 5-6: Organizing Objects in the Active Directory

You've added objects to the Heartland Hospital Active Directory, and you've probably made these additions into the default containers. Is that the best choice for your implementation? What advantages, in terms of efficiency of design and implementation, could be achieved by segmenting your Active Directory implementation with additional OUs? Can you use a revised OU design to improve delegation of administrative authority? If so, use the skills you've learned in this chapter, as well as in Chapter 4, to create and move OUs as necessary.

Case Project 5-7: Moving Objects between OUs

If you decided to create additional OUs in the Heartland Hospital Active Directory, you may need to move objects to their new OUs. Plan the move process carefully, and record your moves using appropriate documentation. Remember to plan before you click. Discuss the planned moves with your partner and/or instructor, then move the objects that you agreed would be better placed in a different OU.

5

6

SECURING AND PROTECTING
THE NETWORK

> **After reading this chapter and completing the exercises,
> you will be able to:**
>
> ♦ Explain basic security concepts in an Active Directory computer network, including discretionary access control lists (DACLs), system access control lists (SACLs), and security principals
> ♦ Demonstrate the use of DACLs to control access to objects in Active Directory
> ♦ Demonstrate the use of DACLs to control access to network resources
> ♦ Describe the user authentication process in an Active Directory domain

In the early chapters of this book, you learned a great deal about the structure of Active Directory and how to design an effective Active Directory forest. In Chapter 5, you learned how to create and manipulate the objects in Active Directory that represent users of your network and some of its available resources. In this chapter, you will see how those objects are used to control access to resources on the network; that is, you will learn how to protect your network by limiting access to your network resources.

There are two important aspects to consider when implementing security (or access control) in a network. First, someone must decide who should have access to what. This is not a trivial decision, nor is it a decision that should be left only to the staff operating the network. It is a business decision. Just like airport security, the more secure things are, the less convenient it is for users. Deciding how much security is enough is a decision that should be made on a case-by-case basis. Secondly, after the roles and policies have been decided, the network administrators have to implement the proper access controls. Accordingly, this chapter will open with a look at DACLs and SACLs, which will lead to a detailed look at security principals, including a close examination of the role of SIDs. We will also look at how groups can make an administrator's job easier. In addition, this chapter provides discussion and examples of how to use inheritance and the delegation of control, based on the granularity available in Active Directory permissions, to manage the protection of your network. This discussion will cover resources such as NTFS, shared folders, and the Windows registry.

We will also examine how the authentication process works, including Kerberos authentication, NTLM authentication, PKI Certificate-based methods, and two-factor authentication.

Of course, there is nothing to stop you from operating a computer network in which every user has full access to all resources. However in doing so, you are just waiting for trouble. Even in a small network at a small business, there is still confidential information, and there are still configurations that should not be changed. In any serious network, security must be in place and access must be controlled appropriately.

SECURITY CONCEPTS IN ACTIVE DIRECTORY

In Chapter 1, you were introduced to the building blocks of Active Directory, including objects and the classes that define objects. If you recall, some of these objects were described as security principals. To review, a security principal is a user object, an iNetOrgPerson object, a computer, or a security group. What makes security principals special is an attribute called the **objectSID**, commonly referred to as the **security identifier (SID)**.

To fully appreciate security, you must first understand the terms that are used for its implementation in a Windows Server 2003 network. Once you understand these terms, you can then discuss how they relate, and hopefully strengthen your understanding of how security is managed in a Windows Server 2003 network.

A security principal is defined as "an account that is automatically assigned a security identifier to control access to resources." In turn, a SID is defined as "a value that uniquely identifies each user, group, computer account, and logon session on a network." A **DACL** is defined as "an access control list that is controlled by the owner of an object and that specifies the access that particular users or groups can have to the object." A **SACL** is defined as "an access control list that controls the generation of audit messages for attempts to access a securable object." Note that for a system access control list, the ability to get or set an object's SACL is a privilege typically held only by system administrators. An access control list (ACL) is a list of security protections that apply to an object. An entry in an ACL is called an **access control entry (ACE)**.

Now that the key terms have been defined, you can learn more about the objectSID attribute defined on a user account (a security principal) and compare this to another object in Active Directory that doesn't contain SID (and is therefore not a security principal).

Activity 6-1: Viewing the objectSID Attribute

Time Required: 5 minutes

Objective: To view the objectSID attribute for selected Active Directory objects.

Description: This activity will reinforce which objects have SIDs and how they are stored. You will examine the objectSID attribute of one of the users you created in Chapter 5, and look at a contact object for comparison. You will also see how the SID is stored in raw, binary format.

1. If necessary, turn on your computer and log on as the administrator from your own domain.

2. Click **Start**, click **Run**, type **adsiedit.msc**, and then click **OK** to open the ADSI Edit console.

3. In the tree pane, expand the domain node until you can see one of the users you created in Chapter 5. Note that the users, like other objects, will appear in the details pane when you click on the OU that contains them.

4. Right-click your user object, and then click **Properties**.

5. Uncheck **Show optional attributes**.

6. In the table labeled Attributes, locate the attribute **objectSID**. If necessary, scroll through the list of attributes to it.

7. Use the scroll bar at the bottom to view as much information as possible.

8. Click the **objectSID** line, and then click **Edit**. (*Warning*: Do not change the values.)

9. If you wish, view the SID in decimal format by changing the settings in the drop-down box.

10. Click **Cancel**.

11. Click **Cancel** again.

12. Locate one of the contacts you created in Chapter 5.

13. Repeat Steps 4–6 on a contact object. Notice that you cannot find the objectSID attribute.

14. Close any property pages that are open by clicking **Cancel**.

15. Close the ADSI Edit console.

16. If you are not proceeding immediately to the next activity, log off your computer.

In general terms, SIDs work in conjunction with ACEs found in DACLs to control access to resources or objects. SIDs also work in conjunction with ACEs in SACLs to control auditing of the use of resources or objects. A SID contains a **relative identifier (RID)** and a **domain identifier**. When accessing a resource, a user presents an **access token** that contains their SID, as well as SIDs from the groups in which they have membership.

Our discussion on security begins by exploring security principals, and then moves on to examine DACLs and SACLs.

 Our discussion of DACLs and SACLs will start with how they apply to objects in the directory, but remember that the same principles apply to NTFS, file shares, and many other resources on the network.

6

Security Principals

A **security principal** can be given permissions to access a resource. In the statement: "Bill is allowed to print to the color printer," Bill is the security principal, the color printer is the resource, and "allowed to print" is the permission. In slightly more technical terms, the user Bill is granted the print permission on the color printer.

Groups can also be granted permissions. For example, a company president might say, "I want everyone who works here to be able to read the Microsoft Word files that contain our company policies." Notice that the president is not giving complete or unlimited permissions. He said that the employees could *read* the files, not delete or change them. The ability to control not only who can access a resource, but also what they can or can't do with that resource is a key feature of network access control.

 Using groups to grant permissions in a network environment is typically considered a best practice because it minimizes the amount of time required to assign access permissions and provide ongoing maintenance.

 When you are talking with nontechnical people in business, they will use plain statements like, "Bill is allowed to change that file," rather than talking about rights and privileges. Sometimes, you will have to translate between terms used by those well-versed in technology, and those who aren't.

It is important to fully understand the role of security principals, and therefore its definition bears repeating: A security principal in Active Directory can be a user, an InetOrgPerson object, a computer, or a security group. Unless specifically noted otherwise, anything you can do with a user object, you can do with an InetOrgPerson object, provided that your domain is set to the Windows Server 2003 functionality level.

It is also important to note that a contact cannot be given permission to access resources because it is not a security principal. The key difference between a security principal, such as a user, and other objects, such as contacts, is the presence of the SID.

Security Identifiers

Microsoft defines the objectSID attribute as a binary value that specifies the SID of the user. The SID is a unique value used to identify the user as a security principal.

There are a number of formats used to display the SID of an object. If you look at the value using ADSI Edit, the default is hexadecimal notation. More often than not, you will see SIDs expressed in a format called **Security Descriptor Definition Language (SDDL)**. A SID expressed in SDDL looks something like this: *S-1-5-21-606747145-436374069-1343024091-1166*. You may have seen this format appear briefly in the Windows tools while the system is searching for the name that matches the SID. Table 6–1 shows SIDs from a test domain.

Table 6-1   Sample SIDs

Security Principal	Security Identifier
User1	S-1-5-21-1993962763-287218729-725345543-1628
User2	S-1-5-21-1993962763-287218729-725345543-2109
User3	S-1-5-21-1993962763-287218729-725345543-1638
User4	S-1-5-21-1993962763-287218729-725345543-1616
User5	S-1-5-21-1993962763-287218729-725345543-1629
Domain Admins	S-1-5-21-1993962763-287218729-725345543-512
BUILTIN\Administrators	S-1-5-32-544
Everyone	S-1-1-0
Group1	S-1-5-21-1993962763-287218729-725345543-1758

A SID in SDDL format begins with S to indicate it is a SID, and is followed by three to seven numbers, separated by hyphens that divide the SID into parts. Normal users and groups will contain all seven parts.

The first number is the revision level of the SDDL format, and hasn't changed since Windows NT was introduced, so it will probably always be 1. Notice the revision level for User1 highlighted in the following example: *S-1-5-21-1993962763-287218729-725345543-1628*.

The next portion of the SID is called the identifier authority, and will be 5 for normal users and groups. The identifier authority for User1 is as follows: *S-1-5-21-1993962763-287218729-725345543-1628*. Most of the SIDs that you will be working with will begin with S-1-5.

SIDs that have an identifier authority of 1 or 3 are special and well known. The term "well known" indicates that it is recognized by all Windows systems to mean the same thing. It also becomes well known in the sense that it is easily recognized by experienced administrators, but the term is technical and refers to the fact that it is known to the operating system. Among the well-known SIDs are: S-1-1-0, which is the everyone group; S-1-3-0, which belongs to the special creator owner group; and S-1-3-1, which belongs to the special creator group.

The next section is called a subauthority identifier. For User1, the subauthority identifier is 21, highlighted in the following example: *S-1-5-21-1993962763-287218729-725345543-1628*. The value 21 indicates that this SID is for a security principal in a domain. Other values can also be used, such as 32, which indicates the BUILTIN groups. It is beyond the scope of this book to delve into the arcane and mysterious history of how and why subauthority identifiers came about. The value 21 is what you will see most often, and SIDS with a 21 in this position will have a domain identifier as well, which will be discussed in the next section.

Domain and Relative Identifiers

When a domain is first created, a set of three long integer numbers is calculated. When used together, these numbers are guaranteed to be unique. Every object that belongs to this domain will have the same three numbers. Each number is 32 bits long, for a total of 96 bits. These bits are called the domain identifier. The domain identifier for User1 is highlighted in the following example: *S-1-5-21-**1993962763-287218729-725345543**-1628*. Notice that all of the other security principals in Table 6-1 are from the same domain and have the same number in this part of their SID.

It is not clear how many domains Microsoft was expecting its customers to create, but 2^{96} (2 to the 96th power) is a very large number—more than 79 octillion. (You can calculate this number by figuring out how many different values can be stored in 96 bits. For example, 8 bits can store 256 different values.)

Another 32 bits is used to uniquely identify the object within the domain, allowing for more than 4 billion individual SIDs within a domain. This number is called the RID because it is *relative* to the domain. The RID for User1 is highlighted in the following example: *S-1-5-21-1993962763-287218729-725345543-**1628***.

Each time an object with a SID is created, the domain assigns it a RID. Each DC has a pool of RIDs available for new objects, and requests more from the RID Master as needed. (The RID Master is one particular DC in a domain. The role of RID Master is discussed in Chapter 9.) The DC combines the domain identifier and the RID to create the last four parts of the object's SID.

Kerberos Tickets and Access Tokens

To access resources on the network, the user's operating system (which will be referred to as the "user's computer") presents either a **Kerberos ticket** or an access token.

Kerberos tickets are used when all of the computers involved in a domain can support Kerberos in compatible implementations, generally on computers running Windows 2000 or newer Microsoft operating systems that participate in an Active Directory domain. When Kerberos authentication is not available, the user's computer uses NTLM authentication. These two types of authentication (Kerberos and NTLM) are covered in more detail later in this chapter.

As part of the authentication process, Windows builds an access token that contains several important pieces of information, including the user's SID. A number of additional SIDs will also be in the user's access token, including the SID for every group of which the user is a member. This access token is then presented whenever a user needs access to a resource. The server protecting the resource will compare the SIDs in the access token to the DACL and SACL on the resource, and either grant or deny access based on this information.

Activity 6-2: Access Tokens

Time Required: 5 minutes

Objective: To view the contents of an access token.

Description: In this activity you will use the whoami utility to show the contents of your access token, including the SID for your account and any groups of which you are a member. Knowing how to use this utility is useful because it can be used to troubleshoot resource access in a network environment.

During this exercise, you will work with another student in the classroom.

1. If necessary, turn on your computer and log on as the administrator from your own domain.

2. Click **Start**, click **Run**, type **cmd**, and then click **OK**.

3. At the prompt, type **whoami /user**, and then press **Enter**.

4. Record your SID for future reference.

5. Compare your SID to your partner's SID. Identify the parts of the two SIDs that are the same and the parts that differ.

6. Compare your SID to that of someone operating a different domain. Identify the parts of the two SIDs that are the same and the parts that differ.

7. To view your group memberships, type **whoami /groups**, and then press **Enter**.

8. Scroll, if necessary, to view all of the groups of which you are a member. Observe which groups have domain SIDs and which are special or well known.

9. Type **exit** and press **Enter**.

10. Close all open windows. If you are not continuing immediately to another activity, log off your computer.

Discretionary Access Control Lists (DACL)

All resources that can be secured have a DACL associated with them. In the case of an Active Directory object, the DACL, along with the SACL and ownership information, is stored in an Active Directory attribute called ntSecurityDescriptor. To help remember the role of a DACL, recall that an object can only be accessed at the discretion of its owner.

A DACL is a list of ACEs, each of which specifies a "who" and a permission. For example, in the statement: "Human Resources staff can modify this object," an ACE grants access to the Human Resources staff (the "who") and specifies the appropriate permission ("modify") to change the object. The Human Resources group would be listed in the ACE not by name, but by SID.

When a member of the Human Resources staff tries to modify the object, Active Directory compares each SID in the user's access token to each ACE until a match is found. In this case, a match would be found on the ACE that gives permission to the group, and the user would be allowed to make the change.

If a user who is not a member of the Human Resources group tries to make the change, what would happen? First of all, let us establish that the user is not an administrator and has not been granted any special permissions. His access token would contain a SID for himself, one for everyone, and probably one for the domain users group. A few other well-known SIDs would also be present, such as the authenticated users SID, and either the interactive or network SID. None of those special groups, however, have been given permissions to change this object. The end result? The system would compare each SID in the user's access token to each ACE and find no matches. Therefore, the user would be denied permission to make the change and would receive an error.

Each ACE can be very specific. An ACE can specify that a security principal is able to read but not change an object. Depending on the class of the object being protected by the DACL, there are various options for what can be included in an ACE. This is a very powerful feature of Windows Server 2003, as it allows control not only of who has access, but of the specific level of access for each user.

System Access Control Lists (SACL)

A SACL has the same structure as a DACL. It contains ACEs that list a SID and a permission. However, instead of determining whether the SID is granted access to the resource, a SACL determines if the access is audited. Auditing allows us to track changes to files, jobs that are sent to a printer, and even attempts to log on to the network. Using a SACL, you can control which user's access is recorded by the system.

Because all users have the everyone SID in their access token, including it in an ACE for a SACL allows an administrator to turn on auditing for everyone accessing the resource in question. By carefully choosing your SACL entries, you can control the level of auditing in your environment.

ACEs that Allow or Deny

When you edit a DACL or SACL, you will notice that you can create ACEs that allow or deny access. It is very important to understand the effects of each type of ACE.

The first thing to remember is that if no match is found between an access token and a DACL, access is not permitted. This is sometimes called an "implicit deny," because the system will automatically deny access, unless it has been explicitly told to allow access. Imagine a doorman at a fancy ball—if someone is not on his list, he or she isn't getting in.

Normally, most access control entries allow access. If you want to allow the Queen of England to come to your party, then you would add her name to the doorman's list. In technical terms, if you had a resource named "party" and the Queen tried to access that resource, the system would match a SID in her access token with the SID in the ACE, allowing her access.

You can also use ACEs to deny access to a resource. For example, if Billy is not welcome at the party, adding his name to the doorman's list with a big warning not to let him in would ensure he was kept out.

The system would match Billy's SID (in his access token) with a SID in the ACE; however this time, the match would say to deny his access to the resource.

You may wonder why this would be necessary. After all, if no ACE match is found, access is denied. The biggest reason that deny ACEs are used, is to change the effect of permissions that a user would otherwise have as a member of a group.

The ability to deny access to a resource can save the administrator a great deal of time. For example, it is easier to grant access to groups of users than to grant it individually. (Remember that group SIDs are also included in the access token.) For example, our doorman's list might say, "admit all reigning monarchs," as opposed to listing them all individually. As a member of that group, the Queen of England's access token would have a SID to match the SID in the ACE, and she would be admitted. However, there may be a member of this group that you don't want to allow in, such as the Queen of Broken Hearts. By employing a deny ACE, her access token would also contain a SID that matches an ACE, but it would deny access instead of granting it.

Remember, a deny permission overrides all other permission. Most users are members of several groups and will match SIDs on several ACEs, allowing them the combined permissions of all their groups. If a user were a member of both group A and group B, he or she would receive the permissions given to both groups, with two exceptions—deny overrides allow and owners can own. Let's look at these exceptions more closely.

As an example of the deny overrides allow exception, suppose you were a member of both group A and group B. What would happen if group A is allowed access and group B is denied? Our doorman would know what to do—the deny always applies first.

> Deny ACEs are listed first in the DACL or SACL, allowing them to be matched first. If a SID in the access token matches a denying ACE, access is denied.

As an example of the owners can own exception, consider what would happen if you removed all of the ACEs from an object's DACL, or you entered an ACE that denied access to the everyone group. Is it possible to lock out everyone, including the administrators of Active Directory? Thankfully, no. Every object in the directory has an owner, as shown in Figure 6-1. The owner of an object can always gain access to that object by resetting its permissions. By default, the owner of Active Directory objects is the Domain Admins Group. An administrator on a DC can also use the take ownership command to become the owner of an object in Active Directory. The owner of an object is always able to access and reset its permissions.

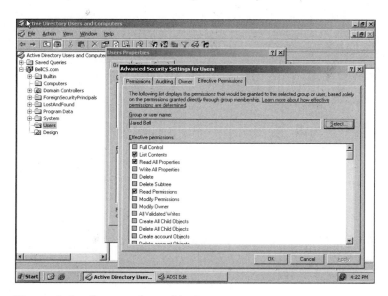

Figure 6-1   Owner of an object

Although an administrator can take ownership, it is important to realize that this is a one-way process. After the ownership of an object is taken, it cannot be given back. The old owner would need to be granted the correct permissions to take back ownership.

Inheritance

Permissions can be applied directly to an object in the directory, or they can be **inherited**. If a directory contains thousands or millions of entries, it would be tedious and time consuming to apply permissions to each individual object. Instead, permissions can be inherited from parent objects, such as OUs.

In Active Directory, each ACE is marked to indicate whether it was directly applied or inherited. If a change is made to permissions on an OU, all objects in that OU are updated with the inherited permissions. You do have control over which permissions are inherited, allowing you to exempt child objects from being granted the same permissions as their parents. To help administrators see which permissions apply, the Active Directory Users and Computers console includes a tab to display the effective permissions on a given object.

Groups in Security

There is no good reason to grant permissions explicitly to individual users. In a large domain, it is nearly impossible to manage, and in a small domain it is a bad habit that usually indicates poor planning in the control of access to resources. In addition to saving administrators from unmanageable headaches, remember that all permissions need an ACE. A DACL consisting of 500 individually granted permissions would be much larger, and take much longer to process.

In a single-domain forest, there is absolutely no difference between the effects of domain local groups, global groups, and universal groups. You should, however be consistent in your choices. Because global groups, such as Domain Admins, are created by default, it is probably a good idea to create your groups as global as well. Some administrators prefer to assign permissions to the global groups, even in a small domain. This is shown in Figure 6-2.

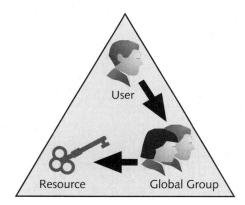

Figure 6-2   Using global groups in a single-domain forest

However, if you plan to use machine local accounts (that is, accounts that can be used only on one server, perhaps a Web server), then you should use machine local groups to grant permissions to the resource, as shown in Figure 6-3.

The situation is more complicated in a multiple-domain forest. There are three main approaches:

- You can use basically the same approach as in a single-domain forest: assign users to global groups, assign global groups to domain local groups, and grant permissions to the domain local groups. This approach, shown in Figure 6-4, works well if you have a small number of domains and only one site. (Sites are discussed in Chapter 7.) This approach is less effective if you have resources that will be accessed by users in many domains or multiple sites.

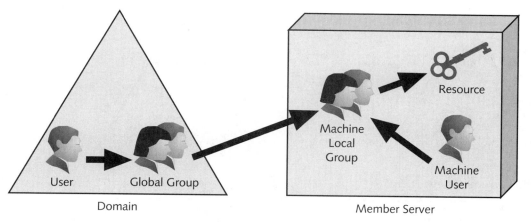

Figure 6-3 Using global and machine local groups in a single-domain forest

- You can choose to use only universal groups. This works well in single-domain environments, but does not work well in a large forest.

- Use domain local, global, and universal groups. This advanced approach requires a great deal of understanding of how information is replicated (discussed in Chapter 8), especially between sites (discussed in Chapter 7). This is probably the best choice if you want the same group of users to access resources in different domains. This approach is illustrated in Figure 6-5.

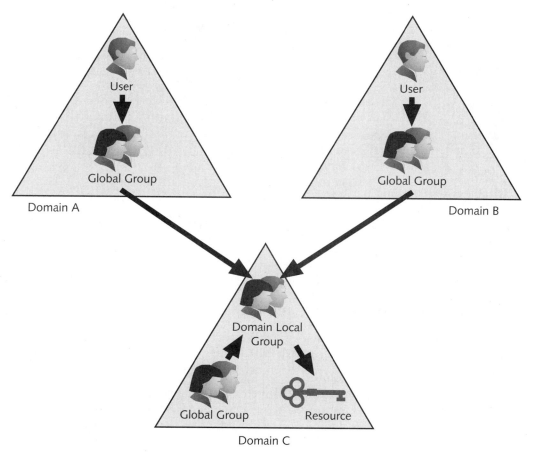

Figure 6-4 Simple approach to groups in multiple domains

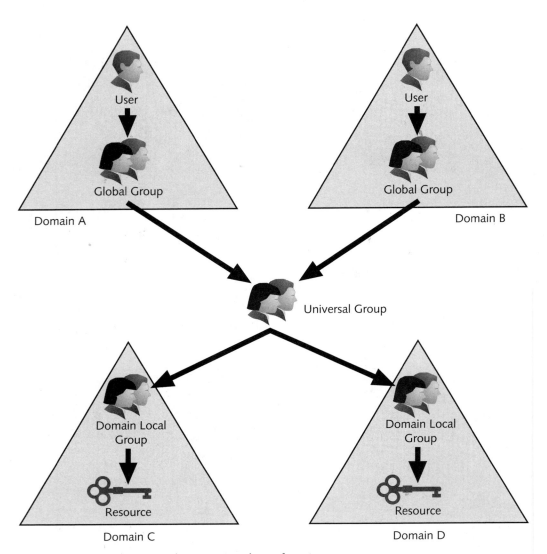

Figure 6-5   Using universal groups in a large forest

 If you are tempted to grant permissions directly to a user, you probably haven't planned your access control well enough.

PROTECTING OBJECTS IN ACTIVE DIRECTORY

Each object in Active Directory has an owner, a DACL, and a SACL. This means that access to any object can be allowed, prevented, or audited. The default permissions work well in a small domain, but are not adequate in a large forest. Active Directory has been designed with security in mind.

To fully appreciate the security available in Active Directory, and to be a pro at manipulating it, it is important to understand two security-related features of Active Directory. First, is the concept of delegation of control and the wizard that assists this task, and second, is the ability to control access on a very granular level.

Delegation of Control

Delegation of control is all about giving data owners the ability to manage their own objects. As discussed in Chapter 3, a service owner is responsible for the operation of the directory service, but a data owner is responsible for its content. Giving data owners the ability to modify only certain objects, or only certain attributes, is called **delegation of control**.

An administrator can delegate control manually, but the easiest, most effective way involves two steps:

- First, organize so that all objects in an OU have the same data owner.

- Second, use the Delegation of Control wizard to create the appropriate ACEs in the DACL on the OU, and then allow them to be inherited to the objects in the OU.

Activity 6-3: Using the Delegation of Control Wizard

Time Required: 10 minutes

Objective: To grant permissions on an OU using the Delegation of Control wizard.

Description: In this activity you will use the Delegation of Control wizard to assign permissions to a group. You will begin by creating a new user and a new group to represent a help desk in the organization. You will then use the wizard to assign appropriate permissions to the group, allowing members of the help desk staff group to reset passwords for some users.

1. If necessary, turn on your computer and log on as the administrator from your own domain.

2. Using the Active Directory Users and Computers console and the skills and knowledge learned in earlier chapters, create the following:

   - An OU called ***xx*-UsersWhoForgetPasswordsOften** (where *xx* represents your assigned student number).

   - A user called ***xx*-HelpDeskUser** (where *xx* represents your assigned student number).

   - A global security group called ***xx*-HelpDeskGroup** (where *xx* represents your assigned student number).

3. Using the Active Directory Users and Computers console and the skills and knowledge learned in earlier chapters, make the new *xx*-HelpDeskUser a member of the new *xx*-HelpDeskGroup.

4. In the Active Directory Users and Computers console, find and select the ***xx*-UsersWhoForgetPasswords Often** OU.

5. On the Action menu, click **Delegate Control**.

6. Click **Next**.

7. Click **Add**.

8. Type ***xx*-HelpDeskGroup** (where *xx* represents your assigned student number).

9. Click **OK**.

10. Click **Next**.

11. Check the **Reset user passwords and force password change at next logon** checkbox.

12. Click **Next**.

13. Review the summary information, and then click **Finish**.

14. If desired, view the properties on your *xx*-UsersWhoForgetPasswordOften OU and use the Security tab to locate the permissions added by the wizard.

15. Close all open windows. If you are not continuing immediately to another activity, log off your computer.

Remember, there is no way to automatically undo the effects of the wizard, so document any changes you make. If you prefer, you can manually create the security settings without the wizard.

Granular Control

In the days of yore when dinosaurs roamed the earth and Windows NT was new, delegation was largely an all-or-nothing proposition. You either were a Domain Admin or you weren't. Administrators were all-powerful and everyone else wasn't. It was nearly impossible to separate data ownership from service ownership in the directory without spending a lot of time or money on custom software or third-party solutions.

With Active Directory however, you can delegate control with precision. Normally, a data owner is given fairly broad permissions over objects contained in an OU. Although, it is possible to be more exact when the situation warrants. Each ACE created on an Active Directory object offers choices for how it is applied:

- Should it apply to all objects or just certain types of objects?

- Should it apply to this container, objects in this container, objects in child containers below this container, or some combination of these?

- Should it apply to all attributes, or just certain attributes?

- To whom are you giving, or from whom are you denying the permission?

 Whenever permissions are changed, either manually or by using the Delegation of Control wizard, you should carefully record or document the changes and the reasons for them.

This ability to granularly control exactly who can do what is an important part of the flexibility of Active Directory. The Advanced Security Settings dialog box in the Active Directory Users and Computers console features a tab to display effective permissions for any user or group, as shown in Figure 6-6, and a command button to reset the DACL to its default state, as shown in Figure 6-7.

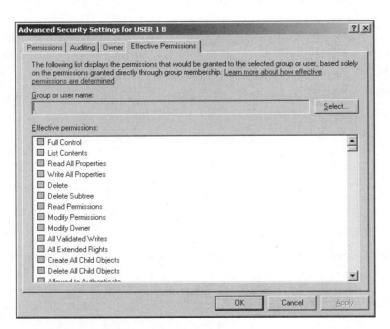

Figure 6-6   Effective Permissions tab

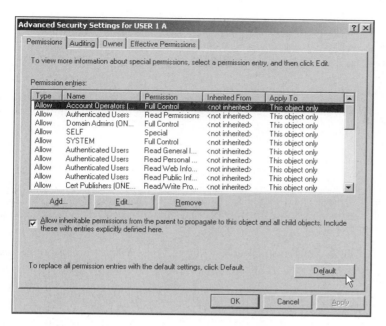

Figure 6-7   Default command button to reset DACL

Activity 6-4: Viewing Effective Permissions on an Active Directory Object

Time Required: 5 minutes

Objective: To view the effective permissions on an object in the directory.

Description: Because of the complex combinations of group memberships, inheritance, and standard and special permissions, it can be difficult to calculate what the effective permissions on an object will be for a given user. In this activity, you will use the Active Directory Users and Computers console to display effective permissions.

1. If necessary, turn on your computer and log on as the administrator from your own domain.

2. Click **Start**, point to **Administrative Tools**, and then click **Active Directory Users and Computers**. If necessary, check the Advanced Features option on the View menu.

3. Use the tree pane to navigate to the *xx*-UsersWhoForgetPasswordsOften OU (where *xx* represents your assigned student number).

4. Create a new user in this OU, named ***xx*-Chap6User** (where *xx* represents your assigned student number).

5. Right-click the new ***xx*-Chap6User**, and then click **Properties**.

6. Click the **Security** tab.

7. Click **Advanced**.

8. Click the **Effective Permissions** tab.

9. Click **Select**.

10. Type ***xx*-Chap6User** (where *xx* represents your assigned student number).

11. Click **OK**.

12. Observe in the Effective Permissions area that some items are now checked. This represents the effective permissions that this user has use of to control his or her own object. The user has the change password permission (because users can change their own password in the default configuration) and several read permissions.

13. Click **Select**.

14. Type **xx–HelpDeskGroup** (where *xx* represents your assigned student number).

15. Click **OK**.

16. Notice that this group has more effective permissions.

17. Repeat Steps 13–15 for the **xx–HelpDeskUser** (where *xx* represents your assigned student number), for **Domain Admins**, and for **Authenticated Users**. Observe the different effective permissions that are available.

18. Click **Cancel**.

19. Click **Cancel** again.

20. Close all open windows. If you are not continuing immediately to another activity, log off your computer.

To make management of permissions easier for administrators, Active Directory offers standard and special permissions.

Standard Permissions

Standard permissions are those permissions that are used for everyday tasks, and are found on the main Security tab of an object, as shown in Figure 6-8. For example, the full control permission is used to grant or deny all possible permissions on an object.

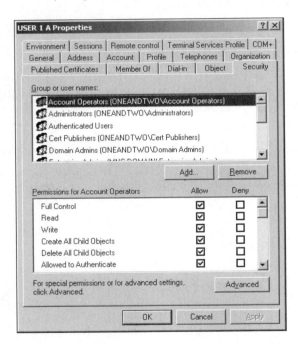

Figure 6-8 Standard permissions in Active Directory

Special Permissions

Special permissions represent the exact and granular permissions available, and can be very specific. To access them, click the Advanced button on the Security tab to open the Advanced Security Settings dialog box. This dialog box is shown in Figure 6-9. Most tasks require only the standard permissions; use special permissions for advanced granular control or special situations.

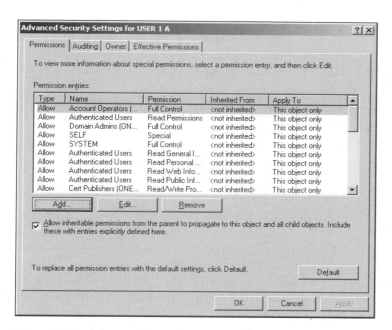

Figure 6-9   Advanced security settings showing special permissions

Activity 6-5: Edit the DACL of an Active Directory Object

Time Required: 10 minutes

Objective: To change the DACL protecting an Active Directory object.

Description: It has been determined that the help desk staff are competent enough to manage all aspects of user objects. In this activity you will remove the permissions created by the Delegation of Control wizard and manually create entries in the DACL that will allow the help desk group to change user objects.

1. If necessary, turn on your computer and log on as the administrator from your own domain.

2. Click **Start**, point to **Administrative Tools**, and then click **Active Directory Users and Computers**.

3. Locate and click the *xx*–**UsersWhoForgetPasswordsOften** OU (where *xx* represents your assigned student number).

4. On the Action menu, click **Rename**, and rename the OU to *xx*–**UsersManagedByHelpDesk** (where *xx* represents your assigned student number).

5. Right-click *xx*–**UsersManagedByHelpDesk** (where *xx* represents your assigned student number), and then click **Properties**.

6. Click the **Security** tab.

7. In the panel labeled Group or user names, click the entry for *xx*-**HelpDeskGroup**, and then click **Remove**. This will remove the entries created by the wizard.

8. Click **Advanced**.

9. Click **Add**.

10. Type *xx*–**HelpDeskGroup** (where *xx* represents your assigned student number).

11. Click **OK**.

12. Click the **Apply onto** drop-down list, and click **User objects**. (You must scroll to the bottom of the list to see the **User objects** entry.)

13. Under **Allow**, check the **Full Control** checkbox.

14. Click **OK**.

15. Click **OK** again.

16. Click **OK** yet again.

17. If desired, review the effective permissions for members of your help desk group using the skills and techniques you learned in Activity 6-4.

18. Close all open windows. If you are not continuing immediately to another activity, log off your computer.

PROTECTING NETWORK RESOURCES

Protecting objects in Active Directory is essential. However, there are a number of other resources on the network that also rely on Active Directory to authenticate users. Most protected resources use a DACL that is similar in format to the one found on Active Directory objects. In the next few sections, you will look at NTFS, printers, shares, and registry keys. Some other related applications will be discussed, such as SQL Servers, which use their own ACL systems for authorization but use Active Directory for authentication.

 Most components of the operating system use the same **security descriptor** and DACL structure. This means that by learning one interface, you can use the same technique with files, shares, printers, and Active Directory objects.

The NT File System (NTFS)

Windows 2003 servers support the **NT File System (NTFS)**. While it is possible to use disks formatted with the simpler **File Allocation Table (FAT)** format, it is not recommend. NTFS is much more robust than FAT, because it uses a journaling or logging system to keep track of changes to a file, so fewer problems occur if the system crashes or loses power during an update. NTFS also assigns a security descriptor to each object, in the same way that Active Directory has security descriptors for Active Directory objects. In fact, the structure of the security descriptors on files and folders is the same as those found on Active Directory objects: Each object in the file system has an owner, a DACL, and a SACL. The DACL and SACL are both composed of a series of ACEs containing SIDs and permissions. The Security tab that is present on all Active Directory objects is also present on files and folders on an NTFS partition. This is an important point because if you format your file system with FAT, you cannot use SACLs and DACLs to control access to these resources.

The difference between an NTFS DACL and an Active Directory DACL is in the types of permissions that can be granted or denied. Rather than permissions that relate to attributes, the NTFS DACL permissions relate to what the users can do with the files and folders. There are also fewer permissions for files, folders, shares, and printers as there are for Active Directory objects. The standard permissions for a file are shown in Figure 6-10, and consist of full control, modify (the ability to change the file or its properties), read and execute, read, and write. In addition to those previously listed for files, a folder also has the standard permission called list folder contents. The standard folder permissions are shown in Figure 6-11.

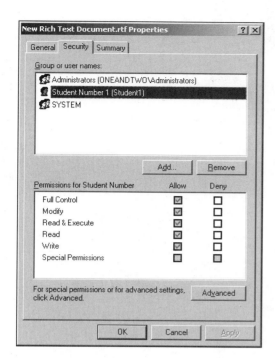

Figure 6-10   Standard file permissions

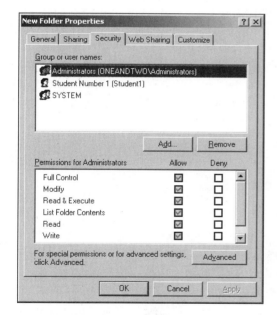

Figure 6-11   Standard folder permissions

NTFS supports a number of special permissions, shown in Figure 6-12.

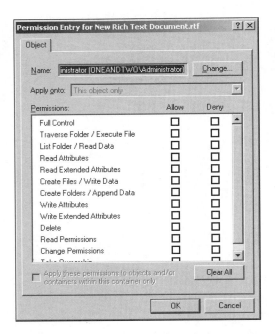

Figure 6-12   NTFS special permissions

The authentication process is where Active Directory plays its biggest role in NTFS security. At logon, the access token is populated to include the user's SID and SIDs from the user's group memberships. When the user accesses a file, the SIDs in the file's DACL are compared to the SIDs in the user's access token in search of a match, just like accessing an Active Directory object. The same rules for allowing and denying access apply.

NTFS permissions can also be inherited. For instance, folders and files inside a folder usually inherit the permissions set on the folder. For example, if *c:\Folder1* has a DACL that includes read permissions for everyone, then that permission is normally inherited to *c:\Folder1\Folder2*. You can add additional permissions to just Folder2 (by adding ACEs to the Folder2 DACL), and/or prevent the inheritance and assign a new DACL to Folder2 that does not contain the inherited ACEs.

Activity 6-6: Controlling Permissions on a File

Time Required: 10 minutes

Objective: To practice managing NTFS permissions on a file.

Description: To comply with corporate IT policy, a log file must be created where the help desk staff can record instances in which they reset a user's password. Only administrators and help desk staff should be able to read or change this log file. In this activity, you will create the file and set appropriate permissions.

1. If necessary, turn on your computer and log on as the administrator from your own domain.

2. Click **Start**, and then click **Windows Explorer**.

3. Using the tree pane on the left, navigate to the root of the C: drive.

4. Create a new folder on C: called **Help Desk Logs** by right-clicking in the details pane, clicking **New**, and then clicking **Folder**. Name the folder **Help Desk Logs**.

5. Double-click the **Help Desk Logs** folder.

6. Right-click in the details pane, click **New**, and then click **Text Document**.

7. Name the new file **Password Change Log File.txt**.

8. Right-click the new file, and then click **Properties**.

9. Click the **Security** tab.

10. Click **Users**.

11. Click **Remove**.

12. Because this is an inherited permission, you cannot remove it directly, so an error appears. Read the message that appears, and then click **OK**.

13. Click **Advanced**.

14. Uncheck the **Allow inheritable permissions from the parent** checkbox.

15. Read the message that appears, and then click **Copy**.

16. Click **OK**.

17. Click **Users**.

18. Click **Remove**. Now, the removal succeeds.

19. Click **Add**.

20. Type *xx*-**HelpDeskGroup** (where *xx* represents your assigned student number), and click **OK**.

21. Click the entry for *xx*-**HelpDeskGroup** so that it is highlighted.

22. Check the checkbox under **Allow** and beside **Full Control**.

23. Click **OK**.

24. Close all open windows. If you are not continuing immediately to another activity, log off your computer.

Activity 6-7: Creating a SACL to Audit File Access

Time Required: 10 minutes

Objective: To create a SACL on a file resource so that access to the file can be monitored.

Description: In this activity you will create a SACL on the file you just created that will instruct the operating system to record all types of access to the file to monitor who is accessing it. This is a useful skill, because as a network administrator, you will need to activate auditing on your servers to monitor access and watch for intrusion attempts.

1. If necessary, turn on your computer and log on as the administrator from your own domain.

2. Click **Start**, and then click **Windows Explorer**.

3. Using the tree pane on the left, navigate to the **Help Desk Logs** folder created in Activity 6-6 on the C: drive.

4. Right-click in the details pane, right-click the **Password Change Log File.txt** file created in Activity 6-6, and then click **Properties**.

5. Click the **Security** tab.

6. Click **Advanced**.

7. Click the **Auditing** tab.

8. Click **Add**.

9. Type **Everyone**, and click **OK**.

10. Under Successful, check the **Full Control** checkbox. This will cause all of the Successful checkboxes to be checked and instruct the system to audit all successful access attempts.

11. Under Failed, check the **Full Control** checkbox. This will cause all of the Failed boxes to be checked and instruct the system to audit all unsuccessful access attempts—that is, requests that are denied.

12. Click **OK**.

13. Click **OK** again.

14. Click **OK** yet again.

15. Close all open windows. If you are not continuing immediately to another activity, log off your computer.

Activity 6-8: Viewing Attempts to Access a File

Time Required: 10 minutes

Objective: To view the auditing entries created by the system when users access a file with a SACL that includes their SID.

Description: Now that the text file has an appropriate SACL, in this activity, you will simulate access to the file and then view the resulting audit entries. Even though the file has a SACL, you must first activate auditing for the file system.

1. If necessary, turn on your computer and log on as the administrator from your own domain.

2. Click **Start**, point to **Administrative Tools**, and then click **Domain Controller Security Policy**.

3. Using the tree pane, expand items and navigate to **Security Settings**, **Local Policies**, and **Audit Policies**.

4. Click **Audit Policy** in the tree pane.

5. In the details pane, double-click **Audit object access**.

6. Make sure that the **Define these policy settings**, **Success**, and **Failure** checkboxes are checked.

7. Click **OK**.

8. Close all open windows.

9. Click **Start**, and then click **Command Prompt**. At the command prompt, type **gpupdate /force** and press **Enter**. This command forces the policy changes you just made to take effect immediately.

10. Type **exit** and then press **Enter**.

11. Click **Start**, and then click **Windows Explorer**.

12. Using the tree pane on the left, navigate to the **Help Desk Logs** folder created in Activity 6-6 on the C: drive.

13. In the details pane, double-click the **Password Change Log File.txt** file created in Activity 6-6 to open the file in Notepad. The file should be empty; do not add text or change anything in the file at this point.

14. Close the **Notepad** window.

15. In the details pane, double-click the **Password Change Log File.txt** file created in Activity 6-6 to open the file in Notepad. This time, change some of the text in the file.

16. On the **File** menu, click **Save**.

17. Close the Notepad window.

18. Click **Start**, point to **Administrative Tools**, and then click **Event Viewer**.

19. In the tree pane, click the **Security** node.

20. In the details pane, examine the entries related to your logon name and object access by double-clicking an entry. Use the next and previous arrows to locate entries related to opening, closing, and writing changes to the file.

21. Close all open windows. If you are not continuing immediately to another activity, log off your computer.

Printers

In Windows Server 2003, a printer also has a security descriptor with an owner, a DACL, and a SACL. The standard permissions allow you to choose who can print to a printer, who can change printer settings, and who can manage documents. These standard printer permissions are shown in Figure 6-13. Note the use of the special, well-known security principal, creator owner, which allow users to manage their own documents without being able to manage others.

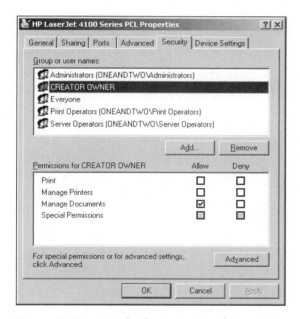

Figure 6-13   Standard permissions for a printer

 Do not confuse the DACL on the printer with the DACL on the Active Directory printer object that may exist for a shared printer. The DACL on the printer controls who can print, while the DACL on the Active Directory object controls who can search for the printer in Active Directory, and who can change the Active Directory object.

File Shares

When accessing files from a network share, the user must first be allowed access to the share, and then access to the file (if it is on an NTFS file system). Share permissions control access via the network. To access the share permissions, click Permissions on the Sharing tab of the folder's property sheet, as shown in Figure 6-14.

Share permissions have very few choices; they are not as granular as either Active Directory permissions or NTFS permissions. With standard permissions, you can allow or deny full control, change, or read access, as shown in Figure 6-15. There are no special permissions for file shares. In situations where more flexibility is needed, ensure that the actual folder is on a hard disk partition formatted with NTFS, and then use NTFS permissions to further restrict access to the folder. Remember, both the NTFS DACL and the share DACL are combined to control access for users who are connecting via the share.

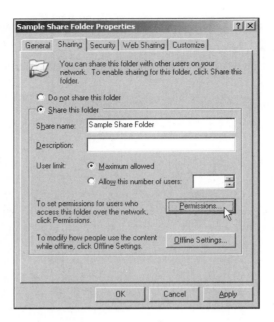

Figure 6-14   Accessing share permissions

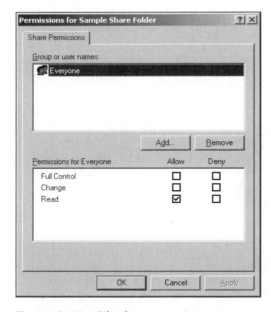

Figure 6-15   File share permissions

 As with printers, do not confuse the DACL on the share with the DACL on the Active Directory shared folder object that may exist for a shared folder. The DACL on the share itself controls who can access files through that share. The DACL on the Active Directory object controls who can search for the shared folder in Active Directory, and who can manage the Active Directory object.

Registry Keys

To control the operation of the computer, Windows operating systems use a hierarchical database called the registry. The registry is divided into **registry hives**, each of which store a particular type of setting. The two most important hives are HKEY_LOCAL_MACHINE (or HKLM) for system-wide configuration settings, and HKEY_CURRENT_USER (or HKCU) for user-specific settings. Many applications also store settings in the registry.

Within each hive there is a set of **registry keys**. A registry key can contain more registry keys, values, or both. The logical layout of a registry key is similar to the nesting structure of OUs and folders. As an example, Figure 6-16 shows the registry keys that keep track of printer settings.

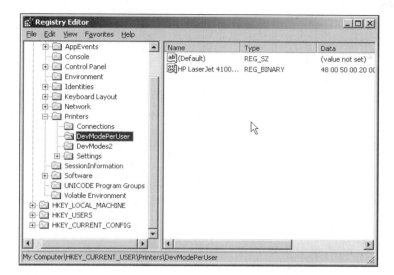

Figure 6-16 The registry, showing printer settings

Values stored in the registry control how the computer system operates. Registry values can enable or disable functionality. There may be times when you won't want users or programs to be able to change certain values in the registry. For example, nonadministrative users can change fewer settings than users who are administrators.

To allow for the control of access to the registry, each registry key has the typical Windows 2003 security descriptor with a SACL, a DACL, and an owner specified. Figure 6-17 shows the standard permissions that can be set on a registry key. Figure 6-18 shows the special permissions.

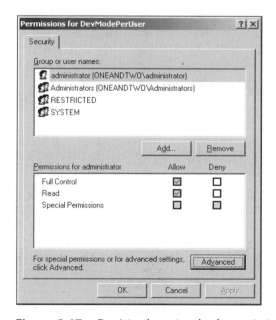

Figure 6-17 Registry key standard permissions

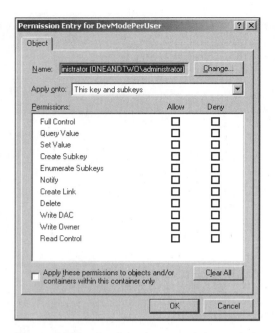

Figure 6-18   Registry key special permissions

 Setting registry key permissions incorrectly or changing registry values can render your computer inoperable.

Activity 6-9: Controlling Access to a Registry Key

Time Required: 10 minutes

Objective: To examine DACLs on a registry key.

Description: In this activity you will examine the security settings on some registry keys to see how the system restricts access to parts of the registry. Knowing how to do this is useful in situations where you want to give only specific users the ability to remotely connect to the registry, or where users need very specific permissions to launch a particular application.

1. If necessary, turn on your computer and log on as the administrator from your own domain.

2. Click **Start**, and then click **Run**.

3. Type **regedit** and press **Enter**.

4. Expand the nodes in the tree pane until the HKEY_USERS node is visible. Expand it so that the .DEFAULT node is also visible.

5. The .DEFAULT node is copied to a new user's registry settings the first time the user logs on to the computer. Right-click the **.DEFAULT** node, and then click **Permissions**.

6. Examine each of the permissions in the DACL on this node. Observe that administrators can make changes but other, authenticated users can only read values. This allows them to copy the values to their own registry when it is created.

7. Click **Cancel** to close the Permissions dialog box.

8. Under HKEY_USERS, locate the node matching your own SID. If you have forgotten what your SID is, open a command prompt and type **whoami /user**.

9. Right-click your own user registry key and click **Permissions**.

10. Examine each of the permissions in the DACL on this node. Note that you have permission on your own registry keys.

11. Click **Cancel** to close the Permissions dialog box.

12. Close all open windows. If you are not continuing immediately to another activity, log off your computer.

Other Applications

In Chapter 1, you learned that applications are becoming more Active Directory-aware and are starting to use Active Directory to control access to the application. There are several approaches in use, ranging from a tightly integrated application like Exchange 2000 Server, to loosely integrated applications that use just NTFS security. Which approach is used usually depends on whether the application is using Active Directory for authentication, authorization, both, or neither.

As described in Chapter 1, authentication is the process of identifying and proving who you are. This is usually performed with a username and password. Authentication will be examined in more detail later in this chapter. Authorization occurs when the system determines whether you are allowed access to a specific resource—you don't have to authenticate again; the system already knows who you are. The system does, however, need to verify your access permissions to the resource.

Many applications do not perform any authentication or authorization. For example, anyone can run Notepad, even on a Windows 98 machine that can't be authenticated. Notepad has no security awareness. However, even within this category, most applications can be given a certain amount of access control by setting NTFS permissions on their executable files or directory. If you were to create a DACL on the Notepad.exe file that only permitted administrators to read it, you would, in effect, prevent nonadministrators from using Notepad.

Some applications perform authentication and authorization internally. You can recognize these applications when they prompt you for a username and password after you have already logged on to the domain. These applications can also gain added protection using NTFS permissions.

More sophisticated applications often use Active Directory for authentication, but provide their own authorizations. Microsoft SQL Server is a good example. When connecting to the SQL Server, a user provides his or her access token, just like accessing a shared folder over a trusted connection. SQL is aware that the user has been authenticated, and can see who the user is by examining his or her name and SID.

Microsoft SQL Server maintains its own DACLs (called access control lists, or ACLs) internally, which are different in format from a security descriptor used by Windows. SQL Server provides its own authorization mechanisms, but can rely on the operating system and Active Directory for authentication. See Figure 6-19 for an example of Active Directory authentication with SQL Server.

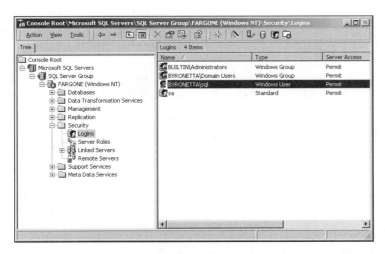

Figure 6-19   SQL Server security using Active Directory security principals

Microsoft Exchange 2000 Server is a complex and full-featured e-mail and group collaboration server. Unlike earlier versions of Exchange, Exchange 2000 relies on Active Directory to be the directory for e-mail. Exchange 2000 extends the Active Directory schema, adding several new classes and attributes. By setting DACLs on the objects it uses (including users that have mailboxes), Exchange 2000 uses Active Directory not only for authenticating users, but also for authorizing access to mailboxes and other Exchange 2000 resources.

UNDERSTANDING THE USER AUTHENTICATION PROCESS

In the last section of this chapter you will examine, in greater depth, exactly what happens when users log on to the network and are authenticated. To many administrators, the authentication process is like a black box—it either works or it doesn't. Many administrators operate their networks without a clear understanding of what is going on "under the hood." However, just like the driver of a car, the more you know about what happens under that hood, the easier it is to troubleshoot problems and deal with issues that might arise.

We will look at the two authentication methods used in Windows Server 2003: Kerberos and NTLM. Then we'll discuss how to handle authentication from other down-level clients, and move on to discuss two-factor authentication and the use of certificates and smart cards.

Kerberos Version 5

Kerberos v5 authentication is the default protocol for network authentication for all Windows Server 2003 computers. Windows XP Professional and the Windows 2000 also use Kerberos for authentication. Kerberos v5 is based on Request for Comments (RFC) number 1510 and will interoperate with other servers and clients that follow this RFC specification. Unfortunately, most implementations, including Microsoft's, vary slightly from the RFC specifications. This is because most vendors want to provide their product with additional functionality that might not be present in the standard protocol.

Kerberos is used for both network authentication and authorization for access to network resources. The components involved in Kerberos include:

- The security principal who is requesting access
- The Key Distribution Center (KDC), which is the Active Directory DC
- The server holding the resource or the service that is being requested

In the Windows Server 2003 implementation of Kerberos, the KDC is the DC that stores the directory database containing all users and passwords. (In theory, a KDC could be some other database, but in Active Directory, it is the DC.) The KDC provides two main services for the security of the network:

- **Authentication Service** — Authenticates and issues ticket granting tickets (TGTs) to users
- **Ticket-Granting Service** — Issues session tickets for access to network resources

Authentication Service

The process of authenticating and granting access to resources requires two tickets from the KDC. The first ticket is the **ticket granting ticket (TGT)** and is issued to the user when he or she is first authenticated during a successful logon. The TGT simply allows the user to request session tickets.

By default, a TGT is valid for 10 hours. This allows the user to request session tickets for the entire length of a normal business day, without needing to go back to the KDC for a new TGT. It also means that a TGT has to be occasionally refreshed, even if a user never logs off. This default lifetime can be adjusted in the security policy of the domain.

Ticket-Granting Service

Each time a user needs to access a resource, the TGT is submitted to the ticket-granting service on the KDC. The KDC sends two copies of a **session ticket** back to the user's machine. One copy is encrypted for the user's computer and is stored in the client computer's ticket cache system. The second copy is encrypted for the server that is hosting the desired resource.

Each time that the user needs to access the resource or service, the client presents the session ticket to the target resource. The session ticket has a default lifetime of 600 minutes (10 hours), which can also be adjusted in the security policy of the domain. The target resource unpacks its copy of the session ticket and examines the user's access token, which is contained in the session ticket. For Windows Server 2003 resources, the SIDs in the access token are compared to SIDs in the ACEs of DACLs. For other types of resources, the session ticket and user access token contain enough information for the target resource to make an authorization decision according to whichever mechanisms the target resource uses.

Kerberos in Action

The process of Kerberos authentication and granting access to network resources involves many steps. RFC 1510, which details how Kerberos v5 works, is about 112 pages long. Figure 6-20 illustrates the process in a simpler manner.

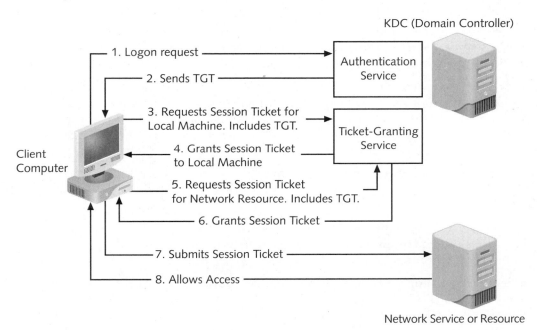

Figure 6-20   Overview of the Kerberos process

Step 1

Logging on by typing a username and password prompts the client computer to send a packet to the KDC. (In technical literature, this request is called the Kerberos Authentication Service Request or KRB_AS_REQ packet.) The packet includes:

- The username
- A secret key, derived from a hash of the user's password
- A timestamp
- A request for a TGT

The entire packet, except for the username, is encrypted using a secret key. This secret key is the user's password. The computer sending the packet knows the user's password because the user has just typed it in. The KDC knows the secret key because it is stored in Active Directory.

When the packet arrives at the server, the server looks at the username and then searches the directory database for the secret key (password) associated with the user's account. The server then decrypts the data in the packet using the user's secret key and checks the timestamp. If the decryption is successful and the timestamp is within five minutes of the current time on the server, the user is authenticated.

If the packet cannot be decrypted, then the password must be wrong, so the authentication will fail. If the timestamp is more than five minutes old, or if the KDC cannot find the user, the authentication will also fail.

The reason for requiring that the timestamp be fairly recent, is to prevent an attacker from capturing and recording the authentication packets and then replaying them at a different time. The maximum allowable time difference can be configured on the domain security policies.

Step 2

After the user is authenticated, the KDC generates a TGT, which can be used to request more tickets. The TGT contains the user's access token, as well as a session key that will later be used to encrypt other things. This key will be called the AS session key to avoid confusing it with other session keys. After being time-stamped, the TGT is encrypted with the KDC's secret key.

The reply packet also contains another copy of the AS session key. The entire packet is also timestamped and encrypted using the secret key (the user's password). Why two copies of the AS session key? Because the copy inside the TGT cannot be read or decrypted by the client computer.

When the packet arrives at the client computer, the user's secret key is used to decrypt the packet. If the decryption is successful and the timestamp is valid, then the user's computer knows that the KDC is authentic because it knew the user's secret key. The TGT is then cached on the local machine for 10 hours. Bear in mind however, that the user's computer now has a newly issued AS session key, but cannot read or change the contents of the TGT because it doesn't know the KDC's private key.

Steps 1 and 2 are the authentication service exchange.

Steps 3 and 4

It may seem silly, but it's true—the user still hasn't logged on to the local computer. In other words, the user has been authenticated but not yet authorized. The user needs a session ticket valid for his or her own workstation in order to proceed.

This is the first ticket-granting service exchange, and it begins with the client building a ticket-granting service request or KRB_TGS_REQ packet. This request packet is sent to the KDC and contains the TGT that the client received from the Kerberos authentication service. It also contains the name of client, the name of the server for which access is desired (in this case, the local workstation), and a timestamp. The timestamp is encrypted with the AS session key issued in Step 2.

The KDC needs to decrypt both the TGT and the timestamp. The KDC knows its own master key so it can decrypt the TGT. Inside the TGT is a copy of the AS session key, which the KDC can use to decrypt the timestamp. The KDC can now verify that the TGT and the timestamp are both valid, and issue a service ticket.

The KDC then creates a new session key that will be used by the client and the server; it will be referred to as the CS session key. A copy of the CS session key and the user's access token are encrypted with another key that is known only to the server hosting the resource and the KDC. The key is not known to the user. This encrypted block is called a **service ticket (ST)**.

The service ticket and an encrypted copy of the CS session key are returned to the client. The client can use the existing keys to decrypt the new CS session key, but because the client does not know the server's password, the client cannot decrypt the service key.

 The KDC does not decide if the user is entitled to access the resource unless the TGT or timestamp is invalid, or unless domain logon restrictions are in place. The KDC does not check DACLs on the resource.

In this particular case, because the resource is on the same machine, the logon process (running as the user) presents the service ticket to the Local Security Authority (LSA) to gain access to the workstation. The LSA can decrypt the service ticket because it knows the computer's password, which was used by the KDC to encrypt the service ticket.

On the local computer, the user's access token is expanded by the LSA to add the machine local groups of which the user may be a member. By definition, those machine local groups are not known outside of the local machine.

Steps 3 and 4 exemplify the ticket-granting service exchange.

Step 5

When the client needs access to a network resource, such as a file on a file server, the request is sent to the KDC for another session ticket. The request includes the TGT and a timestamp that is encrypted with the AS session key.

Step 6

The server decrypts and verifies the data in the packet. If the data is acceptable, the server will issue the session ticket to the client using the same process followed in Step 4.

Steps 5 and 6 exemplify a ticket-granting service exchange, as do Steps 3 and 4.

Steps 7 and 8

Steps 7 and 8 represent the client/server authentication exchange, and are a bit different than the previous steps because there is no need to go back to the KDC or any other third party.

The client possesses a copy of the CS session key, which is used to encrypt a timestamp. The client sends this encrypted timestamp, along with the service ticket, to the server in a KRB_AP_REQ packet.

The server cannot decrypt the timestamp until after it has decrypted the service ticket. Because the service ticket was encrypted with the server's master key (known to the server and to the KDC), the server can decrypt the service ticket to obtain the CS session key and the user's access token. The server validates the timestamp and uses DACLs and SIDs (or similar mechanisms) to authorize the user's access to the desired resource.

If the client needs subsequent use of the resource or service, the session ticket is pulled up from the ticket cache and reissued to the target resource server. If the session ticket has expired, the client has to return to the KDC to obtain a new ticket.

This process of obtaining a session ticket from the KDC before accessing a network resource is completely different than the process used in Windows NT. When trying to access a resource on a Windows NT server, the client would connect directly to the resource and request access. The server holding the resource would then use a process of pass-through authentication and connect to the DC to see if the user has the right level of permission. With Kerberos, the client does not connect to the resource until it has received a session ticket from the KDC, but the server doesn't need to contact a DC to make the decision to authorize.

Activity 6-10: Changing the Kerberos Ticket Lifetime

Time Required: 10 minutes

Objective: To view and change Kerberos settings for the domain. This activity will require you to work with a partner.

Description: Because Multinational Mega Corporation's staff often work 12-hour shifts, it decided to increase the default ticket lifetime from 10 hours to 12 hours. In this activity, you will examine and change the account policy settings that control how Kerberos behaves in your domain. Note that these Kerberos settings can be changed only at the domain level.

1. Because you are changing a domain policy, work with your partner and perform this activity from one of the two computers in the domain.

2. If necessary, turn on your computer and log on as the administrator from your own domain.

3. Click **Start**, point to **Administrative Tools**, and then click **Domain Security Policy**.

4. In the tree pane, expand the following nodes: **Security Settings** and **Account Policies**.

5. Click **Kerberos Policy**.

6. In the details pane, observe the Kerberos settings that can be changed.

7. Double-click **Maximum lifetime for service ticket**.

8. Change the value from 600 to **720**.

9. Click **OK**.

10. Read the notice that appears, and then click **OK**.

11. Click **Close**.

12. Close all open windows. If you are not continuing immediately to another activity, log off your computer.

NTLM Authentication

NTLM authentication is the second option when authenticating a user on a network, and is supported mainly for backward compatibility with Windows NT 4.0 and Windows 9x client computers, although it is occasionally used by newer clients as well. This protocol is used in various scenarios, as follows:

- A Windows 95/98/NT-based computer authenticates to a Windows 2000 or Windows Server 2003 DC

- A Windows 2000/XP/2003 computer authenticates to a Windows NT-based server

- A log-on request is sent to a Windows 2000 or 2003 standalone server (i.e., one that is not in a domain)

- A security principal (such as a user) needs to be authenticated by a DC that is running as part of a Windows 2000 cluster server environment

- A security principal needs to be authenticated for access to a resource in a different forest, using an external trust relationship between forests (or between a forest and a Windows NT domain)

This NTLM protocol is significantly less secure than Kerberos, and many password-cracking tools have been developed to decrypt NTLM authentication. With Windows NT 4.0 Service Pack 4, Microsoft introduced a new version called NTLMv2. This new version includes additional security, such as a unique session key for each time a new connection is established and an advanced key exchange to protect the session keys.

As Figure 6-21 illustrates, the NTLM authentication process is much different than the Kerberos process. First, an NTLM challenge and response is sent from the client computer to the server holding the resource that the user wants to access. Although the user's password is not sent on the network, it is easier to capture this challenge and use hacking tools to discover the password than it is with Kerberos. With Kerberos, it is impossible to do so in any reasonable period of time.

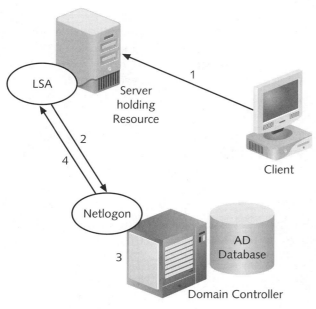

Figure 6-21   The NTLM authentication process

Next, the application on the server uses the server's LSA process to log on to the domain by contacting the netlogon process on a DC. The netlogon process then queries the Active Directory database using a special filter designed to support NTLM and allow the verification of the user's existence and correct password.

Finally, the authenticating DC sends the user's SID and group SIDs back to the server. In NTLMv2, the communication between the server and the DC (arrows 2 and 4) is encrypted. It is highly recommended that you use only the NTLMv2 flavor of NTLM.

All Windows 2000 clients should be required to use Kerberos. This is the default configuration for Windows 2000, but if the Windows 2000 client cannot use Kerberos (for example, if the Kerberos authentication ports are blocked on a router), then the client would fall back on NTLM. If your network requires a high level of security, then your security plan should include a recommendation to upgrade all clients to Windows 2000 to ensure that only Kerberos is used for authentication.

Down-Level Client Authentication

Almost all large corporate networks have a mixture of client operating systems, which may include Windows 95, Windows 98, Windows NT 3.51 or 4.0, Windows 2000, Windows XP, and possibly even Windows Me. These older clients (pre-Windows 2000) are referred to as **down-level clients**. These down-level clients (Windows 95/98/Me and NT) create a security concern when implemented within a Windows 2000/2003 network. In particular, Windows 95/98 clients are the most vulnerable because they use LAN manager (LM) authentication, which is one of the weakest authentication protocols available. Windows NT 4.0 uses NTLM, which can be updated to version 2 in Service Pack 4.

To help remedy these security concerns, the Directory Services Client is available as an add-on component to Windows 95/98, enabling these clients to use NTLMv2 on the Windows 2000/2003 network. The Directory Services Client, which is also available for Windows NT, implements additional features such as Active Directory site awareness, search capabilities in Active Directory, and the ability to connect to any DC to change passwords rather than having to connect to the PDC emulator.

There are certain features that the Directory Services Client does not provide, such as Kerberos or Group Policy support, IPSec support, dynamic DNS support, and user principal name authentication capabilities. To use these features, an upgrade to Windows 2000 Professional, Windows XP, or Windows Server 2003 is required.

The Directory Service Client software for Windows 95/98 and Windows NT 4.0 is available from Microsoft. Note that in its default configuration, a Windows 95 or 98 computer cannot authenticate to a Windows Server 2003 DC. (Windows 95 is no longer an officially supported product.)

 NTLMv2 authentication can be implemented on a Windows NT machine by installing Service Pack 4.0 or later.

Activity 6-11: Preventing the Use of NTLM v1

Time Required: 10 minutes

Objective: To prevent clients who are not using Kerberos or NTLMv2 from connecting.

Description: Because of the security vulnerabilities in down-level clients, Multinational Mega Corporation has decided to require all clients to use Kerberos or NTLMv2. This will require Windows 95/98 or Me clients to have the Active Directory extensions installed. In this activity, you will change the domain security policy to support this decision.

1. Because you are changing a domain policy, work with your partner and perform this activity from one of the two computers in the domain.

2. If necessary, turn on your computer and log on as the administrator from your own domain.

3. Click **Start**, point to **Administrative Tools**, and then click **Domain Security Policy**.

4. In the tree pane, expand the following nodes: **Security Settings** and **Local Policies**.

5. Click **Security Options**.

6. In the details pane, locate and double-click **Network security: LAN Manager authentication level**.

7. Check the **Define this policy setting** checkbox.

8. Click the drop-down list and select **Send NTLMv2 response only\refuse LM & NTLM**.

9. Click **OK**.

10. Close all open windows. If you are not continuing immediately to another activity, log off your computer.

Two-Factor Authentication

Traditionally, security experts have described three possible factors that help identify you for authentication:

■ Something you know — a password, a PIN, or a secret phrase

■ Something you have — a key to your house, a bankcard, or a signet ring from a medieval king

■ Something you are — an indelible characteristic that can't be imitated, your fingerprint, your signature, or your DNA

In general, the more of these factors you use in security, the more secure your resource will be. For example, you can't access a bank account at an automated teller without both a card (something you have) and a PIN (something you know). It would be too easy to have cash stolen if all you needed was the card, and most agree that it would also be too easy to find out the PIN.

Traditional name and password combinations rely on only one factor—something that you know. A number of systems are available to increase the security of a network or computer system by introducing a second factor. This is called **two-factor authentication**. By way of example, RSA Security Corporation markets a product line, SecurID, which requires a user to have a small portable device (the size of a key). This device displays a changing number that must also be entered as part of the logon process. The device by itself is not sufficient—the user still needs a password.

Several companies market biometric devices that scan hands, fingerprints, or retinas. The cost of these devices is coming down, but user acceptance remains an issue, except in the most secure environments. Some manufacturers are starting to integrate facial recognition software into computer programs that can be used with low-cost Web cams. Though facial recognition may not be ready for mainstream use, new products are released every week.

Unlike certificates and smart cards (discussed in the next section), these types of products require additional hardware or software, and are not directly supported by Active Directory or Windows. Though they add cost and complexity to your network, they do make it more secure.

Public Key Infrastructure for Authentication with Smart Cards

Active Directory does support the use of smart cards and certificates to enhance the security of the logon process. Smart cards and certificates are part of a PKI. To understand PKI, you need to delve a little bit into the science of cryptography.

Most encryption is done with **symmetric keys**. In symmetric key cryptography, the same secret key can be used to encode and decode a message. The effectiveness of the encryption is based, in part, on the length of the key and, in part, on the quality of the algorithm used to generate the encrypted text. However, the biggest problem has always been how to keep the key secret, while at the same time getting it to the people who need it. In this kind of encryption, you have to be absolutely sure that no one is eavesdropping when you tell someone the key that you're using to encrypt a document.

Recently, public key cryptography has come to the forefront as a solution to this problem. In public key cryptography, two different keys—which are numbers that have a very special mathematical relationship—are used. If I use one key to encrypt something, the other key, and only the other key, can decrypt it. These related numbers, called a **key pair** or a private/public key pair, are usually very large.

One of the keys is called the private key, and is held privately by its owner. It is never sent with a message or disclosed to another party. On the other hand, the public key can, and should, be widely distributed. It can be painted on billboards, published in the newspaper, or stored in an electronic directory for anyone to find. If you wish to send me an encrypted message, you can find my public key anywhere you like and then use it to encrypt your message, knowing that only I can read it.

 In practice, public key encryption is comparatively slow, so it is often used to encrypt a symmetric key sent with a message. The receiver decrypts the symmetric key and then uses it to quickly decrypt the message.

One possible hiccup remains. If Joe gives you a public key and says, "Here's Bill's public key," how would you know whether it was really Bill's public key? If someone has replaced Bill's key with their own, they could read messages you intended for only Bill. Certificates help address this issue.

In PKI, the term certificate usually refers to an **X.509 digital certificate**, which contains information about the person or entity it represents (called the subject of the certificate). It also contains the public key and a digital signature of the person who issued the certificate. (Digital signing is another feature of public key cryptography.)

There is a *Star Trek* episode where the android Data has to give the computer his complex password. Because the *Star Trek* computer is voice activated, he lists off a long string of numbers, spoken very quickly. As an android, he can repeat this sequence flawlessly. In the real world, however, even professional actors would have a hard time remembering private or public keys, which are often several hundred or even thousands of bytes long.

Active Directory can be used as a repository for X.509 certificates, so you can easily find someone's public key. Private keys can be stored on a hard drive, but most organizations that invest in a PKI system are not comfortable with the possibility that someone in possession of the hard drive and the user's password could compromise the key. Private keys are, therefore, usually stored on removable media, or better still, on a smart card.

Smart cards are much more common in Europe and Asia than in North America. In the United States and Canada, many of our bankcards have a magnetic stripe that can store information, such as an account number. In theory, a private key could be written to a magnetic stripe and read when necessary; however, that would mean that as the key is passed from card reader to computer, it could be intercepted or recorded.

A smart card is different. It provides nonvolatile memory that stores the owner's certificate and private key, as well as a small amount of computing power to perform the encryption and decryption requiring the public key on the card itself. The smart card is called smart because it contains a small CPU. The private key is never read off the card. For more details about the internal workings of smart cards, visit the Web sites of some of its major manufacturers, such as Datakey (*www.datakey.com*) or the Smart Card Alliance (*www.smartcardalliance.org*).

You can use smart cards and certificates to increase the security of the Windows-authentication process. Windows Server 2003 supports extensions to Kerberos that allow the authentication session to be changed slightly. Rather than employing the user's password (or any derivative of it) to encrypt the timestamp, the system uses the user's private key. The KDC then employs the public key of the user (stored with the user's certificate in the Active Directory database) to decrypt it.

However, because the user's private key is stored on the smart card, decryption can only occur if the card is present. Smart cards also require the user to enter a PIN to access the private key functions.

You can configure your domain to require smart-card logons, make them optional, or require them for some users, but not others. Recently, Microsoft Corporation began requiring smart-card logons for remote connections to its corporate network, a decision that affected thousands of employees. Including smart cards and PKI in its domain adds complexity and cost to your network, but increases security substantially.

Activity 6-12: Requiring the Use of Smart Cards

Time Required: 20 minutes

Objective: To require use of smart cards on all computers in the domain.

Description: In this activity you will change domain security settings to require the use of smart cards. The settings will not be put into effect, because you do not have smart cards and readers available. You will work with your partner for this activity.

Manufacturers, such as Datakey, will sometimes make demonstration equipment available to classrooms. If you have smart-card equipment available, your instructor will provide alternate instructions.

1. Because you are changing a domain policy, work with your partner and perform this activity from one of the two computers in the domain.

2. If necessary, turn on your computer and log on as the administrator from your own domain.

3. Click **Start**, point to **Administrative Tools**, and then click **Domain Security Policy**.

4. In the tree pane, expand the following nodes: **Security Settings**, **Local Policies**, and **Security Options**.

5. Locate and double-click the setting **Interactive logon: Require smart card**.

6. Check **Define this policy setting**.

7. Click **Enabled**.

8. Click **OK**.

9. *Important*: Make certain that both you and your partner are logged on to a computer as an administrator in the domain. When instructed to log off in Step 11, you will log off from only one machine. You and your partner need to decide who is going to log off.

10. Click **Start**, click **Run**, and then type **gpupdate /force** and press **Enter**.

11. After the gpupdate command has completed, close all open windows and either you or your partner should log off your computer. Only the user agreed upon in Step 9 should log off.

12. Attempt to log on to your computer. Observe that you will receive an error message stating that you must use a smart card.

13. Have your partner repeat Steps 3–6 on his or her computer.

14. Have your partner click **Disabled**, not Enabled.

15. Have your partner close the Domain Security console.

16. Enjoy a coffee break, or perhaps a gentle stroll through the campus to allow time for replication and group policy updating to occur. After these have occurred (anywhere from 3 to 20 minutes), you should be able to log on to your computer again. If this fails, your instructor can use an enterprise administrator logon to reset your domain.

17. When complete, log off your computer.

CHAPTER SUMMARY

❑ Security principals are special because the have a SID. SIDs work with ACEs in DACLs to control access to resources or objects and with ACEs in SACLs to control auditing of resource use.

❑ Security principals can be granted specific permissions to access resources. There are standard permissions for common applications and special permissions for advanced purposes.

❑ DACLs are a list of ACEs. Each ACE specifies a SID and the type of permission being granted or denied. The system compares each SID in a user's access token to the SID in each ACE. If a match is found, the defined action (allow or deny) is taken. If no match is found the user is denied access.

❑ Always grant permissions to groups instead of individual users. In large or complicated forests with multiple domains and a site structure, you will probably need to use domain local, global, and universal groups.

❑ Delegation of control refers to assigning permissions on Active Directory objects so that data owners can manage their own objects. There is a Delegation of Control wizard to assist with setting permissions for common tasks.

❑ NTFS provides the same security descriptor structure for files and folders as for Active Directory objects. Each file and folder has an owner, a DACL, and a SACL that work in the same way as the Active Directory equivalent. Printers, file shares, and registry keys are protected in a similar manner.

❑ Permissions in NTFS and Active Directory can be inherited from a parent level to a child level for simpler administration.

❑ Other applications may use Active Directory for authentication, authorization, both, or neither. Even applications that do not use Active Directory for authentication can still be made more secure by protecting their executables and data files with NTFS permissions.

❑ The two primary user authentication methods in a Windows Server 2003 network are NTLM and Kerberos. Two-factor and biometric authentications are available, but add complexity and cost to your network. Most two-factor or biometric solutions are third-party add-ons for Active Directory and Windows.

❑ Active Directory supports smart cards and X.509 certificates with extensions to the Kerberos protocol, enabling asymmetric encryption during the exchange.

KEY TERMS

access control entry (ACE) — An entry in a DACL or SACL that lists a security principal (by SID), a type of permission (such as read or write), and whether that SID is allowed or denied the permission.

access token — A binary structure that lists the identity, rights, and group membership of a user on the network. An access token contains, among other items, the user's SID and the SID of each group to which the user belongs.

asymmetric keys — *See* public/private key pair.

delegation of control — Refers to assigning permissions on Active Directory objects so that data owners can manage their own objects. There is a Delegation of Control wizard to assist with setting permissions for common tasks.

discretionary access control list (DACL) — A list of ACEs used to control access to an object or resource.

domain identifier — Three 32-bit numbers that are statistically unique and identify a particular domain.

down-level client — A computer running an operating system that is not Active Directory-aware or Kerberos capable, such as Windows 3.x, Windows 95/98, Windows Me, or Windows NT.

File Allocation Table (FAT) — An older file format used by down-level clients and DOS. FAT disks do not support file-based permissions, auditing, or journaling.

inheritance — The concept that a security setting on one object can be inherited by objects lower in the hierarchy. Examples include folders inheriting settings from other parent folders, or OUs inheriting settings from parent OUs.

Kerberos — A network protocol first developed at MIT to allow for a wide-area, distributed method of securely authenticating users before they are allowed to access network resources.

Kerberos ticket — One of several types of binary constructs contained in Kerberos messages. Kerberos tickets are used in authentication and authorization.

key pair — *See* public/private key pair.

NT File System (NTFS) — Known almost exclusively by its initials, NTFS is the robust file system used by Windows NT, Windows 2000, Windows XP, and Windows Server 2003. NTFS supports the ability to control and audit access, and uses a journaling system to minimize corruption.

NT LAN Manager (NTLM) — More commonly known by its initials, NTLM is the older network authentication protocol used by all Windows systems prior to Windows 2000. It is still used with Windows 2000, Windows XP, and Windows Server 2003 in certain circumstances.

objectSID — The Active Directory attribute that stores a security principal's security identifier (SID).

Public Key Infrastructure (PKI) — An organized system that issues and manages certificates and key pairs to support the use of public key cryptography in an organization.

public/private key pair — A set of two mathematically related keys used in public key cryptographic (or asymmetric encryption). If a message is encrypted with one key, it can only be decrypted with the other. The public key is widely distributed; the private key is closely guarded.

registry hives — Major sections of the Windows registry. Originally, each hive was stored in its own file.

registry key — One or more related settings stored in the Windows registry. A key is similar to a folder in the file system; it can contain other keys or values.

relative identifier (RID) — A 32-bit number, unique within the domain, that makes up part of a security principal's SID.

security descriptor — A package of binary information associated with an object or a resource, which contains the DACL, SACL, object owner, and related security information. For Active Directory objects, the security descriptor is an attribute of all objects and is called ntSecurityDescriptor.

Security Descriptor Definition Language (SDDL) — A format that efficiently describes SIDs, ACEs, DACLs, SACLs, and related constructs. SDDL is both reasonably compact and easily read by humans.

security identifier (SID) — A binary number that uniquely represents a security principal. For most security principals, the two key components are a domain identifier and a RID that are unique within the domain.

security principal — An object in the directory to which resource permissions can be granted. In Active Directory, security principals are users (including InetOrgPersons), computers, and security groups.

service ticket (ST) — A Kerberos ticket presented to a resource server, allowing it to authorize access.

special permission — A specific, granular permission available from the Advanced dialog box when setting permissions.

standard permissions — Permissions shown on the main Security tab in an object's properties that represent the most common permissions granted to users. A standard permission represents several related special permissions.

symmetric keys — Encryption keys that can be used to encrypt or decrypt a message. The same key is used for both encryption and decryption.

system access control list (SACL) — A list of ACEs used to determine which actions are audited or logged for a particular resource.

ticket granting ticket (TGT) — A Kerberos ticket used to request service tickets from a KDC.

two-factor authentication — Authentication systems that require possession of a physical object (or present a biometric) and a password or PIN.

X.509 digital certificate — A specially structured electronic document that describes the identity of a person or service. The certificate is digitally signed by its issuer.

REVIEW QUESTIONS

1. All objects in Active Directory have an objectSID attribute to control who can modify that object. True or false?

2. The _____ access control list controls auditing.

3. The share \\SERVER\Download is a security principal. True or false?

4. Access to a resource is granted by:

   a. Comparing the user's SID to the SAM database on the DC

   b. Comparing the user's SID to the DACL on the resource

   c. Comparing the user's password against the resource password

   d. Comparing the user's access token to the SACL

5. A SACL controls _____.

   a. Auditing on a resource

   b. System account permissions

   c. Services configured to run as a user

   d. User system access

6. Changing permissions on an NTFS object is done in the same way as changing permissions on an Active Directory object. True or False?

7. Each time a user requires access to a resource, the user's computer sends a request to the KDC. True or False?

8. When a user first logs on, he or she sends which of the following to the KDC?

   a. A timestamp

   b. A service ticket

   c. A password

   d. A private key

9. A security principal can be recognized because it has the _____ attribute.

10. SIDs are usually displayed to humans in the _____ format.

11. The SID *S-1-1-0* should be recognized by all security administrators because it represents
    _____.

    a. Domain Admins

    b. Everyone

    c. Nobody (that is, no matching user could be found)

    d. BUILTIN\Administrators

12. Assume that a user with a UPN of *tonyb@lan.commons.gov.uk* has a SID of *S-1-5-21-1993962763-287218729-725645543-1642*. The _____ part of the SID represents his or her domain, and the _____ part of the SID represents his or her RID.

13. Which information contained in a user's access token is used to allow servers to decide if the user should be authorized access to a resource?

14. The _____ of an object can always reset its permissions to allow access to the object.

15. It is preferable to assign permissions directly to users, not groups. True or False?

16. Global groups are only used in forests with a single domain. All multidomain forests must use universal groups. True or False?

17. All classes of objects have the same special permissions available. True or False?

18. Which of the following is a security principal? (Choose all that apply.)

    a. OUs

    b. Users

    c. Distribution groups

    d. Computers

19. On which file system can you most exactly control access to files and folders?

    a. Compact Disc File System (CDFS)

    b. File Allocation Table (FAT)

    c. 32-bit File Allocation Table (FAT32)

    d. NT File System (NTFS)

20. For each of the following applications, indicate whether they use Active Directory for authentication, authorization, neither, or both.

    a. Notepad: _____

    b. SQL Server: _____

    c. Exchange 2000: _____

21. Number the following authentication protocols from most to least secure:

    a. NTLMv2: _____

    b. NTLM: _____

    c. Kerberos: _____

    d. Kerberos with smart cards: _____

22. A smart card has a magnetic stripe that stores the user's private key, which is read back by swiping the card through a reader. True or False?

HEARTLAND HOSPITAL CASE PROJECTS

Now that the Heartland Hospital Active Directory is beginning to come together, some meetings have been taking place with the key staff involved in shaping the network and its infrastructure. In one of these meetings, the staff began the process of formulating the security model for Active Directory. The following personnel were present: Leah Bailey, Marti Macauly, Michael Garabaldi, Ami Mavani, and Mary Firth. (You can refer to the organization chart introduced in Chapter 3 (Figure 3-1) for more details on the participants.) The meeting centered on the basic concepts of security in the Heartland Hospital Active Directory.

Mary has been fighting to maintain an initially simple, clean security implementation and phase in additional security protection over the course of a year. These are Mary's arguments:

a. Let's get everyone used to Active Directory before turning on the bells and whistles.

b. Jenn and I simply don't have the bandwidth available on a day-to-day basis to run all over creation fixing problems for people who aren't yet ready for this. Let's keep things simple and reasonably secure initially, and then lock it down as we go along. Also, Jenn and I don't yet fully understand what we're turning on, and if you're not going to allow us to receive training, we need to learn this on the job. Even if we get a class scheduled, who is going to manage the network while we are in class?

c. As a hospital, do we fully understand all the implications of the new HIPAA requirements, along with everything else that we need to do on a daily basis?

Michael had different concerns and objectives. As the hospital's security chief, he would like to see all of the bells and whistles turned on—yesterday. He also feels that as the responsible party for physical security, he should also be responsible for infrastructure security—not necessarily in terms of implementation, but of the requirements and design of the hospital's security policy. Because of his extensive security experience, Mary didn't express any concerns over Michael's ability to design or define security, but she still maintains the concerns she voiced earlier regarding the effects of his security initiative on both staff and employees. Some of Michael's concerns were:

a. There are a lot of bad guys out there. I don't think we should just blindly commit all of our confidential and business information to a system without locking everything down first.

b. I want smart cards for everyone who draws a paycheck, *before* they're allowed to access the system.

c. I want strict local settings on the computers. I don't want users to be able to use their floppy drives or CDs for anything. I want the desktop and list of applications standardized and the Web sites controlled...*everything*.

d. I want to know, specifically, how the HIPAA law (when it goes into effect) is going to impact the security plan and its implementation.

Leah is concerned that hospital users will only be given access to the resources needed to perform their jobs. She feels that strict access controls should be balanced against any perceived infringement of personal freedoms. Though recent case law has sided with corporations that restrict user access and use of corporate computer networks, such cases are expensive to litigate and win. Leah wants to avoid any such possibilities for the time being.

Leah is also concerned about the possibility of revealing confidential information. She reminded the others in the meeting of what happened last year when the payroll process was changed and employees' social security numbers and bank routing numbers were printed on the paycheck stubs.

Leah is also concerned that patient information could leak out, or that the medical staff will not have access to vital patient information. Her arguments include:

a. I want to make sure that we don't do something that will invite a lawsuit. We don't have the budget right now to handle a major incident.

b. Can't we just roll out this Active Directory thing and keep the security we have now? Why do we need to switch anything at all?

c. I still don't understand everything that's being discussed, and I think that the legal department needs to exercise more control and have more input into the process.

Ami is concerned that the medical staff will be impacted by new training on the computer systems, and that vital, need-to-know patient information won't be available to her staff. However, she is generally in favor of Mary's concept of slowly rolling out the additional security features after everyone has gotten used to dealing with Active Directory on a daily basis. Some of her comments include:

a. I like Mary's idea of slowly rolling out additional features for the hospital. I don't think we should hit everyone with everything at the same time. Give everyone a chance to get used to what is happening.

b. One concern is that my staff wouldn't be able to access vital information when needed, and I'd like to meet off-line with Mary to go over possible solutions to eliminate this potential problem. I'm also interested in finding out what this new technology can do to help our patients...can we use this new system to improve the quality of their time here?

c. Can we add additional functionality for my staff using this tool? I'd like to reduce the amount of paperwork that my people need to deal with on a daily basis. I'd also like to explore some new technologies that will help my doctors get the information they need to treat patients more effectively.

Marti is concerned with the hospital's Active Directory implementation being in compliance with the new HIPAA standards. The new law is very complex, and no one fully understands all of the various provisions associated with it. Like most regulations coming from Washington, it was designed to impress voters, but is very difficult to understand and implement.

a. I don't care so much about how we get from point A to point B, as long as we comply with the regulations as they exist now.

b. We'll need something that is flexible and able to adapt quickly as the law and standards change. It also has to be able to control who can see and access specific information. I don't want someone in the laundry able to pull up a patient's medical information because they were just killing time and decided to see if they could.

c. I want some input on how this is going to be implemented in terms of HIPAA compliance. I want control over what is going to be configured to deal with the standards for which I'm responsible.

There are a lot of issues being brought to the table in terms of securing and protecting the Heartland Hospital Active Directory network infrastructure, and many differing views from each of the primary stakeholders. You should now begin the process of planning this implementation.

Note that network design is frequently an exercise in compromise. You will need to design something that satisfies the largest number of stakeholders and addresses their issues while still providing an implementation that is usable and secure. You may need to refer to the Heartland Hospital organization chart and network diagram (Figures 3-1 and 3-2) to complete these exercises.

Case Project 6-1: Identifying Staff Responsible for Security

Use Table 6-2 to identify the primary security stakeholders for each department in the hospital. Identify which of the staff attending the meeting described in the introduction would be the primary stakeholder, from a security point of view, for each of the areas listed in Table 6-2. You can also refer to the hospital organization chart (Figure 3-1) from Chapter 3. The first entry has been filled in for you. Be prepared to explain your selections to your instructor or class.

Case Project 6-2: Defining Groups for Security

Review the existing groups that you created in Chapter 5 to see if they can be used to control access to the resources on the network. Determine what scope your groups should have and which departments should have access to which resources. You may need to create appropriate groups where none exist.

After you determine what groups to use, create a document that lists these groups and their membership. Be careful not to place a user into a group unnecessarily. The objective of this exercise is to control access by restricting access. You may be asked to present your solutions to the class.

Create at least three folders on your hard disk representing resources and then assign permissions to the folders based on your groups.

Table 6-2 Key security stakeholders

Department Name	Primary Security Stakeholder
Administration & Finance	Leah Bailey
Admissions	
Physicians, Nursing & Clinical Services	
Ethics & Legal	
HIPAA Compliance	
Human Resources	
Medical Records	
Administration & General Services	
Physical Facilities	
Security	

Case Project 6-3: Delegating Control in Active Directory

You have looked at who the possible data owners are, as well as who the key security stakeholders are. Who should have permissions over objects in Active Directory? Who should be Domain Administrators? Should any one person or group have complete control to access every object in Active Directory? Should particular data owners manage some OUs?

If necessary, create additional group objects in your Heartland Hospital Active Directory. Work with your partner and make certain to select unique names for your objects. Use the Delegation of Control wizard to grant appropriate control over designated OUs to the appropriate groups.

Case Project 6-4: Planning to Upgrade and Deploy Resources

With some basic permissions now configured for Active Directory, you will need to configure security settings for your network resources. Mary Firth was recently able to purchase two network file servers—NAS1 and NAS2, respectively—and some resources are stored on these servers. However, many file shares are still located on departmental servers and have not yet been migrated to the new servers.

Permissions on the departmental file servers are so confused that Mary has decided to simply decommission those machines and completely rebuild them after their file shares have been moved to the new servers. To do so, any shared printers located on the departmental servers will be redeployed to a neighboring department's server as an interim measure. After the specific department server has been rebuilt, the department's shared printer will be returned to the original host server and reconfigured.

Using the resources available to you, design the deployment document for this process. Work with a partner and create a document for each department. Determine which department should be moved first, where its printer should be positioned, and if possible, a time frame for the process. You will also need to move all remaining file shares from the departmental servers to the NAS servers. The two NAS servers are both using Windows Server 2003, Enterprise Edition and are both member servers in the Heartland Hospital Active Directory domain.

This activity can be completed individually, with your partner, in a small group, or as a class discussion, as decided by your instructor.

Case Project 6-5: Limiting Access to an Application

You learned from Ami that her department uses a software-based accounting solution, and that the department has instituted the multiuser version of the application. This means that one common copy of the central file exists on a file server centrally. You will need to maintain access for all users in her department and all management team members for these files.

Create a folder called **Accounting Solution** on a hard drive. Share this folder and decide how to protect it using NTFS and/or share permissions. Discuss your plans with your instructor. After your plan is approved by management (represented by your instructor), assign the appropriate permissions to the share and/or the folder using groups and follow the principles in this chapter.

Case Project 6-6: Weighing User Authentication Options

In an effort to ease Michael Garabaldi's concerns regarding Active Directory security, Mary Firth has decided to implement either certificate-based smart-card authentication or another two-factor authentication scheme for user logons.

Mary would prefer to delay this implementation as long as possible, for several reasons, not the least of which is the cost of hardware such as card readers. Also, she hasn't been able to obtain the buy-in of Dr. Thompson for the added expense. He has asked Mary and Michael to prepare a document justifying the need.

Prepare a "decision paper" (not to exceed one page in length) for his consideration, which either recommends or discourages the use of smart card-based certificates. Do your best to estimate the cost by acquiring current information from the Internet or your instructor. Create a short, cost-benefit analysis in which you compare the cost to the perceived benefits.

In preparing your recommendation, use all available resources, such as the online material at *www.msdn.microsoft.com*, *www.reskit.com*, or TechNet, which is also available at *www.microsoft.com*. Case studies are also published at other manufacturer's Web sites, such as *www.rsasecurity.com*, *www.datakey.com*, and *www.smartcardalliance.org*.

This activity can be completed individually, with your partner, in a small group, or as a class discussion, as decided by your instructor. Your instructor will advise you as to the final format of your report.

7

ACTIVE DIRECTORY SITES

> **After reading this chapter and completing the exercises, you will be able to:**
>
> ◆ Describe the role of sites in Active Directory and understand how they represent the physical structure of a network
>
> ◆ Describe the objects and components of Active Directory that relate to sites
>
> ◆ Understand how to plan for the implementation of sites in Active Directory and consider how the topology of your network will affect your design
>
> ◆ Understand how to create a site and related objects—including subnets, site links, and site link bridges—using the appropriate administrative tools and management consoles

As you know, objects in Active Directory represent objects in the real world. So far in this book, you've learned about objects that represent things—users, printers, and groups. In this chapter, you will learn about objects that represent the structure or physical topology of your network. A **site** is the most important object that Active Directory uses to represent your physical network.

A site is made up of one or more Internet Protocol (IP) subnets that are well connected. Sites allow you to control the timing of replication of information within Active Directory, and provide a method to ensure that users access certain resources in the most efficient and effective way. (This is discussed in more detail later in this chapter, as well as in Chapter 9.)

After working through this chapter, you will have a firm understanding of sites, their use, and their creation. As with all other parts of an Active Directory network, you will learn that planning your design before implementation is crucial to success.

UNDERSTANDING SITES

As you just learned, a site is one or more IP subnets that are well connected. This means that a site represents a single physical area of your enterprise. This could be one building, one campus, one city, or even one region, depending on how well connected the network subnets are. The term "well connected" is commonly understood to refer to a local area network (LAN) environment, as opposed to a wide area network (WAN). LANs are usually connected at high speeds using Ethernet or fiber-optic cabling, and offer a continual connection. In contrast, a WAN has slower connections using modems or slower frame-relay circuits, or may rely on dial-on-demand telephone connections.

As an example, consider a small office building that contains five IP subnets that are connected through a 10/100 Ethernet switch. Since these five subnets are considered to have "good" connectivity (or to be well connected), this building and the five subnets could constitute a site. The site object (and related objects) in Active Directory represents the physical network, and is sometimes called the "logical" description of the "physical" network. Although the logical site is separate from the physical network, the Active Directory designer would normally try to ensure that the logical description matched the physical network.

Although uncommon, a well-connected physical network can be divided into multiple sites to control replication or the way in which resources are accessed. Doing so is an advanced skill.

A very basic example of a site will serve to introduce the following sections, which will examine the various network components that can make up a site in an Active Directory environment.

ACTIVE DIRECTORY OBJECTS RELATED TO SITES

To understand the role of sites in Active Directory, you must first understand how several components of Active Directory interact. We will, therefore, review and expand on our earlier discussion of particular elements in Active Directory.

We will begin by reviewing the naming contexts of logical containers (i.e., partitions) that are involved in the implementation of sites, and continue on to specific implementations of specialized DCs and advanced tools for determining the appropriate replication topologies connected to the Active Directory sites.

Naming Contexts (Partitions)

In Chapter 1, you learned about the NCs of Active Directory. NCs are also called partitions. You will usually see the term "naming context" in Active Directory tools, commands, and technical documentation. However, in common speech, and in more casual writing, the term "partition" seems to be more popular. As an Active Directory administrator, you need to be familiar with both terms, but you can consider them equivalent.

The three most important NCs to site implementation are the Configuration NC, Schema NC, and the Domain NC. You can review the information in Chapter 1 for a refresher on how these NCs make up parts of the Active Directory database. Activity 7-1 introduces you to a tool that Active Directory administrators use to view detailed information in the Active Directory database.

Activity 7-1 Using LDP to View Naming Partition Information

Time Required: 10 minutes

Objective: To use the Active Directory Ldp tool to discover information about the NCs contained in the Active Directory.

Description: To reinforce the concepts of the Active Directory NCs, you will use the Ldp tool (installed with the Active Directory support tools) to view information directly from Active Directory. You will also examine the type of information stored in Active Directory.

1. If necessary, turn on your computer and log on as the administrator from your own domain.

2. Click **Start**, click **Run**, type **ldp.exe**, and click **OK**.

3. Using the menu bar for the Ldp tool, select the **Connection** menu item and then choose **Connect**.

4. In the Connect pop-up box, accept the name of the server as well as the default settings and click **OK**. If a server does not appear in the Server box, enter the name of a DC and confirm a port setting of 389, then click **OK**.

5. Maximize the screen if desired.

6. Using the information returned by LDP as a source, determine the supported LDAP version.

7. Identify the defaultNamingContext and the rootDomainNamingContext.

8. Select the **Connection** menu again and choose the **Bind** option.

9. Using the Domain Administrator account name and password where indicated, bind to Active Directory and confirm a successful authentication.

10. When finished, select the **Connection** menu and choose the **Disconnect** option.

11. Open the **Connection** menu and choose **Exit** to close the Ldp tool.

12. If you are not proceeding immediately to the next activity, log off your computer.

Figure 7-1 contains the capture of a live Active Directory listing from a Windows Server 2003 Enterprise Server with Active Directory installed and configured.

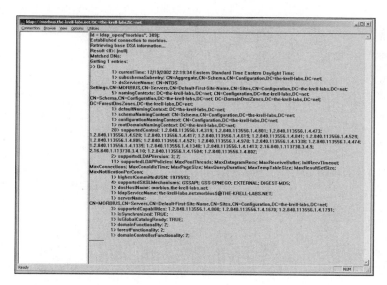

Figure 7-1 LDAP listing

The information in Figure 7-1 was collected using the Active Directory Administration Tool, also known as ldp.exe, which is installed with the Windows Server 2003 support tools. This is a useful GUI-based tool that should be part of every administrator's Active Directory tool set. Detailed instructions on the use of this tool may be found in the *Microsoft Active Directory Programmer's Guide*, which is available from Microsoft as a five-volume set.

Based on an examination of the data returned by ldp, Admin1 is the name of the DC that was queried for the listing shown. This information is contained in the first line of output from Ldp. Next, you should see the default NC. You will find that the 14th line of returned data contains the information: "defaultNamingContext: DC=HeartlandHospital,DC=org;." The next three lines of information should contain records for the Configuration NC, Schema NC, and Domain NC for the Heartland Hospital Active Directory.

The Configuration NC contains information about DCs and domains and sites, as well as other information as diverse as the USN-Changed date and NT Security Description for a schema object. The Configuration NC replicates to all DCs and sites that belong to the same Active Directory forest. Membership in a child domain is not a limiting factor when discussing or determining the scope of replication for the Configuration NC, because all child objects of the same Active Directory forest root receive this NC. You can consider the Configuration NC as mapping directly against and describing the topology of your Active Directory infrastructure.

Without knowledge of the Configuration NC, DCs in a site would not be able to obtain the information required to implement replication with either the domain or the forest. Additionally, the Configuration NC is used by the Knowledge Consistency Checker (KCC) and the Intersite Topology Generator (ISTG) to construct the replication objects. Chapter 9 covers Active Directory replication in more detail.

The Schema NC contains the attributes and classes that describe each object that exists in Active Directory. As discussed in Chapter 1, the schema is an extensible database that can be accessed programmatically, either by schema-enabled applications and services, such as Exchange 2000 or Visio 2002, or by Active Directory administrators using a variety of programming languages. The Schema NC replicates to all DCs in all domains that belong to the same Active Directory forest. Therefore, all DCs in a forest contain the same Schema NC, regardless of the domain of which they are members.

As you've learned, Active Directory can contain other types of information, such as binary (e.g., an employee photograph) or textual. It is the schema's ability to be extended (or added to) that allows an enterprise to include these types of information. You can view the Schema NC by registering the Active Directory Schema snap-in. After the snap-in is registered, an administrator may open the schema and receive a view similar to the one shown in the Figure 7-2.

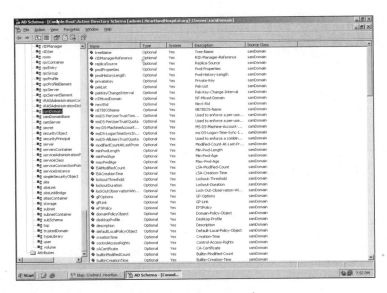

Figure 7-2 Active Directory Schema tool

Activity 7-2: Registering the Active Directory Schema Snap-in Tool

Time Required: 5 minutes

Objective: To register the schema tool for use by Active Directory administrators in an MMC.

Description: In this exercise you will register the schema tool in order to access schema components (which is not enabled by default) for administrative purposes.

1. If necessary, turn on your computer and log on as the administrator from your own domain.

2. Click **Start**, click **Run**, then type **regsvr32 schmmgmt.dll**, and click **OK**.

3. A message will appear telling you that registration of the DLL succeeded. Click the **OK** button to proceed.

4. Click **Start**, then click **Run**, type **mmc**, and click **OK**. An empty MMC console will appear.

5. Click **File** and **Add/Remove Snap-in**. Click **Add** and then click **Active Directory Schema**. Click **Add**, click **Close**, and then click **OK**.

6. Expand the Active Directory Schema root node and all child nodes. Explore the classes and attributes that form the schema.

7. When finished, click **File** and then click **Exit** to close the snap-in. When prompted to save settings, click **No**.

8. If you are not proceeding immediately to the next activity, log off your computer.

By selecting objects within the schema admin tool, administrators can access the contents of the Schema NC directly. This tool allows administrators who are members of the Schema Admins security group to alter the contents of the Active Directory schema. Use caution when accessing this tool, because any changes made to the schema using this tool are immediate and will replicate to all DCs in the forest.

The Domain NC contains Active Directory information that is specific to the domain for which it is named. In this regard, the Domain NC is different from the other two NCs we are discussing. While there will be only one Schema NC and one Configuration NC for each Active Directory forest, there can be many Domain NCs, depending on the number of domains in your Active Directory environment. If an Active Directory forest contains five child domains, which are all children of the Active Directory forest root domain, then there will be six Domain NCs—one for the forest root and one for each child.

The Domain NC can be viewed using several tools, including the Active Directory Domains and Trusts console and the Active Directory Users and Computers console. The Domain NC replicates only to DCs in a particular domain, not to DCs in other domains—whether they are in the same forest or not. Therefore, any changes to the local domain are reflected only in the Domain NC for that specific domain, not in the Domain NCs for other domains.

If you need to view the NCs in Active Directory, the most useful tool (in addition to those previously mentioned) is probably ADSI Edit. Review the information from Chapter 1 if you need to install ADSI Edit or other support tools. The ADSI Edit tool is shown in Figure 7-3.

As you examine Figure 7-3, notice that all three NCs are shown using this tool. This is particularly useful for an administrator and will simplify your work with Active Directory. The ADSI Edit tool will also permit the administrator to bind to different Active Directory components in foreign domains. This functionality makes ADSI Edit a particularly useful, and potentially dangerous, tool for day-to-day administration of an Active Directory environment.

ADSI stands for "Active Directory Services Interface"—the underlying components used by ADSI Edit and other programs to access the Active Directory database.

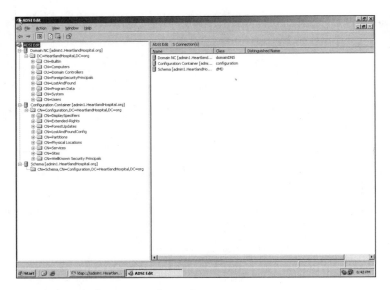

Figure 7-3   The ADSI Edit tool

Activity 7-3: Using the ADSI Edit Tool with Active Directory

Time Required: 10 minutes

Objective: To gain familiarity with ADSI Edit by launching the tool and using it to discover its functionality.

Description: As an administrator, you will need to be familiar with the administrative tools available in the Windows Server 2003. ADSI Edit is a particularly powerful tool for administration of the Active Directory environment.

1. If necessary, turn on your computer and log on as the administrator from your own domain.

2. If the support tools have not been installed, review the steps in Chapter 1 to install them.

3. Click **Start**, then click **Run**, type **adsiedit.msc**, and click **OK**. With ADSI Edit now open, you should see all three Active Directory NCs at once.

4. Explore the tool by expanding the schema object, and click the **CN=Schema**. Scroll down to find the object **CN=Address** and right-click it, and click Properties to view its properties.

5. When the CN=Address Properties box opens, note the options that are available to control which attributes to view. You can choose to show mandatory attributes, optional attributes, or both, and you can also limit the display to only attributes that are populated with values. (As time permits, you may change these settings to see how the list of attributes shown changes.)

6. Click the **Security** tab to see the default security permissions associated with this object, and then click **Cancel**.

7. Next, double-click the **Configuration Container** and then expand the child objects until you have located the object named CN=Partitions. Right-click the **CN=Enterprise Schema** object, click **Properties**, and view the information located there. Notice the default security permissions. Be careful not to modify any settings or you may damage the Active Directory of your domain. When finished, click Cancel.

8. When you have finished examining the contents of the Active Directory with ADSI Edit, you may close it.

9. If you are not proceeding immediately to the next activity, log off your computer.

Site Objects

As stated in the first part of the chapter, a site in Active Directory is a region of your network infrastructure made up of one or more well-connected IP subnets. Site objects are used in Active Directory to allow all Active Directory clients belonging to the same physical network area to access services from the servers in close proximity, rather than from servers located far away—across slow, expensive WAN links.

Some of the important services are DCs, GC servers, and DNS servers, among others. As an example of this functional usage of the Active Directory site, take a look at Figure 7-4, which illustrates a simple Active Directory site.

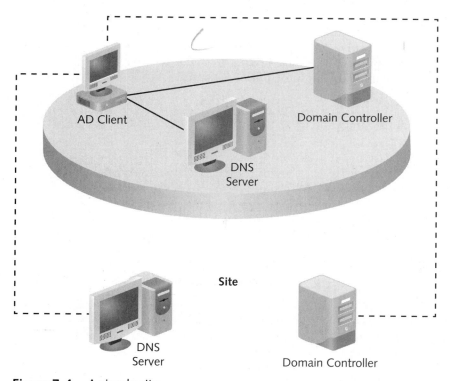

Figure 7-4   A simple site

As you examine the site diagram, notice that the clients within the site have access to various servers, such as a DC, without being required to cross the site boundary and initiate a logon session across a slow WAN connection. Should the client be unable to contact a server within their own site or require services that do not exist within the site, then the client would cross the site boundary and use the WAN to obtain those services. The Active Directory site serves to localize client traffic within a defined part of your network.

Note that sites generally map the physical structure of your network, but it is up to the administrator to define sites in a manual process (you might use a program or script to help create the site objects in a large network, but it is not automatic). You will need to plan carefully, as all other sites are created according to your implementation plan, with the exception of the initial site created when Active Directory was installed.

Activity 7-4: Creating a Site Using Active Directory Sites and Services

Time Required: 10 minutes

Objective: This exercise is designed to familiarize you with the process used to create a site in Active Directory using the Active Directory Sites and Services snap-in.

Description: When administering Active Directory, you will need to create sites that enable connectivity in your Active Directory infrastructure. Sites form the basis of many different services in Active Directory.

1. If necessary, turn on your computer and log on as the administrator from your own domain.

2. Click the **Start** button and then select the **Manage Your Server** tool. Under the domain controller section, choose the **Manage sites and services** option to open the Active Directory Sites and Services snap-in.

3. Right-click the **Sites** object and select **New Site** from the menu.

4. In the **New Object–Site** dialog box, type **MySiteXX** (where XX is your assigned student/computer number) as the name for the new site and then select a site link object to add to the new site. Choose **DEFAULTIPSITELINK** as the Site Link Object, and then click **OK** to continue. You will see a message box that lists other steps related to creating a site, and that suggests additional procedures. Click **OK** in the message box. This message only appears once per session. You will complete most of these steps in later hands-on activities.

5. Close the Active Directory Sites and Services snap-in.

6. If you are not proceeding immediately to the next activity, log off your computer.

Subnet Objects

Because a site is a group of one or more IP subnets, Active Directory uses subnet objects to identify what constitutes a subnet. A subnet object simply tells Active Directory which IP addresses are in a subnet.

Activity 7-5 Creating an Active Directory Subnet

Time Required: 10 minutes

Objective: To understand the process used to manually create a subnet object in Active Directory prior to creating a bridgehead server.

Description: Before configuring the specifics of any Active Directory site, you will need to first create one or more subnet objects using Active Directory Sites and Services. Because sites and subnets affect all domains in the forest, you will need to use an account that is a member of the Enterprise Admins group.

1. If necessary, turn on your computer and log on as the user **ea** from the forest root domain (ad.multinatcorp.com). The password is "Forestpw1".

2. Click the **Start** button and then select the **Manage Your Server** tool. Under the Domain Controller section, choose the **Manage sites and services** option to open the Active Directory Sites and Services snap-in.

3. Expand the **Sites** object, then right-click the **Subnets** object, and choose **New Subnet** from the menu.

4. Using the New Object-Subnet dialog box, enter the subnet address in the address field. For this example, use the subnet address assigned to your DC. You must also enter the subnet mask manually. Active Directory will generate the appropriate network mask/bits value.

5. Next, select the site you created in the previous activity (MySiteXX, where XX represents your assigned student/computer number) as the site object for this new subnet and click **OK**.

6. If the Subnets folder is not expanded already, expand it now.

7. You can now right-click the newly created subnet object and choose **Properties** to view the properties associated with this object. When you have examined the properties, click **Cancel** to close the object.

8. You may now exit the Active Directory Sites and Services snap-in tool.

9. If you are not proceeding immediately to the next activity, log off your computer.

Domain Controllers

At this point in the course, you should understand the concept and purpose of a DC in an Active Directory environment. As defined earlier, a DC is a Windows server computer that maintains a copy of the domain database. Users and computers use DCs for authentication, which allows access to domain resources and information. The DCs also contain information about the Active Directory environment in the form of the NCs. These NCs are replicated between DCs, and the replication process is affected by how sites are defined.

As part of the underlying process and implementation of sites in Active Directory, DCs are automatically placed into sites when they join the Active Directory domain, preferentially by IP subnet membership. That is, DCs and Active Directory are site-aware, so when a DC joins Active Directory, its site membership is determined according to the IP subnet that maps to a specific site within Active Directory. This functionality is illustrated with several sites in Figure 7-5.

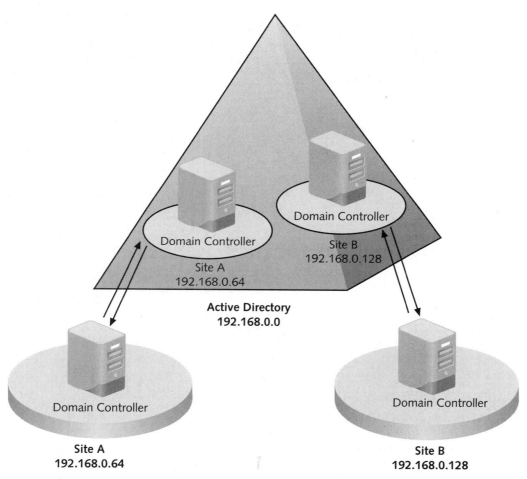

Figure 7-5   Basic DC/site functionality

As shown in Figure 7-5, as DCs join Active Directory domains, the Active Directory Installation Wizard ("dcpromo") examines the IP address being used by the DC and places the DC into the appropriate site. This process occurs without intervention from the Active Directory administrator, and ensures that DCs enter the Active Directory sites they were intended to support. After they are placed in the site by Active Directory, the DCs begin receiving replicated information for their own domain, as well as information about the forest.

Bridgehead Servers

A **bridgehead server** is used to designate a particular DC for replication purposes. Before getting into the specific operation of a bridgehead server, you will need to understand the basics of the replication process, as well as a little history. First, we will look at the replication process implemented in a Windows NT 4.0 domain so that you can then contrast that model against the new model implemented in Windows Server 2003.

Windows NT 4.0 domains follow the architectural model known as single master replication. (You may have heard of the single master domain model, but that is not the same thing.) Single master replication describes the situations in which one single master DC, called the primary domain controller (PDC), contains the read/write copy of the directory database. One or more other DCs, called backup domain controllers (BDCs), have read-only copies of the same database. All changes are made at the PDC and then sent (or replicated) to the BDCs.

By default, the PDC sends replicated domain information to 10 BDCs per replication session. A session begins when either a large number of changes have been made (by default, 2,000) or when at least one change has been made and five minutes have gone by. Figure 7-6 shows a typical Windows NT 4.0 domain environment with the PDC and a number of BDCs.

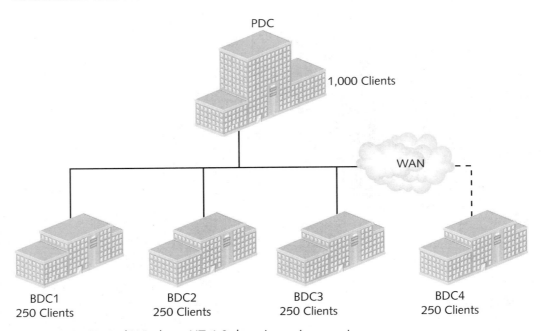

Figure 7-6   Typical Windows NT 4.0 domain environment

In Figure 7-6, the five DCs support 2,000 users located in five separate physical locations, including an administration building. Three of the BDCs (BDC1, BDC2, and BDC3) enjoy good connectivity to each other and the PDC using LAN. However, BDC4 is connected to the domain using an unreliable WAN connection (denoted by the dashed line).

In our example, the LAN network has a connection speed of 10 Mbps and the WAN connection has a speed of only 384 kbps. It is obvious that BDC4 will experience difficulties maintaining up-to-date domain information, particularly if there are large or frequent changes to the directory database. In fact, this DC may never catch up! It could become locked in a perpetual state of replication with the PDC, never able to receive a complete domain update.

This situation with BDC4 can become even more critical if several additional DCs are added to the BDC4 location. When more than one BDC exists at an NT 4.0 remote location, all BDCs receive domain updates at once, as shown in Figure 7-7, which builds upon Figure 7-6.

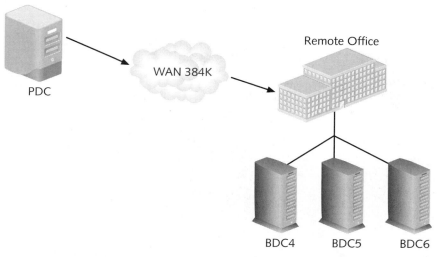

Figure 7-7   Additional BDCs at a remote location

In Figure 7-7, two additional DCs have been added to the remote location of BDC4. Now, instead of replicating the directory database to just one BDC across a WAN connection, the PDC replicates the directory database to three BDCs across the same WAN connection simultaneously, thereby degrading the performance of the WAN even further. If you add clients to this remote location who are also attempting to make use of the WAN for access to network resources located on the other side of the WAN, the situation becomes worse.

The preceding discussion illustrates the default behavior of the NT 4.0 directory replication mechanism. A method did exist to configure scheduled replication from the PDC to the BDCs; however, this needed to be configured at each BDC individually.

In many Windows NT 4.0 environments, the solution for this infrastructure design problem is to create the remote location as a separate Windows NT 4.0 domain with its own PDC. This eliminates replication issues across the WAN link. In exchange, though, it introduces issues related to the trust relationships, and might still require the placement of a BDC from the primary domain in the remote location to support client logons.

To counter these problems in the Active Directory environment, the infrastructure makes use of designated DCs called bridgehead servers. The bridgehead server is a DC that has been either automatically selected by the ISTG, or has been selected by the Active Directory designers to be a bridgehead server. Once configured in a site, the bridgehead server functions as the single point of contact for all replication information from its parent domain.

Note that an Active Directory site may contain several bridgehead servers. Some may belong to the same domain and serve a back-up role in case the designated bridgehead server becomes unavailable. Others may belong to other domains in the forest and provide the same functionality for their domains.

The use of bridgehead servers eliminates the problem that was encountered in the Windows NT 4.0 environment when replicating to remote locations. Instead of providing replication information to all member DCs in a site, Active Directory replicates domain information to only the bridgehead server. Once the bridgehead server has replicated fully with its replication partner from the other site, the now updated bridgehead server replicates to its partners in the same site using LAN connectivity. Figure 7-8 illustrates this process.

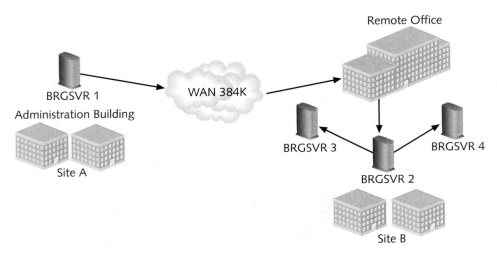

Figure 7-8   Bridgehead server functionality

In Figure 7–8, two Active Directory sites exist—Site A, which contains the administration building and the forest root, and Site B, which is a remote office and contains remote users. The network topology between these two sites is a single, 384K demand-dial link that, as a demand-dial connection, is only active when required. Site A contains a single bridgehead server named BRGSVR1, while Site B contains three bridgehead servers, named BRGSVR2, BRGSVR3, and BRGSVR4, respectively. The primary bridgehead server at the remote office location is BRGSVR2. All four DCs belong to the same domain and, therefore, must contain identical NCs for this domain.

In operation, the bridgehead server in Site A, BRGSVR1, collects domain NC information that must be replicated from Site A to Site B. BRGSVR1 initiates communications using the demand-dial connection. Once the network establishes the connection, the primary bridgehead server in Site B, BRGSVR2, accepts the replicated information. When BRGSVR2 has replicated completely with its opposite in Site A, the WAN connection is terminated because it is no longer required (assuming, of course, that there is no traffic for users or other services).

At this point in the replication process, BRGSVR2 replicates with its two partners in its own site, BRGSVR3 and BRGSVR4. Once these two DCs receive updated replication information from BRGSVR2, the process is complete. Instead of sending the same replication information to all DCs at the same time, the replicated information is sent to only one DC, which then replicates this information (if necessary) to other DCs in that site.

If you contrast this process with the older methods used in Windows NT 4.0, you will see that this way is much better. Active Directory has greatly reduced the need for multiple domains. The decision to create an additional domain is now more of a business decision than one based on technology or topology.

There are additional details related to bridgehead servers that need to be discussed. Most importantly, you must be aware that the selection of a bridgehead server can be either automatic or manual. Normally, the ISTG component makes the selection; however, an administrator could override the automatic selection and choose a specific server. Servers selected in this way are called **preferred bridgehead servers (PBSs)**.

You might choose to override this automatic selection if the DC selected by Active Directory is underpowered—that is to say, it may have limited system resources, such as RAM or CPU speed. For example, the ISTG may select a Pentium III computer with 512 MB of RAM as the bridgehead server; however, you may have acquired a new Pentium 4 with 2 GB of RAM that you wish to install in its place.

Another possible reason may be that the automatically selected server is leased, and you may want to designate a server that your company owns, even though it may be less powerful than the leased computer.

There are negatives associated with a manual selection of the bridgehead server, and the details of that implementation will be examined next.

The method used to automatically select a bridgehead server is controlled by two components: the **Inter-Site Topology Generator (ISTG)** and the **Knowledge Consistency Checker (KCC)**. The KCC functions in an intrasite environment, managing and optimizing the replication process for DCs within each site in Active Directory. Using an algorithm, the KCC dynamically determines replication paths for DCs, ensuring that domain NC information will replicate across a site within a time span no greater than 15 minutes. The ISTG functions in a similar manner to optimize the replication links between sites.

The process used by the KCC for the selection of a bridgehead server involves an examination of several parameters associated with both Active Directory and the individual DCs. The first step in the KCC process determines whether any PBSs have been selected. The implementation of a PBS causes the KCC to stop its bridgehead server selection process and use only the DC designated as the PBS by the Active Directory administrator. Although this manual configuration process may seem simple, and there may be perfectly valid reasons for using it in your environment, be advised that if the KCC has selected the bridgehead server, it will also manage the selection for you. If the bridgehead server selected by the KCC becomes unavailable or fails, the KCC will automatically perform a failover selection of a new bridgehead server without administrator intervention. If, on the other hand, you have elected to designate a PBS, the KCC will not manage the bridgehead server process, and there will be no automatic failover selection. Instead, you will need to examine the remaining DCs and manually select a server for the role.

The first step in manually creating a bridgehead server requires the creation of at least one subnet object. You created a subnet object in Activity 7-5. Now you will have an opportunity to manually create a bridgehead server.

Activity 7-6: Creating a Bridgehead Server Manually in an Active Directory Subnet Object

Time Required: 10 minutes

Objective: To understand the procedure for manually creating a bridgehead server in an Active Directory subnet object.

Description: In a normal operation, the KCC will determine, install, and manage bridgehead servers in a Windows Server 2003 Active Directory domain environment. A significant advantage in allowing the KCC to manage this process is that bridgehead servers created automatically are managed automatically. The KCC will also provide auto-failover if the KCC-designated bridgehead server fails. However, you may have justifiable business reasons for manually selecting a designated bridgehead server in your environment. This exercise will allow you to create such a server. Because sites and subnets affect all domains in the forest, you will need to use an account that is a member of the Enterprise Admins group.

1. If necessary, turn on your computer and log on as the user **ea** from the forest root domain (ad.multinatcorp.com). The password is "Forestpw1".

2. Click the **Start** button and then select the **Manage Your Server** tool. Under the Domain Controller section, choose the **Manage sites and services** option to open the Active Directory Sites and Services snap-in.

3. Expand the **Sites** object, then expand the Default-First-Site-Name site, then expand the **Servers** object that contains the DC you wish to add as the preferred bridgehead server.

4. Right-click the name of your server, and choose **Properties**.

5. The Servername Properties dialog box will appear. Select the IP transport protocol to be used by this bridgehead, and then click **Add**. Next, click **OK** to commit the change.

As other students complete this activity, additional preferred bridgehead servers will be designated.

6. You have now created a preferred bridgehead server. If this server becomes unavailable, you will need to manually select another DC in this site to replace it. When finished, close the Active Directory Sites and Services console.

7. If you are not proceeding immediately to the next activity, log off your computer.

After determining whether any PBS-designated servers exist, the KCC will continue the selection process by determining which DCs in the site can communicate using the designated replication protocol (RPC over IP or SMTP). Following this determination, all DCs within the site are ranked according to GUID. GUID ranking is used to determine which DC in each site has been running the longest without being restarted. After the runtime of the DCs has been determined, the first DC on the list is selected to become the bridgehead server for that site. After all of the DCs in a site have been sorted and ranked, they are considered equal in terms of bridgehead server selection criteria.

The process governing the ISTG is similar, and begins with the KCC. However, while the KCC runs on every DC in an Active Directory site, the ISTG runs on only one DC per site. The selection of ISTG is made using the same ordered list that controls the enumeration of the bridgehead server, as governed by the KCC. The senior DC on the list, in terms of GUID, assumes the role of ISTG. In the event that two servers in a site claim the role of ISTG (which sometimes happens), the two DCs will resolve the problem during the domain replication event by propagating up-to-date information through the Active Directory replication process to all DCs within the site.

Connection Objects

A connection object is a logical construct that exists in Active Directory to provide a representation of the connection between two or more DCs within a site, or between two sites for the purpose of regulating and controlling Active Directory replication. Connection objects are created in one of two ways—either automatically by the KCC and ISTG or manually by the Active Directory administrator.

Although the connection object created by the KCC or ISTG is similar to the one created by the administrator, one key difference exists. The KCC and ISTG will not optimize any connection objects created using a manual process. If you, as an administrator, elect to create connection objects manually, then you are wholly responsible for maintaining them in the event of misconfiguration issues or unavailability. Connection objects have specific characteristics that you will need to be aware of when configuring sites in Active Directory.

Connection objects are unidirectional (one-way), not bidirectional (two-way). The KCC and ISTG create a pair of matching connection objects for each Active Directory site link. However, if you are creating connection objects for a site link manually, you will need to create one in each direction—one outbound connection object and one inbound connection object for each DC or site with which you wish to establish a replication link.

Connection objects are created in Active Directory using the Active Directory Sites and Services snap-in tool. To create a new connection object, right-click the desired NTDS settings object (as shown in Figure 7-9) and choose the New Active Directory Connection menu option.

After selecting the New Active Directory Connection menu, complete the wizard to finish installing a new connection object. Using this process, additional connection objects can be created in Active Directory for either intrasite or intersite connections.

Activity 7-7: Creating a Connection Object in Active Directory

Time Required: 15 minutes

Objective: To provide an understanding of the process for manually creating a connection object using the Active Directory Sites and Services snap-in tool.

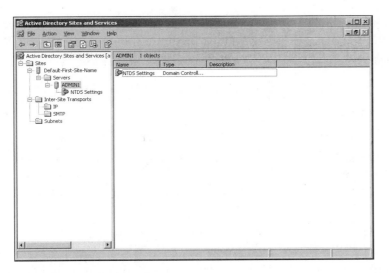

Figure 7-9 NTDS settings

Description: Normally, connection objects are created automatically when a DC is added to a domain. This exercise will demonstrate the process of adding an object manually.

1. If necessary, turn on your computer and log on as the user **ea** from the forest root domain (ad.multinatcorp.com). The password is "Forestpw1".

2. Click the **Start** button and then select the **Manage Your Server** tool. Under the Domain Controller section, choose the **Manage sites and services** option to open the Active Directory Sites and Services snap-in.

3. Expand the **Default-First-Site-Name** site, expand the **Servers** object, expand the **MNC-FRDC** server object, right-click the **NTDS Settings** object, and choose the **New Active Directory Connection** object.

4. From the Find Domain Controllers dialog box, select the name of your own server to create a connection object between MNC-FRDC and your DC, and then click **OK**.

5. If you receive a warning that a connection already exists, it means that the KCC or ISTG has automatically created a connection. Click **Yes** to create a new manual connection object.

6. Accept the default name provided by clicking **OK**.

7. Repeat this procedure to build a connection object between your server and MNC-FRDC (the reverse of the one you just created).

8. When you finish the procedure, click **File**, and then click **Exit** to close the Active Directory Sites and Services snap-in.

9. If you are not proceeding immediately to the next activity, log off your computer.

Global Catalog

The GC is a DC that fulfills a specific role in the Active Directory environment. Its purpose in an Active Directory site is to provide clients with a means for locating Active Directory resources that are outside of the domain in which they participate. GC servers contain a subset of information from every object in the entire forest. (You can review the details of GC servers in Chapter 1).

Sites are very important to the efficient operation of the GC process. One of the uses of a site in Active Directory is to localize Active Directory resources for users on a subnet-by-subnet basis. This means that when a client needs to use a GC server, it uses one from its own site.

With multiple domains and sites, users at each site will require information about available resources in Active Directory. As you design your Active Directory implementation, be certain to provide your users with adequate GC coverage at all sites, particularly those that are remote or sporadically connected.

Activity 7-8: Creating Additional GC Servers in an Active Directory Site

Time Required: 10 minutes

Objective: To demonstrate the process of adding a GC server to an Active Directory site.

Description: You may wish to optimize your site infrastructure by adding additional GC servers to Active Directory sites. This can be done to provide redundancy within a site—a second GC server in the event that the first one should fail. Most Active Directory sites require at least one GC server for functional use of Active Directory sites.

1. If necessary, turn on your computer and log on as the user **ea** from the forest root domain (ad.multinatcorp.com). The password is "Forestpw1".

2. Click the **Start** button and then select the **Manage Your Server** tool. Under the Domain Controller section, choose the **Manage sites and services** option to open the Active Directory Sites and Services snap-in.

3. If necessary, expand the **Default-First-Site-Name** site, expand the **Servers** object, expand the server object for your server, right-click the **NTDS Settings** object for your server, and then choose **Properties**.

4. You will now see the NTDS Settings Properties dialog box. You will see a number of configuration settings on the General page, including the Global Catalog checkbox. To enable this DC as a GC server, check this box and click the **OK** button.

5. You have configured this computer as a GC server for this site. You may now close Active Directory Sites and Services.

6. If you are not proceeding immediately to the next activity, log off your computer.

PLANNING AND DESIGNING SITES

Planning and designing your Active Directory site implementation is an important task that needs to be completed prior to implementing the sites themselves. As with all other features of the Active Directory environment, failure to plan your sites carefully and understand the overall goals of the implementation will complicate the implementation and could ultimately lead to the failure of your Active Directory infrastructure. To help you plan, consider two different aspects of your network—the physical network and the logical site topology.

Physical Network

All networks require one basic physical component to function. This is true regardless of whether your network is a basic, peer-to-peer network comprised of only two nodes, or it's the latest Windows Server 2003 Active Directory enterprise infrastructure supporting thousands of users and computers.

The physical network represents the actual physical objects that deliver a message from one place to another. From the simplest object, such as a child's toy made from a piece of string stretched between two tin cans, to the most complex, such as an optical network supporting terabytes of information transfer, all physical networks have three things in common: a point of transmission, a transmission medium, and a point of reception. (Of course, most modern computer networks have many points of transmission and many points of reception.) All other features and functionalities build upon these three basic concepts.

Begin planning your Active Directory sites by creating a diagram of your physical network infrastructure. There are several ways to determine the exact nature of your physical infrastructure, ranging from the original blueprints to various automated solutions. One particular automated solution is Microsoft Visio 2002 Enterprise, which is not an easy tool to configure, but has the ability to dynamically scan your network infrastructure and create a diagram that illustrates the details of the physical network. This diagram can serve as an excellent starting point as you plan your implementation. Your diagram should include the following information:

- Cable types—including Ethernet, thinnet, thicknet, fiber, ISDN, and digital and analog communication lines—and the lengths and cable grades associated with these items.

- Approximate paths of cable routing, including Ethernet, thinnet, thicknet, fiber, ISDN, and digital and analog communication lines.

- Server maps with detailed information about each server, including its role, IP address, name, domain membership (if any), and the owner's name and contact information.

- Peripheral devices, such as print devices, infrastructure devices (hubs, switches, routers, etc.), proxy servers, firewall servers, modems, and wireless access points (WAPs).

- WAN connections, including details such as the type of connection, available bandwidth for each connection, information about responsible parties, and contact information for the ISP providing the service.

- The number of users and computers located at each physical location.

- Any nonstandard implementations.

You should also thoroughly document all firmware versions being used in your infrastructure, as well as the DHCP and static IP settings of all network-enabled hosts. Pay attention to name-resolution services, such as WINS or DNS, and document the configuration of those servers, as well as any responsible parties or owners of these servers. Document any routing and remote access services (RRASs) or other dial-in servers or modem pools to include in your site implementation plans. After thoroughly documenting your physical network, you are ready to begin documenting your site topology.

 The person who pays the phone bill is a great resource when trying to find out where leased network connections exist.

Site Topology

With your newly created physical network map in hand, you are now ready to begin designing your site topology. Remember that the site topology is a logical representation of your physical network and does not necessarily map to the actual physical topology. The arrangement of subnets (specifically the well-connected ones) within your physical network is a key factor that will allow you to delineate your site topology. You should consider one or more well-connected subnets to constitute a site in your Active Directory design. As you assemble these subnets into sites, be sure that all sites can reach each other. (In network terms, this is called having a full-routed network.) If this is not possible, you will have to plan more advanced site links and site link bridges, which will be discussed later in this chapter.

Site Links

As you create your site topology and assemble your subnets into sites, you will probably find that you have a collection of disjointed objects, comprised of well-connected subnets that have no connectivity defined. When you reach this point, you are ready to begin assembling your site using site links.

A **site link** is the logical link that connects two LAN networks. It is a logical object that exists in Active Directory, not a physical object. You cannot reach out and touch a site link. Site links may already exist in your physical network, waiting for you to recognize and add them to the logical representation in Active Directory.

Microsoft's documentation describes site links in this way: "Site links are used to model the amount of available bandwidth between two sites. As a general rule, any two networks connected by a link that is slower than LAN speed is considered to be connected by a site link. A fast link that is near capacity has a low effective bandwidth, and can also be considered a site link."

The experience of administrators and designers allow them to make the call on what is considered well connected and what is not. If you have a cable modem in your home, are you well connected? What about a T-1 link at 1.55 Mbps? While some guidelines have been published by Microsoft and others experts, each situation is different. The amount of traffic that crosses the network and the available resources will also affect your decisions.

Several parameters are associated with site links. The first is the cost of the site link, which is a purely arbitrary value—meaning it is made up, not an actual dollar figure—that is assigned by the administrator. When deciding which of several possible routes to use, Windows will choose the route with the lowest cost. In other words, the cost determines which site links should be used preferentially when calculating replication connections. Figure 7-10 illustrates this concept.

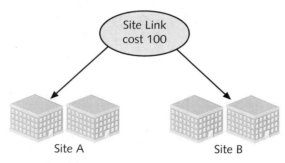

Figure 7-10   Site link costs

This simple diagram illustrates how a site link spans a WAN to provide connectivity to two otherwise disconnected sites. As you examine the site link, notice the site link cost. When configuring site link cost, it is strongly suggested that you not use a value of 1 for a preferred link. The reason for this is simple. If you assign a site link cost of 1 to a preferred link, what will happen if, at some point in the future, you install a faster connection technology for this site? If you have already given the existing site link a cost of 1, how can you designate the new link as the preferred link with a lower numeric value than 1?

Many designers choose a value such as 100 or 500 to represent the default value, allowing them to add higher or lower cost links in the future.

Another parameter associated with site links and site topology is the replication schedule. The replication schedule configuration will be covered in more detail in Chapter 8, but briefly stated, it defines the hours during the day when the site link is available for intersite replication. The replication schedule is manually configured and requires some consideration when determining the appropriate settings.

In addition to the replication schedule, is the replication interval, which will also be discussed in more detail in Chapter 8. The replication interval controls the polling interval used by the replication process to contact a DC at the other end of the site link for replication update changes.

The final parameter associated with the site link is the transport protocol used for intersite replication. The choice of a replication transport protocol is very important, as the wrong choice can have far-reaching consequences. The two available protocols are RPC over TCP/IP and SMTP. Each protocol is intended for specific circumstances that may exist when configuring the site links, and each has specific characteristics when used for Active Directory intersite replication. When you examine the site link container object in Active Directory for the site link being considered, you will notice two child objects below the site link. These child objects are the IP container object and the SMTP container object. Each contains settings and parameters specific to the named protocol.

The decision of when to use a specific replication protocol should be based on the quality of network connectivity between the two sites in question. The speed of the link is not necessarily an indication of connection quality, although it may be a deciding factor in the selection. The availability of a connection should be the primary criterion used to determine the replication transport protocol. If you have reliable connectivity between the sites—for example a 128K demand-dial link that is reliable—then your transport protocol should be RPC over TCP/IP. If the two sites have only intermittent or unreliable connectivity, then you should implement SMTP as a transport protocol. The specific differences between these two protocols will be examined in Chapter 8.

Site Link Bridges

Another issue that may arise when configuring site links occurs when two sites do not have a routed IP environment available to them for connectivity. In a properly functioning IP environment, all devices on your network are able to exchange packets with other devices on your network. In other words, IP connectivity can be established between sites using the normal IP connectivity process—following paths through network routers and other hardware. If you are able to use the *ping* command to send packets from a computer in one Active Directory site to a computer in another Active Directory site, then you have normal connectivity, and you do not need any special site implementations.

However, if you cannot ping from one site to another, then you will need to design and plan the site connections using additional objects called **site link bridges**. A site link bridge is composed of a minimum of three sites, as illustrated in Figure 7-11.

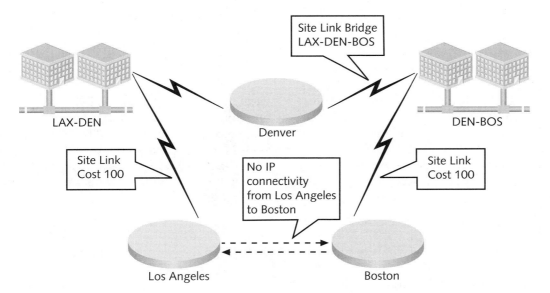

Figure 7-11 Site link bridges

There are three Active Directory sites in Figure 7-11: one in Los Angles (LAX), one in Denver (DEN), and one in Boston (BOS). The LAX site does not have network connectivity with the BOS site, and BOS does not have connectivity with LAX. However, both LAX and BOS have connectivity with DEN. Therefore, two site link bridges can be created, one between LAX and DEN, and another between DEN and BOS to mimic an IP-routed infrastructure. This site link bridge would be called LAX-DEN-BOS. Notice that in the diagram, a site link cost of 100 has been assigned to each leg of the LAX-DEN-BOS site link bridge, for a total cost of 200. If an additional site link bridge is installed, then the result would be as shown in Figure 7-12.

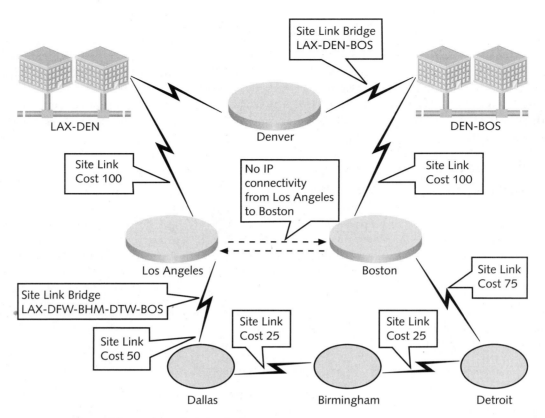

Figure 7-12   Additional site link bridges

This new site link bridge connects LAX and BOS via the route from LAX to DFW to BHM to DTW and finally to BOS. Again, each segment of this new site link bridge has been assigned a per-segment cost. The total cost of this new site link bridge is only 175; therefore LAX-DFW-BHM-DTW-BOS would become the preferred site link bridge (instead of LAX-DEN-BOS) based on the total cost of the assigned links. Figure 7-12 also illustrates that even though the LAX-DEN-BOS site link bridge is logically a simpler route, simplicity is not necessarily a consideration when configuring the site links or site link bridges. Route selection is determined when you assign link costs to the segment links.

Transitivity

Another concept to consider with site links and site link bridges is transitivity. By default, all site links are transitive connections with the "bridge all site links" setting enabled. This means that all site links are visible to each other and will be used to duplicate a fully routed IP infrastructure. If your network is not fully routed, you will need to disable this setting and configure site link bridges as described above.

The most important point to remember about site links and site link bridges is that unless your infrastructure is not fully routed or is unusually large (more than 200 sites), you do not need to enable site link bridges. A normally routed IP network will enable connections between sites.

CREATING AND MANAGING SITES

There are a number of ways to create and manage sites in Windows Server 2003 Active Directory. The most common tool is the Active Directory Sites and Services console, which is installed when the Active Directory Installation Wizard is first used to promote a server to a DC. It can also be installed as part of the administrative tools, as described in Chapter 1.

You can also create and manage sites using the Manage Your Server page, which offers administrators a convenient place to manage many aspects of a server. This tool is shown in Figure 7-13 as it appears in Windows Server 2003 with Active Directory installed. The Manage Your Server tool will be discussed again later in this section.

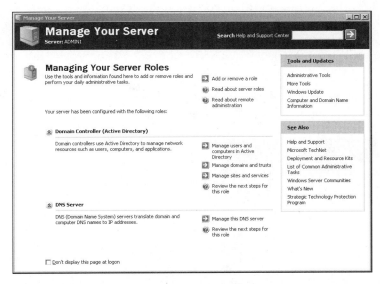

Figure 7-13 The Manage Your Server tool

Another tool for adding and administering sites is ADSI Edit, which has been discussed several times previously. ADSI Edit is a very powerful tool that offers administrators complete control over Active Directory, and should be used with care since it accesses Active Directory at a lower level than the other two tools.

Assigning Computers to Sites

The placement of DCs occurs automatically during the Active Directory installation process, which was described earlier in this chapter. It is important to remember that DCs are not automatically reassigned if/when your site is reconfigured or the IP address of a DC is changed. The administrator can move the DC to a different site by selecting a DC in a specific site and choosing the Move option.

Clients are placed into Active Directory sites according to their subnet membership. However, unlike DCs, clients (including servers that are not DCs) are assigned to a site each time they start up. This makes sense because clients are more likely to move between sites (especially mobile clients like laptop computers), and many are assigned addresses dynamically, such as with DHCP.

There is no option to move client computers using Active Directory Sites and Services. The client IP address must be changed and the computer must be restarted to change site membership.

Creating Sites

The process for creating a new site is very simple, provided that you have completed your preliminary site planning and design. Once this aspect of your site implementation has been finalized, use one of the tools described previously to create the required sites. In this book, we will use the Active Directory Sites and Services console and ADSI Edit to complete the hands-on activities. For detailed instructions on the use of ADSI Edit, refer to the *Microsoft Active Directory Programmer's Reference Guide, Volume 3, Active Directory Service Interfaces Programmer's Guide*.

Using these tools to create sites in Active Directory is fairly straightforward. You used the Active Directory Sites and Services console earlier in this chapter.

The Manage Your Server tool can be accessed using two different methods. The first method requires the administrator to leave the checkbox in the lower left corner of the interface labeled "Don't display this page at logon" unchecked, because this tool opens by default whenever an administrator logs on to a Windows server. Otherwise, the Manage Your Server tool can be accessed from the Start menu.

Once the tool has been started, click the option for Manage sites and services. This opens the Active Directory Sites and Services console, which is the standard tool for administering and creating sites in Active Directory. The Active Directory Sites and Services console is accessible either through the Administrative Tools menu, the Control Panel, Manage Your Server, or by creating a new instance of the snap-in in another MMC console.

ADSI Edit is available only if the support tools found on the Windows Server 2003 Server CD have been installed. Then the ADSI Edit tool can be found in the path shown in Figure 7-14.

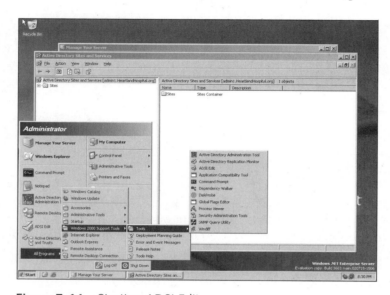

Figure 7-14   Starting ADSI Edit

Now that you know how to open these three tools, you can begin to add and modify sites in Active Directory using the Active Directory Sites and Services console.

Activity 7-9: Creating a Site Using ADSI Edit

Time Required: 10 minutes

Objective: To create a site in Active Directory using the Active Directory Scripting Interface tool.

Description: You are already familiar with the process required to create a site in Active Directory using the Active Directory Sites and Services snap-in. This activity presents another method that can be used to create the same type of object. As an additional note concerning this method, ADSI Edit is a scriptable tool that allows for the mass creation of multiple sites using VB scripts. This process speeds the creation of large numbers of sites and removes a possible source of creation/configuration errors.

1. If necessary, turn on your computer and log on as the user **ea** from the forest root domain (ad.multinatcorp.com). The password is "Forestpw1".

2. Click **Start**, click **Run**, type **adsiedit.msc**, and then click **OK**.

3. Expand the **Configuration** container object and then expand the object whose name begins **CN=Configuration,DC=…**'. When this object is expanded, you will see the object named CN=Sites.

4. Expand the **CN=Sites** object to view all child objects that presently exist.

5. Next, right-click the **CN=Sites** object, point to **New**, and then click **Object**. From the **Create Object** dialog box, select **site**, and then click **Next**.

6. In the Value property box, type a name for the new site. For this exercise use the name **ADSI-SITE**, and then click the **Next** button. At the next screen, click **Finish**. You do not need to configure additional attributes.

7. Now that you have added the new site object, you may close ADSI Edit.

8. If you are not proceeding immediately to the next activity, log off your computer.

Modifying the Default-First-Site-Name Site

When Active Directory is installed on the forest root DC, the IP subnet that contains the forest root DC becomes the first site in the forest and is given the name Default-First-Site-Name. One of the first things you should do is change this name to reflect your own infrastructure. To change the name of this site, double-click the container object, right-click the container, choose the **Rename** option, and then type in the new name. Keep in mind that you cannot use a name that contains special characters or spaces. After changing the name, press **Enter** to commit the change. The process is similar using ADSI Edit. Since there is only one Default-First-Site-Name in the classroom, you will rename the site you created earlier.

Activity 7-10: Renaming a Site Using ADSI Edit

Time Required: 5 minutes

Objective: To demonstrate the use of ADSI Edit as an administrative tool for managing Active Directory.

Description: Using ADSI Edit, you will rename the Default-First-Site-Name site object to gain experience using this administrative tool. ADSI Edit is a fully scriptable tool using VB, and can be used for many different purposes in Active Directory.

1. If necessary, turn on your computer and log on as the administrator from your own domain.

2. Click **Start**, click **Run**, type **adsiedit.msc**, and click **OK**.

3. Expand the **Configuration** container object and then expand the object whose name begins **CN=Configuration,DC=...**'. When this object is expanded, you will see the object named CN=Sites.

4. Expand the **CN=Sites** object to view all child objects that presently exist.

5. Locate the object named **CN=MySiteXX** (where XX represents your assigned student/computer number) and right-click it.

6. Select the **Rename** option and change the name to **Administration-Building-XX** (where XX represents your assigned student/computer number). Press the **Enter** key.

7. Look at the site object to visually confirm that its name was changed.

8. Close ADSI Edit.

9. If you are not proceeding immediately to the next activity, log off your computer.

Configuring Site Links

Actually performing the steps to create a site link is not difficult. If you completed the previous activities in this chapter, you now have at least two sites. According to our examples, these two sites are named Administration-Building and ADSI-SITE. If you do not have these two sites set up, consult with your instructor for assistance. It may take a few minutes for the new sites to replicate to all DCs in the classroom.

Activity 7-11: Configuring the Parameters for a Site Link in Active Directory

Time Required: 10 minutes

Objective: To configure the required parameters for an Active Directory site link object.

Description: After creating a site link object, there are four different parameters that need to be configured for functionality of the site link. You will configure those parameters in this activity.

1. If necessary, turn on your computer and log on as the user **ea** from the forest root domain (ad.multinatcorp.com). The password is "Forestpw1".

2. Click the **Start** button and then select the **Manage Your Server** tool. Under the Domain Controller section, choose the **Manage sites and services** option to open the Active Directory Sites and Services snap-in.

3. If necessary, expand Sites, then expand the **Inter-Site Transports** object, and then double-click the **IP** object.

4. In the right window, select the newly created **My Site Link XX** and right-click it, and choose **Properties**. You will now see the Site-Link Properties dialog box.

5. The first setting to be configured will be for cost. Change the Cost setting from the default of 100 to a value of **200**.

6. Next, adjust the Replicate every setting from its default of 180 minutes to **360 minutes**.

7. Next, click the **Change Schedule** button and configure the replication schedule to exclude the hours between 8:00 a.m. and 4:00 p.m., Monday through Friday. Allow replication at any other time, including Saturday and Sunday. Note that the fourth replication setting, for a transport protocol, was accomplished in Step 3 when you selected the IP object.

8. Click **OK**.

9. Click **OK** to commit the changes. You should see the newly configured cost and replication interval in the properties for this site link.

10. When finished, you may close Active Directory Sites and Services.

11. If you are not proceeding immediately to the next activity, log off your computer.

Configuring Site Link Bridges

There is very little to configure in a site link bridge object. All of the settings governing replication are set on the individual site links, and the site link bridge can almost be considered the sum of its parts.

Activity 7-12: Configuring Site Link Bridges in Active Directory

Time Required: 10 minutes

Objective: To configure the Active Directory setting that controls the transitive bridging of site links for site link connectivity.

Description: Although Active Directory sites are automatically bridged, you may at some point have a need to disable this feature. This activity will illustrate the process of disabling transitive bridging of site links.

1. If necessary, turn on your computer and log on as the user **ea** from the forest root domain (ad.multinatcorp.com). The password is "Forestpw1".

2. Click the **Start** button and then select the **Manage Your Server** tool. Under the Domain Controller section, choose the **Manage sites and services** option to open the Active Directory Sites and Services snap-in.

3. If necessary, expand the **Sites** object and then expand the **Inter-Site Transports** object. Right-click the IP object and select **Properties**. Note: The process is exactly the same for the SMTP object.

4. To disable site link bridging, remove the checkmark from the **Bridge all site links** checkbox and click **OK**.

5. Close Active Directory Sites and Services.

6. If you are not proceeding immediately to the next activity, log off your computer.

Chapter Summary

❏ Active Directory sites are composed of one or more well-connected subnets, where the term well connected is generally accepted to mean a LAN. Two or more sites are connected by a WAN.

❏ The object connecting two or more sites is called a site link. The site link is an object in Active Directory and has parameters attached to it. The parameters include site link cost, replication interval, replication schedule, and transport protocol.

❏ If a routed IP network does not exist between sites, then the administrator will construct another type of object in Active Directory called a site link bridge, which defines the path that will be followed by replication traffic through a number of sites. Site link bridges are composed of existing site links and have an associated overall cost made up of the cumulative site links in the site link bridge.

❏ Bridgehead servers are dedicated DCs that are used in the replication process and serve as a point of contact from one site to another. Replication packets travel between sites from one bridgehead server to another, and are then distributed to other DCs within each site.

❏ DCs are placed into the appropriate site based on their IP address and can be moved later by an administrator.

❏ Client computers are placed into sites based on their IP addresses each time they start.

❏ Sites may be created in Active Directory using the Active Directory Sites and Services snap-in, the Manage Your Server tool, or the ADSI Edit tool.

Key Terms

bridgehead server — A dedicated DC that serves as the point of contact from its own parent domain to its site container and serves as replication bridge for the replication of naming context partitions.

Intersite Topology Generator (ISTG) — Creates and manages the intersite replication of Active Directory naming partitions.

Knowledge Consistency Checker (KCC) — Creates and manages the intrasite replication of Active Directory naming partitions.

preferred bridgehead server (PBS) — A bridgehead server that has been selected by an administrator, not by an automatic process.

site — Two or more well-connected IP subnets.

site link — An object that exists in Active Directory to define the logical connection between two sites in a fully routed IP network. Site links are transitive by default.

site link bridge — An object that exists in Active Directory to define the logical connection between three or more sites in a nonrouted IP network. A site link bridge may be formed from more than three sites and is manually created. Site link bridges are not transitive.

REVIEW QUESTIONS

1. The _____ controls intersite replication of Active Directory naming contexts in a Windows Server 2003 Active Directory infrastructure.

2. If configuring connectivity between sites in a nonrouted IP environment, you should disable _____ first.

   a. All bridgehead servers

   b. All site link replication intervals

   c. Site link transitivity

   d. IP routing

3. When a new DC is added to an Active Directory domain, the administrator must manually select which site to join it to. True or False?

4. A connection object is _____. (Choose all that apply.)

   a. A logical object

   b. A network object

   c. The connection defined between two Active Directory sites

   d. An object that uses SMTP as its transport technology across a reliable WAN connection

5. When configuring bridgehead servers in a site, if a PBS is manually selected and subsequently fails, the ISTG will select a new bridgehead server to fill the role of the failed bridgehead server. True or False?

6. By default, the _____ selects the DC that will assume the role of bridgehead server in a site. (Choose all that apply.)

   a. Administrator

   b. Intersite Topology Generator

   c. Bridgehead selection algorithm

   d. Knowledge Consistency Checker

7. When configuring bridgehead servers in a site, if a PBS is manually selected and subsequently fails, the KCC will not select a new bridgehead server to fill the role of the failed bridgehead server. True or False?

8. New sites can be added to Active Directory using _____. (Choose all that apply.)

   a. LDAP.EXE

   b. ADSI Edit

   c. Manage Your Server

   d. Active Directory Sites and Services

9. The GC is a _____ that fulfills a specific role in the Active Directory environment.

   a. Member server from a domain

   b. Modified DNS server

   c. Secondary forest root DC

   d. DC

10. By default, all site links are transitive connections with the Active Directory setting of Bridge all site links enabled. True or False?

11. A site link is an object in Active Directory with parameters that include _____: (Choose all that apply.)

    a. Site link transitivity, replication interval, replication schedule, and transport protocol

    b. Site link cost, replication interval, replication schedule, and transport protocol

    c. Site link bridge cost, SMTP replication compression setting, replication schedule, and transport schedule

    d. Site link cost, replication interval, replication schedule, and RPC transport schedule

12. The process used to create a site link bridge is identical to the process used to create a site link, with the exception of which of the following? (Choose all that apply.)

    a. Site link bridges have no settings for site link cost or replication interval

    b. Site link bridges require configuration of SMTP transport protocol settings

    c. Site link bridges do not require configuration of SMTP transport protocol settings

    d. Site link bridges can only be configured using GC servers as endpoints

13. The Configuration NC contains information about DCs, domains and sites, and the NT Security Description for a schema object. True or False?

14. *Default-First-Site-Name* is created automatically when Active Directory is first installed, and except for this first site, all other sites are created _____. (Choose all that apply.)

    a. Automatically as child domains are created and joined to the Active Directory

    b. Automatically as remote GC servers are created in Active Directory

    c. As dictated by your site implementation plan

    d. Manually as your Active Directory implementation grows over the course of time

15. Sites in Active Directory allow the administrator to control the replication process for Active Directory information. True or False?

16. Remember that the site topology is a logical representation of your physical network and does not necessarily map to the actual physical topology. The key factor that will allow you to delineate your site topology will be _____. (Choose all that apply.)

    a. The number of nonrouted IP subnetworks in your network infrastructure

    b. The arrangement of subnets within your physical network

    c. The classes of IP addresses used in your infrastructure

    d. The number of IP host nodes assigned per subnet

17. It is not possible to change the name of the *Default-First-Site-Name* site container. True or False?

18. When creating site links, the administrator must configure a cost for the site link. The range of values for the site link cost is from _____. (Choose all that apply.)

    a. 0-5,000

    b. 1-500

    c. 1-99,999

    d. 1-10,000

19. Site link costs are cumulative. Therefore, if Site Link A has a cost of 50, Site Link B has a cost of 75, Site Link C has a cost of _____, and Site Link D has a cost of 251, then the total cost for this site link bridge is 487.

    a. 112

    b. 115

    c. 110

    d. 111

7

20. If the choice of a replication transport protocol is wrong, there can be far-reaching consequences. The protocol available is _____ over TCP/IP or SMTP. (Choose all that apply.)

    a. SNMP

    b. ARP

    c. UDP

    d. RPC

HEARTLAND HOSPITAL CASE PROJECTS

Now that the Heartland Hospital Active Directory implementation is starting to take form, it is time to turn your attention to some of the physical aspects of the hospital's Active Directory implementation. Working with Mary, you have begun the process of implementing sites in Active Directory. Examine the map in Figure 7-15 to understand why multiple sites may be necessary for Heartland Hospital.

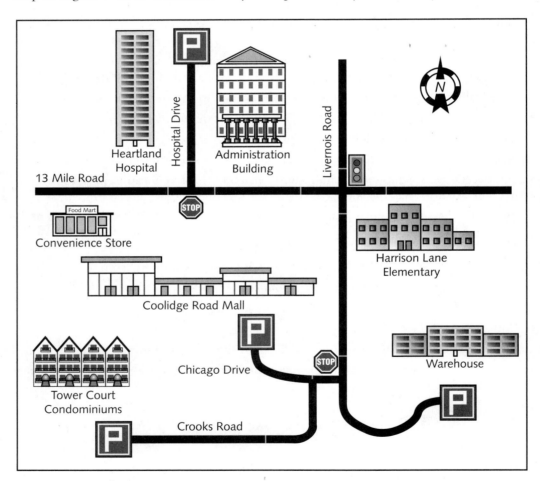

Figure 7-15   Heartland Hospital map

Case Project 7-1: An Introduction to Sites

In Figure 7-15, notice the layout of the different buildings that comprise the Heartland Hospital complex. The warehouse facility is approximately 5 km (3 miles) from the administration building. Using the map above, work with Mary to make some basic design decisions for the Heartland Hospital Active Directory site implementation.

1. From your first examination of the map, how many sites do you think should be implemented in this particular site model?

2. Examine the details carefully. Would the fact that the warehouse building, which is an older facility that Heartland Hospital purchased, still uses a token ring network affect your site design?

3. The hospital building and the administration building are located across the street from one another, a distance of approximately 60 m (200 ft). Is this separation sufficient to require multiple sites or a single site for these two buildings?

Case Project 7-2: IP Address Assignment

Refer to the previous chapters and the figures in those case projects. Table 7-1 shows a part of the network documentation that describes the IP addressing scheme defined for Heartland Hospital.

Table 7-1   Heartland Hospital IP Subnet Chart

Subnet	Mask	Subnet Size	Host Range	Broadcast
192.168.0.0	255.255.255.192	62	192.168.0.1 to 192.168.0.62	192.168.0.63
192.168.0.64	255.255.255.192	62	192.168.0.64 to 192.168.0.126	192.168.0.127
192.168.0.128	255.255.255.192	62	192.168.0.129 to 192.168.0.191	192.168.0.191
192.168.0.192	255.255.255.192	62	192.168.0.193 to 192.168.0.254	192.168.0.255

1. What kind of IP address is represented in Table 7-1?

2. Use Table 7-1 and Figure 7-16 to define an IP addressing scheme based on the number of floors in each building. Determine whether to assign a range of IP addresses on a floor-by-floor basis, have one range per building, or determine another addressing scheme with your partner.

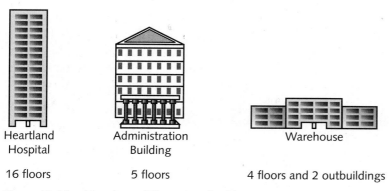

Heartland Hospital — 16 floors

Administration Building — 5 floors

Warehouse — 4 floors and 2 outbuildings

Figure 7-16   Number of floors per building

Case Project 7-3: Benefits of Using Sites

Using the update network map shown in Figure 7-17, consider the possible network flow and design for your replication traffic and client-logon traffic.

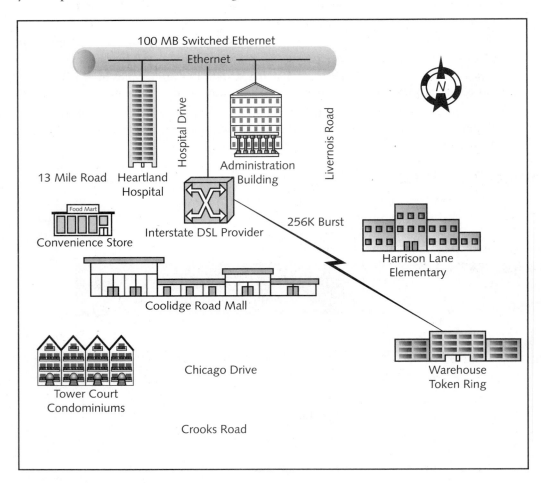

Figure 7-17   Heartland Hospital WAN

1. A decision has been made not to place a DC in the warehouse building. However, a resource server (file/print and other network services) will be placed at this location. The administration building will contain the forest root DC, as well as at least one resource server. The hospital building will contain at least one DC, as well as one resource server. Refer to the previous chapters and work with your partner to create a replication design.

2. Will you need to implement any site links or site link bridges?

3. Is there any justification for implementing a suggestion by Michael Garabaldi to adjust the replication schedule to replicate Active Directory information between the administration building and the hospital building on a 16-hour replication cycle?

4. Why would he suggest this detail and how could it be implemented, given the diagram above?

Case Project 7-4: Creating and Using Sites

You and Mary may need to configure the cost, as well as other properties of site links.

1. Using Figure 7-18, determine the link cost between the hospital site and the warehouse site.

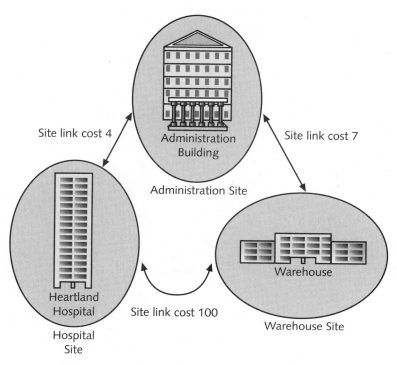

Figure 7-18   Heartland Hospital site link costs

2. What would the effect on the network be if the direct link between the hospital site and the administration building were unavailable?

3. What would the effect on the network be if the direct link between the hospital site and the warehouse site were unavailable?

4. You should plan for some redundancy in your network design. Using Figure 7-18 as a reference, is it necessary to place administrative servers (such as DCs or GC servers) at any additional sites?

8

ACTIVE DIRECTORY REPLICATION

After reading this chapter and completing the exercises, you will be able to:

♦ Describe and understand how Active Directory replication works

♦ Describe the Active Directory replication topology

♦ Manage Active Directory replication

♦ Monitor Active Directory replication

♦ Understand the role of operations masters

♦ Troubleshoot Active Directory replication

In normal day-to-day administration, changes are made to objects in Active Directory. New users are added, passwords are changed, and objects are deleted. These changes need to be updated on all DCs in the network to ensure they have the most up-to-date information. This process of updating Active Directory changes to all DCs on the network is called replication.

In this chapter, you will learn how replication allows Windows Server 2003 to work with multiple copies of the Active Directory database and make changes at any replica.

Specifically, this chapter will examine the inner workings of Active Directory replication, replication topology, how to manage and monitor replication, and some other issues that can arise. This chapter will also discuss operations master roles, where they appear, and why they are significant. Finally, we will look at troubleshooting Active Directory replication.

THE REPLICATION PROCESS

Active Directory uses a **multi-master model** for replication. This means that changes to Active Directory can be made on any DC, and those changes will then be replicated to other DCs. This is a significant enhancement over the replication in Windows NT, which has only one master (or writeable) copy. In a Windows NT domain, only the PDC can change the domain database. This means that if the PDC is not available, changes—such as adding users to the network, or even changing a password—cannot occur.

When a change is made to Active Directory, such as adding a new user or changing a user's telephone number, the replication process begins. Replication is performed at the attribute level, not the object level. For example, if a user's fax number is changed, then only the new fax number of that user object is replicated. Other attributes of the user object that were not changed are not replicated, making the replication process in Windows Server 2003 very efficient.

The use of a multi-master model does, however, introduce a different consideration: It is possible for two DCs in the same domain to show different information, even for the same object. This is caused by **latency**, which is the idea that the replication process takes some time. The latency could be only a few seconds, but most often it is a few minutes. In large, geographically dispersed networks, the latency could be hours. Once replications have finished and all DCs contain the same information for every object, the directory database is said to have reached **convergence** (or to have converged).

The membership attribute of a group object is treated differently by Windows Server 2003 than by Windows 2000. If the forest functionality level is set for Windows 2003 Server, then only changes to group membership are synchronized. If it is set at a lower functionality level, then the entire membership is replicated when new users are added or removed from the group. If a group membership is large, this can create a significant amount of replication traffic. You will learn more about forest functionality levels in Chapter 12.

 The way in which group membership changes are replicated is one of the most important differences between Windows Server 2003 and Windows 2000. The membership of a group is a single attribute—albeit a large one—which Windows 2000 must handle as a single unit.

Tracking Replication

Since changes to Active Directory can be made on any DC, there must be a mechanism to track those changes and ensure that updates are replicated properly. DCs track these object changes using **Update Sequence Numbers (USNs)**.

Each DC maintains its own USN, and every time the Active Directory database on a DC is modified, the USN is incremented by one. The changed objects and attributes are then stamped with the USN.

To ensure that the latest updates are received, each DC maintains a table that lists the USNs it has received from the other DCs, as well as the highest USN from each DC. When a DC sends a change notification, each receiving DC checks its USN table for the last USN it received from the sending DC. If the USNs are the same, then no update is required. If the USN on the source DC is higher (newer) than the last USN seen on the destination server, then an update is required and the changes are replicated. This eliminates the reliance on timestamps for updates, although they are sometimes used for conflict resolution.

Replication Timing

Replication is either intra-site or inter-site. **Intra-site replication** is the process of updating DCs within the same site. **Inter-site replication** is the process of updating DCs between sites. (Sites were discussed in Chapter 7.)

Intra-site replication is automatic and cannot be scheduled or compressed. Replication is based on change notification, and the replication process begins when an object is modified at a DC. This change could be made initially at that DC, or could be received by replication from another DC. By default, the DC will wait a few seconds after the first change is made and then send out a notification to each of its **replication partners**. When many small changes are made to Active Directory at almost the same time, they are collected into batches to enhance the efficiency of Active Directory replication. This makes sense since administrators often make many changes to several objects or one change that affects many attributes. This brief delay reduces the overhead otherwise involved in sending many small changes.

Once the replication partners receive the change notification, they will request updates. Recall from Chapter 7 that DCs in the same site have high-speed, reliable connectivity between them, so they can handle the comparatively high number of updates.

On the other hand, inter-site replication is time-based and is determined by a schedule set in a site link. The administrator can configure the replication to occur during specific times, and compress it to make better use of available bandwidth. The default replication schedule between sites is every three hours. This is an important consideration for most organizations. You will need to fine-tune your inter-site replication, based on your WAN links, to meet the needs of your organization.

Urgent Replication

Urgent replication occurs immediately within a site. No delay between updates is observed.

Events that trigger urgent replication are:

- An account lockout—If an account lockout policy is in place, accounts will be locked after the defined number of log-on failures.

- A Local Security Authority (LSA) secret change—LSA secrets store passwords used for establishing trust relationships and service accounts.

- The RID master role is assigned to a new server—The RID master is a single master operations role covered later in this chapter.

When considering these items, notice that they each represent something critically important, where all DCs must be in agreement immediately. If you think about it, there would be no point in locking out an account at one DC if the other DCs continue to act as if nothing is wrong.

 Change notification can be configured on site links to force urgent replications to occur between sites. However, this will cause normal, nonurgent replication traffic between sites to increase. If change notification is configured on a site link, then the change notification that occurs within a site can also traverse the site link.

Password Replication

It is important for passwords to be synchronized between DCs more frequently than the default. Normally you would have no control over which DC authenticates a particular user. If a user's password is changed on a particular DC, but the user's next logon didn't happen to be authenticated by the same DC, what would happen? The user would be refused access when he or she used the new password! Clearly, this is not acceptable. To avoid such situations, password changes are replicated a bit differently than urgent or nonurgent replication.

The most important part of password replication is the **PDC emulator**. Each domain has one DC that holds the role of PDC emulator. (Roles are discussed in detail later in this chapter.) When the password of a user object is changed on a DC, the change is replicated immediately to the PDC emulator. This occurs whether the PDC emulator is in the same site or a different site. Normal replication of the password change also updates the other DCs.

If the update to the PDC emulator fails, then only the normal, nonurgent replication process is used.

When a user attempts to log on using an incorrect password—such as the old one—the DC being contacted (called the authenticating DC) will not immediately deny the logon. The authenticating DC will first contact the PDC emulator to see if the password has been recently changed. If there is an updated password that matches the password supplied by the user, then the user will be allowed to log on.

REPLICATION TOPOLOGY

A **replication topology** is the combination of paths used to replicate changes between DCs. Not every DC within a site communicates directly with every other DC when changes are made. As you learned in Chapter 7, there is also a system to control replication between sites.

Active Directory Partitions

Active Directory information is divided into separate parts, called partitions or NCs:

- Schema partition—This partition contains the definitions, attributes, and rules for all objects that can be created in Active Directory. This partition is replicated to all DCs in the forest.

- Configuration partition—This partition contains information about the forest's structure, including domains, sites, trust relationships, DCs, and services. This partition is also replicated to all DCs in the forest.

- Domain partition—This partition stores information on all objects in the domain, including OUs, users, printers, and groups. This partition is only replicated to other DCs in the same domain. A forest may have multiple domain partitions.

- Application partition (optional)—These partitions are optional, so there may be many, or they may not exist at all. They can contain any type of object except security principals, and can exist on any chosen DC in the forest. Application partitions are normally used to store information for an application in which you need flexibility regarding which DCs have replicas of the partition. The integrated DNS Server in Windows Server 2003 is the first application to make use of application partitions, using them to store Active Directory integrated DNS zones.

As described in Chapter 1, the copy of an Active Directory partition held on a DC is called a **replica**. For example, every DC holds a replica of the schema and configuration partition. Every DC in a single domain holds a replica of its specific domain partition.

Intra-site Replication

When an Active Directory site is created, the KCC creates the replication topology automatically. The KCC runs on every DC at set intervals to determine which DCs will replicate with other DCs, creating replication partners. The replication topology is constantly updated by the KCC as new domains and DCs are added or removed.

The default replication topology is a bidirectional ring that provides fault tolerance and reliability. A bidirectional ring creates a minimum of two replication paths between DCs.

For example, imagine yourself as part of group of people standing in a circle, holding hands. In this circle, every time your hand is squeezed, you would squeeze the hand of the person on the other side of you. So if the person on your left squeezes your hand, you would squeeze the hand of the person on your right, and so on. A hand squeeze would travel all around the circle until it got back to its originator. (This is one of the few network administration topics that can be turned into a party game.)

You could send a squeeze to the person on your left by simply squeezing your left hand. But what if you weren't able to keep your hands together and the ring was broken? You could send a squeeze to the person on your left by sending it around to your right—through all of the other people in the circle. This is the concept of a fault-tolerant ring. Messages can travel either way around the ring to bypass a break in one spot.

The KCC also ensures that no more than three hops are required to replicate a change between all the DCs in a site. If less than seven DCs are in a site, then a simple ring is sufficient. If more than seven DCs are present, then additional connections are created between members of the ring to reduce the number of hops.

The replication paths between DCs are called connections. If a DC is not available, the KCC will automatically create additional **connection objects** to ensure replication is successful. The administrator can also create connection objects to better manage replication.

Connection objects can be configured using Active Directory Sites and Services. Figure 8-1 shows two connections generated automatically by the KCC.

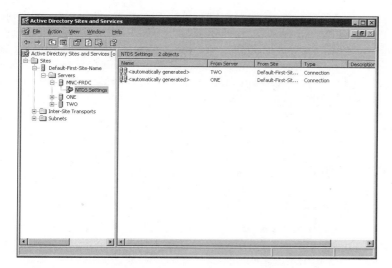

Figure 8-1   Automatically generated connection objects

 To manually force a replication, right-click a connection object, and then click **Replicate Now**. This is useful for troubleshooting.

Inter-site Replication

The inter-site replication topology is also generated by the KCC, based on information in Active Directory regarding sites, subnets, and costs to create the best connections between sites.

The first DC in a site will take on the role of ISTG, which is responsible for choosing a bridgehead server. The first DC retains the role of ISTG until it becomes unavailable for 60 minutes, at which point another DC in the site will take over the role.

 You cannot control which DC is given the ISTG role, but you can verify which one it is in Active Directory Sites and Services. In a site, right-click **NTDS Settings**, then click **Properties**.

A **bridgehead server** is a DC in the local site that performs replication to and from other sites and then updates other DCs within its own site. Normally the bridgehead server is automatically chosen by the ISTG, as discussed in Chapter 7. However, you can specify a server as a PBS (as you practiced in Activity 7-6), therefore ensuring that it becomes a bridgehead server.

Replication Updates

Replication involves two types of updates—originating updates and replicated updates. An **originating update** is a change to Active Directory that was made on the local DC. For example, if a user's password is changed on Server1, then it is an originating update on Server1.

A **replicated update** is a change that was made through replication. For example, if a user's password is changed on Server1, and the change is replicated to Server2, then it is a replicated update on Server2.

Updates to Active Directory are replicated to replication partners until all DCs are updated. However, because replication is a ring, DCs will eventually attempt to replicate with other DCs that are already updated.

To prevent updates from happening more than once, a process called **propagation dampening** is used. Each DC keeps a list of DC pairs and the last USN received from each. This is called the **up-to-dateness vector**. When a destination DC requests changes, it provides its up-to-dateness vector to the source DC (remember, it will have a unique up-to-dateness vector for each replication partner). By comparing this value on the source and destination DC, the source DC can determine that the destination does or does not have an up-to-date value for an attribute, and sends updates accordingly. If the destination already has an up-to-date value, the source DC does not send that attribute.

Replication Conflicts

As you've learned, a multi-master model allows changes to be made on any DC. These changes are then replicated to the other DCs. This can cause problems when changes are made to the same object at the same time on different DCs. Active Directory has built-in safeguards to avoid or resolve these conflicts for you.

First of all, replicating at the attribute level minimizes replication conflicts. In other words, only the changed attribute is replicated, not the entire object. A conflict will only occur if the same attribute is changed on the same object at the same time on two different DCs. If the department attribute of a user object is changed on DC1 and the fax number of the same user is changed on DC2, there won't be a conflict. This helps minimize the number of conflicts that occur in Active Directory.

If the same attribute is changed on two different DCs at the same time before replication is complete, a timestamp is used to resolve the conflict. When a DC receives both updates, the update with the most recent timestamp will be written to the directory. In the event that the timestamps are the same, the update with the highest **globally unique identifier (GUID)** is used.

 Since GUIDs are, in part, random numbers, they are not generated in sequence. Therefore, using the GUID to resolve a conflict will not guarantee which change is the "better" choice. However, it does ensure that all DCs use the same information.

MANAGING ACTIVE DIRECTORY REPLICATION

The primary means for managing replication is through the use of sites. As you learned in Chapter 7, a **site** is a group of well-connected subnets with high-speed, permanent network connectivity. Intra-site replication is automatic, cannot be scheduled, and cannot be compressed. Inter-site replication is controlled by site links and can be configured by the administrator. Therefore, to control replication you need to use sites.

To control replication, sites are sometimes set up between areas of a network that have high-speed, reliable connections.

In a fully routed network, inter-site replication is automatically configured, and the administrator does not need to create additional site links. However, the administrator might want to change the replication schedule or manually configure which sites replicate with other sites where particularly slow WAN links exist.

Using Sites

As you learned in Chapter 7, a site named Default-First-Site-Name is automatically created when the first DC in the forest is created. All DCs are automatically placed in that site unless the administrator created other sites and subnets. Therefore, all DCs will be placed in the same site by default. This is an optimum arrangement if all DCs have a high-speed connection to one another and to all of their client computers. If some DCs or client computers are connected through a WAN link, additional sites should be created to better manage replication traffic and control how clients access the servers. By creating additional sites you can control how often replication occurs (through site links), as well as between which DCs it occurs.

Activity 8-1: Creating Sites

Time Required: 5 minutes

Objective: To create multiple sites to configure replication.

Description: In this activity you will create separate sites between DCs, and then create a custom replication schedule for inter-site replication. This will reduce the amount of replication traffic between the two DCs. You practiced some of these steps in Chapter 7, and the activities in this chapter reinforce and build on the activities in Chapter 7.

1. If necessary, turn on your computer and log on as the user **ea** from the forest root domain (ad.multinatcorp.com). The password is "Forestpw1".

2. Start **Active Directory Sites and Services**.

3. Right-click **Sites** and click **New Site**.

4. Type **Computer-Site** (where *Computer* is the name of your computer and *Site* is its location), as shown in Figure 8-2. Click **DEFAULTIPSITELINK** and click **OK**.

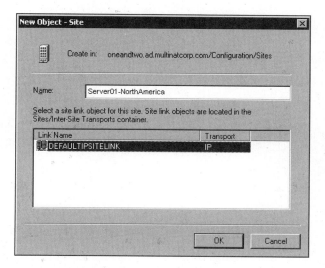

Figure 8-2   Creating a new site

5. Click **OK**.

6. Double-click **Default-First-Site-Name**, then double-click **Servers**.

7. Right-click your server name and click **Move**.

8. Click your **Computer-Site**, then click **OK**.

9. Double-click **Computer-Site**, then double-click **Servers**.

10. Double-click your server name and click **NTDS Settings**. Notice the replication connections to other DCs. These were automatically created by the KCC.

11. Close **Active Directory Sites and Services**. If you are not proceeding immediately to the next activity, log off your computer.

Activity 8-2: Manually Creating Active Directory Connections

Time Required: 10 minutes

Objective: To create manual connections to configure replication.

Description: You want to manually configure the replication topology to make better use of network bandwidth. In this activity you will be working with a partner to manually create an Active Directory connection between your DCs that will manage replication between multiple sites.

1. If necessary, turn on your computer and log on as the administrator from your own domain.

2. Start **Active Directory Sites and Services**.

3. Double-click **Sites**, then double-click your **Computer-Site**.

4. Double-click **Servers**, then double-click your server name.

5. Click **NTDS Settings**.

6. Delete all automatically generated connections with other DCs by right-clicking each connection and clicking **Delete**. Click **Yes** to delete the object. Do this for each connection object listed.

7. Create a site link to your partner's site by right-clicking **NTDS Settings**, then clicking **New Active Directory Connection**.

8. Click your partner's server name from the list and click **OK**.

9. Click **OK** again.

10. Right-click the connection object you just created, then click **Replicate Now**. Notice the dialog box that appears, as shown in Figure 8-3. Click **OK**.

11. Close **Active Directory Sites and Services**. If you are not proceeding immediately to the next activity, log off your computer.

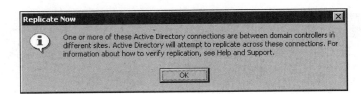

Figure 8-3   Replication message

Site Links

Once sites have been created, you can create a site link that connects them. A site link is used to control the replication of Active Directory changes from one site to another. As shown in Figure 8-4, when creating a site link you must configure the following parameters:

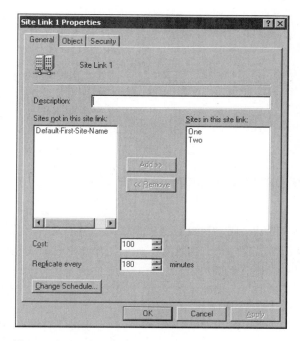

Figure 8-4   Site link properties

- Transport—You must specify which network transport will be used to transfer data between the sites. You can choose either **Remote Procedure Call (RPC)** or **Simple Mail Transfer Protocol (SMTP)**. RPC is the default replication protocol within a site and is used when the sites have high-speed connectivity. SMTP is generally used over slow links or when the connection is not reliable. The major disadvantage to using SMTP is that it cannot be used to replicate the domain partition to DCs in the same domain.

- Member Sites—You can include two or more sites in a site link as long as the sites use the same replication protocol.

- Cost—Costs are used to assign priorities to site links. Replication will try to use the lowest cost connector when possible. Costs can range from a minimum of 1 to a maximum of 32767. Generally, costs are used to identify the speed of a network connection. A 56 Kbps ISDN connection should have a higher relative cost than a T1 connection.

- Schedule—Site link schedules can be customized. For example, you can configure a link so that it is available only during the evening, ensuring that replication does not occur during regular business hours. You can also configure the schedule for specific hours. For instance, Figure 8-5 shows a replication schedule set so replication will only occur from 7:00 a.m. to 8:00 a.m., noon to 1:00 p.m., 3:00 p.m. to 4:00 p.m., 6:00 p.m. to 7:00 p.m., and all day Saturday.

Replication Interval

You can configure how often replication will occur during the schedule. The maximum is every 15 minutes and the minimum is every 10,080 minutes.

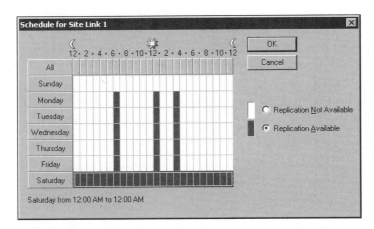

Figure 8-5   Sample replication schedule

Activity 8-3: Creating and Configuring Site Links

Time Required: 5 minutes

Objective: To configure a new site link with a custom replication schedule.

Description: In this activity you will reduce the amount of replication traffic during business hours by configuring a site link between two sites. You will then configure this site link to replicate every 15 minutes during the evening, after business hours (9:00 a.m. to 5:00 p.m.), as well as during the lunch hour from Monday to Friday.

1. If necessary, turn on your computer and log on as the administrator from your own domain.

2. Start **Active Directory Sites and Services**.

3. Double-click **Sites**, then double-click **Inter-Site Transports**.

4. Right-click **IP** and select **New Site Link**.

5. Provide an intuitive and unique name for the site link.

6. Select the sites that this site link will connect. Select **Add**, and then click **OK**.

7. Double-click **IP**.

8. Right-click the name of the site you created in Step 5, then click **Properties**.

9. Click **Change Schedule**. Configure the schedule as shown in Figure 8-6. When finished click **OK**.

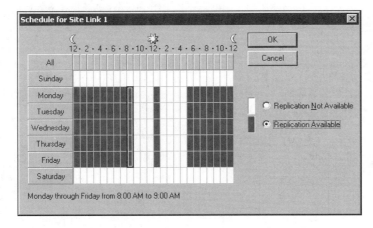

Figure 8-6   Replication schedule to be configured

10. In the **Replicate every** box, change the value to **15** and click **OK**.

11. Close the **Active Directory Sites and Services** console. If you are not proceeding immediately to the next activity, log off your computer.

MONITORING ACTIVE DIRECTORY REPLICATION

Active Directory replication occurs transparently over the network, making it difficult to verify that it is functioning. The symptoms of replication failure include log-on failure due to Active Directory updates not being replicated to other DCs, as well as other inconsistencies in Active Directory.

To monitor replication, Microsoft created **Active Directory Replication Monitor**, which is included in the Windows Server 2003 Support Tools. Replication Monitor can be used to:

- Monitor replication traffic between DCs
- Display a list of DCs in a domain
- Verify replication topology
- Manually force replication
- Check a DC's current USN and unreplicated objects
- Display bridgehead servers and trusts

The Active Directory Replication Monitor window is shown in Figure 8-7.

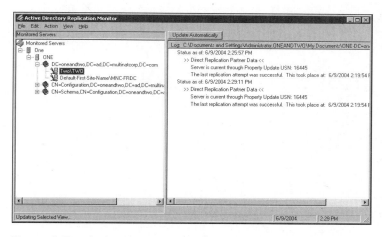

Figure 8-7   Active Directory Replication Monitor window

In the next activity you will use Replication Monitor (otherwise known as replmon) to verify replication. When you open replmon, notice that you can select the name of the DC that you want to monitor (Figure 8-8).

Alternately, you can choose to search the directory for the server to be monitored, as shown in Figure 8-9. Specify the name of the domain to search, and then click **Next**.

Expand the desired site, click the server to be monitored, and then click **Finish**.

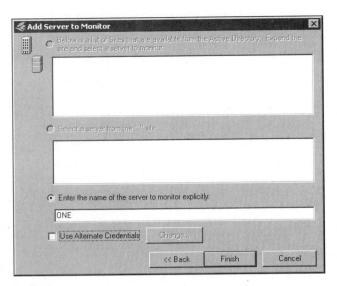

Figure 8-8   Adding a server explicitly in Replication Monitor

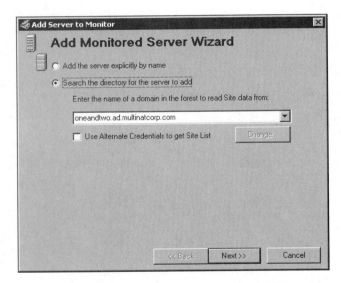

Figure 8-9   Adding a server by searching Active Directory in Replication Monitor

Activity 8-4: Verifying Replication

Time Required: 20 minutes

Objective: To verify Active Directory replication between two DCs.

Description: Now that you have changed the replication topology, you will verify that replication between two DCs in different sites is functioning.

1. If necessary, turn on your computer and log on as the administrator from your own domain.

2. Click **Start**, then point to **All Programs**.

3. Point to **Windows Support Tools**, then click **Command Prompt**.

4. Type **replmon** and press **Enter**.

5. Right-click **Monitored Servers**, then click **Add Monitored Server**.

6. Select **Add the server explicitly by name** and click **Next**.

7. Type the name of your server and click **Finish**. (The time required to complete this activity may vary considerably.)

8. Right-click your server name, then click **Check Replication Topology**. Click **OK**.

9. Right-click your server name, then click **Show Domain Controllers in Domain**. How many DCs do you see? Click **OK** to close the window.

10. Expand the domain partition by double-clicking the first one in the list.

11. Click your partner's server within the domain partition. When was the last replication? Was it successful?

12. Right-click the server name, then click **Synchronize with this Replication Partner**. Click **OK**.

13. Refresh the display by pressing **F5**.

14. Scroll down to the bottom of the list and verify that the replication was successful.

15. Expand the **Schema** partition and verify that it was replicated successfully to the other DCs listed.

16. If you are not proceeding immediately to the next activity, log off your computer.

Activity 8-5: Generating a Replication Report

Time Required: 20 minutes

Objective: To generate a replication report.

Description: In this activity, you will generate a status report showing your server's replication partners, USN numbers, and partition information to document the network topology for a backup administrator.

1. If necessary, turn on your computer and log on as the administrator from your own domain.

2. Click **Start**, then point to **All Programs**.

3. Point to **Windows Support Tools**, then click **Command Prompt**.

4. Type **replmon** and press **Enter**.

5. Right-click your server name and click **Generate Status Report**.

6. Type *Servername* **Status Report** (where *Servername* is the name of your own server). Save the report to the desktop.

7. Configure the report options as shown in Figure 8-10, then click **OK**. (The time required to complete this activity may vary considerably.)

8. When the report is complete, click **OK**.

9. Close Active Directory Replication Monitor.

10. Double-click the *Servername* **Status Report.log** file on the desktop (where *Servername* is the name of your server). Scroll through the report.

11. For the directory partition, what was the last USN number updated from your replication partners? Why are the numbers different?

12. When was the last change notification for the directory partition?

13. Review the report contents. When you're finished, close the report.

14. If you are not proceeding immediately to the next activity, log off your computer.

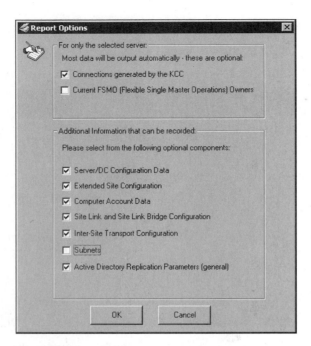

Figure 8-10   Configuring report options

OPERATIONS MASTERS

Some Active Directory tasks cannot tolerate the risk of inconsistency created by the multi-master replication process used for most Active Directory changes. In other words, there are a few things that are so important that there can *never* be a risk of conflict or different data in two different places. Therefore, specific servers are designated to perform certain types of updates. The servers that perform these critical tasks are called **operations masters**. There are five types of operations masters:

- Schema master

- Domain naming master

- Relative identifier (RID) master

- Primary domain controller (PDC) emulator

- Infrastructure master

 It's funny how some terms stick around. During the development of Active Directory, these roles were called "Flexible Single Master Operation" roles, or FSMO for short. You will still see this acronym used, even in some of the support tools, although it doesn't appear in the consoles. You will even hear experienced administrators use the term, pronounced "fizz-mo."

In the case of the schema master and the domain naming master, only one DC in each forest can hold these roles. In the case of the other operations masters, only one DC per domain can hold those roles.

Schema Master

The **schema master** is the only source for originating updates to the **schema partition** of Active Directory. This DC alone can write changes to the schema partition. In order to do so, the administrator must be connected to this DC and be a member of the Schema Admins Group.

After the schema master has made an originating update, the change is replicated to all other DCs in the forest using standard, nonurgent replication.

As you learned in Chapter 1, the schema is a critical part of Active Directory that lists objects and attributes that can be stored in Active Directory. Using a single source for changes ensures that there will never be a replication conflict relative to the schema. The schema is updated very rarely, so there is no need for multiple replicas to accept changes.

By default, the first DC in the forest will be the schema master.

Schema changes can be reversed in Windows Server 2003, which was not possible in Windows 2000.

Domain Naming Master

For each forest there is one **domain naming master** that is responsible for controlling the addition and removal of domains in the forest. If the domain naming master is unavailable, new domains cannot be added and old domains cannot be removed.

When a new domain is added to the forest, the domain naming master ensures that its name is unique within the forest. To do this, it queries a GC server, which contains a subset of Active Directory information from all domains in the forest, including domain names.

A domain naming master must be a GC server. This ensures that a GC server can always be reached. By default, the first DC in the forest will also be the domain naming master. As with schema changes, domains are not added or removed on a regular basis, so the domain naming master is not a bottleneck for the network.

The domain naming master also verifies the uniqueness of site names. New sites cannot be created if the domain naming server cannot be contacted, or if you are attempting to create a duplicate site name.

RID Master

A **RID** is used in the creation of Active Directory objects. Users, groups, and computer objects are assigned a SID when they are created. This SID includes the domain ID and a RID, as detailed in Chapter 6.

The **RID master** generates RIDs and distributes a range of them to each DC. A DC requests additional RIDs from the RID master when required. If a DC is out of RIDs and the RID master is unavailable, then new users, groups, and computer objects cannot be created.

Having only one DC in a domain responsible for generating RIDs ensures that SIDs will be unique within the domain. Using the domain ID as part of the object SID ensures that SIDs will be unique within the forest, as no two domains have the same domain ID.

When objects are moved between domains, the move must be initiated on the RID master. This ensures that the object is not accidentally moved to multiple domains at the same time. By default, the first DC in a domain is the RID master.

PDC Emulator

A PDC emulator performs a variety of important tasks for a domain. Many of these tasks provide backward compatibility with older Windows clients and servers.

The replication model for Windows NT has a single PDC that controls changes to the domain database, as well as many backup DCs (BDCs) that copy changes from the PDC. Windows NT Servers that are configured as DCs do not understand the multi-master replication used by Active Directory DCs. Consequently, only one DC in a domain can act as a PDC to Windows NT BDCs. The PDC emulator performs this role.

 When a domain is switched to native mode, a PDC emulator will not synchronize with Windows NT BDCs. This is important because once you switch to native mode you can't switch back.

If a user is logged on to a pre-Windows 2000 client, such as Windows NT or Windows 95, the computer must contact a PDC in order for the user to change his or her domain password. The PDC emulator performs this role for legacy clients.

Time synchronization is critical for the correct timestamping of Active Directory changes. Each DC in a domain synchronizes its time with the PDC emulator. The PDC emulator for a domain sets its time by a DC in a parent domain. The PDC emulator in the forest root domain should be configured to set its time by a reliable external time source, such as an atomic clock on the Internet, a GPS receiver, or a similarly accurate device.

Password changes for a domain are replicated to the PDC emulator first. Then, if any DC is unable to authenticate a user because of an incorrect password, the authenticating DC will pass the authentication request to the PDC emulator.

By default, the first DC in a domain will be the PDC emulator.

Infrastructure Master

This operations master role is the most confusing of them all. In a multiple-domain forest, a group in one domain may contain security principals from another domain, but the group object itself exists only in its own domain. Within the attributes of the group object, there are references to the security principals that are members of the group, but exist in a different domain. The infrastructure master is responsible for updating these references to objects in other domains. To do this, it compares its own information with a GC server, which contains information about those objects.

The references that are updated include new distinguished names of objects that are renamed or moved to a new OU. The SID will also be updated if the object is moved to a new domain.

If a GC server is located on the server acting as infrastructure master, then the infrastructure master will not function. If a domain has more than one DC, then the infrastructure master should not also be a GC server.

If you have only one domain in your forest, the infrastructure master is not needed, as there are no cross-domain references to worry about.

TROUBLESHOOTING ACTIVE DIRECTORY REPLICATION

Most problems with Active Directory replication are caused by administrator error or network infrastructure glitches. A few of the most common problems are:

- Slow replication between sites—The most likely causes of slow replication between sites are slow WAN links and poorly configured site links. A slow WAN link will limit the amount of changes that can be synchronized. The default time schedule for site links is every three hours. If faster replication is required between sites, you must configure the site links manually.

- DNS errors—Windows Server 2003, like Windows 2000, relies on DNS to locate DCs when replicating. If a DC has the wrong DNS Server configured or the DNS entries are incorrect, replication to other DCs will fail. Verify that all DCs can be resolved in DNS.

■ Stopped replication between sites—The most likely cause of stopped replication between sites is failed WAN links. In addition, if no site link is configured, replication will not occur.

■ Time differences between servers—This is an error that occurs when the time on two DCs is more than five minutes apart. Although time synchronization between DCs should be automatic, it will occasionally fail. To fix it, reset the time properly.

■ Excessive network traffic—If you use a relatively congested 10-Mbps LAN, then Active Directory synchronization traffic between servers may be excessive. Because replication traffic within a site cannot be controlled, you should upgrade to a faster network or build a dedicated segment between DCs for Active Directory traffic. If traffic is excessive across a WAN link, ensure that sites are properly configured and adjust the site links to control replication as required.

■ Slow authentication when using new passwords—If a user logs on quickly after a password is reset, then it is likely the DC he or she is authenticating to has not received the new password. In this case, the authenticating DC will attempt to verify the password with the PDC emulator for the domain. If the PDC emulator is across a slow WAN link, then the logon will be slow. To prevent this, change passwords using a DC that is local to the user, or move the PDC emulator to a location with faster network connectivity.

8

Chapter Summary

❑ Active Directory uses a multi-master model for replication, which means changes can be made on any DC and are replicated to other DCs.

❑ Replication of changes is performed at the attribute level, and not the object level. The exception is the membership attribute of group objects in Windows 2003 Server Forest Native Mode, where only the changes to the membership are replicated.

❑ Intra-site replication occurs every five minutes via RPC and cannot be compressed. Inter-site replication is controlled with site links, and can be done via RPC or SMTP transports.

❑ Urgent replication, such as an account lockout, is performed immediately within a site but is limited by site links between sites.

❑ Password changes are replicated immediately to the PDC emulator for a domain, regardless of site links. Standard intra-site and inter-site replication is issued to synchronize password changes with other DCs.

❑ The replication topology for inter-site and intra-site replication is created by the KCC. A bidirectional ring is used for intra-site replication. Inter-site replication topologies are based on the configuration of site links.

❑ Replicating attribute-level changes minimizes replication conflicts. On the rare occasion that a conflict does occur, a timestamp is used to choose the correct value.

❑ Active Directory Replication Monitor can be used to view both intra-site and inter-site replication information.

❑ Operations masters are used for critical Active Directory operations that cannot be trusted to multi-master replication.

Key Terms

Active Directory Replication Monitor — A tool used to monitor, troubleshoot, and verify Active Directory replication.

bridgehead server — A DC that is configured to perform replication to and from other sites.

connection object — A connection between two DCs used for replication.

convergence — The state when all replicas of a database have the same version of the data. (In Active Directory, this means that all DCs have the same set of information.)

domain naming master — The operations master that controls the addition and removal of domains in the forest.

globally unique identifier (GUID) — A 16-byte value generated by an algorithm that guarantees it will be different from every other GUID generated anywhere in the world. A GUID is used to uniquely identify a particular device, component, item, or object.

infrastructure master — The operations master for a domain that updates references to objects in other domains.

inter-site replication — Replication occurring between sites.

intra-site replication — Replication occurring within a site.

Knowledge Consistency Checker (KCC) — A process that runs on each DC to create the replication topology for the forest.

latency — The delay or "lag time" between a change made in one replica being recognized in another.

multi-master model — The replication model used by Active Directory. Changes to Active Directory objects can be performed on any DC in the domain. Changes are then replicated to other DCs.

operations masters — DCs that manage specific changes to Active Directory that would be impractical to manage using a multi-master replication model. (Also called Flexible Single Master Operations roles, or FSMO.)

originating update — A change to Active Directory made by an administrator on a local DC.

PDC emulator — An operations master for a domain that simulates a Windows NT 4 PDC for backward compatibility with older Windows clients and servers.

propagation dampening — The process of preventing a DC from replicating with other DCs that have already been updated.

relative identifier (RID) — Combined with the domain SID to create the SID for a user, group, or computer object.

Remote Procedure Call (RPC) — The default replication protocol within a site. An RPC connection requires permanent, high-speed connectivity between the sites.

replica — A copy of an Active Directory partition stored on a DC.

replicated update — A change to Active Directory that was made through replication.

replication — The process of updating Active Directory to all DCs on the network.

replication partner — A DC that replicates with another DC.

replication topology — The set of physical connections used by DCs to replicate directory updates among DCs in both the same and different sites.

RID master — The operations master for a domain that generates RIDs used by DCs when creating user, group, and computer objects.

schema master — The operations master that controls changes to the Active Directory schema.

schema partition — The Active Directory partition that stores definitions, attributes, and rules for all objects in Active Directory. This partition is replicated to all DCs in the forest.

Simple Mail Transfer Protocol (SMTP) — A store-and-forward replication protocol that is generally used when the connectivity between two sites is slow and unreliable.

site — One or more well-connected (highly reliable and fast) TCP/IP subnets. A site allows an administrator to configure Active Directory access and replication topology to take advantage of the physical network.

Update Sequence Number (USN) — A unique number assigned to every object and attribute in Active Directory to track changes. Each DC maintains its own set of USNs.

up-to-dateness vector — A list of DC pairs and the last USN received from each pair.

REVIEW QUESTIONS

1. By default, replication between sites in Active Directory occurs how often?

    a. Every 5 minutes

    b. Every 15 minutes

    c. Every 60 minutes

    d. Every 180 minutes

2. Which Active Directory partition stores information about users, groups, and printers?

    a. Schema partition

    b. Configuration partition

    c. Domain partition

    d. All of the above

3. In a fully routed network, inter-site replication must be manually configured. True or False?

4. A DC in a site that sends and receives updates from other sites is known as what type of server?

    a. Bridgehead server

    b. Originating server

    c. Replicated server

5. Which of the following statements regarding intra-site replication are true? (Choose all that apply.)

    a. Replication occurs just after changes are made

    b. Replication traffic cannot be compressed

    c. Replication is determined by a schedule

    d. Replication occurs, by default, four times per hour

6. Which changes in Active Directory are replicated immediately, regardless of the replication schedule? (Choose all that apply.)

    a. A new user is added

    b. A user's password is changed

    c. A user's group membership is changed

    d. A user account is disabled

    e. A user account is locked out

7. Two administrators change the same user's department attribute in Active Directory on two different DCs at approximately the same time. Which change will be replicated to all DCs?

    a. The update from the DC with the highest GUID

    b. The update with the earliest timestamp

    c. The update with the most recent timestamp

    d. Both updates will be made to Active Directory

8. Two administrators change the same user's properties in Active Directory on two different DCs at approximately the same time. One administrator changes the user's fax number attribute and the other administrator changes the user's city attribute. Which change will be replicated to all DCs?

   a. The update from the DC with the highest GUID

   b. The update with the earliest timestamp

   c. The update with the most recent timestamp

   d. Both updates will be made to Active Directory

9. When all DCs have the same version of the domain directory database, the network is said to have what?

   a. Consistency

   b. Convergence

   c. Replica

   d. State-based replication

10. A site named North America has three site links to a site named South America. Site link one has a cost of 20, site link two has a cost of 100, and site link three has a cost of 15000. Which site link will be used first when attempting replication?

    a. Site link one

    b. Site link two

    c. Site link three

    d. A site link will be chosen randomly

11. SMTP is generally used in which situation(s) as a replication protocol? (Choose all that apply.)

    a. Sites are connected with a high-speed connection

    b. Sites are connected with a slow-speed connection

    c. Sites are connected with an unreliable WAN connection

    d. Replication is between DCs in the same domain

12. You just installed a new DC on the network. By default, in which site will it be placed?

    a. DEFAULT-FIRST-NAME-SITE

    b. DEFAULT-IP-LINK

    c. DEFAULTSITE

    d. DEFAULT-FIRST-SITE-NAME

13. By default, how often does the KCC run on each DC?

    a. Every 15 minutes

    b. Once an hour

    c. Once every three hours

    d. Once a day

14. You have created a new site link between two sites in Active Directory. What is the default replication interval?

    a. Every 15 minutes

    b. Twice an hour

    c. Once an hour

    d. Eight times a day

    e. Once a day

15. The process of preventing a DC from receiving the same update from multiple DCs is called?

    a. Loose consistency

    b. Propagation dampening

    c. Replication latency

    d. Convergence

16. Which Active Directory partitions are stored on all DCs in the forest? (Choose all that apply.)

    a. Schema partition

    b. Configuration partition

    c. Domain partition

    d. Application partition

17. What is used to determine which updates are to be made to the local replica?

    a. Originating server's GUID

    b. USNs

    c. Timestamps

    d. Up-to-dateness vectors

18. The KCC creates a bidirectional replication ring that ensures an originating update does not go through more than how many connections?

    a. One

    b. Two

    c. Three

    d. 15

    e. There is no limit

19. A change to an object in Active Directory made by an administrator on a local DC is called a(n)?

    a. Originating update

    b. Replicated update

    c. Replica

    d. Replication partner

20. Which of the following statements about USNs are true? (Choose all that apply.)

   a. USN numbers are the same on all DCs

   b. Each DC maintains its own USNs

   c. When a change is made, the object's USN is incremented by 10

   d. USNs are used to determine if changes have been made to an object

21. Which operations masters are required once per domain? (Choose all that apply.)

   a. PDC emulator

   b. Infrastructure master

   c. Schema master

   d. Domain naming master

   e. RID master

HEARTLAND HOSPITAL CASE PROJECT

The hospital currently has 25 DCs located in nine departments around the hospital. All DCs are connected through the LAN. Three departments are using older, 10-Mbps hubs, while the other departments are using 10/100-Mbps switches. Between the hours of 8:00 a.m. and 6:00 p.m. the network bandwidth utilization averages 95 percent. A research team just leased office space in a building located across town to house 20 researchers. The new office currently has a 56-Kbps ISDN connection to the hospital that needs to be upgraded to a T1 within the next six months.

Case Project 8-1: Designing Sites for Replication

The IT manager is concerned that there is too much Active Directory replication occurring during the day, consuming the bulk of the available bandwidth in the hospital. You just found out that the researchers will be using Active Directory to store research subject data that will be constantly updated and modified. Senior researchers at the hospital will review this data. You are concerned this will cause network slow-downs at the hospital. How should you design the hospital's replication topology to minimize the amount and frequency of replication during the day?

Case Project 8-2: Replication Conflicts

The head of the new research facility is concerned that crucial subject records will be deleted when two researchers are editing different fields in the same record in Active Directory. What can you tell him about Active Directory that will address his concerns?

Case Project 8-3: Optimizing Operations Master Roles

You received a call from a researcher in the new facility informing you that its ISDN line is temporarily down. You try to create a new site in Active Directory Sites and Services, but are unable to do so. What is the problem and how can it be avoided in the future?

9

ACTIVE DIRECTORY MAINTENANCE AND DATA RECOVERY

After reading this chapter and completing the exercises, you will be able to:

♦ Describe the file structure used by Active Directory

♦ Describe how data is written to the Active Directory database

♦ Defragment the Active Directory database

♦ Move the Active Directory database to a different location on disk

♦ Back up Active Directory

♦ Recover the Active Directory database and restore it, if necessary, from a backup

♦ Manage which DCs hold the operations master roles

The goal of every administrator is to protect data from hardware or software failure, including the failure of Active Directory. When implemented properly, Active Directory is very stable. It is based on a fault-tolerant, transactional database that is designed to maintain data integrity after any system failure. Employing best practices, such as using multiple DCs, will help minimize the risk and scope of problems.

However, some unavoidable events, like a complete server failure or a hard disk controller failure, may prevent Active Directory from running. If this happens, it may be necessary to manually restore parts of Active Directory, or perform a complete Active Directory restore to another computer.

ACTIVE DIRECTORY FILE STRUCTURE

Active Directory uses a transactional database based on the **Extensible Storage Engine (ESE)**. This database uses log files to store changes to Active Directory. A simple log file can be modified much faster than a database, and changes are written to the log files before they are made in Active Directory.

Each addition, modification, or deletion in Active Directory is called a **transaction**. In processing a transaction, the database changes are recorded first in the log files, and are then made to the actual database files. Finally, when the transaction is complete, a pointer is written to a checkpoint file, enabling the system to quickly locate the last completed transaction. In the event of a failure, incomplete (or partially complete) transactions are removed from the database files. This is called **rollback**, or rolling back a transaction. Changes that have been recorded in the log file but not applied to the database can then be recorded in the database using the information in the log files. (This, as you may have guessed, is called **roll forward**, or rolling a transaction forward.)

Active Directory uses the following files to maintain data integrity, as shown in Figure 9-1:

- NTDS.DIT
- EDB.LOG
- EDB*xxxxx*.LOG
- EDB.CHK
- RES1.LOG and RES2.LOG
- TEMP.EDB

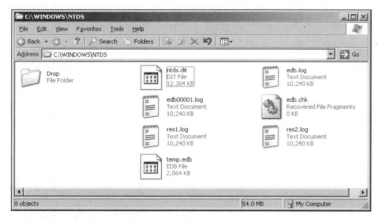

Figure 9-1   Active Directory files

NTDS.DIT

The **NTDS.DIT** file is the actual Active Directory database. It stores all objects and their attributes in Active Directory. By default, this file is located in the %SYSTEMROOT%\NTDS folder on the DC. The size of the database file may vary between DCs because of the way changes are replicated, and because each DC may hold replicas of a different set of partitions (or NCs).

 %SYSTEMROOT% is a placeholder (or variable) that represents the path to your Windows Server 2003 installation, such as *c:\windows*.

NTDS.DIT is made up of three parts: schema table, link table, and data table. The **schema table** stores information on the types of objects that can be created, including the optional and mandatory attributes for each type of object. The **link table** contains linked attributes that point to other objects in Active Directory. For example, group membership is linked to the group and to the user object in Active Directory. The **data table** stores the values for each attribute of objects in Active Directory.

EDB.LOG

EDB.LOG is the current transaction log file. All changes to Active Directory, either through an originating update or a replicated update, are written first to the transaction log file. The updates are then written to NTDS.DIT.

It is very important that changes are written to this file quickly. Active Directory changes that are held only in memory are at risk of being lost if there is a power interruption. Following a system failure, changes that are written to the log can be applied to Active Directory after the system restarts.

The size of EDB.LOG is always 10 MB, even when it is first created. When a variable-sized file is expanded, it takes a small amount of time. Keeping EDB.LOG a consistent size allows changes to be written to disk faster, and reduces the risk that Active Directory changes will be lost while in memory before being written to disk.

 If the EDB.LOG file is not 10 MB in size, then it may be corrupted, and you should investigate the situation. You may need to restore the database from a backup.

EDB*XXXXX*.LOG

EDB*XXXXX*.LOG files are the log files that contain all previous transactions that have been written to the Active Directory database and can be used for disaster recovery. When EDB.LOG is filled, it is renamed to EDB*XXXXX*.LOG, where *XXXXX* is a number increased by one each time a new log file is created. For example, EDB*00001*.LOG, EDB*00002*.LOG, EDB*00003*.LOG, etc. (This is a hexadecimal number.) A new transaction log file named EDB.LOG is then created.

EDB.CHK

EDB.CHK is the checkpoint file used by the ESE to keep track of what data in the transaction logs has been written to the database. If the system needs to recover from a failure, it uses the EDB.CHK file to determine what data still needs to be written to the database and what data has already been confirmed.

RES1.LOG and RES2.LOG

RES1.LOG and **RES2.LOG** are reserve log files. If the DC runs out of free disk space, changes to Active Directory are written to the reserve log files, preventing Active Directory from losing updates when it runs out of disk space. When installing Active Directory, it is important that you include additional free space that will store the Active Directory database as it grows.

TEMP.EDB

TEMP.EDB is a temporary storage space. The system uses this file to hold large transactions while they are in process, and during some maintenance operations.

HOW DATA IS WRITTEN TO ACTIVE DIRECTORY

When a change is made to an object in Active Directory, the change is not written directly to the database. Instead the updates are written to the transaction log files. This minimizes corruption to the Active Directory database in the event of an unexpected shutdown.

When a change is made in Active Directory, the following occurs:

1. The data to be modified is loaded into RAM. This allows Windows Server 2003 to make multiple changes to objects in memory with fewer read/write operations to disk. (If the entire transaction will not fit into memory, TEMP.EDB will be used.)

2. The transaction is recorded in EDB.LOG. The change is written to the log file first, to prevent the data from being lost in the event of a system failure.

3. The transaction is then written to NTDS.DIT, the Active Directory database. This may not happen immediately, especially if the system is busy doing other things for clients. Active Directory will update the files when it has free cycles or during a clean shutdown.

4. The EDB.CHK file is updated with a new pointer, indicating that transaction has been successfully written to the database.

If a DC is shut down improperly—that is, if it crashes without the proper shutdown procedure—inconsistencies can develop in the Active Directory database. When the DC is restarted, the log files will be checked and any outstanding transactions will be written to the database.

Managing Deleted Objects

When an object is deleted from Active Directory, it is not immediately purged from the database. Instead, the object is marked for deletion and moved into the Deleted Objects folder. This creates a **tombstone** for the object, which will remain in the database until its tombstone expires.

To understand the importance of the tombstone, consider this example of the replication process: Imagine that you have two DCs, named DC1 and DC2, respectively. If you were to delete an object on DC1, completely removing it from the database so no trace remained, what would happen during the next replication cycle? First of all, it would never be deleted from DC2, and in some cases, DC2 would happily send a copy of the object back to DC1!

Tombstones are used to ensure that deleted objects are removed from all DCs. When an object is marked for deletion, it is said to be tombstoned, and the tombstone information is replicated to all other DCs holding a copy (or partial copy) of this object.

The administrator can configure how long deleted objects remain in the database by specifying the tombstone lifetime using ADSI Edit. The default is 60 days.

Care must be taken when changing the **tombstone lifetime** because it will affect Active Directory backups and restores. Backups older than the tombstone lifetime cannot be restored. For example, changing the tombstone lifetime to seven days would create problems restoring Active Directory objects from a backup older than seven days.

The accuracy of the database can only be guaranteed if the backup is more recent than the oldest possible tombstone. For example, say a backup is taken on day one, the tombstone lifetime is seven days, and on day four a user object is deleted. If the backup is restored on day six when the deleted user object is restored, the tombstone's status is newer and will ensure that the user object stays deleted. If the restore were allowed after the tombstone expired, then the user object would be restored and there would be no way to tell this user apart from any other valid user. And, having user accounts that shouldn't exist could result in security holes. (We will discuss how to restore a deleted object that you do want to keep, later in this chapter.)

DEFRAGMENTING THE DATABASE

Over time, Active Directory will become fragmented as new objects are added and deleted. Fragmentation in a database, just like in hard drive files, means that related information is spread out in little chunks instead of being neatly collected. As the database becomes more fragmented, it will take longer to find information. Just like a hard drive, the database needs to be defragmented to rearrange the data and optimize the data store. It does this by physically grouping related information together in the file. There are two types of defragmentation—online and offline.

Online Defragmentation

Online defragmentation on DCs occurs every 12 hours by default. Online defragmentation is also called **garbage collection** because deleted objects whose tombstone lifetimes have expired are purged from the database. However, the database is not compacted. The server does not have to be taken offline to run an online defragmentation, so users are not affected.

Offline Defragmentation

Offline defragmentation is performed when you want to compact the database. The database gets larger as new objects and attributes are added. However, it does not reduce in size when objects are deleted. The database cannot be compacted while Active Directory is running; the server must be offline during the defragmentation process.

An offline defragmentation only needs to be performed if there are many deletions in Active Directory that are taking up a large amount of space, such as a child domain or the contents of an entire, large OU. Performing an offline defragmentation to remove these items may free up a substantial amount of space.

When an offline defragmentation is performed, the existing database is not modified. A new, compacted copy is created, reducing the risk of a corruption error. The new, compacted copy of the database is created in a temporary location. Only when it has been created error free is the new, defragmented database copied over the old fragmented version. Figure 9-2 shows what the output of an offline defragmentation would look like.

Figure 9-2   Compacting the Active Directory database

 To perform an offline defragmenation, the amount of free disk space must be equal to the size of the existing Active Directory database. This is required in order to hold the fragmented and defragmented versions of the database simultaneously.

Activity 9-1: Defragmenting and Compacting the Active Directory Database

Time Required: 10 minutes

Objective: To defragment and compact the Active Directory database.

Description: In this activity you will perform an offline defragmentation of the Active Directory database to compact the database files and free up disk space.

1. If your computer is turned off, turn it on and proceed to Step 6.

2. Click **Start**, and click **Shut Down**.

3. At the Shut Down Windows dialog box, click **Restart**.

4. In the Shutdown Event Tracker section, click the drop-down arrow, then click **Operating System: Reconfiguration (Planned)**.

5. Click in the Comment section and type **Restart in DSRM for Offline Defragmentation of the Ntds.dit database** and click **OK** to restart the computer.

6. Press **F8** to see the Windows Advanced Options Menu.

7. Using the down arrow on your keyboard, select Directory Services Restore Mode (Windows domain controllers only), then press **Enter**.

8. The computer will boot into safemode – Directory Services Repair. The words Safe Mode will appear in all four corners of the display screen.

9. Log on as an administrator using the Directory Services Restore Mode Administrator Account password. (This password was assigned during the planning activities in Chapter 2, when you promoted this computer to a DC.)

10. In the dialog box that tells you Windows is running in safe mode, click **OK**. This dialog box will remind you that you are in a special diagnostics mode used to fix problems, and that some of your devices may not be available in this mode.

11. Click **Start**, point to **All Programs**, point to **Accessories**, and click **Command Prompt**.

12. In the command prompt window, type **Ntdsutil** and press **Enter**.

13. At the Ntdsutil prompt, type **files** and press **Enter**.

14. At the file maintenance prompt, type **info** and press **Enter**. This will show the current location of the Active Directory database as well as the size of the database and the log files.

15. Type **compact to C:\Temp** and press **Enter**, as shown in Figure 9-2. Note the information displayed regarding this procedure. Also note the instructions telling you that you will need to copy c:\temp\ntds.dit to the C:\WINDOWS\NTDS\ntds.dit and delete the old log files del C:\WINDOWS\NTDS*.log.

16. At the file maintenance prompt, type **quit** and press **Enter**.

17. At the Ntdsutil prompt, type **quit** and press **Enter**.

18. Type **copy C:\temp\ntds.dit c:\windows\ntds\ntds.dit** and press **Enter**.

19. When asked if you'd like to overwrite C:\Windows\ntds\ntds.dit, type **Y**, and press **Enter**.

20. Type **del C:\Windows\Ntds*.log** and press **Enter**.

21. Close the command prompt window.

22. Click **Start**, and click **Shut Down**.

23. At the Shut Down Windows dialog box, make sure that **Restart** is selected.

24. In the Shutdown Event Tracker section, click the drop-down arrow under Option, and click **Operating System: Reconfiguration (Planned)**.

25. Click in the Comment section and type **Restart after compacting Ntds.dit**, then click **OK**.

26. Restart Windows normally.

MOVING THE ACTIVE DIRECTORY DATABASE

By default, Active Directory is installed in the %SYSTEMROOT%\NTDS folder. As mentioned, problems can occur if the partition storing Active Directory runs out of space. To prevent this, you may want to place Active Directory on a dedicated partition.

The location of Active Directory can be selected during the initial installation using dcpromo, or moved after installation. You have the option of moving just the database or the log files as well.

To move the database file, restart the DC in Directory Services Restore Mode by pressing **F8**, as you did in Activity 9-1. Run Ntdsutil and use the **files** command. Type **move db to *path*** (where *path* is the target drive and folder to store NTDS.DIT) and press **Enter**. Use the **quit** command to move up the Ntdsutil structure and exit the program, then restart the DC.

To move the transaction log files to a new drive or folder, use the **files** command in Ntdsutil. Type **move logs to *path*** (where *path* is the target drive and folder to store the log files) and press **Enter**. Exit and restart the DC.

9

BACKING UP ACTIVE DIRECTORY

It is important to regularly back up Active Directory and its components. Multiple DCs provide a fault tolerance by having multiple copies of the Active Directory database, but do not allow you to recover from some types of failures, like accidentally deleting the wrong user account—or worse, a whole OU.

It is important to have a back-up copy of Active Directory in the event that a user error occurs, or something destroys all of your DCs (like a fire, explosion, or flood).

 Most organizations will have at least one back-up copy stored in a different physical location, such as a safety deposit box at the bank.

Active Directory is backed up as part of the **system state**. System state, shown in Figure 9-3, includes the following:

- Active Directory
- Boot files
- COM+ class registration database
- Registry
- SYSVOL (system volume)

In addition to the Active Directory database files, the system state includes SYSVOL, which contains other components of Active Directory, including the NetLogon share, user log-in scripts, group policy templates, and the other files copied by the File Replication Service.

The system state can be backed up while the server is online. Using Windows 2003 Server's Backup Utility, you can only back up the system state on the local computer. The Windows Server 2003 Backup Utility cannot be used to back up the system state of a remote DC.

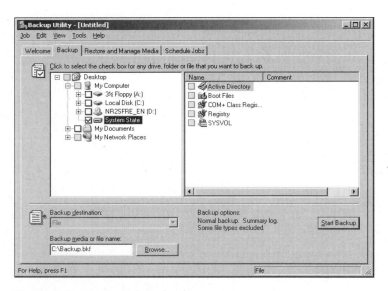

Figure 9-3   System state backup

System state information can be backed up remotely when third-party back-up software, such as Veritas BackupExec or Computer Associates ArcServe is used. Make sure that the version you select is approved for Windows Server 2003.

It is also important to note that you cannot perform an incremental backup of the system state. You must perform a normal backup. This is not a problem if you are performing a full backup of your DC, including data files, nightly. However, if you are performing incremental daily backups, you might want to schedule a separate, full backup for the system state each day.

Activity 9-2: Performing an Active Directory Backup

Time Required: 15 minutes

Objective: To make a backup of Active Directory.

Description: In this activity you will back up the system state to a file on the hard drive. This backup will be used to restore Active Directory in a later exercise.

1. If necessary, start your computer and log on as the administrator from your own domain.

2. Click **Start**, point to **All Programs**, point to **Accessories**, point to **System Tools**, and click **Backup**. The Backup or Restore Wizard will start automatically.

3. Click **Next** on the Welcome page.

4. Accept the defaults to back up files and settings, then click **Next**.

5. Click **Let me choose what to back up**, then click **Next**.

6. On the Items to Back Up page, expand **My Computer**, then click **System State** under My Computer. (*Note*: If you choose to back up the system state, it will automatically back up Active Directory, the boot files, the COM+ class registration database, the registry, and the SYSVOL.)

7. Click in the checkbox next to System State, then click **Next**.

8. On the Backup Type, Destination and Name page, under Choose a place to save your backup, click **Browse**.

9. In the Save As dialog box, click the drop-down arrow in the Save in field and click **Local Disk (C:)**.

10. Click in the File name section and type **AdBackup**, then click **Save**.

11. In the Backup Type, Destination, and Name page, click **Next**.

12. On the Completing the Backup or Restore Wizard page, review your selections and click **Finish**. The Backup progress dialog box will appear.

13. When the backup is completed, click **Close**.

14. If you are not proceeding immediately to the next activity, log off your computer.

RECOVERING ACTIVE DIRECTORY

As mentioned, Active Directory uses a fault-tolerant transactional database to store its data. When a DC restarts after a system failure, or after any sort of improper shutdown, any transactions that exist in the log files but not in the database files will be written to the Active Directory database automatically as part of the start-up process. A server restart is often all that is required to fix problems in Active Directory files.

On rare occasions, Active Directory can become corrupted, in which case a reboot may not help. The corruption may be due to hardware or software problems, such as a bad hard disk controller, a faulty memory chip, a serious virus, or a corrupted system file. In those cases, there are four options for recovering Active Directory:

- Perform soft recovery of the Active Directory database

- Perform a repair of the Active Directory database

- Restore Active Directory from a backup

- Reinstall Active Directory

 Although they sound similar, restore and recover have different meanings when talking about fault-tolerant databases such as Active Directory. To **restore** the database means to replace the current copy (or part of it) with a back-up copy. To **recover** the database means to repair it—to return it to a consistent state or to fix some sort of corruption. If you have to restore your database, you will probably have to recover it as well (in fact, the system will perform some integrity checks as part of a restore). However, you can sometimes recover the database without restoring it.

Soft Recovery

Windows Server 2003 includes a utility called Esentutl.exe, which can be used to recover or repair a damaged Active Directory database. (Although Esentutl is a separate program, it is also used by Ntdsutil.) A recover is used to scan the log files to ensure that all transactions have been written to the database. This recovery, in effect, replays the log files to ensure the database is in a consistent state with no outstanding transactions.

To perform a **soft recovery**, use the files > recover command of Ntdsutil to start esentutl, while the DC is in Directory Services Restore Mode. The soft recovery process is shown in Figure 9-4.

Repairing Active Directory

If a soft recovery does not fix the Active Directory database, the next step is to try repairing it. In Active Directory terminology, repair has a specific meaning. A repair performs a low-level rebuild of the Active Directory database. The repair command can only fix data that it can find; data that is missing or incomplete cannot be repaired.

Practice extreme caution when using the repair option, as it can cause more damage to the database if you do not follow the process exactly. If additional damage is incurred, the only remaining options are to restore Active Directory from a recent backup or reinstall it.

Figure 9-4   Recovering the Active Directory database using Ntdsutil

To run a repair, start the DC in Directory Services Restore Mode and log on, as learned in Activity 9-1. Start a command prompt and change to the folder that contains the Active Directory database, which is C:\WINDOWS\NTDS by default. Type **esentutl /p ntds.dit** and press **Enter**. Type **files** and press **Enter**. Type **repair** and press **Enter**. Click **OK** to accept the warning message, as shown in Figure 9-5.

Figure 9-5   Repair warning message

Once the repair process completes, enter **quit** twice to exit the Ntdsutil prompt. Reboot the server and start Windows 2003 Server normally.

Restoring Active Directory

If you cannot successfully recover or repair Active Directory, the next step is to restore it from a recent backup. There are two types of restores that can be performed: a **non–authoritative restore** or an **authoritative restore**.

Non-Authoritative Restore

A non-authoritative restore is used to restore a damaged Active Directory database from a good system state backup made before the database was corrupted. The older copy of the database will be restored to the DC, and changes will then be replicated from other DCs during the next replication interval. A non-authoritative restore is usually performed when there are multiple DCs in the domain.

 If you have only one DC in the domain, you will loose any changes made after the backup was created. This is one of the main reasons that most Active Directory installations have at least two DCs.

A non-authoritative restore cannot be used to restore a deleted object to Active Directory. When the deleted object is restored from the backup, its USN at the time of the deletion is also restored. Other DCs will have a newer USN for the deleted object and will replicate the tombstone information to the restored Active Directory database. To restore a deleted object, you must perform an authoritative restore, as discussed in the next section.

You must be an administrator on the DC to perform a restore.

To perform a non-authoritative restore of Active Directory, restart the DC in Directory Services Restore Mode, as learned in Activity 9-1, then proceed to Activity 9-3.

Activity 9-3: Performing a Non-Authoritative Restore from a Backup

Time Required: 30 minutes

Objective: To restore a damaged Active Directory from a valid backup.

Description: In this activity you will restore the system state to the DC, and verify that Active Directory is functioning by creating a new user and testing replication. You will perform this activity with a partner, in three parts. You will need the back-up file you created in Activity 9-2.

Perform the following steps on the DC with the lower computer number:

1. If your computer is not turned on, turn it on and proceed to Step 7. Otherwise, log on as the administrator from your own domain.

2. Click **Start**, and click **Shut Down**.

3. At the Shut Down Windows dialog box, click **Restart**.

4. In the Shutdown Event Tracker section, click the drop-down arrow and click **Operating System: Reconfiguration (Planned)**.

5. Click in the Comment section and type **Restart in DSRM for Non Authoritative Restore**, then click **OK**. The computer will restart.

6. During the boot process, press **F8** to see the Windows Advanced Options Menu.

7. Using the up or down arrow key on your keyboard, select **Directory Services Restore Mode** (Windows domain controllers only) and press **Enter**.

8. When prompted to choose which operating system to start, choose **Windows Server 2003**, by selecting it with the up and down arrow keys and pressing **Enter**.

9. The computer will boot into safemode – Directory Services Repair. The words Safe Mode will appear in all four corners of the display screen.

10. Press Ctrl+Alt+Del and then log on as an administrator using the Directory Services Restore Mode Administrator Account password that you assigned to the computer during Active Directory installation.

11. Read the information regarding safe mode, then click **OK**.

12. Click **Start**, point to **All Programs**, point to **Accessories**, point to **System Tools**, then click **Backup**.

13. On the Welcome to the Backup or Restore Wizard page, click **Next**.

14. On the Backup or Restore page, click **Restore files and settings**, then click **Next**.

15. On the What to Restore page under Items to restore, expand **File**. Expand **AdBackup.bkf** (which is the file you created in Activity 9-2).

16. Click the checkbox next to System State, then click **Next**.

17. On the Completing the Backup or Restore Wizard page, click **Finish**.

18. Click **OK** at the warning message telling you that Restoring System State will always overwrite current System State unless restoring to an alternate location. The Restore Progress dialog box will appear.

19. When the restore is complete, click **Close**.

20. At the Backup Utility dialog box, a message will appear telling you that a restart is required to complete the restore. Wait until your partner completes the following steps.

> Prior to restarting the computer, your partner will create objects on the DC with the higher computer number, which will be replicated to the other DC when it restarts. These objects are not in the system state backup that you just restored. Have your partner perform the following steps on the DC with the higher computer number (i.e., the computer that has not been used in Steps 1–20).

Perform the following steps on the DC with the higher computer number:

21. Log on as an administrator in your own domain.

22. Click **Start**, point to **All Programs**, point to **Administrative Tools**, and click **Active Directory Users and Computers**.

23. Expand the name of your domain.

24. Right-click your domain name and click **New**, then click **Organizational Unit**.

25. In the New Object-Organizational Unit dialog box, type **Demo OU** and click **OK**.

26. In the Demo OU, create a new user, employing the skills you learned in Chapter 5. The user will be John Doe, with a username "jdoe" and a password of "Password1". If you have trouble with this task, review Chapter 5 or consult with your instructor for assistance.

27. Exit Active Directory Users and Computers.

> Perform the following steps on the computer with the lower number; that is, the computer used in Steps 1–20 that has just been restored. This server is now in Directory Service Repair Mode, and has therefore not received replication of the objects your partner just created. Those objects do not exist in the backup you just restored on the first server.

Perform the following steps on the DC with the lower computer number:

28. At the prompt, "Do you want to restart the computer now?" click **Yes**.

29. Once the computer has restarted, wait about five minutes to allow replication to complete, then log on as an administrator in your own domain.

30. Click **Start**, point to **All Programs**, point to **Administrative Tools**, then click **Active Directory Users and Computers**.

31. Expand your domain name. Note that the Demo OU created on the other DC (while this DC was offline to be restored) now appears. Select Demo OU and note that the John Doe user account has been replicated and appears in the details pane. If these items do not yet appear, refresh the display (by choosing refresh from the menu or pressing F5) every few minutes until replication is complete. If they do not appear within a few minutes, consult your instructor for assistance.

32. Exit Active Directory Users and Computers.

33. If you are not proceeding immediately to the next activity, log off your computer.

Authoritative Restore

An authoritative restore is a special restore performed on an Active Directory DC to restore objects that were mistakenly deleted or modified. It does this by incrementing the object's USN by 100,000 to ensure that the newly restored object's USN is the highest and will then be replicated to other DCs in the domain. An authoritative restore is only used to undo changes or deletions, as it will overwrite any changes to Active Directory that were performed after the backup was made, no matter which DC processed those changes. The database will be reset to the state it was in when the backup was made.

You can choose to restore the entire Active Directory database during an authoritative restore, or a selected part of it, such as one OU or even one object.

After an authoritative restore, you will need to wait for restored objects to be replicated to all DCs in the domain. Depending on your replication topology, this can take anywhere from five minutes to more than 24 hours.

Activity 9-4: Performing an Authoritative Restore from a Backup

Time Required: 30 minutes

Objective: To perform an authoritative restore of an object from a valid backup.

Description: In this activity you will perform an authoritative restore to restore an OU that was accidentally deleted in Active Directory. You will perform this activity with a partner, in three parts, using both DCs.

Perform the following steps on the DC with the lower computer number.

1. If necessary, turn on your computer and log on as the administrator from your own domain.

2. Click **Start**, point to **All Programs**, point to **Accessories**, point to **System Tools**, then click **Backup**.

3. On the Welcome to the Backup or Restore Wizard page, clear the checkbox next to Always start in wizard mode, then click **Next**, then click **Cancel** and exit the Backup Utility.

4. Restart the Backup Utility from the menu. Notice how the Backup Utility displays four tabs. Click the **Backup** tab.

5. Click the checkbox next to System State.

6. Click in the field under Backup media or file name and type **C:\adbackup2.bkf**, then click **Start Backup**.

7. In the Backup Job Information dialog box, click **Start Backup**.

8. When the backup is complete, click **Close**.

9. Exit the Backup utility.

You now have the new OU and user account saved in a recent backup. Your partner will now delete them, after which they will be restored using an authoritative restore.

Perform the following steps on the DC with the higher computer number.

10. On the DC with the higher number, log on as an administrator in your own domain.

11. Click **Start**, point to **All Programs**, point to **Administrative Tools**, click **Active Directory Users and Computers**.

12. Expand your domain name.

13. Right-click the **Demo OU** and click **Delete**.

14. Click **Yes** to confirm the deletion.

15. A message will appear stating that the Demo OU is a container and contains other objects. Click **Yes**. (You have now deleted the Demo OU and the John Doe user account, tombstoning these objects in the Active Directory database.)

16. Exit Active Directory Users and Computers.

 You will now shut down the first server (with the lower computer number) in order to perform an authoritative restore. Perform the following steps on the DC with the lower computer number.

17. Click **Start**, and click **Shut Down**.

18. In the Shut Down Windows dialog box, make sure **Restart** is selected.

19. Under Shutdown Event Tracker, click the drop-down arrow and click **Operating System: Reconfiguration (Planned)**.

20. Click in the Comment section and type **Restart in DSRM for Authoritative Restore** and click **OK**.

21. Windows will restart. Press **F8** to see the Windows Advanced Options menu.

22. Use the down arrow on your keyboard to highlight Directory Services Restore Mode (Windows DCs only) and press **Enter**.

23. Windows will boot into Safe Mode-Directory Services Repair. The words Safe Mode will appear in all four corners of the display.

24. Log on with the Directory Services Restore Mode Administrator Account password.

25. A message will appear telling you that this is a special diagnostics mode of windows. Click **OK**.

26. Click **Start**, point to **All Programs**, point to **Accessories**, point to **System Tools**, then click **Backup**.

27. Click the **Restore and Manage Media** tab.

28. Expand file, then expand **adbackup2.bkf**.

29. Click the checkbox next to System State.

30. Make sure the Restore files to setting is set to the Original location, then click **Start Restore**.

31. A message will appear telling you that restoring System State will always overwrite current System State unless restoring to an alternate location. Click **OK**.

32. In the Confirm Restore dialog box, click **OK**.

33. When the restore is complete, click **Close**.

34. A message will appear telling you that some of the files and settings restored require you to restart your computer to complete the restore. Click **No**.

35. Exit the Backup Utility.

36. Click **Start**, click **Run**, type **Ntdsutil**, and click **OK**.

37. In the command prompt window, type **authoritative restore** and press **Enter**.

38. At the authoritative restore prompt, type **restore subtree "ou=Demo OU, dc=*oneandtwo*, dc=ad, dc=multinatcorp, dc=com"** (where *oneandtwo* represent your assigned classroom domain) and press **Enter**.

39. Click **Yes** to confirm the restore.

40. The utility will open the database, update the records, and when complete a message will appear stating that the authoritative restore completed successfully.

41. At the authoritative restore prompt, type **quit** and press **Enter**.

42. At the Ntdsutil.exe prompt, type **quit** and press **Enter**.

43. Click **Start**, and click **Shut Down**.

44. In the Shut Down Windows dialog box, make sure **Restart** is selected.

45. Click the drop-down arrow under the Shutdown Event Tracker and click **Operating System: Reconfiguration (Planned)**.

46. Click in the Comment section and type **Authoritative Restore Restart** and click **OK**.

47. Restart your server normally.

48. Click **Start**, point to **All Programs**, point to **Administrative Tools**, then click **Active Directory Users and Computers**.

49. Expand your domain name. Notice that Demo OU has been restored. Expand Demo OU and note that the John Doe user account has also been restored.

50. Exit Active Directory Users and Computers.

51. If desired, you can confirm that the objects also appear on the other DC in your domain. (Remember that replication may take a few minutes.)

52. If you are not proceeding immediately to the next activity, log off your computer.

Reinstalling Active Directory

Another option for fixing Active Directory corruption is reinstalling Active Directory. This is only a valid option if there is at least one other DC that can supply the current contents of Active Directory by replication, or if you are willing to completely rebuild your domain. There are two steps involved in reinstalling Active Directory. The first is to run dcpromo to demote the DC with the corrupt database to a member server. Then, run dcpromo again to promote it to a DC. Note that if DCs are separated by a slow WAN link, it will take some time for the complete contents of Active Directory to be replicated.

OPERATIONS MASTER ROLES

In a multi-master domain model, all DCs can accept updates to Active Directory. This can lead to problems if conflicting changes are made to the same object at the same time on different DCs.

Some Active Directory tasks are so critical that the risk of this occurring is unacceptable. To prevent this from happening for these critical tasks, a specific DC or controllers are assigned master operations roles, as you learned in Chapter 8. In this section, you will learn how to determine which DC holds a master operations role, and how the role can be moved from one DC to another.

In the next few activities, you will determine which DC holds each of the master operations roles in your classroom forest and your own domain.

Activity 9-5: Verifying the Schema Master

Time Required: 5 minutes

Objective: To identify which DC is assigned the schema master role.

Description: In this activity you will identify the DC assigned the schema master role and verify that it is functioning.

1. If necessary, turn on your computer and log on as the administrator from your own domain.

2. Click **Start**, click **Run**, type **regsvr32.exe %systemroot%\system32\schmmgmt.dll**, then click **OK**. This command registers the schema master snap-in for the MMC console.

3. At the Regsvr32 dialog box, click **OK** to close the message that states DllRegisterServer in C:\Windows\System32\schmmgmt.dll succeeded.

4. Click **Start**, click **Run**, type **mmc**, then click **OK**.

5. In the Console1 Window, click **File**, then click **Add/Remove Snap-in**.

6. In the Add/Remove Snap-in dialog box, click **Add**.

7. In the Add Standalone Snap-in dialog box, click **Active Directory Schema**, then click **Add**.

8. Click **Close** to exit the Add Standalone Snap-in dialog box.

9. Click **OK** to close the Add/Remove Snap-in dialog box.

10. In the Console1 window, click **Active Directory Schema**.

11. Right-click **Active Directory Schema**, then click **Operations Master**.

12. In the Change Schema Master dialog box, note the name of the computer listed under Current schema master.

13. Click **Close** to exit the Change Schema Master dialog box.

14. Close the Console1 window. When asked if you would like to save the settings to the Console1 window, click **No**.

15. If you are not proceeding immediately to the next activity, log off your computer.

Activity 9-6: Verifying the Domain Naming Master

Time Required: 5 minutes

Objective: To identify which DC is assigned the domain naming master role.

Description: In this activity you will identify the DC assigned the domain naming master role and verify that it is functioning.

1. If necessary, turn on your computer and log on as the administrator from your own domain.

2. Click **Start**, point to **All Programs**, point to **Administrative Tools**, then click **Active Directory Domains and Trusts**.

3. Right-click **Active Directory Domains and Trusts** in the console tree.

4. Click **Operations Master**. The Change Operations Master dialog box will appear.

5. Under Domain naming operations master, note the name of the current role holder.

6. Click **Close** to exit the Change Operations Master dialog box.

7. Exit Active Directory Domains and Trusts.

8. If you are not proceeding immediately to the next activity, log off your computer.

Activity 9-7: Verifying the Operations Masters for the Domain

Time Required: 5 minutes

Objective: To identify which DCs are assigned the domain-specific roles.

Description: In this activity you will identify the DCs assigned the PDC emulator, RID master, and infrastructure master roles.

1. If necessary, turn on your computer and log on as the administrator from your own domain.

2. Click **Start**, point to **All Programs**, point to **Administrative Tools**, then click **Active Directory Users and Computers**.

3. Right-click the name of your domain.

4. Click **Operations Masters**.

5. The Operations Masters dialog box will open. Notice the three tabs, RID, PDC, and Infrastructure.

6. Click the tabs to view the current role holder for each. Note that only one server in the domain performs this role.

7. Click **Close** to exit the Operations Masters dialog box.

8. Exit Active Directory Users and Computers.

9. If you are not proceeding immediately to the next activity, log off your computer.

Changing the Holder of Operations Master Roles

Normally you do not need to reassign operations master roles to other DCs. However you may want to reassign the roles to more powerful servers in the domain or in preparation for the removal of a DC from the domain. You have two options for changing the master operations roles—transferring the role or seizing the role

Transferring the Role

A transfer is performed when both the DC holding the role and the target DC are available on the network. During the transfer process, the current role holder is contacted and the appropriate data is transferred to the new DC. The process is graceful and no data is lost.

Transferring the Schema Master Role To transfer the schema master role, start **Active Directory Schema**. Right-click **Active Directory Schema** and click **Change Domain Controller**. Select the DC to become the new schema master and click **OK**. Right-click **Active Directory Schema** and click **Operations Master**. Click **Change**. Click **Yes** to confirm the transfer. When finished, click **OK** and close Active Directory Schema.

Transferring the Domain Naming Master Role To transfer the domain naming master role, start Active Directory Domains and Trusts. Right-click **Active Directory Domains and Trusts** and click **Change Domain Controller**. Select the DC to become the new domain naming master and click **OK**. Right-click **Active Directory Domains and Trusts** and click **Operations Master**. Click **Change**. Click **Yes** to confirm the transfer. When finished, click **OK** and close Active Directory Domains and Trusts.

Transferring the PDC Emulator, RID Master, or Infrastructure Master Role To transfer these roles, you can use Active Directory Users and Computers. These three roles exist within each domain, and so you and your partner will work together to transfer the roles between DCs in your own domain.

Activity 9-8: Transferring the PDC Emulator Role

Time Required: 10 minutes

Objective: To transfer the PDC emulator role.

Description: In this activity you will take the current PDC emulator offline for maintenance and transfer the role to another DC. This activity will be performed on a DC that is not the PDC emulator.

1. If necessary, turn on your computer and log on as the administrator from your own domain.

2. Click **Start**, point to **All Programs**, point to **Administrative Tools**, then click **Active Directory Users and Computers**.

3. Right-click **Active Directory Users and Computers**, then click **Connect to Domain Controller**. (*Note*: You have two options for what you may do at this point—either type the name of the DC to which you'd like to transfer the role or select the name of an available DC from a list.)

4. Click the DC that is not currently assigned the PDC emulator role, and click **OK**.

5. Right-click the domain name, then click **Operations Masters**.

6. In the Operations Masters dialog box, click the **PDC** tab. Note the name of the current PDC emulator under Operations Master. Beneath is the name of the DC to which you are transferring the role. Click the **Change** button.

7. When asked if you're sure you want to transfer the role, click **Yes**.

8. Click **OK** to acknowledge the change.

9. Click **Close** to exit the Operations Master dialog box.

10. Exit Active Directory Users and Computers.

11. If you are not proceeding immediately to the next activity, log off your computer.

The transfer process is similar for the RID master and Infrastructure Master Roles. Time permitting, you may practice the skills you just learned by transferring these roles as well.

Seizing the Role

Seizing the role is done when the DC holding the role is not available on the network. For example, the DC crashed and will not be brought back online within a reasonable amount of time, or it is damaged beyond repair. You should only seize the role if it cannot be transferred.

In Activity 9-9, you will use Active Directory Users and Computers to seize the PDC role, and in Activity 9-11 you will do the same thing with the Ntdsutil command. In both cases, the system will first try to contact the existing master and gracefully transfer the role. If that is not possible, the role is seized. It is possible to lose some data during a seizure, which is why the system will always try a transfer first.

You must also confirm that you want to seize a role. Figure 9-6 shows a typical role seizure confirmation dialog box.

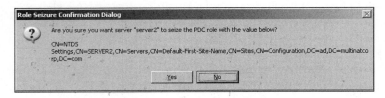

Figure 9-6   Role seizure confirmation message

Activity 9-9: Using the GUI to Seize the PDC Emulator Role

Time Required: 5 minutes

Objective: To seize the PDC emulator role.

Description: The current PDC emulator crashed and you do not know when it will be brought back online. In this activity you will seize the role with the participation of your partner. The activity contains two sections—each performed on one of the DCs.

The following steps will only be performed on the DC that is the current PDC emulator.

1. If necessary, turn on your computer and log on as the administrator from your own domain.

2. Click **Start**, then click **Shut down**.

3. In the Shut Down Windows dialog box, click the drop-down arrow, then click **Operating System: Reconfiguration (Planned)**.

4. In the Comment section of this tab, type **Shutdown to Perform PDC Role Seizure**, then click **OK**.

5. Wait until the computer is completely shut down.

Complete the remainder of this activity on the other DC.

6. Log on as the administrator from your own domain.

7. Click **Start**, point to **All Programs**, point to **Administrative Tools**, then click **Active Directory Users and Computers**.

8. Right-click your domain name and click **Operations Masters**.

9. Click the **PDC** tab. Note the text under Operations master that states: The current operations master is offline. The role cannot be transferred.

10. Click **Change**.

11. Click **Yes** to confirm the change.

12. When prompted with the message: This computer is a non-replication partner. Transferring the PDC role to this computer may cause a full sync of NT4 BDCs. Do you still want to continue with the transfer? Click **Yes**.

13. If you see a message stating: The requested FSMO operation failed. The current FSMO holder could not be contacted. The current operations master cannot be contacted to perform the transfer. Under some circumstances, a forced transfer can be performed. Do you want to attempt a forced transfer? Click **Yes**.

14. Click **OK** to acknowledge the change.

15. Exit Active Directory Users and Computers.

16. If you are not proceeding immediately to the next activity, log off your computer.

Activity 9-10: Verifying the Role Seizure

Time Required: 5 minutes

Objective: To verify that the PDC emulator role was successfully seized.

Description: In this activity you will verify that the seizure of the PDC emulator role was successful, and see what happens when the previous PDC emulator is brought back online.

The following steps will only be performed on the DC that was shut down in Activity 9-9.

1. If necessary, turn on your computer and log on as the administrator from your own domain.

2. Click **Start**, point to **All Programs**, click **Administrative Tools**, then click **Active Directory Users and Computers**.

3. Right-click your domain name and click **Operations Masters**.

4. Click the **PDC** tab. Note which server appears as the operations master.

5. Click **Close** to exit the Operations Master dialog box.

6. Exit Active Directory Users and Computers.

7. If you are not proceeding immediately to the next activity, log off your computer.

Activity 9-11: Using Ntdsutil to Seize the PDC Emulator Role

Time Required: 5 minutes

Objective: To seize the PDC emulator role using Ntdsutil.

Description: In this activity you will seize the role of the PDC emulator using Ntdsutil.exe.

The following steps will only be performed on the DC that is the current PDC emulator.

1. If necessary, turn on your computer and log on as the administrator from your own domain.

2. Click **Start**, then click **Shut Down**.

3. In the Shut Down Windows dialog box, click the drop-down arrow under the Shut Down Event Tracker section and click **Operating System: Reconfiguration (Planned)**. In the Comment section, type **Shutdown to Test Ntdsutil PDC Role Seizure** and click **OK**.

4. Wait until the computer has completely shut down before completing the rest of the activity.

   Perform the following steps on the DC that is still running.

5. Log on as the administrator from your own domain.

6. Click **Start**, point to **All Programs**, point to **Accessories**, then click **Command Prompt**.

7. In the command prompt window, type **ntdsutil** and press **Enter**.

8. At the Ntdsutil prompt, type **roles** and press **Enter**.

9. At the fsmo maintenance prompt, type **connections** and press **Enter**.

10. At the server connections prompt, type **connect to server** *name* (where *name* is the fully qualified domain name of the current server) and press **Enter**.

11. At the Server connections prompt, type **quit** and press **Enter**.

12. At the fsmo maintenance prompt, type **seize PDC** and press **Enter**.

You could also use one of the following commands to seize other roles:
- Seize schema master to seize the schema master role
- Seize domain naming master to seize the domain naming master role
- Seize rid master to seize the RID master role

13. The Role Seizure Confirmation dialog box will appear. Click **Yes** to confirm the change.

14. Note that a safe transfer of the PDC FSMO will be attempted before seizure. Once the procedure has completed, type **quit** and press **Enter** to exit FSMO maintenance.

15. Type **quit** and press **Enter** to exit Ntdsutil.

16. Close the command prompt window.

17. Log off your computer.

CHAPTER SUMMARY

❏ NTDS.DIT is the Active Directory database.

❏ EDB.LOG is a transaction log for changes to NTDS.DIT and maintains a constant size of 10MB. EDB*xxxxx*.LOG is an old version of EDB.LOG.

❏ EDB.CHK is a checkpoint file that tracks which transactions in EDB.LOG have been written to NTDS.DIT.

❏ RES1.LOG and RES2.LOG are used as reserve space if the disk holding EDB.LOG runs out of disk space.

❏ Deleted objects are not removed from Active Directory immediately. They are marked with a tombstone for 60 days, by default. When restoring Active Directory, the age of the backup must be less than the tombstone lifetime.

❏ Online defragmentation of Active Directory is automatically performed every 12 hours, but does not compact the database.

❏ Offline defragmentation of Active Directory must be performed manually in Directory Services Restore Mode. This is done with Ntdsutil and does compact the database.

❏ The location of the Active Directory database and log files can be moved.

❏ Active Directory is backed up as part of a system state backup on a DC.

❏ A soft recovery of Active Directory uses Esentutl to scan log files and ensure that all transactions are written to the database.

❏ A repair of Active Directory uses Esentutl to perform a low-level rebuild of the database. This is a structural rebuild only, and does not repair missing or incomplete data.

❏ When a non-authoritative restore of Active Directory is performed, the restored data will be overwritten with newer changes from other DCs. It is used to replace a corrupted database, not objects in Active Directory.

❏ An authoritative restore will overwrite objects on other DCs. This is used to replace accidentally deleted or corrupted objects.

❏ The five flexible single master operations are: schema master, domain naming master, PDC emulator, RID master, and infrastructure master.

❏ FSMO roles are transferred to another DC when the DC performing the role is removed. When the DC performing an FSMO role is unavailable, the role must be seized.

9

KEY TERMS

authoritative restore — An Active Directory restore that allows you to restore deleted or modified objects and have those changes replicated to other DCs in the domain.

data table — The portion of NTDS.DIT that stores the attributes and properties for objects in Active Directory.

domain naming master — The DC responsible for adding or removing domains from the forest. There is only one domain naming master per forest.

EDB.CHK — The checkpoint file that tracks which transactions in EDB.LOG have been written to the Active Directory database.

EDB.LOG — The transaction log used by Active Directory. It is always 10 MB.

EDBXXXXX.LOG — Old versions of the transaction log used by Active Directory.

Extensible Storage Engine (ESE) — A database design that uses log files to provide fault tolerance and improved performance.

garbage collection — The process of purging deleted objects from Active Directory.

infrastructure master — The DC responsible for updating references in other domains to an object in the local domain. There is one infrastructure domain for each domain in the forest.

link table — The portion of NTDS.DIT that stores linked attributes that point to other objects in Active Directory.

non-authoritative restore — A restore of Active Directory used to restore a damaged database. Updates are replicated from other DCs in the domain.

NTDS.DIT — The Active Directory database.

offline defragmentation — The process of compacting the Active Directory database to free up space.

online defragmentation — A process that runs every 12 hours to purge deleted objects from Active Directory.

operations master roles — Roles assigned to specific DCs in the forest to prevent conflicts in Active Directory.

PDC emulator — A DC that emulates a Windows NT primary DC for domain synchronization and password changes for pre-Windows 2000 DCs. There is one PDC emulator for each domain in the forest.

recover — To repair a database; to return it to a consistent state; to fix corruption therein.

relative identifier (RID) master — The DC that is responsible for distributing a range of RID numbers to DCs in the domain. There is one RID master for each domain in the forest.

RES1.LOG and **RES2.LOG** — Files used for transaction logging if the disk runs out of space.

restore — To replace the current copy of a database (or part of it) with a back-up copy made previously.

rollback (*or* rolling back a transaction) — The process used by transactional database systems (including the ESE data engine used by Active Directory) to remove partially completed transactions from the database files.

roll forward (*or* rolling forward a transaction) — The process used by transactional database systems (including the ESE data engine used by Active Directory) in which a log file is used to ensure that partially completed transactions are fully recorded in the database files.

schema master — The DC designated as the schema master has the authority to make changes to the schema in the forest. There is only one schema master per forest.

schema table — The portion of NTDS.DIT that stores information on the types of objects that can be created in Active Directory.

soft recovery — The process of scanning log files to ensure that all transactions have been written to the Active Directory database.

system state — A collection of critical operating system files including the registry, Active Directory components, SYSVOL, and start-up files that can be backed up as a single unit on DCs.

tombstone — A marker in the Active Directory database that indicates an object has been deleted.

tombstone lifetime — The time period after which deleted objects are purged from Active Directory. The default is 60 days.

transaction — Any addition, deletion, or modification to Active Directory.

REVIEW QUESTIONS

1. The Active Directory database is named?

   a. Active Directory.LOG

   b. EDB.LOG

   c. EDB.CHK

   d. NTDS.DIT

2. The size of each Active Directory log file is?

    a. 5 MB

    b. 10 MB

    c. 20 MB

    d. Varies

3. Which of the following is not backed up as part of the system state?

    a. Registry

    b. SYSVOL

    c. User's home folders

    d. Start-up files

4. When performing an authoritative restore, Windows 2003 Server increments the restored object's USN by?

    a. 1

    b. 10

    c. 1000

    d. 100,000

5. Which operations master roles are forest-wide? Select all that apply?

    a. Schema master

    b. PDC emulator

    c. RID master

    d. Infrastructure master

    e. Domain naming master

6. Which operations master role is used to synchronize time on DCs in the domain?

    a. Schema master

    b. PDC emulator

    c. RID master

    d. Infrastructure master

    e. Domain naming master

7. The default tombstone lifetime is?

    a. 7 days

    b. 30 days

    c. 60 days

    d. 90 days

    e. Unlimited

8. On a DC, garbage collection occurs every?

    a. 12 hours

    b. 24 hours

    c. 7 days

    d. 60 days

9. You accidentally deleted the wrong user account from Active Directory. What type of restore should you perform to restore the user account?

   a. Authoritative

   b. Non–authoritative

   c. Offline

   d. Directory services restore

10. You are trying to install a new child domain in the forest but are unsuccessful. Which operations master is responsible for adding new domains?

    a. Schema master

    b. PDC emulator

    c. RID master

    d. Infrastructure master

    e. Domain naming master

11. Which tool is used to transfer the RID master role?

    a. Active Directory Schema

    b. Active Directory Domain and Trusts

    c. Active Directory Sites and Services

    d. Active Directory Users and Computer

12. Each addition, deletion, or modification to Active Directory is called a(n)?

    a. Update

    b. Transaction

    c. Originating update

    d. Replicated update

13. Which file is used by Active Directory to keep track of what information in the log files has been written to the Active Directory database?

    a. NTDS.DIT

    b. EDB.LOG

    c. EDB.CHK

    d. EDB00001.LOG

    e. RES1.LOG

14. When a change has been made to Active Directory, which file is the data written to first?

    a. NTDS.DIT

    b. EDB.LOG

    c. EDB.CHK

    d. EDB00001.LOG

    e. RES1.LOG

15. Which of the following statements regarding an offline defragmentation are correct? (Select all that apply.)

    a. An offline defragmentation can free up disk space

    b. The Active Directory database cannot be mounted during an offline defragmentation

    c. An offline defragmentation runs every 12 hours by default

    d. An offline defragmentation is also called garbage collection

16. Which tool is used to perform an offline defragmentation?

    a. DEFRAG.EXE

    b. COMPACT.EXE

    c. NTDSUTIL.EXE

    d. NTDSDEFRAG.EXE

17. Which of the following backups cannot be performed when backing up the system state?

    a. Normal

    b. Incremental

    c. Differential

    d. Copy

18. A low-level rebuild of the Active Directory database is called a?

    a. Repair

    b. Soft recover

    c. Hard recover

    d. Defragmentation

19. By default, the first DC installed in a child domain is assigned which FSMO role(s)? (Select all that apply.)

    a. Schema master

    b. PDC emulator

    c. RID master

    d. Infrastructure master

    e. Domain naming master

20. Which tool is used to transfer the domain naming master role?

    a. Active Directory Schema

    b. Active Directory Domain and Trusts

    c. Active Directory Sites and Services

    d. Active Directory Users and Computer

9

HEARTLAND HOSPITAL CASE PROJECTS

Case Project 9-1: Designing a Disaster Recovery Plan

Heartland Hospital has asked you to create a disaster recovery plan that will allow the hospital to continue operating in the event of an IT disaster. The goal of the disaster recovery plan is to:

❑ Ensure that Active Directory can be restored on any and all DCs.

❑ Ensure that Active Directory can be restored to a new server, if required.

❑ Prevent the crash of a single DC from negatively affecting the performance and functionality of the forest if the DC cannot be brought back online within four hours.

Outline the steps you would take to ensure the goals listed above are met.

Case Project 9-2: Planning Operations Master Role Assignment

As part of the budget, the hospital has allocated enough money to upgrade the hardware for one-third of the DCs each year (meaning that no DC will be older than three years old). In the upcoming year, the first DC in the forest root domain will be replaced.

What operations master role issues must you address before you can replace the selected DC? What would you recommend for operations masters in the forest? How would your recommendations change if you had more domains in the forest?

Case Project 9-3: Recovering Active Directory Databases

The hospital began experiencing random power outages, causing the DC to shutdown unexpectedly. The staff is worried that changes they made to data in Active Directory will be lost when the power fails and the DC stops.

What can you tell them regarding Active Directory to eliminate their fears?

10

USING ACTIVE DIRECTORY AS A TOOL TO ENFORCE CORPORATE POLICY

After reading this chapter and completing the exercises, you will be able to:

♦ Understand and describe the purpose of Group Policy

♦ Describe how group policies are applied

♦ Manage desktop computers using Group Policy

♦ Distribute software using Group Policy

♦ Analyze and configure security settings using Group Policy

♦ Troubleshoot Group Policy

Group Policy is used to configure workstations and servers that are part of an Active Directory forest. It can be used to manage the configuration of computers, control the settings and options available to users, manage or enforce security policies, and distribute software across the network.

Group Policy is nothing short of amazing. It can be used in the smallest organization or the largest enterprise to bring consistency and enforce the wishes of the organization's management. This chapter will help you understand how Group Policy is created and managed, as well as how group policy objects (GPOs) integrate with Active Directory. You will learn to manage users' desktops and distribute software with group policies. This chapter will also cover the analysis and configuration of security settings, as well as troubleshooting Group Policy settings.

GROUP POLICY

To understand Group Policy in Active Directory, it helps to have some background. The ability to use **policies** to manage Windows desktop computers was first introduced with Windows 95 and Windows NT. These older operating systems used a feature called system policies to change a number of registry entries that controlled desktop settings. A system policy file created on a DC would either enable or disable a particular setting on the client computer.

System policies are stored in a policy file that must be placed in the **netlogon share**, a share found on every DC in a domain. Client computers using system policies download the policy file from the DC during the authentication process.

Once policies are applied to these client computers, the registry entries in the policies are permanently set on these computers. Therefore, with Windows 95, Windows 98, Windows Me, and Windows NT, these settings still apply unless they were deliberately removed. For example, if Bob logs on with a policy that restricts access to the display properties, and his computer is disconnected from the network or the policy file is merely deleted from the DC, he would still be restricted from accessing the display properties.

This effect of permanently changing the registry is known as **tattooing the registry**.

System policies can still be used by Windows XP, Windows 2000, or Windows 2003 clients that participate in a Windows NT domain. When authenticating to an Active Directory DC, though, these newer clients use Group Policy instead of system policies.

If you have both Windows NT and Active Directory DCs in your domain, the Windows 2000 and newer clients will prefer the Active Directory DCs, and only use the Windows NT DC if no Active Directory DC responds. Once the client starts using Group Policy, it will not go back to system policies.

Group Policy, introduced in Windows 2000 and enhanced in both Windows XP and Windows Server 2003, is still largely a collection of registry entries. However, management of the policies has been significantly enhanced. These enhancements include:

- Automatic replication—Group policies are automatically replicated to all DCs for a domain.

- Transient policy settings—The registry entries applied by Group Policy are automatically removed when the policy no longer applies.

- Expanded capabilities—The system policies in older operating systems allowed basic user interface controls. Group Policy can control security auditing, IPSec settings, software distribution, and desktop restrictions. Windows Server 2003 has introduced more than 200 policy settings that were not available in Windows 2000.

Administrative Templates

Most group policies are based on **administrative templates**, which are files with an .adm extension. These administrative templates describe registry settings that can be configured in a policy or Group Policy.

Several administrative templates are included with Windows Server 2003, but you can also create your own. Creating your own administrative templates allows you to create customized registry settings to configure the operating system and applications on your network, ensuring that all of your systems are configured to a corporate standard. You can control any setting in the registry with a custom administrative template, however, some settings can only be managed in custom templates by tattooing the registry, in the same way that system policies do.

For more information on creating your own administrative templates, visit *http://msdn.microsoft.com/ asp?url=/library/en-us/policy/policy/administrative_template_file_format.asp*. (The Microsoft Web site is frequently reorganized as content is updated. If the file is not found at this URL, then search the Microsoft site using the term "group policy administrative templates.")

The administrative templates included with Windows Server 2003 are:

- System.adm—This administrative template contains a variety of system settings that restrict the operation of the operating system. It includes security settings and desktop restrictions.

- Inetres.adm—This administrative template controls settings for Internet Explorer. It includes the ability to set and restrict access to settings such as menu items and proxy servers.

- Wmplayer.adm—This administrative template includes settings for Windows Media Player. It is not applicable to 64-bit versions of Windows XP or Windows Server 2003.

- Conf.adm—This administrative template has settings for Microsoft NetMeeting. It is not applicable to 64-bit versions of Windows XP or Windows Server 2003.

- Wuau.adm—This administrative template controls settings for Windows Update. It allows administrators to control where and when client computers receive operating system updates.

Group Policy Storage

Group policies are stored on DCs and on local computers. Every computer capable of using Group Policy (Windows 2000, Windows Server 2003, and Windows XP) holds a local policy object in a hidden folder called *systemroot*\system32\GroupPolicy. This local GPO, referred to as a **local computer policy**, applies only to the local computer. Figure 10-1 shows an example of the storage of a local computer policy on Windows XP.

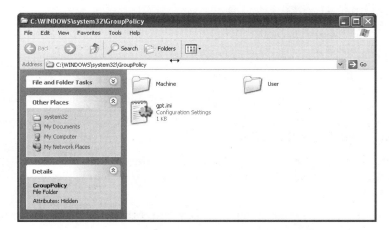

Figure 10-1   Local computer policy stored on Windows XP

Local computer policies are great for a workgroup environment because they still allow you to configure policies that apply to each computer. However, they must be configured on each system individually.

When talking about Group Policy, though, one is almost always referring to Group Policy managed in a domain or forest, where GPOs are stored on DCs as part of Active Directory. Group polices are centrally managed, and a single group policy will affect many users and computers.

 Some people are confused by the term group policy object (GPO), since it isn't really an object and it isn't linked to groups—although it can apply to groups of people or computers. Think of a GPO as a group of policy settings.

Group Policy in a forest is managed in sets of GPOs. These GPOs are stored on DCs, and are *virtual* objects—meaning that what you see and manipulate as one object or policy is really made up of several components. A GPO is not a single object in the directory the way a user or contact is.

One part of a GPO is stored in the Active Directory database, while the other is stored in the **SYSVOL share**. (SYSVOL is automatically replicated between all DCs.) The Active Directory portion of a group policy is called the **group policy container (GPC)**. The GPC contains information regarding the version of individual GPOs, software installation, folder redirection information, as well as settings made in any of the administrative templates used to create the GPO. The GPC is used to track the status of the GPOs.

Clients, however, do not read the GPO from the Active Directory database directly. The portion of the GPO stored on the SYSVOL share is referred to as a **group policy template (GPT)**. A GPT is a collection of subfolders stored in *systemroot*\sysvol\sysvol*domainname*\policies. Each GPT is stored in a separate subfolder named with the GUID of the GPO. An example of the full path to a GPT would be *C:\WINDOWS\ SYSVOL\sysvol\ad.multinatcorp.com\Policies\\{0DE5A83B-B9DA-40FF-A2F2-A8390CBC3468}*, as shown in Figure 10-2.

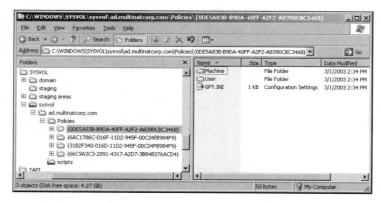

Figure 10-2   GPT stored on a DC

The subfolders that may be present within a GPT folder include:

- Adm—Contains all of the custom administrative templates (.adm files) used to create the GPO.

- USER—Contains a registry.pol file that holds registry settings that are applied to users. The registry entries are applied in HKEY_CURRENT_USER.

- USER\applications—A subfolder in the user folder, which contains application advertisement scripts (.aas) used to distribute and install applications through Group Policy. These are for applications associated with users.

- MACHINE—Contains a registry.pol file that holds registry settings that are applied to computers. The registry entries are applied in HKEY_LOCAL_MACHINE.

- Machine\applications—A subfolder in the machine folder, which contains application advertisement scripts (.aas) used to distribute and install applications through Group Policy. These are for applications associated with computers.

Do not confuse a GPT with an administrative template used for Group Policy.

Activity 10-1: Viewing Local Group Policy Settings

Time Required: 5 minutes

Objective: To view the contents of the local GPO on your server.

Description: Each Windows Server 2003 DC has a local group policy. In this activity you will view its contents using the Group Policy snap-in.

1. If necessary, start your computer and log on as the administrator from your own domain.
2. Click **Start**, click **Run**, type **mmc**, then press **Enter**.
3. Click **File**, then click **Add/Remove Snap-in**.
4. Click **Add** to add a new Snap-in to the MMC.
5. In the Add Standalone Snap-in, scroll through the list of snap-ins and double-click **Group Policy Object Editor**.
6. Confirm that **Local Computer** is listed in the Group Policy Object box, then click **Finish**.
7. Click **Close**, then click **OK**.
8. Double-click **Local Computer Policy**. You should see two areas: Computer Configuration and User Configuration.
9. Double-click **User Configuration** to view the components inside.
10. Double-click **Administrative Templates** to view the contents inside.
11. Double-click **Start Menu and Taskbar**, then click **Remove user's folders from the Start Menu**. A description of this option is now displayed, and includes the versions of Windows that support it.
12. View the description for some other settings that look interesting.
13. Close the MMC. If you are asked to save the console settings, click **No**.
14. If you are not proceeding immediately to the next activity, log off your computer.

Activity 10-2: Edit a GPO Stored on a DC

Time Required: 5 minutes

Objective: To edit the Default Domain Controllers Policy for your domain.

Description: The Default Domain Controllers Policy for your domain limits the ability of users to log on to DCs. Average users on the network cannot sit down at the keyboard of a DC to log on (referred to as an interactive logon). Normally this is an excellent security procedure. However, to test Group Policy application in later activities, you must allow authenticated users to log on locally to the DCs in your domain. You will do so in this activity.

1. If necessary, start your computer and log on as the administrator from your own domain.
2. Click **Start**, point to **Administrative Tools**, then click **Active Directory Users and Computers**.
3. If necessary, expand the entry for your domain. Then, right-click **Domain Controllers**, and click **Properties**.
4. Click the **Group Policy** tab to view the existing GPOs.
5. Double-click **Default Domain Controllers Policy** to edit it.
6. Under Computer Configuration, double-click **Windows Settings**, double-click **Security Settings**, double-click **Local Policies**, then click **User Rights Assignment**.
7. In the right pane, double-click **Allow log on locally**.

8. Click **Add User or Group**, type **Authenticated Users**, then click **OK**.

9. Click **OK** to close the **Allow log on locally Properties** window.

10. Close the Group Policy Object Editor.

11. Click **OK** to close the Domain Controllers Properties window.

12. Close Active Directory Users and Computers.

GROUP POLICY APPLICATION

Group policies are composed of user configuration settings and computer configuration settings. The user configuration settings apply only to users, and the computer configuration settings apply only to computers. User and computer settings are applied according to where they are located in Active Directory and how the GPOs are attached or linked to the containers in Active Directory.

GPOs stored on DCs are **linked** to sites, domains, and OUs. A GPO applies to the user and computer objects that exist in the container (and child containers) to which they are linked. For example, when a GPO is linked to a domain, it will apply to all computers and users in the domain. If it were linked to an OU, then it would apply to all computers and users in that OU and in child OUs.

Linking a GPO to a site is a little different. When a GPO is linked to a site, it will apply to computers assigned to that site (by IP number and subnet, as discussed in Chapter 7), and to users who log on to computers in that site, regardless of their domains or OUs. Linking a GPO to a site is usually done because there is a particular setting that needs to apply in only one specific geographic location.

A single GPO can be linked with multiple OUs, sites, or even domains. However, they are always stored on the DCs of a single domain. You should avoid linking GPOs between domains, as it will make user logons less efficient.

Most networks are designed to allow users to authenticate to a local DC for their domain; however, retrieving the GPO from another domain might involve crossing a WAN link or a second DC.

For example, a GPO created in ad.multinatcorp.com is replicated to all DCs for that domain. You can link this GPO to the oneandtwo.ad.multinatcorp.com domain, and it will be applied to users and computers in that domain. However, since the GPO is not replicated to DCs in oneandtwo.ad.multinatcorp.com, when a user in that domain logs on, the GPO must be retrieved from a DC in ad.multinatcorp.com—even though the rest of the logon is processed at a DC in oneandtwo.ad.multinatcorp.com.

If a DC for ad.multinatcorp.com is not in the same site, then the GPO would be retrieved across slower WAN links, which is normally something that should be avoided.

Group Policy Priority

GPOs are applied and processed in a specific order. First we'll discuss the order in which GPOs are applied, then why the processing order is important.

1. The first policy to be applied is the local computer policy. These policies only affect users of the one computer, and are *always* overridden by group policy settings, if any exist.

2. Second, any GPO linked to the site is applied.

3. Third, any GPOs linked to the domain are applied. GPOs for the domain set options for the entire domain, and additional GPOs are used for settings that are more specific to each OU.

4. Fourth, GPOs linked to OUs are applied by working down from the domain to the OU that holds the computer object or user account object.

This process is followed twice—once for the computer when it starts up and once for the user at logon. The default processing sequence is illustrated in Figure 10-3. There are settings that will override this default sequence. You will learn more about them later in this chapter.

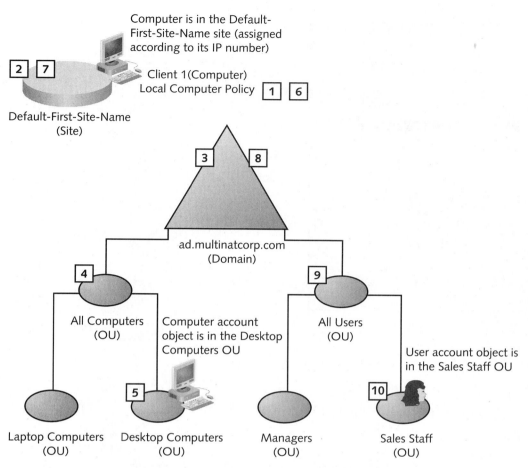

1 to 5: Default GPO sequence for computer settings
6 to 10: Default GPO sequence for user settings

Figure 10-3   Default GPO processing sequence

 You may see the acronym SDOU in reference to GPOs. It stands for site, domain, and OUs, and was created to help you remember which containers can be linked with a GPO, and the order in which they apply. You might hear a techie say, "link the GPO to a SDOU," meaning link the GPO to the appropriate container—a site, domain, or OU.

Different group policy settings from multiple GPOs can be combined, as long as they do not conflict. For example, if a GPO linked to the domain removes the run command from the Start menu, and another GPO linked to an OU adds the My Computer icon to the Windows XP desktop, then both settings will be applied.

However, if there is a conflict between GPOs that linked at different levels and configure the same setting, then the last GPO to be applied will win the conflict and configure the setting (unless you change this behavior). Local computer policy objects always have the lowest priority, and therefore always lose. For example, if the run command is removed from the Start menu in a GPO linked to the site, and the run command is added to the Start menu in a GPO linked to the domain, then the run command will be present in the Start menu. You can also consider it this way: GPOs that are "closer" to the user or computer have higher priority.

If multiple GPOs are linked to a single site, domain, or OU, as shown in Figure 10-4, the administrator will have to choose which one has the highest priority. When viewing the GPOs that are linked to a site, domain, or OU, the GPO at the top of the list will have the highest priority. You can change the order of GPOs by highlighting a GPO and clicking the Up and Down buttons.

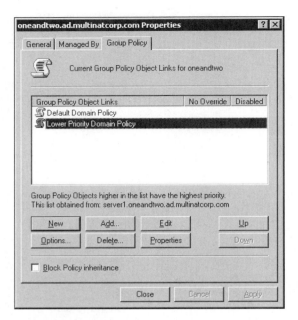

Figure 10-4   Multiple GPOs linked to an OU

Activity 10-3: Creating a GPO for an OU

Time Required: 20 minutes

Objective: To create a GPO that is linked to an OU.

Description: Most organizations design their Active Directory structure to reflect the hierarchy of their organization, whether by department, geography, or even functions. Remember from Chapters 3 and 4 that the application of Group Policy is one thing to keep in mind when making choices regarding your Active Directory structure. Since policies are most often applied to OUs, it's a good idea to define OUs to hold objects that need similar policies.

1. If necessary, start your computer and log on as the administrator from your own domain.

2. Click **Start**, point to **Administrative Tools**, then click **Active Directory Users and Computers**.

3. Right-click your domain, point to **New**, then click **Organizational Unit**.

4. In the name box, type *yourname***OU** (where *yourname* is your name), then click **OK**.

5. Right-click **yournameOU**, point to **New**, then click **Organizational Unit**.

6. In the name box, type **Sales**, then click **OK**.

7. Right-click **yournameOU**, point to **New**, then click **Organizational Unit**.

8. In the name box, type **IT**, then click **OK**.

9. In yournameOU, right-click **Sales**, point to **New**, then click **User**.

10. In the First name box, type **Bob**, in the Last name box type **Smith**, in the User logon name box type *yourname***Bob** (where *yourname* is your name, to ensure uniqueness), then click **Next**. Remember that user logon names must be unique within a domain. Assign the user a password of "Password1".

11. Click **User must change password at next logon** to deselect it, click **Next**, then click **Finish**.

12. In yournameOU, right-click **IT**, point to **New**, then click **User**.

13. In the First name box, type **Susan**, in the Last name box type **Jones**, in the User logon name box type *yourname***Susan** (where *yourname* is your name, to ensure uniqueness), then click **Next**. Assign the user a password of "Password1".

14. Click **User must change password at next logon** to deselect it, click **Next**, then click **Finish**.

15. Right-click **yournameOU** and click **Properties**.

16. Click **Group Policy** to view the tab.

17. Click **New** to create a new GPO, type *yourname***GPO** (where *yourname* is your name) to name the new GPO, then press **Enter**.

18. Click **Edit** to edit the contents of the GPO.

19. Under User Configuration, double-click **Administrative Templates**, then click **Control Panel**.

20. Double-click **Prohibit access to the Control Panel**, click the **Enabled** option button, then click **OK**. This enables the setting for all users in yournameOU.

21. Close the Group Policy Object Editor and click **Close**.

22. In yournameOU, right-click **IT** and click **Properties**.

23. Click **Group Policy** to view the tab.

24. Click **New** to create a new GPO, type *yourname***IT** (where *yourname* is your name) to name the new GPO, then press **Enter**. Though it appears that GPOs are stored as part of the OU, they are actually stored by domain and must have unique names.

25. Click **Edit** to edit the contents of the GPO.

26. Under User Configuration, double-click **Administrative Templates**, then click **Control Panel**.

27. Double-click **Prohibit access to the Control Panel**, click the **Disabled** option button, then click **OK**. This disables the setting for all users in the IT OU.

28. Close the Group Policy Object Editor and click **Close**.

29. Close Active Directory Users and Computers.

30. Test the application of Group Policy by logging on as yournameBob, and yournameSusan. YournameBob will not be able to access the control panel because the users in the Sales OU inherit the setting configured at yournameOU. YournameSusan will be allowed access because the GPO linked to the IT OU disables the setting and has higher priority.

Modifying Group Policy Priority

In most situations, the standard priority of Group Policy application meets the needs of network administrators. However, the priority can be modified by configuring **No Override**, **Block Policy Inheritance**, and **Loopback Processing Mode**.

No Override

When No Override is enabled on a policy, it always has the highest priority. This is useful when enforcing organizational or departmental settings, like creating a GPO linked to the domain that disables a common peer-to-peer file sharing application. You might be concerned that an administrator who has control over some OUs will configure a GPO for his or her OU that allows the program to run. By configuring No Override on the GPO at the domain level, you ensure that GPOs linked to child OUs cannot override your GPO. Figure 10-5 shows No Override enabled on a group policy link.

10

Figure 10-5   No Override enabled on a GPO

If two GPOs are configured with No Override, then the first policy object processed will be in effect. This means that a site-linked GPO with No Override has priority over a domain-linked GPO with No Override.

If multiple GPOs linked to the same OU have No Override turned on, and they try to configure the same setting, which GPO would win? The one higher in the list. This may not be intuitive, but it does make sense. When using No Override, always test your group policies carefully to be sure that you understand the effect.

Block Policy Inheritance

When Block Policy Inheritance is configured on a site, domain, or OU, GPOs higher in the tree do not apply (unless No Override is set). This allows for exemptions from corporate policy for a particular OU (or department). For example, say you've created several GPOs that contain settings that lock down user desktops. You've linked them to the domain and an upper-level OU, but don't want the restrictions to apply to users in the IT department. Rather than create an additional GPO that removes all of these settings, you could configure Block Policy Inheritance on the OU containing the IT staff. This would ensure that the GPOs associated with the domain and other OUs will not affect the IT staff, allowing them unrestricted access to repair the organization's computers. However, all settings (without No Override) are blocked, including those that distribute software or configure settings that are beneficial. Block Policy Inheritance is shown in Figure 10-6.

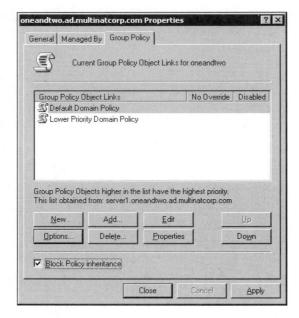

Figure 10-6   Block Policy Inheritance enabled on an OU

Block Policy Inheritance cannot be used to stop a No Override. This means that administrators of larger parts of the forest can always force a policy to apply.

Loopback Processing Mode

Loopback Processing Mode controls how user-based group policy settings are applied. It is a computer configuration setting and can be used to replace or modify the standard method of applying Group Policy.

Remember that Group Policy applies to computers and to users. In each GPO, there are settings for both computers and for users. Look back to Figure 10-3 and consider what would happen to user settings in a GPO that is linked to the Desktop Computers OU. What would happen to computer settings in a GPO that is linked to the Sales Staff OU? Normally, computer settings apply at startup, when processing Group Policy for the computer, and user settings apply at logon, when processing Group Policy for the user.

Loopback Processing Mode lets us modify that behavior by applying user settings based on the location of the computer's object in Active Directory.

 Loopback Processing Mode is commonly used on computers in a public area or kiosk. No matter who logs on to that computer, specific user settings will apply, even if a user account has other settings assigned.

Loopback Processing Mode has two settings—replace and merge. When Loopback Processing is enabled and set in replace mode, the user settings are taken from the GPOs that apply to the computer, not the user. The group policy engine does not even bother to look up the group policies that apply to the user's account.

When Loopback Processing is enabled and set in merge mode, the user configuration settings from the computer are added to the user configuration settings that apply to the user. The user settings that apply to the computer are applied last, and have a higher priority than the user settings that apply to the user.

For example, in Figure 10-7, the object for the user Bob is located in the Sales OU. Normally, when Bob logs on to a computer, his user configuration comes from GPOs linked to the domain, Users OU, and Sales. But, if Bob logs on at WS5 (which has Loopback Processing enabled in replace mode), then the normal process for applying user configuration settings is not used. Instead, the user configuration settings for Bob will be read from GPOs linked to the domain, Computers OU, and Restricted.

Activity 10-4: Changing Group Policy Priority

Time Required: 15 minutes

Objective: To change the default process that Group Policy uses to apply settings.

Description: In most situations the default method for Group Policy processing is appropriate. In this activity, you will explore a way to prevent the control panel setting from applying to users in the IT OU. You will then force the control panel setting to apply.

1. If necessary, start your computer and log on as the administrator from your own domain.
2. Click **Start**, point to **Administrative Tools**, then click **Active Directory Users and Computers**.
3. In yournameOU, right-click **IT** and click **Properties**.
4. Click the **Group Policy** tab.
5. Confirm that yournameIT is selected, then click **Delete**.
6. Click **Remove the link and delete the Group Policy Object permanently**, then click **OK**.

10

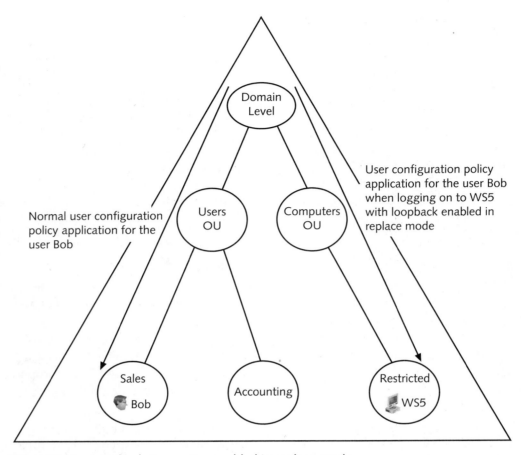

Figure 10-7   Loopback Processing enabled in replace mode

7. Click **Yes** to confirm the deletion and click **Close**.

8. Close Active Directory Users and Computers.

9. The IT OU is now prohibited from using the control panel because the GPO linked to yournameOU will apply. To test the restriction, log off and log on as yournameSusan.

10. After you have confirmed that yournameSusan is prohibited from using the control panel, log off and log on as an administrator.

11. Click **Start**, point to **Administrative Tools**, then click **Active Directory Users and Computers**.

12. In yournameOU, right-click **IT** and click **Properties**.

13. Click the **Group Policy** tab.

14. Click **Block Policy Inheritance** to select it, and click **OK**. This prevents GPOs from other levels being applied to users in the IT OU.

15. Close Active Directory Users and Computers.

16. Users in the IT OU are now allowed to use the control panel because the group policy setting has been configured to block the inheritance of higher-level group policy settings. To test this ability, log off and log on as yournameSusan.

17. After you have confirmed that yournameSusan is able to access the control panel, log off, and log on as an administrator.

18. Click **Start**, point to **Administrative Tools**, then click **Active Directory Users and Computers**.

19. Right-click **yournameOU** and click **Properties**.

20. Click the **Group Policy** tab.

21. Confirm that **yournameGPO** is selected, then click **Options**.

22. Click **No Override: prevents other Group Policy Objects from overriding policy set in this one**, then click **OK**.

23. Click **OK**, then close Active Directory Users and Computers.

24. Users in the IT OU are once again prevented from using the control panel. The GPO linked to yournameOU cannot be blocked by the Block Policy Inheritance setting on the IT OU. This is because the No Override setting takes precedence over the Block Inheritance setting. To test this restriction, log off and log on as yournameSusan.

25. After you confirm that yournameSusan is prohibited from accessing the control panel, log off.

Controlling Group Policy Application with Permissions

GPOs cannot be linked to groups. To control the way Group Policy is applied to different users, those users must be placed in different OUs, unless you change the default permissions.

The application of Group Policy for users and groups can be controlled through permissions. The standard permissions available to a GPO are full control, read, write, create all child objects, delete all child objects, and apply group policy.

A user or computer must have the read and apply group policy permissions on a GPO in order for the policy to apply to that user or computer. By default, the authenticated users group, which includes all computers and all users (except the guest account), has these permissions. To configure a GPO that only applies to a specific user or group of users, you would assign the read and apply permissions to the user or group. You would then specify the users and groups that should be exempted from the policy by denying them these permissions. You can also remove the authenticated users group from the list of groups with permissions.

For example, you might create a GPO that applies to the IT staff, enabling them access to all desktop settings to perform routine maintenance on workstations. However, the user objects for the IT staff are located in multiple OUs, making it harder to apply the policy at the OU level.

To configure a GPO that applies only to the IT staff, you would link it to the domain and remove the default ACE that assigns read and apply group policy permissions to the authenticated users group. You would then add a new ACE granting the IT staff the read and apply group policy permissions.

Activity 10-5: Restricting Group Policy for a Single User

Time Required: 10 minutes

Objective: To limit access to a GPO for a single user.

Description: It may be useful to restrict the application of Group Policy to a specific user in an organization. Users are normally grouped into OUs for the application of Group Policy. However, this is not always granular enough. In this activity you will restrict the application of Group Policy to a user by modifying the permissions assigned to the GPO.

1. If necessary, start your computer and log on as the administrator from your own domain.

2. Click **Start**, point to **Administrative Tools**, then click **Active Directory Users and Computers**.

3. Right-click **yournameOU** and click **Properties**.

4. Click the **Group Policy** tab.

5. Confirm that **yournameGPO** is selected, then click **Properties**.

6. Click **Security** to view the security configuration for the GPO.

7. Click **Add**.

8. Type **yournameSusan**, then click **OK**.

9. Click **Susan Jones**, click the checkbox to **Deny Read** permission, then click the checkbox to **Deny** the **Apply Group Policy** permission. Based on these permissions, Susan will not be able to read or apply the settings in this GPO. Therefore, she will have access to the control panel.

10. Click **OK** to save the changes, then click **Yes** to continue. Then, click **OK** to close the Properties window.

11. Close Active Directory Users and Computers.

12. To test the new settings, log off and log on as yournameSusan. After confirming that yournameSusan is able to access the control panel, log off.

Windows Management Instrumentation Filters

Windows Management Instrumentation (WMI) filters can be used to restrict the application of GPOs. There is a WMI filter tab in the properties of each GPO. Figure 10-8 shows the property page that allows you to specify a WMI filter.

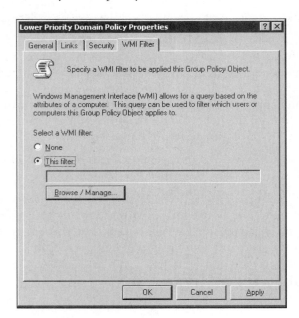

Figure 10-8   Specifying a WMI filter

WMI filters control access based on computer configuration. For example, access can be controlled based on a hardware configuration, file existence or attributes, applications being installed, and ping times.

WMI filters are written in WMI Query Language (WQL). For more information on creating WMI filters, read the WMI solution developer kit at http://msdn.microsoft.com/library/default.asp?url=/library/en-us/wmisdk/wmi/wmi_start_page.asp.

Windows 2000 does not understand WMI filters on GPOs, and will therefore apply the GPO regardless of the filter.

DESKTOP MANAGEMENT WITH GROUP POLICY

Desktop management is one of the primary goals that can be accomplished with Group Policy. Using group policy settings, you can restrict access to or change Windows settings, reduce user errors, redirect folders to a central location, and define scripts to create standardized environments for users.

Restricting Windows

Many Windows functions are restricted based on group membership. For example, you must be a member of the administrators local group or power users local group to add printers to a workstation. However, there are many Windows features that are available to all users, such as desktop wallpaper settings, the run command in the Start menu, and applets in the control panel.

Restricting access to Windows features can protect users from their own mistakes. For example, a user that accidentally changes the proxy setting in Internet Explorer cannot access the Internet. Restricting the ability to change the proxy setting in Internet Explorer ensures that this will never happen.

Or, you may simply wish to have a consistent and professional image throughout your operations. More than one company has restricted users from changing desktop wallpaper after complaints about too many swimsuit models (or worse!).

Folder Redirection

Folder redirection allows you to change the location of default Windows folders. Centralizing the contents of these folders on a server allows users to access this information from any computer on the network. It backs up the information as part of the daily backup of the server and protects it from the loss or failure of an individual computer.

Network administrators can instruct users to save their files on the server, but users don't always remember or want to comply. Many applications save documents to the My Documents folder by default, storing files on the local hard drive. Rather than relying on the users, Group Policy can be used to redirect the folder.

The folders that can be redirected are:

- Application data—Holds user-specific files for various applications. Microsoft Office stores document and spreadsheet templates here.

- Desktop—Contains the files, folders, and shortcuts placed on the user desktop.

- My Documents—Contains files created by users and the My Pictures folder. Many applications use My Documents as the default location for saving data.

- Start menu—Contains the folders and shortcuts that make up the user-specific portion of the Start menu. Start menu items configured for all users are not included.

How and Where to Redirect

There are two ways that folders can be redirected. Basic redirection directs all users affected by the GPO to the same location. Advanced redirection allows the administrator to specify different locations for different security groups.

When folders are redirected using basic or advanced redirection, there are four options to specify where the folder is redirected, as shown in Figure 10-9.

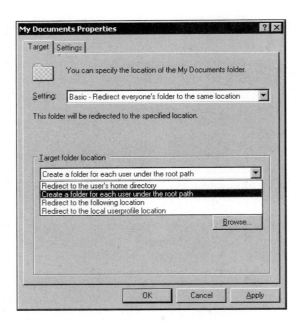

Figure 10-9   Options for folder redirection

The options are:

- Redirect to the user's home directory—Places the folder in the home directory specified in the Active Directory user object on the Profile tab. This option is only available for the My Documents folder.

- Create a folder for each user under the root path—Allows the administrator to specify a location where subdirectories will be created for each user's redirected folder. When the folder is created, the NTFS permissions are automatically set to allow only that user to access the folder. This option is not available for the Start menu.

- Redirect to the following location—Allows the administrator to set a single location to be shared by all users. This is useful when you want all users to share the same Start menu, store all files in the same location, or share application files. The administrator can also use variables such as %USERNAME% to create a folder that is specific to each user.

- Redirect to the local userprofile location—Redirects the folder back to the default location on the local machine.

Other Folder Redirection Settings

There are a number of other folder redirection settings regarding security, folder contents, and removing the policy. Figure 10-10 shows these settings for the My Documents folder.

When "Grant the user exclusive rights to My Documents" is selected, only the local system and the user have rights to this folder. Not even the administrator is able to access it. This is enforced by setting NTFS permissions when the group policy engine creates the folder. (If the folder already exists, and permissions are incompatible with this setting, an error will be logged in the event log and the folder will not be redirected.)

If the option "Move the content of My Documents to the new location" is selected, then the contents of the existing My Documents folder are copied to the new location. This is useful when My Documents is redirected to a private storage area on the server. However, this option should not be used when My Documents is redirected to a shared location for all users, as their files will become disorganized and may be overwritten as multiple files with the same name are copied from various computers.

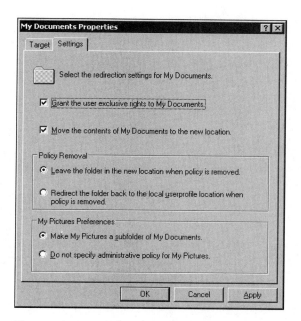

Figure 10-10 Other folder redirection settings

For policy removal you can choose the "Leave the folder in the new location when policy is removed" option, which allows the redirection to continue even after the policy is removed. To stop the redirection and force the folder back to the default location on the local machine, a new GPO must be configured. If "Redirect the folder back to the local userprofile location when policy is removed" option is selected, then the redirected folder will automatically return to its default location when the policy is removed.

The settings for My Pictures are only available when redirecting My Documents. It is recommended that My Pictures be kept as a subfolder in My Documents so that they can be stored in a central location. Since My Pictures always appears as a subfolder in My Documents, users will be very confused if they are told that My Documents is stored on the server and backed up, but My Pictures is not.

Activity 10-6: Redirecting My Documents

Time Required: 15 minutes

Objective: To redirect the My Documents folder to a share on the network.

Description: The hard drive on a workstation in your network has just crashed. Despite the training you've provided on how to save files to the network, this user has been saving all of his files in My Documents. To ensure this never happens again, you will redirect the My Documents folder for all users to a shared folder on the server.

1. If necessary, start your computer and log on as the administrator from your own domain.
2. Click **Start**, then click **Windows Explorer**.
3. Click **My Computer**, then click **Local Disk (C:)**.
4. Click **File**, point to **New**, then click **Folder**.
5. Type **ShareDoc** and press **Enter**.
6. Right-click **ShareDoc** and click **Sharing and Security**.
7. Click **Share this folder**, then click **Permissions**.
8. Click the checkbox to allow **Full Control**, click **OK**, then click **OK** again.
9. Close Windows Explorer.

10

10. Click **Start**, point to **Administrative Tools**, then click **Active Directory Users and Computers**.

11. Right-click **yournameOU** and click **Properties**.

12. Click **Group Policy**, then double-click **yournameGPO**.

13. In User Configuration, double-click **Windows Settings**, then double-click **Folder Redirection**.

14. Right-click **My Documents** and click **Properties**.

15. In the Setting box, click the down arrow, then click **Basic–Redirect everyone's folder to the same location**.

16. Confirm that the Target folder location is configured to **Create a folder for each user under the root path**.

17. In the Root Path box, type ***yourservername*\\ShareDoc** (where *yourservername* is the name of your server).

18. Click **Settings**.

19. Confirm that **Grant the user exclusive rights to My Documents** is selected.

20. Click **Redirect the folder back to the local userprofile when policy is removed** in the policy removal section.

21. Click **OK,** close the Group Policy Object Editor.

22. Click **OK,** and close Active Directory Users and Computers.

23. Log off and log on as **yournameBob**.

24. Click **Start**, then click **Windows Explorer**.

25. Confirm that **My Documents** is selected, click **File**, point to **New**, then click **Text Document**.

26. Type **FileOnServer.txt** and press **Enter**.

27. Click **My Computer**, click **Local Drive (C:)**, click **ShareDoc**, click **yournameBob**, then click **yournameBOB's Documents**. Notice that your document is here because the My Documents folder has been redirected here.

28. Close Windows Explorer.

29. Log off and log on as an administrator.

30. Click **Start**, then click **Windows Explorer**.

31. Click **My Computer**, click **Local Drive (C:)**, click **ShareDoc**, click **yournameBob**, then click **My Documents**. You will receive an error message indicating that you do not have permission to view this folder. Only yournameBob has permission to view the contents of this folder.

Scripts

GPOs can contain **logon**, **logoff**, **startup**, and **shutdown scripts**, which can be written in **Visual Basic Script (.vbs)** or **Jscript (.js)**. Both types are processed by Windows Script Host on the computer that is connecting to the network or logging on. For example, if a user is logging on to the domain at a Windows XP client, then the logon script will be processed on the Windows XP client, not the DC. Batch files (.bat) and command files (.cmd) can also be used.

Scripts must be stored in a location that is accessible to the users running them. The netlogon share on a DC is the most common location for storing scripts. Startup and shutdown scripts are run when the client computer boots up and shuts down, respectively. They run under the system account because they are processed before a user logs on. These scripts are assigned to computers.

Logon and logoff scripts are run when the user logs on or logs off the network. They run with the security privileges of the user that is logging on or off. These scripts configure the environment for users by performing various tasks, such as mapping drive letters to network shares. Logon and logoff scripts are assigned to users.

APPLICATION DISTRIBUTION WITH GROUP POLICY

Group Policy can be used to deliver applications to users and computers. When an application is delivered to a user, it will be available on every computer used by that user (providing of course, that the computer is able to process Group Policy and is joined to a domain in the forest). When software is delivered to a computer, the application will remain on that computer and all users that log on to it may use the software.

Applications can be either **assigned** or **published** using Group Policy. Assigned software is immediately available to users and computers. When applications are assigned to a computer, they are installed when the computer is booted up, before a user logs on. When applications are assigned to a user, they are advertised by placing shortcuts in the Start menu and on the desktop. When a user clicks on a shortcut, the application is installed. Additionally, if a user clicks on a file associated with an assigned application, the application will be installed. For example, if the application Adobe Acrobat is assigned to a user named Bob, and Bob double-clicks on a file with the .pdf extension, then Adobe Acrobat will be installed to view the file.

 Assigned applications are resilient. If a user deletes an application—or a particular program file is overwritten—the file will be reinstalled when required. (Of course, this doesn't protect the user's documents from accidental deletion.)

Published applications are different from assigned applications in several ways. They are only assigned to users, not computers, and are not advertised with desktop shortcuts or Start menu items (that is, they do not appear until after they are manually installed).

When applications are published, they are listed in Add or Remove Programs. Users can manually install the applications from there. If there are many published applications, it may be difficult to find a particular one in a list containing all applications. You can subdivide the applications into categories to make it easier for users to find the applications they wish to install.

File name extensions for published applications are registered in Active Directory. When a user double-clicks an unknown file type (unknown to the workstation), a query is sent to Active Directory to find the associated application(s) for that specific file type. If an associated application is found (and has been published to the user), it will be installed. This process of installing an associated application is known as **document activation**.

Application Types

Older versions of Windows programs were often installed using a setup.exe program. This file was responsible for installing the software application by reading various source and configuration files. Newer applications can use the Windows Installer service, which is a preferred method. Group Policy relies on the Windows Installer to assign and publish most types of applications.

To deploy applications, two components are required:

- **Windows Installer service**—A service that runs on client computers. It is responsible for installing, repairing, and uninstalling applications.

- **Windows Installer package**—This contains the information required to install an application. The package is an .msi file that has the instructions required to install the application, and often contains the application files as well.

When an application is assigned or published using Group Policy, it will most likely be done using an .msi file. The GPO may also contain a **transform (.mst)** file that is added to the .msi file. An .mst file contains changes that are applied to an .msi file during distribution. This allows administrators to configure the installation of applications without intervention from users.

A **.zap file** is a text file used to distribute older applications that do not use the Windows Installer service. The text file contains the commands to install the application. The command to install the application specifies the location of setup.exe and any switches it requires. Switches are commonly used to specify an answer file that eliminates the need for user interaction during the installation. These files are used in place of an .msi file.

A .zap file does not provide most of the advantages that Group Policy does when deploying applications. A .zap file is not resilient and requires the user to have all permissions and privileges to complete the install.

Activity 10-7: Configuring Group Policy to Deliver an Application

Time Required: 10 minutes

Objective: To configure a GPO to publish an application.

Description: You would like all members of the IT staff to have the Administrative Tools, such as Active Directory Users and Computers, available to them when they log on to workstations around the company. In this activity you will publish the Administrative Tools as part of a GPO configured for the IT OU.

1. If necessary, start your computer and log on as the administrator from your own domain.

2. Click **Start**, click **Run**, type **cmd**, then press **Enter**.

3. Type **copy c:\windows\system32\adminpak.msi c:\ShareDoc**, then press **Enter**. The installation file for the application must be available on a share to be installed remotely. This copies the application installation file to a shared folder that you created previously.

4. Close the command prompt.

5. Click **Start**, point to **Administrative Tools**, then click **Active Directory Users and Computers**.

6. In yournameOU, right-click **IT** and click **Properties**.

7. Click the **Group Policy** tab.

8. Click **New**, type **yournameApps** (where *yourname* is your name), and press **Enter**.

9. Double-click **yournameApps**.

10. In User Configuration, double-click **Software Settings**, then click **Software installation**. There are no applications currently configured.

11. Right-click **Software installation** and click **Properties**.

12. Click the **Categories** tab, click **Add**, type *yourname***Tools** (where *yourname* is your name), click **OK**, then click **OK** again. You created a new category in which to place your application. Users will see this category in Add or Remove Programs.

13. Right-click **Software installation**, point to **New**, then click **Package**.

14. Click **My Network Places**, double-click **Entire Network**, double-click **Microsoft Windows Network**, double-click **yourdomain**, double-click **yourserver**, double-click **ShareDoc**, then double-click **adminpak.msi**.

15. Confirm that **Published** is the selected deployment method and click **OK**.

16. Double-click **Windows Server 2003 Administration Tools Pack**.

17. Click the **Categories** tab, click **yournameTools**, then click **Select**. This adds the Administrative Tools Pack to the yournameTools category.

18. Click **OK**, close the Group Policy Object Editor, click **Close**, then close Active Directory Users and Computers.

19. Log off and log on as **yournameSusan**.

20. Click **Start**, click **Control Panel**, and double-click **Add or Remove Programs**.

21. Click **Add New Programs**. You will now see the application you configured for the IT OU.

22. In the Categories box, click the down arrow, then click **yournameTools**. You should still see the application you configured for the IT OU. If many applications are being distributed through Group Policy, categories will make it easier for users to find applications.

23. Close **Add or Remove Programs**, close the Control Panel, and log off.

Maintaining Applications

The applications used on a network are constantly changing as new versions are installed, old versions are removed, and patches—such as security improvements or bug fixes—are deployed. Group Policy can help manage software throughout its entire life cycle. Using GPOs, you can push out mandatory and optional upgrades to replace existing applications, force the reinstallation of applications, and even remove applications that are no longer needed.

Upgrading an Application

Upgrades to existing software are created as separate applications in a GPO. The new application package will then be configured as an upgrade of an existing application.

Upgrades can be mandatory or optional. A **mandatory upgrade** is automatically installed the next time the user runs the application. An **optional upgrade** is performed only when and if the user chooses to do so.

Mandatory upgrades should only be performed after you have tested the compatibility of the new version with data files from the previous version. You should be particularly careful with applications that are shared among many users, such as databases. Sometimes a new version of a database application will upgrade the database and make it unreadable to anyone with the older version.

Redeploying an Application

Many applications have **patches** available to fix small bugs that appear after the release of the product. If the patch is distributed as an **.msp** file, then you will need to **redeploy** the application after it has been patched. For example, the enterprise edition of the Microsoft Office Suite (Office XP) works in this way. You must upgrade the installation on the server, and then redeploy the package.

An .msp file contains file changes that can be applied to an .msi file, or directly on a computer with the application installed. When Group Policy is used to distribute an application, the .msp file is used to update the original .msi file. The application is then redeployed to distribute the patched version.

To patch an .msi file, use the following command: msiexec /p *patchfile.msp* /a *originalapplication.msi*. Depending on the location of the files, you may need to specify the full paths to the .msp file, .msi file, or both. Always follow the instructions provided by the software publisher.

10

To redeploy the patched software, right-click the application in the Group Policy Object Editor, point to **All Tasks**, and click **Redeploy application**.

When dealing with upgrades and redeployments, it's wise to fully test your plans in a test environment. It wouldn't look good to accidentally force a large application like Microsoft Office to reinstall on a thousand desktops when everyone comes in on Monday morning.

Removing an Application

Applications installed by Group Policy can be removed when they are no longer required. You can force the removal of an application or allow users the option of removing it.

When an application is removed, you are presented with a dialog box giving two options, as shown in Figure 10-11. If "Immediately uninstall software from users and computer" is selected, then the software will be deleted from the computer the next time it is rebooted or the next time a user logs off. If "Allow users to continue to use the software but prevent new installations" is selected, then the software is not removed but it is no longer available to be installed. In both cases, the application is no longer advertised with desktop shortcuts and Start menu items, nor is it listed in Add or Remove Programs.

Figure 10-11   Remove Software dialog box

Activity 10-8: Remove an Application

Time Required: 5 minutes

Objective: To remove the Administrative Tools application.

Description: You have decided to administer your servers remotely, rather than by using the Administrative Tools on the local machine. You want to remove the Administrative Tools application.

1. If necessary, start your computer and log on as the administrator from your own domain.

2. Click **Start**, point to **Administrative Tools**, then click **Active Directory Users and Computers**.

3. In yournameOU, right-click **IT** and click **Properties**.

4. Click the **Group Policy** tab.

5. Double-click **yournameApps**.

6. In User Configuration, double-click **Software Settings**, then click **Software installation**.

7. Right-click **Windows Server 2003 Administrative Tools Pack**, point to **All Tasks**, then click **Remove**.

8. Click **Allow users to continue to use the software, but prevent new installations**, then click **OK**.

9. Close the **Group Policy Object Editor**, click **OK**, then close Active Directory Users and Computers.

SECURITY MANAGEMENT WITH GROUP POLICY

GPOs have a variety of security-related settings. This collection of settings is known as a **security policy**. These settings are located in all GPOs, whether they are on a local machine or stored on DCs.

The security policy settings that apply to users are found in the User Configuration section of a GPO, under Windows Settings, Security Settings. Only public key policies and software restriction policies exist here. Public key policies can be used to control the way users receive certificates used for authentication and encryption. Software restriction policies restrict the ability to run and install software.

The majority of security policy settings apply to computers. In a GPO, the security settings that apply to computers are found in the Computer Configurations section, under Windows Settings, Security Settings. The categories of security settings that exist for computers are shown in Figure 10-12. We will examine some of the more important areas in the next few sections.

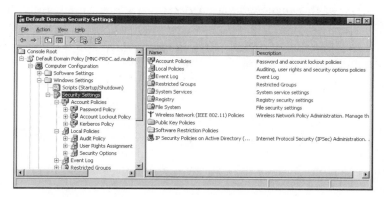

Figure 10-12 Computer security policy categories

Account Policies

Account policies must be configured in a GPO linked to the domain in order to affect domain accounts. If these settings are configured at any other level, they will affect only local accounts on member servers and workstations.

 Remember that DCs do not have local accounts. In practice, account policy settings are almost always managed in the Default Domain Policy GPO.

Account policies include:

- Password policy—Configures password aging and complexity requirements.

- Account lockout policy—Configures how many incorrect logon attempts can be made with a user account before it is locked out. This is useful for preventing brute force hacking attempts to guess passwords.

- Kerberos policy—Configures a variety of Kerberos settings, including ticket lifetimes and time synchronization tolerance. This has no effect when configured for any level other than the domain.

Local Policies

Local policies contain a wide variety of settings, including:

- Audit policy—Establishes the auditing configuration for all computers for which it applies. This includes tracking of file access, user logons, and use of rights. If this is set at the domain level, it will affect all computers except DCs. The Default Domain Controllers Policy, which is linked to the domain controllers OU, disables auditing. To configure auditing for, DCs you must configure the Default Domain Controllers Policy.

- User rights assignment—Configures a user's rights to modify some system configuration options when logging on to a computer. Each user right has a list of security principals that is able to perform a specified task. Two important user rights that can be configured are "Allow log on locally" and "Deny log on locally." In the Default Domain Controllers Policy, these are configured to allow only administrators to log on locally. This means that average users on the network cannot log on to a DC at the keyboard, via terminal services, or as an authenticated user to Internet Information Services (IIS).

- Security options—Contain a large number of operating system security features that can be enabled or disabled. These are not dependent on the user that logs on. Options include cryptography settings, disabling the guest account, and disabling operating system features.

Restricted Groups

Restricted groups define the users that are allowed membership to specific groups. An attempt to add an undefined user to a restricted group will be denied. This prevents administrators from accidentally adding users to sensitive groups, such as Domain Admins, Enterprise Admins, Schema Administrators, or Administrators.

System Services

System services define which services will be started, stopped, or disabled on computers. You can configure security for services, which allows you to define which users can start and stop them. This is an effective way to disable unnecessary services on client computers and servers to increase security.

Registry Settings

Registry defines security permissions for registry entries. These permissions are then applied to all computers affected by the GPO and can be used to change permissions if you wish to restrict access to some registry settings that are part of a new application.

This section of a GPO controls access to the registry or parts of it. Do not confuse it with administrative template settings, which change the *values* stored in the Windows registry.

File System

File system defines the NTFS permissions that are applied to the local hard drives of computers affected by the GPO. It can be used to enhance security by removing the read permission, which all users are assigned in Windows Server 2003 and Windows XP.

Wireless Network Policies

Wireless network (IEEE 802.11) policies define settings for wireless network connectivity. They allow you to configure which wireless networks' workstations can connect to and automatically configure Wireless Encryption Protocol (WEP). One of the largest security holes in many networks today is a wireless infrastructure without WEP configured. Wireless network policies reduce that problem by automating configuration.

IP Security Policies

IP security policies in Active Directory define IPSec settings, such as authentication configuration. By enabling these policies, you can enable IPSec for an entire network with very little effort.

The settings covering public key policies and software restriction policies perform the same functions for computer settings as for user settings. A computer security setting will override the same setting for a user, if both are defined.

Security Templates

Security templates are .inf files that contain options for some or all of the computer settings in a security policy. They can be applied to a local computer or imported into a GPO.

Using a security template, you can test security configuration in a test lab environment and then easily apply the tested security template to the production network. For example, suppose you would like to restrict access to the local file system on workstations. You decide to create a security template that restricts access to the file system. This first attempt causes the test workstation to crash because the permissions are too limited for the local system account. After several modifications, the template works properly. You can then copy the security template onto a floppy disk, log on to your workstation, and import the security settings into a GPO that applies to all user workstations.

You can create your own security templates using the **Security Templates snap–in**. However, there are a number of default security templates that are included with Windows Server 2003. Table 10-1 lists these default security templates.

10

Table 10-1   Default security templates

Template	Description
setup security.inf	Contains the default settings applied during the installation of the server. It is created during installation and the contents will vary depending on whether it is a new installation or an upgrade. If it is an upgrade, it will vary depending on the original configuration of the server. This security template is very large and should not be applied using Group Policy. DCs cannot apply this policy.
DC security.inf	Contains the default security setting for a DC. It is created when a server is promoted to a DC.
compatws.inf	Contains settings that allow the local group users to run older applications that do not run properly with the default security settings applied to workstations. Applications designed for Windows 2000 and newer do not require this security template. This template also removes all users from the power users group.
securews.inf	Contains settings for workstations and member servers that enforce the use of NTLM or Kerberos authentication. This means that Windows 9x clients must be using the Directory Services Client, and Windows NT clients must have Service Pack 4 installed. Anonymous connections are prevented from listing available shares and account names. SID-to-name and name-to-SID conversions are disabled. Finally, Server Message Block (SMB) signing is enabled. This ensures that network requests are not modified while in transit.
securedc.inf	Performs the same functions for DCs that securews.inf performs for member servers and workstations.
hisecws.inf	This is an enhancement of securews.inf. Additional settings include restricting authentication to NTLMv2 and Kerberos, and enforcing the use of SMB signing. All users are removed from the power users group, and only Domain Admins, and the local administrator account are members of the local group administrators.

Table 10-1   Default security templates (continued)

Template	Description
hisecdc.inf	Performs the same functions for DCs that securews.inf performs for member servers and workstations. However, membership in power users and administrators is not affected because they do not exist on DCs.
rootsec.inf	Defines the permissions applied to the root folder of the system partition. It can be used to redefine those permissions if they are changed. It will not override explicit permission assignments that are made on lower-level folders.
notssid.inf	By default, a terminal server SID is assigned permission to certain files and registry entries. This is required when running the terminal server in application compatibility mode. This security template removes the permission assigned to the terminal server SID if it is not required. (This file may not be present on computers that are not terminal servers.)

You can view the detailed settings in the default security templates using the Security Templates snap-in.

Activity 10-9: Importing a Security Template into a GPO

Time Required: 10 minutes

Objective: To import a security template into a GPO so it can be applied to the computers in the domain.

Description: After upgrading all of your workstations to Windows XP, some of your older applications are not able to run. In your test lab you found that applying the compatws.inf security template allowed these applications to run. To apply this template to many computers at once, you will import it into a GPO.

1. If necessary, start your computer and log on as the administrator from your own domain.

2. Click **Start**, point to **Administrative Tools**, then click **Active Directory Users and Computers**.

3. Right-click **yournameOU** and click **Properties**.

4. Click the **Group Policy** tab.

5. Double-click **yournameGPO**.

6. In Computer Configuration, double-click **Windows Settings**.

7. Right-click **Security Settings**, then click **Import Policy**.

8. Double-click **compatws.inf**. The settings from compatws.inf have now been imported into this GPO. These settings will be automatically distributed to all workstations in yournameOU within approximately 90 minutes, although some settings may not take effect until the computer is restarted.

9. Close the Group Policy Object Editor, click **OK**, then close Active Directory Users and Computers.

Analyzing Security

Security templates can be used to analyze an existing security configuration. When analysis is performed, the security template is the baseline. The results indicate which settings on the computer being analyzed are not configured according to the template settings.

Security analysis can be performed graphically, using the **Security Configuration and Analysis snap-in**, as shown in Figure 10-13. This graphical analysis is effective when only one or a few computers are being analyzed. When performing security analysis for many computers, the command line utility Secedit is more efficient, as it allows you to automate security analysis commands as part of a startup or logon script.

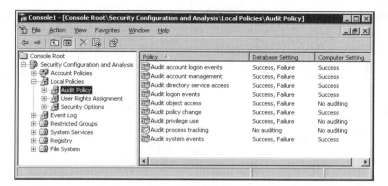

Figure 10-13   Security Configuration and Analysis snap-in

Activity 10-10: Using Security Configuration and Analysis

Time Required: 10 minutes

Objective: To compare the security configuration on your server with the hisecdc.inf security template.

Description: The standard security configuration for DCs in your company is the default security setting. You are considering upgrading your security level by applying the hisecdc.inf security template to all DCs. However, before you do this, you want to see what changes will be made.

1. If necessary, start your computer and log on as the administrator from your own domain.

2. Click **Start**, click **Run**, type **mmc**, then press **Enter**.

3. Click **File**, then click **Add/Remove Snap-in**.

4. Click **Add**, in the Available Standalone Snap-in box, double-click **Security Configuration and Analysis**, click **Close**, then click **OK**.

5. Click **Security Configuration and Analysis**. This displays the instructions for using the snap-in.

6. Right-click **Security Configuration and Analysis** and click **Open Database**.

7. There is not an existing database. Therefore, any filename can be entered here. Type **MyDB**, then click **Open**.

8. Click **hisecdc.inf**, then click **Open**. This is the security template that is compared to the configuration of the local computers.

9. Expand the node labelled **Security Configuration and Analysis**, then right-click the same node and click **Analyze Computer Now**.

10. Click **OK** to accept the default error log path.

11. After the analysis is complete, double-click **Local Policies**, then double-click **Audit Policy**.

12. Most of the audit settings are not configured as strongly as the security template. An icon with a red x indicates a setting that is weaker than the security template. An icon with a green checkmark indicates a setting that is equal to or stronger than the security template.

13. Browse through any other settings that interest you.

14. Close **MMC**. If asked to save the console settings, click **No**.

15. If you are not proceeding immediately to the next activity, log off your computer.

TROUBLESHOOTING GROUP POLICY

The most important thing to be aware of when implementing group policy is how the links to containers, priority ordering by administrators, No Override, Block Inheritance, ACL permissions, Loopback Processing Mode, and WMI filters all interact to determine how and when a GPO applies. It can be complicated, but you must gain an understanding of them to be successful with Group Policy.

Most Group Policy issues occur when GPOs do not apply in the priority they should. If this happens, look for the following situations:

- Do any of the group policy links have No Override enabled? If so, then this GPO may apply regardless of the settings on any other GPOs.

- Is Block Policy Inheritance enabled on an OU? If so, then GPOs from other locations may not apply.

- Is Loopback Processing enabled for Group Policy? If so, then the user settings will be taken from the GPOs that apply to the computer and possibly the user (depending on the mode).

- Is the GPO newly created or linked? If so, workstations and member servers only refresh group policy information every 90 minutes by default. DCs refresh group policy information every 5 minutes. (A few settings, including software installation, will not apply until a restart or new logon.) To force the refresh of group policy information, you can reboot the computer or use the Gpupdate.exe utility.

- Is Group Policy applied over a slow link? A slow link is calculated based on the ping time between the client and DC. By default, a ping time of more than two seconds is considered a slow link. Some parts of Group Policy will not apply if a client is connected by a slow link. However, security settings and settings based on administrative templates will be applied over slow links. You can control which parts of your policies will be applied over slow links.

Troubleshooting Tools

There are several tools to help you troubleshoot group policy configuration:

- **Resultant Set of Policy (RSoP)**—This is an MMC snap-in. When used in logging mode, it allows you to see the group policy settings that apply to a particular user when logged on to a particular computer. It also tells you which GPO the setting came from. When used in planning mode, RSoP can show you how policies would vary in different scenarios, such as for users in different containers in different security groups, if slow links are in effect, and for other configured variables. Some RSoP functions are also available from menus within Active Directory Users and Computers when working with GPOs.

- **Gpresult**—This is a command-line utility that performs the same task as RSoP in logging mode. It is useful when documenting settings for many users or computers through logon scripts.

- **Gpupdate**—This is a command-line utility that can be used to force the update of group policy information on the local workstation. It saves time when testing new GPOs. Without this utility, workstations would need to be rebooted to ensure that group policy information was refreshed.

- **Dcgpofix**—This is a command-line utility that resets the Default Domain Controller Policy and the Default Domain Policy back to their default configuration. This is useful if one of these policies has been accidentally deleted or misconfigured. All previous changes to these GPOs would be lost.

Microsoft is developing a new tool called the Group Policy Management Console (GPMC). Although GPMC isn't included on the Windows Server 2003 CD, it is a free download for Windows Server 2003 customers. GPMC brings together tools and options that have been accessible from a number of different tools, including Active Directory Sites and Services, Active Directory Users and Computers, and the Gpresult command, and lets you access them from one console. GPMC also adds new functionality—such as the ability to back up or restore a GPO separately from the system state. We highly recommend this tool, as it makes working with Group Policy much easier. For more information, visit *http://www.microsoft.com/ windowsserver2003/gpmc/default.mspx*. (The Microsoft Web site is frequently reorganized, especially as software is first released. If the link does not work, search the site using the term "Group Policy Management Console.")

Activity 10-11: Using RSoP

Time Required: 10 minutes

Objective: To use the RSoP snap-in to see where the configuration settings on your server come from.

Description: In this activity you will use the RSoP snap-in to see which GPOs are affecting your server.

1. If necessary, start your computer and log on as the administrator from your own domain.
2. Click **Start**, click **Run**, type **mmc**, then press **Enter**.
3. Click **File**, then click **Add/Remove Snap-in**.
4. Click **Add**. Then, in the Available Standalone Snap-in box, double-click **Resultant Set of Policy**, click **Close**, then click **OK**.
5. Click **Resultant Set of Policy**.
6. Click **Action**, then click **Generate RSoP Data**.
7. Click **Next** to start the Resultant Set of Policy wizard.
8. Confirm that **Logging mode** is selected, then click **Next**.
9. Confirm that **This computer** is selected, then click **Next**.
10. Click **Do not display user policy settings in the results (display computer policy settings only)**, then click **Next**.
11. View the selection summary, then click **Next**.
12. Click **Finish**.
13. Double-click **Computer Configuration**, double-click **Windows Settings**, double-click **Security Settings**, double-click **Local Policies**, then double-click **Audit Policy**.
14. You will see that all of the audit policy settings are configured in the Default Domain Controllers Policy.
15. In Security Settings, double-click **Account Policies**, then click **Password Policy**.
16. You will see that all of the account policy settings are configured in the Default Domain Policy.
17. Browse any other settings that interest you.
18. Close **MMC**. If asked to save the console settings, click **No**.
19. Log off your computer.

10

CHAPTER SUMMARY

❑ Group Policy is a way to apply a group of settings to users and computers in a site, domain, or OU. It can also be set in a local GPO that exists on each workstation and server.

❑ The local computer policy (sometimes called a local GPO) is stored on the hard drive. Nonlocal GPOs are stored in Active Directory and in the SYSVOL share on DCs.

❑ The order of application for GPOs is local, site, domain, OU. The last GPO applied has the highest priority. You can modify the default priority settings for GPOs by using No Override, Block Policy Inheritance, Loopback Processing, security permissions, and WMI filters.

❑ When using Group Policy for desktop management, you can restrict Windows functions, redirect folders, and define scripts for logon, logoff, startup, and shutdown.

❑ Group Policy can be used to distribute applications to users and computers. The applications can be either published or assigned. Published applications appear in Add or Remove Programs, and must be installed manually by the user or through document activation. Assigned applications advertise their presence with desktop shortcuts and Start menu items. Applications assigned to computers are installed at startup. Applications assigned to users are installed on first use.

❑ Security management using Group Policy is accomplished with security templates. Security templates are .inf files with security settings configured and can be imported into a GPO. Security templates can also be used as a baseline to examine security settings using the Security Configuration and Analysis snap-in.

❑ The main tools used to troubleshoot Group Policy are the RSoP snap-in, Gpresult, Gpupdate, and Dcgpofix (and the upcoming GPMC).

KEY TERMS

account policies — Configuration settings for passwords, account lockouts, and Kerberos. They must be linked to the domain to affect settings for the domain.

administrative templates — Files containing settings used by the GPO Editor to define the registry key that should be changed, the options, and a description of the effects.

assigned — An assigned application is advertised on the desktop and in the Start menu. When an application is assigned to a user, it is installed on first use. When an application is assigned to a computer, it is installed when the computer boots up.

Block Policy Inheritance — A setting in the group policy configuration for a site domain or OU that prevents settings from GPOs higher in the tree from being inherited.

Dcgpofix — A command-line utility that recreates the Default Domain Policy and the Default Domain Controllers Policy.

document activation — The automatic installation of a published application when a user opens an associated file type.

file system — A security policy setting that defines permissions applied to the file system.

folder redirection — A user configuration setting that redirects folders from the local user profile to the server. Basic redirection redirects all users' folders to the same path (although variables such as %USERNAME% can be used). Advanced redirection allows completely different paths based on security group memberships.

Gpresult — A command-line utility that is equivalent to RSoP.

Gpupdate — A command-line utility that forces the update of Group Policy on a workstation.

Group Policy — An enhancement to Windows 9x and Windows NT policies. Group policy settings are stored on DCs as virtual objects.

group policy container (GPC) — The collection of objects in Active Directory that holds GPOs and their settings.

group policy template (GPT) — A set of files and folders in the SYSVOL folder that holds settings and files for a GPO.

IP security policies — Security policy settings relating to IPSec configuration.

Jscript (.js) — A scripting language that can be used to write logon, logoff, startup, and shutdown scripts. It is similar to JavaScript.

link — GPOs are assigned to a site, domain, or OU by linking them. A single GPO can be linked to multiple locations.

local computer policy — A GPO that is stored on the local computer, and is only available on the local computer. It is sometimes called the local GPO.

local policies — A wide variety of settings for auditing, user rights, and security options.

logoff script — A script that runs when a user logs off.

logon script — A script that runs when a user logs on.

Loopback Processing Mode — A computer configuration setting that changes the processing of user configuration settings. When in effect, a user's settings from the GPOs that apply to the computer will be used rather than the GPOs that apply to the user.

mandatory upgrade — An upgrade that is performed automatically the next time a user runs the application.

netlogon share — A default share that is available on all DCs. It is commonly used to hold logon scripts and policies. It is part of the SYSVOL.

No Override — A link setting that prevents policies linked at a lower level from having priority over the settings in the GPO.

optional upgrade — An upgrade that users can run manually at their discretion.

patch (.msp) — An update to a Windows Installer package that fixes bugs.

policies — Collections of registry entries that are used to control Windows 9x and Windows NT workstations.

published — A published application appears in Add or Remove Programs and must be installed manually by the user or through document activation.

redeploy — Forces an application to redistribute the next time it is used. This is done after an .msi file has been patched.

registry — A security policy setting that defines security permission to be applied to registry entries.

restricted groups — A security policy setting that defines group membership.

Resultant Set of Policy (RSoP) — A tool used to show how settings are applied, and which GPO supplied a particular setting.

Security Configuration and Analysis snap-in — An MMC snap-in that compares a security template with the existing configuration on a computer, or applies a security template to a computer.

security policy — The collection of user configuration and computer configuration settings located in Windows Settings, Security Settings. These can be updated using security templates.

security template — An .inf file that contains settings for some or all of the computer settings in a security policy.

Security Templates snap-in — An MMC snap-in that edits existing security templates or creates new ones.

shutdown script — A script that runs when a computer is shut down.

startup script — A script that runs when a computer boots up.

system services — A security policy setting that defines which services will be started, stopped, or disabled.

SYSVOL share — A folder that is shared by default on DCs. It holds parts of the scripts, administrative templates, and registry files for GPOs.

tattooing the registry — The normally undesired effect of leaving permanent changes in the Windows registry, even after the policy no longer applies.

transform (.mst) — Customized settings for a Windows Installer package that are applied during installation.

Visual Basic Script (.vbs) — A scripting language that can be used to write logon, logoff, startup, and shutdown scripts. It is based on Visual Basic and is sometimes called Visual Basic Scripting Edition.

10

Windows Installer package (.msi) — A Windows application that is installed by the Windows Installer service.

Windows Installer service — A Windows service that is responsible for installing applications using the extensions .msi, .mst, and .msp.

Windows Management Instrumentation (WMI) — The Windows implementation of Web-Based Enterprise Management (WBEM) that uses a common set of interfaces to present information about a computer system in a consistent way across a variety of tools and platforms.

wireless network (IEEE 802.11) policies — Security policy settings that configure settings for wireless access.

.zap file — A text file that is used by Group Policy to install older applications that use a setup.exe file.

Review Questions

1. Which of the following describe Group Policy? (Choose all that apply.)

   a. Policy files must be manually copied to each DC

   b. Replication is automatic between DCs

   c. Registry entries are permanently applied to workstations

   d. Group Policy can be used to distribute applications

   e. Group Policy can only be used with Windows 2000

2. When a GPO is stored on a DC, it has a unique name in the SYSVOL folder. What is the name based on?

   a. The name of the GPO

   b. The GUID of the GPO

   c. The SID of the GPO

   d. The GUID of the user that created the GPO

   e. The domain SID and the SID of the GPO

3. Which folders on SYSVOL may contain a file named registry.pol, which contains registry settings? (Choose all that apply.)

   a. Adm

   b. Scripts

   c. User

   d. Machine

   e. Applications

4. In what order are GPOs applied?

   a. Site, local, domain, OU

   b. Local, OU, domain, site

   c. Site, domain, OU, local

   d. Local, site, domain, OU

5. A single GPO can only apply to computers in a single domain. True or False?

6. A group policy linked at what level will have the lowest priority?

   a. Local

   b. Site

   c. Domain

   d. OU

7. Which of the following settings is applied to a group policy link?

   a. No Override

   b. Block Policy Inheritance

   c. Loopback

   d. Security permissions

8. Which of the following settings is applied to a site, domain, or OU?

   a. No Override

   b. Block Policy Inheritance

   c. Loopback

   d. Security permissions

9. Which of the following settings is used to force the user configuration settings from the computer policies?

   a. No Override

   b. Block Policy Inheritance

   c. Loopback

   d. Security permissions

10. Which group policy feature can be used to point the My Documents folder to a location on the server rather than the local hard drive?

    a. Folder redirection

    b. Windows restrictions

    c. Security settings

    d. Administrative templates

11. Which languages can be used to write logon, logoff, startup, and shutdown scripts? (Choose all that apply.)

    a. Visual Basic

    b. Visual Basic Script

    c. Java

    d. Jscript

    e. C++

12. When installing an older application with Group Policy, which type of file is used?

    a. .msi

    b. .mst

    c. .zap

    d. .msp

    e. .aas

13. Which type of file modifies the installation settings of an application?

    a. .msi

    b. .mst

    c. .zap

    d. .msp

    e. .aas

10

14. Which methods can be used to install a published application? (Choose all that apply.)

   a. Click a desktop shortcut

   b. Click a Start menu item

   c. Add or Remove Programs

   d. Document activation

15. When would you redeploy an application?

   a. When a new version of the application is available

   b. When an application has been patched

   c. When you would like to add a new feature

   d. When you would like to change registry entries

16. Which policies must be linked to the domain to have an effect?

   a. Account policies

   b. Local policies

   c. System services

   d. Restricted groups

17. Which policies must be linked to the Domain Controllers OU to affect DCs?

   a. Account policies

   b. Local policies

   c. System services

   d. Restricted groups

18. Which security template cannot be applied to DCs?

   a. Setup security.inf

   b. Rootsec.inf

   c. Notssid.inf

   d. Hisecdc.inf

   e. DC security.inf

19. Which utility can use security templates as a baseline to compare security settings?

   a. Gpresult

   b. Gpupdate

   c. RSoP snap-in

   d. Security Configuration and Analysis snap-in

   e. Dcgpofix

20. Which utility can be used to recreate the Default Domain Policy and the Default Domain Controllers Policy?

   a. Gpresult

   b. Gpupdate

   c. RSoP snap-in

   d. Security Configuration and Analysis snap-in

   e. Dcgpofix

HEARTLAND HOSPITAL CASE PROJECTS

Like any other large organization, Heartland Hospital has problems with misconfigured desktop computers, application deployment and version control, and security settings. As she is learning more about Active Directory, Mary Firth asks you if Group Policy can help her and Jenn reduce the amount of time they spend managing these issues.

Case Project 10-1: Windows Restrictions

At Heartland Hospital, some workstations have been misconfigured by users who have attempted to fix their own computers. Most of these computers are located in offices; however, some are located in nursing stations that are shared by many users. It is helpful to have a consistent interface on these computers that is free of unauthorized software—no matter who is logged on.

Describe some of the group policy settings that might be appropriate for the nursing station computers. If some of these settings are user configuration settings, how can you ensure that they apply regardless of who logs on?

Case Project 10-2: Application Distribution

Mary Firth needs to request new software for the next few years. Some software publishers are promoting that their software works with Active Directory and is shipped as MSI files. Others state that they do not support Active Directory, and some make no mention one way or the other. Mary is considering the recommendation that all new software installed on client computers support management by Group Policy.

Would you support this recommendation? If so, help her by describing some of the advantages of using Group Policy for software distribution. Include information about how applications can be upgraded and patched. If you would not support this recommendation, explain why.

Case Project 10-3: Security Baselining

Michael Garabaldi calls you. He is a bit frustrated because neither he nor Mary Firth can be sure whether the current configuration of the Heartland Hospital servers matches the hospital's written security policy. He has been in contact with Marti Macauly to determine how HIPAA requirements will affect data processing. Marti is emphatic regarding the hospital's requirement to demonstrate a set of known policies for system configuration.

You invite Michael, Mary, and Marti to a meeting to help them determine how to proceed. Explain how you can use security templates to generate reports that indicate compliance with hospital policy.

11

INTEROPERABILITY BETWEEN ACTIVE DIRECTORY AND OTHER DIRECTORIES

After reading this chapter and completing the exercises, you will be able to:

♦ Describe and use Lightweight Directory Access Protocol

♦ Understand and use Active Directory Services Interface

♦ Describe Microsoft Metadirectory Services

♦ Describe the Active Directory Connector for Exchange 5.5

The goal of every computer network is to allow as much centralized management as possible within the bounds of security requirements. For some companies, this may mean a completely centralized system in which the head office controls all aspects of the computer system. In other companies, some applications will be centralized and others decentralized.

Real-world computer systems are seldom composed of Active Directory-aware products alone. Many applications—such as e-mail systems, enterprise resource planning, customer relationship management, and internal telephone systems—will not use Active Directory. Enabling communications between theses applications and Active Directory is a good way to increase centralization and efficiency.

LIGHTWEIGHT DIRECTORY ACCESS PROTOCOL

Most common directory services in use today are based on the **X.500** model developed by the **International Organization for Standardization (ISO)**. The ISO is the same organization that developed the Open Systems Interconnection (OSI) model for networking standards.

The X.500 standard for directories defines the common elements like containers and users that are found in every directory service. It also defines a protocol for querying directories, called **Directory Access Protocol (DAP)**.

DAP is rich in features, but has never been widely implemented. The large number of features that it supports makes it very resource intensive and difficult to implement.

Lightweight Directory Access Protocol (LDAP) was developed to address the shortcomings of DAP. Because it has fewer features—concentrating instead on the essential ones—it is easier to implement and requires fewer resources from the computers running the directory service. Currently, the Internet Engineering Task Force (IETF) publishes the LDAP standard and provides a way for the industry to suggest changes and improvements while keeping the simplicity and interoperability that are the hallmark of LDAP.

The term **LDAP server** is commonly used to identify any directory that supports LDAP queries. LDAP is a protocol for querying a directory, not a directory type itself.

A Common Protocol for Directory Access

As the Internet began to gain popularity in the early 1990s, the need for a common directory access protocol became apparent. Many different directories of information were available on the Internet, but there was no standardized mechanism for retrieving data from them. Even before consumers started using the Internet en masse, businesses, government departments, and academic institutions wanted to be able to easily locate each other's e-mail addresses. Each e-mail vendor had a different mechanism for retrieving address book information from e-mail servers, which required you to use their client software to look up addresses on that server.

To resolve this problem, LDAP was implemented as the standard method for accessing information in a directory, though most database systems will still support **Structured Query Language (SQL)**. LDAP is now used as the standard method for retrieving address book information from e-mail servers, and is implemented in most e-mail client software, including Microsoft Outlook, Lotus Notes, Microsoft Outlook Express, and Eudora, to name a few. Figure 11-1 shows how to configure an LDAP server to look up addresses in Outlook Express.

From a software developer's perspective, a standardized method for accessing directories significantly reduces the complexity involved in writing an application. For example, imagine there are three common directory services used by your client—say, Microsoft Exchange, Lotus Notes, and a Novell Directory Service (NDS) network. Since each of these directory services uses its own protocol for access, you would have to create three different versions of your software. If all directory services supported a single-access protocol, then you would only have to create one version.

Most applications that require a directory service now use LDAP to access those directories. Developers now need to write only one version of their software, and it can access data in all of the commonly implemented LDAP-compliant directories.

While LDAP and X.500 are standards, not all directory services are 100 percent compatible. Watch for subtle differences that may cause problems.

Having a standardized method for directory access prevents you from being locked into a single vendor for directory services. If the applications you implement use a standardized directory access method (like LDAP), then you can choose from the many vendors who provide directories that support that standardized method.

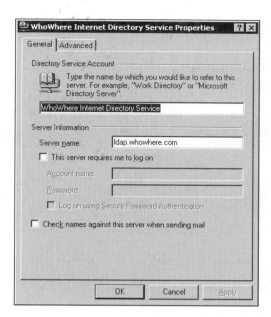

Figure 11-1 LDAP configuration in Outlook Express

In the past, administrators were forced to implement the directory service that was distributed with the applications they purchased. Now, since most commonly used applications support LDAP, they can choose their directory service based on available features, price, and performance, not just brand loyalty.

From the network administrator's point of view, the biggest benefit of standardized directory access is the centralization of directory services. If all applications support LDAP, then all applications can use a single directory service. This means that a single directory can support the e-mail system, human resources software, telephone system, and network access.

LDAP and Active Directory

Active Directory supports LDAP requests natively, meaning that they do not need to be translated before Active Directory can understand and respond to them. Active Directory uses LDAP by default, not as an add-on, making Active Directory a suitable directory service for any application requiring an LDAP server.

Windows Server 2003 has several new Active Directory features that add to its value as an LDAP server. These include:

- InetOrgPerson as a security principal—InetOrgPerson is the object type used by some other LDAP applications to represent users. Active Directory now supports this object type as a security principal. This is important when defining access control for LDAP queries based on the user making the query.

- Password for InetOrgPerson—Passwords are now supported for InetOrgPerson objects. This is important because every security principal should be authenticated.

- Convert InetOrgPerson objects—InetOrgPerson objects can be converted to standard user objects, and standard user objects can be converted to InetOrgPerson objects. This simplifies data migration from other LDAP-compliant directories to Active Directory.

- Dynamic auxiliary classes—This feature allows you to extend only certain instances of an object class with new attributes, rather than all instances of that object. For example, it would allow an e-mail application to add e-mail attributes to user objects with e-mail accounts only, rather than to all user accounts. In large directories this can significantly reduce performance degradation when a new application is implemented.

11

LDAP Naming

LDAP names describe where an object is located in a directory. Each object's name is composed of a portion of the object's attributes. Table 11-1 lists the LDAP attributes used in naming most objects in Active Directory. Commas are used to separate the attributes in an LDAP name.

Table 11-1   LDAP name attributes supported by Active Directory

Attribute	Name	Description
DC	Domain Component	A part of the LDAP name that corresponds with part of the DNS system. For example, DC=com.
OU	Organizational Unit	An organizational unit in Active Directory. For example, OU=sales.
CN	Common Name	The "friendly" name of the object. Usually a short name that is easily recognized.

Activity 11-1: Finding the LDAP Name of an Object

Time Required: 5 minutes

Objective: To view the LDAP name of a user.

Description: Your sales department uses a customized application to track client orders. The vendor just modified the application to use an LDAP driver, rather than a proprietary database, to obtain the list of users. As part of testing the new driver, a technician from the vendor would like the LDAP name of a user to query. In this activity you will find the LDAP name of a user.

1. If necessary, start your computer and log on as the administrator from your own domain.

2. Click **Start**, point to **Administrative Tools**, then click **Active Directory Users and Computers**.

3. Click **View**, then make sure that Advanced Features is checked. (If you did not turn on the viewing of advanced features in earlier activities, click **Advanced Features** to activate this option.)

4. Double-click *yourname***OU**, then click **Sales**

5. Right-click **Bob Smith** and click **Properties**.

6. Click the **Object** tab. In the **Canonical name of object** box is the full name of Bob Smith. It is not in LDAP format; you must convert it. For example, the name listed is *oneandtwo.ad. multinatcorp.com/yournameOU/Sales/BobSmith*. This name, when converted into LDAP format, will be *CN=Bob Smith,OU=Sales,OU=yournameOU,DC=oneandtwo,DC=ad, DC=multinatcorp, DC=com*.

7. Click **OK**, then close Active Directory Users and Computers.

8. If you are not proceeding immediately to the next activity, log off your computer.

LDAP Distinguished Names

When an LDAP name refers to exactly where an object is located in the directory, it is called a **distinguished name (DN)**. A DN works in the same way as a complete telephone number described with country code, area code, and local phone number. Each DN is completely unique in the directory (in this case, in an Active Directory forest).

The following are examples of distinguished names:

- CN=Bob Smith,OU=Sales,DC=ad,DC=multinatcorp,DC=com
- CN=Susan Jones,OU=IT,OU=NYC,DC=ad.DC=multinatcorp,DC=com

LDAP Relative Distinguished Names

The part of an LDAP distinguished name that uniquely identifies the object within its parent container is a **relative distinguished name (RDN)**. Going back to the telephone number example, I remember when you only had to dial four digits to call a neighbor—all other parts of the phone number were assumed. In the same way, a RDN is unique within the container (such as an OU) and not necessarily unique in the whole directory.

The following are example RDNs for Bob Smith and Susan Jones:

- CN=Bob Smith

- CN=Susan Jones

LDAP URLs

Within some programming environments and some applications, you can use **LDAP URLs** to specify the location of an object in the directory. The URL lists LDAP:// as the protocol, then specifies the server and naming attributes of the object. In this case, the naming attributes are separated by forward slashes (/).

The following are examples of LDAP URLs:

- LDAP://*servername*/CN=Bob%20Smith/OU=Sales/DC=ad/DC=multinatcorp/DC=com

- LDAP://*servername*/CN=Susan%20Jones/OU=IT/OU=NYC/DC=ad/ DC=multinatcorp/DC=com

 URLs should not have spaces in them. Spaces in an LDAP name are replaced with %20, since 20 is the ASCII code for a space. This is the standard for encoding special characters in a URL.

Lightweight Directory Interchange Format

Lightweight Directory Interchange Format (LDIF) is a standardized file format for moving information in and out of directories using LDAP. LDIF files are simple text files with lists of information that can be imported into a directory using LDAP. Many directories also support exporting data to an LDIF file. Figure 11-2 shows the contents of an LDIF file.

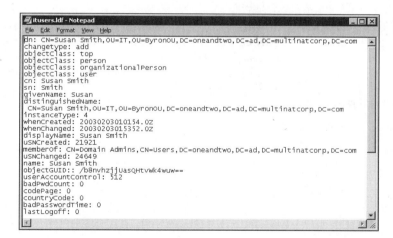

Figure 11-2   An LDIF file

Active Directory uses the utility **LDIFDE.EXE (LDIF Directory Exchange)** to import and export directory information in LDIF format. It is typically used to import large amounts of data that already exist elsewhere in a different format. For example, at the beginning of the school year a database of incoming students could be exported (from another application) in LDIF format and imported into Active Directory to create user objects for the students. If there are several hundred students, this could save days of manual data entry.

LDIFDE.EXE can also be used to change user information in the directory. Again, this is useful when there are large amounts of data that already exist in the directory, but require updating. For example, say a large corporation stores phone numbers as part of the Active Directory user objects for employees. If a new phone system is implemented and the phone numbers change, LDIFDE.EXE could be used to export the user object information into an LDIF file. The phone number data could then be updated by the telephone system or a data-entry clerk and imported back into the directory. Changing the phone numbers in Active Directory by importing an LDIF file would be much faster and more accurate than changing each phone number manually.

Exported information can also be moved into a nonnetworked application. For example, say a list of company employees is required for a new database. Rather than entering the information manually, the data can be exported from an existing database in LDIF format and imported into the new database.

 Another tool for importing large amounts of data into Active Directory is the **CSVDE.EXE** (CSV Directory Exchange) utility. Rather than using LDIF, it uses text in comma-separated values (CSV) format.

Activity 11-2: Exporting Active Directory Information with LDIFDE.EXE

Time Required: 5 minutes

Objective: To export data from Active Directory into an LDIF file.

Description: You are configuring a new application that uses a proprietary database. The application cannot conduct LDAP queries directly; however, it is able to import LDIF files to create user accounts. In this activity you will use LDIFDE.EXE to get a list of users in the IT department.

1. If necessary, start your computer and log on as the administrator from your own domain.
2. Click **Start**, click **Run**, type **cmd**, then press **Enter**.
3. Type **cd ** and press **Enter**.
4. Type **ldifde /?** to view the options for LDIFDE.EXE. Use the scroll bar in the command prompt to view any information that has been pushed past the screen.
5. Type **ldifde –f itusers.ldf –s** *yourserver* **–d "ou=IT,ou=***yourname***OU,dc=***yourdomain***, dc=ad,dc=multinatcorp,dc=com" –r "(objectClass=user)"** then press **Enter**. Be sure to substitute the proper name for *yourserver, yourname, yourdomain*. You should receive a response indicating that one entry has been exported and the command has completed successfully. (The –r command allows you to restrict the objectclass that is exported; in this case, only user objects in the defined container are exported.)
6. Type **edit itusers.ldf**, then press **Enter**.
7. Scroll through the file to view the information that was exported for Susan Jones.
8. To close, press **Alt**, press **f**, then press **x**.
9. Close the command prompt.
10. If you are not proceeding immediately to the next activity, log off your computer.

Querying Active Directory Using LDAP

Active Directory acts as an LDAP server. It does not need any extra drivers or services to respond to LDAP queries. Active Directory uses the standard 389 LDAP server port. Because of this, any tool that can query LDAP can query Active Directory.

The LDP utility is included with Windows Server 2003 in \support\tools\support.cab. It is a graphical utility that uses LDAP to browse a directory, as shown in Figure 11-3.

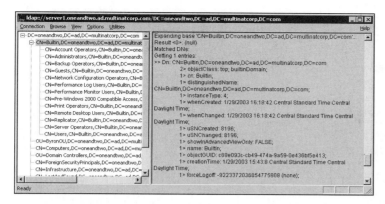

Figure 11-3   The LDP utility

The command line utility DSQUERY.EXE can also perform LDAP queries when the * option is used.

Activity 11-3: Browsing Active Directory with LDP.EXE

Time Required: 5 minutes

Objective: To view the contents of Active Directory using the ldp.exe utility.

Description: The ldp.exe utility can be used to issue any LDAP query or to browse Active Directory using LDAP. Because Active Directory only allows authorized access to objects, first you will authenticate to Active Directory, then you will see the information presented as LDAP results.

1. If necessary, start your computer and log on as the administrator from your own domain.

2. Click **Start**, then click **Windows Explorer**.

3. If you have already installed the Support Tools, proceed to Step 6. Otherwise, click **My Computer**, click the drive or network folder where the Windows Server 2003 installation files are stored, click **support**, click **tools**, then double-click **Suptools.msi**.

4. Click **Next**, click **I Agree**, click **Next**, click **Next**, click **Install Now**, then click **Finish**.

5. Close **Windows Explorer**.

6. Click **Start**, point to **All Programs**, point to **Windows Support Tools**, then click **Command Prompt**.

7. Type **ldp**, then press **Enter**.

8. Click **Connection**, then click **Connect**.

9. In the Server box type *yourserver*, then click **OK**. You will receive information about the LDAP capabilities of your server.

10. Click **Connection**, then click **Bind**.

11. In the User box, type **administrator**; in the Password box, type *yourpassword*; in the Domain box, type *yourdomain*; then click **OK**. This establishes the credentials used to perform LDAP queries.

12. Click **View**, then click **Tree**.

13. In the Tree View window, leave the BaseDN box empty, then click **OK**.

14. You can now browse a tree view of Active Directory using LDAP. Double-click in the left pane to expand containers and view their contents. When you double-click in the left pane, information about the object will appear in the right pane.

15. When you are done browsing, close LDP.

16. Close the command prompt.

17. If you are not proceeding immediately to the next activity, log off your computer.

11

ACTIVE DIRECTORY SERVICES INTERFACE

Active Directory Services Interface (ADSI) is an interface used by programmers and administrators to access a variety of directory services using a consistent set of commands. Programmers and administrators write scripts and programs that communicate with ADSI. ADSI is then responsible for translating requests into a format that the directory service can understand.

> Technically speaking, ADSI is a set of component object model (COM) objects, and can therefore be used for a variety of program languages and scripting tools.

To translate requests for a particular directory service, ADSI is configured with **providers**. The providers included with Windows Server 2003 are for Windows NT, LDAP, **Novell Directory Services (NDS)**, and **Novell NetWare Bindery Services**. The Windows NT provider communicates with the security accounts manager (SAM) database for Windows NT servers. The LDAP provider is used to access Active Directory or any other LDAP server. The NDS provider communicates with Novell NetWare server versions 4, 5, and 6. The Novell NetWare Bindery Services Provider communicates with NetWare 3 servers.

A Common Programming Mechanism for Directory Access

One way to reduce the complexity of accessing information in multiple directories is for all directory services to understand the same language for requests. This is what LDAP provides. However, a common access method is still required for older directories that do not understand LDAP queries. This is what ADSI provides.

ADSI gives programmers a consistent set of commands to access different directories. The command to create a user is the same in a Windows NT directory as it is in an LDAP directory. However, not all directory types support every ADSI command. The commands available for a directory service are based on the capabilities of the directory service and on the functions that are built into the particular ADSI provider.

When a programmer accesses a directory using ADSI, he or she must specify the type of directory that is being accessed with an **ADsPATH**. In addition to specifying the type of directory, the ADsPATH also specifies the object in the directory that is being accessed. Table 11-2 contains examples of ADsPATHs.

Table 11-2   ADsPATH examples

ADsPATH	Description
WinNT://multinatcorp/susan	A user named Susan in the Multinatcorp domain.
LDAP://cn=Susan,ou=IT,dc=ad,dc=multinatcorp,dc=com	A user named Susan in the IT OU in the domain ad.multinatcorp.com.

> Most MMC snap-ins and consoles used to modify Active Directory (such as Active Directory Users and Computers) are written to use ADSI.

Administrative Uses for ADSI

As a network administrator, you are not likely to use ADSI to access multiple directories. However, you may create scripts in VBScript or JScript that use ADSI to access Active Directory.

Scripting is an effective way to automate repetitive maintenance tasks. You can write a script that performs a task, and schedule it to run as often as required using Scheduled Tasks in Control Panel. For instance, you could do a weekly query of Active Directory to create a phone list that is e-mailed to the entire organization.

Scripts written in VBScript and JScript rely on the Windows Script Host to execute. The files cscript.exe or wscript.exe must be present. Cscript.exe executes command-line scripts. Wscript.exe executes scripts that use a graphical interface. Figure 11-4 shows a simple script written in VBScript.

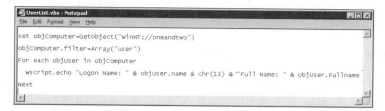

Figure 11-4   Script written in VBScript

Activity 11-4: Listing Users in a Domain with VBScript

Time Required: 10 minutes

Objective: To list all users in a domain.

Description: In the past, your company had problems with user accounts that were not deleted when employees left or were dismissed. Company policy now dictates that each user account in Active Directory corresponds with a current employee. To allow the human resources staff to verify this, you have developed a VBScript that lists all of the users in your domain.

1. If necessary, start you computer and log on as the administrator from your own domain.

2. Right-click the **desktop**, point to **New**, then click **Text Document**.

3. Type **UserList.vbs** and press **Enter**.

4. Click **Yes** to confirm the file extension change.

5. Right-click **UserList.vbs** and click **Edit**. This will open UserList.vbs in Notepad.

6. Type the following:

```
set objComputer=GetObject("WinNT://yourdomain")
objComputer.filter=Array("user")
For each objUser in objComputer
Wscript.echo "Logon Name: " & objUser.name & chr(13) & "Full Name: "
& objUser.Fullname
Next
```

7. Be sure to replace *yourdomain* with your actual domain name (for example, *oneandtwo*). Because WinNT was used to query Active Directory, this script will also work with Windows NT domains.

8. Click **File**, then click **Save**.

9. Close **Notepad**.

10. Double-click **UserList.vbs** to run the script. Click **OK** after viewing each user. When no more windows appear, the list of users is complete. If an error message pops up, you may have made a typographical error. The error message will indicate which line the error is in. If no error message appears and no users are listed, you may have typed your domain name incorrectly.

11. If you are not proceeding immediately to the next activity, log off your computer.

ADSI Edit

The standard tools that administrators use to make Active Directory changes, such as Active Directory Users and Computers, use ADSI to communicate with Active Directory. These standard tools offer you only a limited way to access Active Directory.

The **ADSI Edit** snap-in, shown in Figure 11-5, allows you complete access to the Active Directory information in your domain, as well as the ability to edit the schema for the forest. Performing manual edits of Active Directory information using ADSI Edit is an advanced skill. The administrative snap-ins included with Windows Server 2003 are written by programmers that understand which attributes are safe to change and when they should be changed. These snap-ins are written to prevent you from harming Active Directory. If you have the right permissions on the directory, ADSI Edit does not limit what you can do.

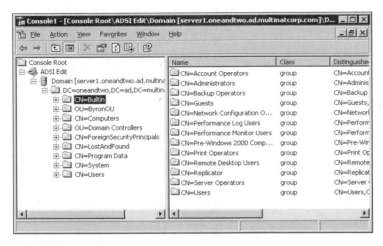

Figure 11-5   ADSI Edit

ADSI Edit is only available on your server if the Windows Support Tools are installed. After they are installed, ADSI Edit will be listed in the available snap-ins when using MMC.

To view the schema, you must first register the schema management dll. To edit the schema using ADSI Edit, you must also be a member of the Schema Admins Group.

Activity 11-5: Viewing the Active Directory Schema

Time Required: 5 minutes

Objective: To view the Active Directory schema using ADSI Edit.

Description: You are installing a new application on your network that uses Active Directory to store information in user objects. The first step for installing the product is to extend the schema. The schema extension adds the attribute appLogins to all user objects. To verify that the schema has been extended, you will use ADSI Edit.

1. If necessary, start your computer and log on as the administrator from your own domain.

2. Click **Start**, click **Run**, type **mmc**, then press **Enter**.

3. Click **File**, then click **Add/Remove Snap-in**.

4. Click **Add**, double-click **ADSI Edit**, click **Close**, then click **OK**.

5. Right-click **ADSI Edit** and click **Connect to**.

6. Confirm that your server is listed in the Path box, then click **OK**.

7. Double-click **ADSI Edit**, then double-click **Domain [*yourserver*]**.

8. Double-click your domain (for example, **DC=oneandtwo,DC=ad, DC=multinatcorp,DC=com**).

9. Double-click **OU=*yourname*OU**, then double-click **OU=IT**.

10. Right-click **CN=Susan Jones** and click **Properties** to view the list of attributes for the user. Look in the list of attributes to see if appLogins is there.

11. Since the attribute appLogins is not present in the user Susan Jones, the schema extension may not have been successful. However, if an attribute is not immediately visible after a schema

extension, the change may not have replicated to the server you are querying. To confirm that a schema extension was not performed properly, you can verify the schema on the schema master.

12. Click **OK** to close the properties for Susan Jones.

13. Close ADSI Edit. If asked to save the changes, click **No**.

14. If you are not proceeding immediately to the next activity, log off your computer.

MICROSOFT METADIRECTORY SERVICES

In many organizations today, it is not uncommon for pieces of employee information to be in several different places. For example, employee information can be contained in Active Directory, a human resources database, and even the e-mail system. Employees are in Active Directory to enable them access to network resources. They are in the human resources database to track payroll, vacations, and tax information. They will also be in an e-mail directory to provide them access to e-mail. Some information, such as a telephone number, may be duplicated in several places.

When new employees are hired, they must be added to all of these directories, and when they leave, they must be removed from all of these directories. Making additions in multiple locations can take a significant amount of time, not to mention the overhead involved in synchronizing information across multiple directories.

When something changes (such as a phone number), it is usually updated in only one directory, resulting in inconsistent information across multiple directories. Obviously, this can create problems.

Ideally, all of the applications could be configured to use the same directory, but that is simply not realistic in large organizations.

Microsoft Metadirectory Services (MMS) can aggregate information from multiple directories into a single directory for centralized management. It can also propagate changes from one directory to other connected directories to synchronize information.

11

Management Agents

MMS uses management agents to communicate with different types of directories. These agents are responsible for receiving changes from and sending changes to external directories.

For example, MMS is used to synchronize information between Active Directory and a human resources system. When a new user is added to Active Directory, a management agent is responsible for informing MMS that a new user exists and for replicating information about that user to MMS. Another management agent then replicates information about the user from MMS to the human resources system to automatically create a record for the user. Other directories, like phone systems, can also be automatically updated.

Using MMS, changes made to one directory are replicated to other directories, so that changes only need to be made once, saving time and ensuring accuracy. It also reduces the administrative overhead associated with synchronizing information across directories.

MMS Version 2.2 ships with a number of management agents configured for common services, as shown in Table 11-3. You can also create your own management agents for customized applications. As of this writing, a new version of MMS is in beta testing. According to the Microsoft Web site, the Standard edition of MMS will be available to all Windows Server 2003 customers within about 90 days of the release of Windows Server 2003, or, in other words, late summer 2003. For more information about MMS, take a look at *http://www.microsoft.com/windows2000/technologies/directory/mms/default.asp*.

MMS can also be used to synchronize two separate Active Directory forests.

Table 11-3   Management agents included with MMS

Category	Supported Items
Directories	Windows NT domains, Active Directory, Novell Directory Services, NetWare Bindery, iPlanet Directory, X.500, Banyan Vines
E-mail	Novell GroupWise, Lotus Notes, Lotus Domino, Lotus cc:mail, Microsoft Exchange
Applications	Peoplesoft, SAP, ERP, telephone switches, XML
Databases	Microsoft SQL Server, Oracle, ODBC
Files	Comma-separated values (CSV), LDIF, delimited

ACTIVE DIRECTORY CONNECTOR

One of the biggest differences between Exchange 5.5 and Exchange 2000/2003 is the way directory information is stored. In Exchange 2000 and Exchange 2003, all directory information—including distribution groups, user e-mail addresses, and the **global address list (GAL)**—is stored in Active Directory. This information is shared between Active Directory and Exchange. In Exchange 5.5, all directory objects are stored in a separate directory service that runs on the Exchange 5.5 server. Mail-related information is separate from user information. Many of the things that Microsoft learned from developing the Exchange directory are applied to Active Directory. The Exchange directory was one of the first Microsoft directories to support multiple-master replication.

When migrating or upgrading from Exchange 5.5 to Exchange 2000 or Exchange 2003, you must exchange directory information between Active Directory and Exchange 5.5's directory service to create the global address list. This is done through the **Active Directory Connector (ADC)**. The ADC is a service that runs on a Windows server and replicates object information between Exchange 5.5 and Active Directory. It does this through **connection agreements** that you configure to manage the replication of information between Exchange 5.5 and Active Directory.

Installing ADC

Before installing the ADC, review the following requirements:

- You must have Windows Server 2003 running Active Directory.

- You must have Exchange 5.5 with Service Pack 3 or higher.

- You must be logged on to Windows Server 2003 as a Domain Administrator in the domain where you will install ADC.

- You must be logged on to the domain as an Enterprise Administrator and a Schema Administrator, because the ADC modifies the Active Directory schema.

The ADC is installed from the Exchange CD in the \ADC\I386 folder. Double-click SETUP.EXE and follow the prompts for the location to store the ADC files and the account name under which to run the ADC service. The installation may take some time because it does modify the schema. Once the ADC is installed, the connection agreements can be created.

Configuring Connection Agreements

A connection agreement defines how object information is replicated to and/or from Exchange 5.5 and Active Directory. You can create two-way or one-way connection agreements. A two-way connection agreement replicates information both ways between Active Directory and Exchange 5.5. A one-way connection agreement can be configured to replicate only from Active Directory to Exchange 5.5 or from Exchange 5.5 to Active Directory. If you plan on running Exchange 2000 or Exchange 2003 and Exchange 5.5 parallel, configure a two-way connection. If you want to import information from Exchange 5.5 into Active Directory and not update Exchange 5.5 with Active Directory information, configure a one-way connection agreement from Exchange 5.5 to Active Directory.

You can configure multiple connection agreements. For example, you may want to configure one connection agreement just to replicate user mailbox information and another to replicate just distribution groups or a specific OU in Active Directory. Since Exchange 5.5 is now several years old, more companies are migrating to Exchange 2000 or to Exchange 2003 (sometimes called "Titanium"), which is also due to be released in 2003. Normally, once you migrate completely from Exchange 5.5 to Exchange 2000 or newer, you would delete the connection agreements and uninstall the ADC software.

CHAPTER SUMMARY

- ❏ LDAP is a standard method for querying directories and is managed by the IETF. Using a standard method to query directories makes software development easier.

- ❏ LDAP names are composed of attributes separated by commas. The name attributes supported by Active Directory are: DC (domain component), OU (organizational unit), and CN (common name). When referring to directory objects using LDAP, you can use distinguished names, relative distinguished names, and URLs.

- ❏ Any LDAP query tool can query Active Directory, as Active Directory natively supports LDAP. The tool LDP.EXE, which can perform LDAP queries, is included in the Support Tools for Windows Server 2003.

- ❏ ADSI is a common programming interface used to access directories. It supports Windows NT, Active Directory, NDS, and NetWare Bindery. It can be accessed using Visual Basic, VBScript, Java, JScript, C++, and others.

- ❏ Microsoft Metadirectory Services uses management agents to aggregate information from multiple directories. It can also synchronize changes between directories.

- ❏ The Active Directory Connector is used to synchronize information between Active Directory and an Exchange 5.5 directory. It can be configured to allow one-way or two-way synchronization. After upgrading to Exchange 2000 or Exchange 2003 it is no longer required.

11

KEY TERMS

Active Directory Connector (ADC) — A service that synchronizes information between Active Directory and the Exchange 5.5 directory.

Active Directory Services Interface (ADSI) — A programming interface that standardizes access to directories.

ADSI Edit — An MMC snap-in that allows you to view detailed information about objects in Active Directory, as well as the structure of Active Directory.

ADsPATH — Describes the type of directory and the location of the object being queried through ADSI.

attribute — In an LDAP name, it is one discrete part of the name. Commas separate the attributes.

common name (CN) — An attribute in an LDAP name that is not an OU or domain component.

connection agreement — Settings that control the replication of information across the Active Directory Connector.

CSVDE.EXE — A utility used to import and export directory information from Active Directory using comma-separated value text files.

Directory Access Protocol (DAP) — A protocol, defined as part of the X.500 standard, for querying directories.

distinguished name (DN) — An LDAP name that refers to the exact location of an object in the directory.

domain component (DC) — An attribute in an LDAP name that corresponds with part of the DNS system.

dynamic auxiliary classes — The ability to add auxiliary class objects. These objects add attributes to other objects, *but only* to a few instances of a class rather than to all instances.

global address list (GAL) — A list of all e-mail addresses in a Microsoft Exchange organization.

InetOrgPerson — Used by LDAP applications to represent users. Support for these objects has been enhanced in Windows Server 2003.

International Organization for Standardization (ISO) — An organization devoted to defining standards for business processes. It has also created standards for computer networking.

LDAP name — The name used to refer to an object in an LDAP query. Commas separate the attributes.

LDAP server — Any directory server that supports LDAP queries.

LDAP URL — A uniform resource locator that defines the location of an object in the directory. The protocol used is LDAP://.

LDIFDE.EXE — A utility used to import and export directory information from Active Directory using LDIF files.

LDP.EXE — A utility included in the Windows Support Tools that queries directories using LDAP.

Lightweight Directory Access Protocol (LDAP) — A simplified version of DAP that is easier to implement and is designed for use on the Internet. This standard is managed by the IETF.

Lightweight Directory Interchange Format (LDIF) — A standardized text file format used to import and export directory information.

Microsoft Metadirectory Services (MMS) — A program that aggregates data from and synchronizes data between multiple directories.

Novell Directory Services (NDS) — A cross-platform directory service originally designed for NetWare 4 and up.

Novell NetWare Bindery Services — A security database used by NetWare Version 3 and earlier.

organizational unit (OU) — An attribute in an LDAP name that represents an Active Directory OU.

provider — An ADSI component that formats ADSI requests for a specific directory service.

relative distinguished name (RDN) — The part of an LDAP distinguished name that uniquely identifies the object within its parent container.

Structured Query Language (SQL) — A standardized language used to query databases.

X.500 — A standard for directory services created by the International Organization for Standardization (ISO).

REVIEW QUESTIONS

1. Which organization is responsible for the LDAP standard?

   a. ISO

   b. OSI

   c. IETF

   d. ICANN

2. Which protocol is defined as part of the X.500 standard?

   a. OSI model

   b. DAP

   c. LDAP

   d. TCP/IP

3. Which of the following are benefits of LDAP? (Choose all that apply.)

   a. Easier to develop software

   b. Not locked into a single directory service vendor

   c. Automated error handling

   d. Centralization of directory services

4. Which Active Directory enhancement in Windows Server 2003 makes it easier to migrate users between Active Directory and other LDAP servers?

   a. Dynamic auxiliary classes

   b. ADSI Edit

   c. The ability to convert InetOrgPerson objects to users and vice versa

   d. Relative distinguished names

5. An LDAP distinguished name describes exactly where to find an object in the directory. True or False?

6. Which character is used to separate the parts of an LDAP name?

   a. Period

   b. Colon

   c. Semi-colon

   d. Comma

7. Which attribute describes the part of LDAP namespace that corresponds with DNS?

   a. DC

   b. OU

   c. CN

   d. DN

8. Which utility is used to import LDIF files into Active Directory?

   a. CSVDE.EXE

   b. LDP.EXE

   c. LDIFDE.EXE

   d. ADSI Edit

9. In which situation are LDIFDE.EXE or CSVDE.EXE most likely to be useful?

   a. Adding many users when a text file must be manually created

   b. Deleting information about two users

   c. Adding many users when data can be exported from an existing data source

   d. Adding one new user

10. Which of the following are LDAP relative distinguished names? (Choose all that apply.)

    a. CN=Bob Smith

    b. OU=Sales

    c. CN=Susan Jones,OU=IT,DC=ad,DC=multinaticorp,DC=com

    d. OU=mktg,DC=ad,DC=multinatcorp,DC=com

11. Which utility performs only LDAP queries?

    a. DSQUERY.EXE

    b. LDP.EXE

    c. LDIFDE.EXE

    d. CSVDE.EXE

12. ADSI Edit makes it harder for programmers to access directories. True or False?

13. What is used in ADSI Edit to define the type of directory that is being accessed?

    a. ADsPATH

    b. NDS

    c. Visual Basic

    d. Distinguished name

14. Which ADSI Edit providers are included with Windows Server 2003? (Choose all that apply.)

    a. Windows NT

    b. LDAP

    c. Active Directory

    d. NDS

    e. StreetTalk

15. Which two files are part of Windows Scripting Host and are required to run Jscript and VBScript?

    a. Jscript.exe

    b. Wscript.exe

    c. Vbscript.exe

    d. Cscript.exe

    e. Winscript.exe

16. Which utility allows you to directly edit objects in Active Directory?

    a. ADSI Edit

    b. Active Directory Users and Computers

    c. Active Directory Sites and Services

    d. LDP.EXE

17. Which service aggregates information from multiple directory services?

    a. Microsoft Metadirectory Services

    b. File Replication Service

    c. Microsoft Megadirectory Services

    d. Active Directory Connector

18. Which service is designed to specifically synchronize information between Active Directory and the Exchange 5.5 directory?

    a. Microsoft Metadirectory Services

    b. File Replication Service

    c. Microsoft Megadirectory Services

    d. Active Directory Connector

19. What controls how the Active Directory Connector synchronizes information?

    a. Site links

    b. Security permissions

    c. Initialization files

    d. Connection agreements

20. ADSI Edit is a programming interface that is important to network administrators. True or False?

HEARTLAND HOSPITAL CASE PROJECTS

Heartland Hospital has a wide range of applications and directories implemented on the network. One of the major challenges facing the IT department is making these directories and applications work together.

Case Project 11-1: Buying a New Application

Heartland Hospital requires a new application for patient tracking. The current application uses a proprietary database to store user information. There is an upgrade available for this product; however, several other vendors offer products based on LDAP servers. Which would you choose? Explain your choice.

Case Project 11-2: Developing a Customized Application

Heartland Hospital has been unable to find commercially available staff scheduling software that meets its needs, so it has decided to contract with a vendor to build customized software. The hospital now needs to choose between two vendors. One has indicated that it will build the application using ADSI. The other has indicated that its solution will use a high-speed proprietary database with higher performance than ADSI. Which vendor would you choose? Explain your choice.

Case Project 11-3: Synchronizing Directories

A Microsoft representative met with the Heartland Hospital management to explain how Microsoft Metadirectory Services can centralize and synchronize information between multiple directories. Which Heartland Hospital directories do you think would benefit from centralization and synchronization?

11

12

UPGRADING A WINDOWS NT OR WINDOWS 2000 DOMAIN

After reading this chapter and completing the exercises, you will be able to:

♦ Enable and understand the different functionality levels of Active Directory

♦ Understand and describe how to upgrade Windows NT domains to Active Directory

♦ Understand and describe how to upgrade Windows 2000 domains to Windows Server 2003

Most organizations already have computer systems in place. It is rare to find even a small company that is not using a computer network in day-to-day operations.

Before you introduce Windows Server 2003 into an existing network, there are a few things you should consider. For example, not all applications will run the same way on a new operating system. The default security settings in Windows Server 2003 are more restrictive than in previous versions. Also, the Web server (Internet Information Services or IIS) is a new version that behaves a bit differently. Changing or upgrading the operating system on your network is not a task that should be taken lightly—you must be aware of the consequences.

There are a number of different methods for integrating Windows Server 2003 into an existing network, and you should understand each in order to choose the best method for a given situation.

ACTIVE DIRECTORY FUNCTIONALITY LEVELS

Because new features have been introduced with each new version of Active Directory, its functionality varies depending on the version of Windows used on the DCs. Some functionality requires that all DCs in the domain use the same version, while other functionality requires that all DCs in the entire forest are able to support the new features.

To handle the different functions provided by different versions, and to allow the administrator to manage how domains and forests behave, Microsoft introduced the concept of functionality levels. In the version of Active Directory introduced with Windows 2000, there were two functionality levels—mixed mode and native mode. In this version of Active Directory, there are four functionality levels:

- Windows 2000 mixed
- Windows 2000 native
- Windows 2003 interim
- Windows 2003 native

There are three forest functionality levels:

- Windows 2000
- Windows 2003 interim
- Windows 2003

 When discussing functionality levels, remember that we are only concerned with DCs. Member servers and client computers can be mixed and matched without affecting the functionality level. You can have a Windows NT Web server in a domain at the Windows 2003 functionality level because it is not a DC.

Activity 12-1: Viewing Domain and Forest Functionality Levels

Time Required: 5 minutes

Objective: To confirm the existing level of functionality in your domain and forest.

Description: In this activity you will view the current functionality levels for both the domain your server is in and the forest. Whenever you are planning an upgrade or a change to Active Directory, it is important that you understand the current configuration.

1. If necessary, turn on your computer and log on as the administrator from your own domain.

2. Click **Start**, point to **Administrative Tools**, then click **Active Directory Domains and Trusts**.

3. Right-click your domain and click **Properties**.

4. The General tab in Properties shows both the domain functional level and the forest functional level. When Active Directory is first installed, the domain functional level is Windows 2000 mixed, and the forest functional level will be Windows 2000. If you completed the activities in Chapter 5, your domain will be at the Windows 2000 native level.

5. Click **Cancel** to close the Properties window.

6. Close Active Directory Domains and Trusts.

7. If you are not proceeding immediately to the next activity, log off your computer.

Windows 2000 Mixed Domains

All domains are mixed-mode domains when they are first created (that is, they have a domain functionality level of Windows 2000 mixed). A mixed-mode domain can contain a combination of DCs running Windows NT, Windows 2000, and Windows Server 2003. The default configuration is shown in Figure 12-1.

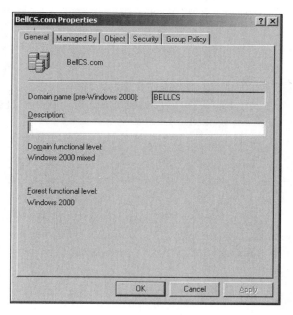

Figure 12-1 Default functionality levels

A Windows 2000 mixed-mode domain has the most limited functionality of the functional levels. (The differences between Windows 2000 mixed and Windows 2000 native are discussed in Chapter 5.) However, Windows Server 2003 running Active Directory in Windows 2000 mixed mode can still do a few things that Windows 2000 Server in mixed mode cannot. The Active Directory enhancements available when Windows Server 2003 is introduced are:

- Install from media

- Global Catalog not required for all logons

- Application directory partitions

Installing from Media

When Windows Server 2003 is promoted to a DC, you have the option to install the directory information using media instead of copying it across the network. Installing from media can save a significant amount of time, especially if it is a large directory being copied across slow WAN links. The most commonly used media are back-up tapes and recorded CD-Rs. Before promoting a server in a remote location, a CD-R or CD-RW containing a replica of the Active Directory information could be shipped to the new site by overnight courier. During the Active Directory installation process, all required Active Directory information could be read from the CD. Normal replication will still update Active Directory, including any changes that occurred between the time the CD was created and Active Directory was installed on the new DC.

Global Catalogs Not Required for All Logons

Windows 2000 servers require access to a GC server to allow logons in multiple-domain forests. If a GC server is not available, then nonadministrative users cannot log on, even with a correct username and password. Windows 2003 can be configured to allow logons even if a GC server cannot be contacted.

 If you are using both Windows 2000 and Windows 2003 in the same domain, the Windows 2000 DCs will not provide this functionality.

Application Directory Partitions

Application directory partitions can be part of Active Directory at this domain functional level. However, only Windows Server 2003 DCs can contain the application partition replicas.

Windows 2000 Native Domains

When all DCs in a domain are Windows 2000 or newer, the domain can be switched to Windows 2000 native mode. This mode is never enabled by default, and therefore must be configured by an administrator.

The Active Directory Domains and Trusts utility is used to switch a domain from Windows 2000 mixed mode to Windows 2000 native mode. To perform this task, right-click your domain and click **Raise Domain Functional Level**. A window, shown in Figure 12-2, will appear, allowing you to raise the domain functionality to Windows 2000 native or Windows 2003.

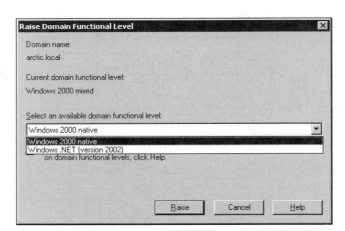

Figure 12-2   Raising the domain functional level

Several useful features are enabled when a domain is switched to Windows 2000 native mode. These include:

- Nesting groups
- Universal groups
- Remote access policies for dial-up and VPN servers
- SIDhistory for domain migration

Nesting Groups and Universal Groups

Nesting groups allows you to make a global group in one domain a member of another global group in the same domain. It also allows you to make a domain local group in a domain a member of a domain local group in the same domain.

Universal groups and their membership are stored on GC servers. Universal groups are used to aggregate the membership of global groups from different domains. Universal groups are not available in the Windows 2000 mixed functionality level. You can review universal groups and the nesting of groups in Chapter 5.

Remote Access Policies

Remote access policies allow you to control VPN and dial-up access based on criteria like time of day, group membership, caller ID, and many others. Without remote access policies, you have only limited ability to control how and when users can dial in or connect via a VPN.

SID History

The **SIDhistory** attribute is used in the migration of users from one domain to another. The SIDhistory attribute of the user in the new domain will contain the SID used in the previous domain. Recall from Chapter 6 that access to resources is controlled by adding SIDs to a DACL on a resource. When a user is migrated from one domain to another, the user receives a new SID. Without the use of SIDhistory, all of the DACLs would need to be updated. Instead, the system uses the SIDhistory to include the old SID in the user's access token, in addition to the new SID. This allows the user to retain access to resources where the DACL contains the old SID.

Activity 12-2: Nesting Groups

Time Required: 10 minutes

Objective: To nest global groups and domain local groups.

Description: In this activity you will create two global groups and make one a member of the other. In addition, you will create two domain local groups and make one a member of the other. The nesting of global groups and domain local groups is only possible when the domain is in Windows 2000 native mode or later.

1. If necessary, turn on your computer and log on as the administrator from your own domain.

2. Create two global groups.

    a. Click **Start**, point to **Administrative Tools**, then click **Active Directory Users and Computers**.

    b. Right-click your domain, point to **New**, then click **Group**.

    c. In the Group name box, type *yourname***G1**.

    d. Confirm that the Group scope selected is **Global**.

    e. Confirm that the Group type selected is **Security**.

    f. Click **OK**.

    g. Right-click your domain, point to **New**, then click **Group**.

    h. In the Group name box, type *yourname***G2**.

    i. Confirm that the Group scope selected is **Global**.

    j. Confirm that the Group type selected is **Security**.

    k. Click **OK**.

3. Make one global group a member of the other.

   a. Right-click **yournameG1** and click **Properties**.

   b. Click the **Members** tab.

   c. Click **Add**.

   d. Type **yournameG2**, and click **OK**.

   e. Click **OK**. The global group yournameG2 is now a member of the global group yournameG1.

4. Create two domain local groups.

   a. Right-click your domain, point to **New**, then click **Group**.

   b. In the Group name box, type *yournameDL1*.

   c. In the Group scope box, click **Domain local**.

   d. Confirm that the Group type selected is **Security**.

   e. Click **OK**.

   f. Right-click your domain, point to **New**, then click **Group**.

   g. In the Group name box, type *yournameDL2*.

   h. In the Group scope box, click **Domain local**.

   i. Confirm that the Group type selected is **Security**.

   j. Click **OK**.

5. Make one domain local group a member of the other.

   a. Right-click **yournameDL1** and click **Properties**.

   b. Click the **Members** tab.

   c. Click **Add**.

   d. Type **yournameDL2**, then click **OK**.

   e. Click **OK**. The domain local group yournameDL2 is now a member of the domain local group yournameDL1.

6. If you are not proceeding immediately to the next activity, log off your computer.

Windows 2003 Interim Domains

Windows 2003 interim domains can contain only Windows NT and Windows Server 2003 DCs. It is meant as a replacement for mixed mode when Windows 2000 DCs are not required.

Within the domain, the functionality at this level is the same as in Windows 2000 mixed mode. However, it does allow for increased functionality at the forest level. The option to enable this level is available during the upgrade of the Windows NT PDC.

Windows 2003 Native Domains

When all DCs in a domain have been upgraded to Windows Server 2003, the domain can be raised to the Windows 2003 native-mode functionality. This mode is never enabled by default, and must be enabled by an administrator using the Active Directory Domains and Trusts console.

Many Active Directory enhancements are enabled with Windows 2003 native mode, in addition to the features that were available in Windows 2000 native mode. These Windows 2003 native-mode features include:

- Replicating a logon timestamp
- User password on InetOrgPerson object
- DC rename

Logon Timestamp

A new attribute for user objects, named **lastLogonTimestamp**, is only used when the domain is in Windows 2003 native mode. This attribute is replicated between DCs and allows administrators to view the last time a user or computer account logged on to the domain. Conversely, the **lastLogon** attribute (included in all versions of Active Directory) is not replicated between DCs, so it only shows the last time a particular DC authenticated a user.

Passwords for InetOrgPerson Objects

Aside from Microsoft products, most directories that use **Lightweight Directory Access Protocol (LDAP)** use the InetOrgPerson object class to identify users that are security principals. Active Directory uses an object class named User to identify network users. In Windows Server 2003, you can create InetOrgPerson objects and assign passwords to them, allowing them to be used as security principals.

DC Rename

Renaming DCs is only possible in the Windows 2003 native mode using the **NETDOM.EXE** utility. NETDOME.EXE ensures that DNS and Active Directory are updated with the new name, and can also be used to manage domains and trust relationships.

NETDOM.EXE is not installed by default. It is located on the Windows Server 2003 CD-ROM in \SUPPORT\TOOLS\SUPPORT.CAB. The tools in this file can be installed by running SUPPORT.MSI, which is located in the same folder.

Changing the name of a DC is a three-step process from a command prompt:

1. **NETDOM computername** *originalDCname* **/add** *newDCname*
   This command adds the new name of the DC to DNS and Active Directory. These changes must be fully replicated before performing Step 2. If the changes are not fully replicated, then users may be unable to access this DC.

2. **NETDOM computername** *originalDCname* **/makeprimary** *newDCname*
   This command marks the new name as the primary name to use when referring to this DC. However, both can be used at this point.

3. **NETDOM computername** *newDCname* **/remove** *originalDCname*
   This command removes references to the original name of the DC from DNS and Active Directory.

Activity 12-3: Converting a Domain to Windows 2003 Native Mode

Time Required: 10 minutes

Objective: To convert a Windows 2000 native-mode domain to Windows 2003 native mode.

Description: In this activity you will convert your domain to Windows 2003 native mode. You will work with a partner because the conversion can only be completed once. In Activity 12-4, you will rename your DC.

1. If necessary, turn on your computer and log on as the administrator from your own domain.

2. Convert your domain to Windows 2003 native mode. Only one partner should complete this step.

    a. Click **Start**, point to **Administrative Tools**, then click **Active Directory Domains and Trusts**.

    b. Right-click your domain and click **Raise Domain Functional Level**.

    c. Confirm that **Windows Server 2003** is selected in the Select an available domain functional level box, then click **Raise**.

    d. Click **OK** to recognize that the functional level cannot be reversed.

    e. Click **OK** to close the confirmation box.

3. Close Active Directory Domains and Trusts.

Activity 12-4: Renaming a DC

Time Required: 10 minutes

Objective: To rename a DC.

Description: Now that the functionality level of your domain has been raised to Windows 2003 native mode, you will test it by renaming your DC.

1. If necessary, turn on your computer and log on as the administrator from your own domain.

2. Install the Windows Server 2003 Support Tools, which includes the NETDOM.EXE utility. Both partners can complete this step. (*Note*: If you completed all earlier activities, then the Support Tools should already be installed, and you can proceed to Step 3.)

    a. Place the Windows Server 2003 CD-ROM in your server.

    b. Click **Start**, click **Run**, click **Browse**, then click **My Computer**.

    c. Double-click the drive letter of your CD-ROM.

    d. Double-click **SUPPORT**, then double-click **TOOLS**.

    e. In the Files of type box, click the down arrow, then click **All Files**.

    f. Double-click **SUPTOOLS.MSI**.

    g. Click **OK**.

    h. Click **Next** to start the installation.

    i. Click **I Agree** to accept the license agreement, then click **Next**.

    j. Click **Next** to accept the default name and organization.

    k. Click **Install Now** to accept the default installation location of C:\Program Files\Support Tools.

    l. Click **Finish**.

3. Add the letter A to the beginning of your DC's name to rename it. Both partners can complete this step.

   a. Click **Start**, click **Run**, type **cmd**, then press **Enter**.

   b. Type **cd "\program files\support tools"** and press **Enter**.

   c. Type **netdom computername . /add A***yourservername* (where *yourservername* is the original FQDN of your server; for example, server1.oneandtwo.ad.multinatcorp.com), then press **Enter**. (Note that the period in the command represents "the current computer".)

   d. The previous step must be replicated before you can proceed to the next step. Intrasite replication takes approximately five minutes. Wait five minutes before moving on to the next step, or force replication using Active Directory Sites and Services.

   e. Type **netdom computername . /makeprimary A***yourservername* (where *yourservername* is the original FQDN of your server), then press **Enter**.

   f. Reboot your server and log on as an administrator.

   g. Click **Start**, click **Run**, type **cmd**, then press **Enter**.

   h. Type **cd "\program files\support tools"** and press **Enter**.

   i. Type **netdom computername .:***yourservername* (where *yourservername* is the original FQDN of your server), then press **Enter**.

   j. Close the command prompt.

4. Confirm the name change.

   a. Click **Start**, right-click **My Computer**, then click **Properties**.

   b. Click the **Computer Name** tab.

   c. The Full computer name field now has the new name of your server.

   d. Close the System Properties window.

5. If you are not proceeding immediately to the next activity, log off your computer.

Windows 2000 Forests

Windows 2000 is the default level of forest functionality. It can accommodate a mix of Windows 2000, Windows NT, and Windows Server 2003 DCs. This is the standard level of forest functionality introduced with Windows 2000.

When a GC is stored on a Windows 2000 server, the entire GC must be replicated each time a new attribute is added. If two GC servers are running on Windows Server 2003, they are capable of replicating only changes. This is a major improvement over Windows 2000 DCs for your GC servers. In a large forest with frequent changes, the use of Windows Server 2003 DCs may considerably reduce the amount of replication traffic between GCs.

Windows 2003 Interim Forests

A Windows 2003 interim forest has been enhanced over a Windows 2000 forest. Only Windows NT and Windows Server 2003 are supported as DCs in this forest level.

Enhancements include:

- Linked value replication
- Improved ISTG algorithms

Linked Value Replication

A linked value attribute is sometimes called a multivalued attribute. The most common example of a multi-valued attribute is the membership attribute of a group, which can contain many members. When raised to this functionality level, Windows Server 2003 DCs implement improved replication of multivalued attributes. The improved replication allows only updates to group membership to be replicated, rather than the entire membership attribute.

Improved ISTG Algorithm

Using an improved replication algorithm, the Inter-Site Topology Generator (ISTG) can make better decisions regarding the replication of Active Directory information between sites. In some circumstances (usually involving lots and lots of small sites), it could take the ISTG (in Windows 2000) so long to calculate the best replication topology that it couldn't complete the calculation before it had to start calculating it again for the next cycle! In a small, single-domain forest you would probably never know the difference, but this feature has been in demand by Microsoft's larger clients for some time.

Windows 2003 Forests

When a forest contains only Windows Server 2003 DCs, it can be raised to a Windows 2003 forest. This enables many new features, in addition to the features available in Windows 2000 and Windows 2003 interim mode. These enhancements include:

- Forest trusts
- Domain renaming
- Deactivation and modification of schema attributes and classes
- Conversion of user objects to InetOrgPerson objects and vice versa
- Dynamic auxiliary classes

Forest Trusts

Forest trusts allow a trust relationship to be established between two forests. A forest trust can be one-way or two-way, and is transitive. These trusts are particularly useful when two organizations merge and need to combine two existing Active Directory forests.

Forest trusts are transitive only between the two forests explicitly chosen. For example, examine Figure 12-3. Forest 1 trusts forest 2, and forest 1 also trusts forest 3. This does *not* mean that forest 2 automatically trusts forest 3—it does not. By saying that forest trusts are transitive, we mean that all domains in forest 1 will trust all domains in forest 2. Thus, a user from domainh.forest3.net could access a resource in domainb.forest1.net, domainc.forest1.net, or domaina.forest1.net. That user could not automatically access a resource in domain3.forest2.net.

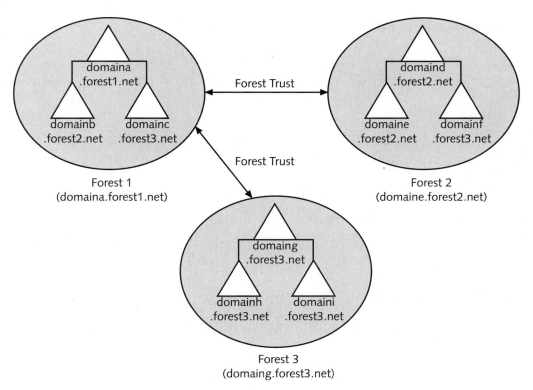

Figure 12-3   Forest trusts

Domain Renaming

In previous versions of Windows and Active Directory, the only way to rename a domain was to remove and recreate it. Now, domains can be renamed, allowing organizations to modify an existing Active Directory structure without migrating users between domains when a name change is required (due to reorganization, poor planning, or some other reason).

 Do not let this feature be a substitute for good planning and design! Microsoft describes a domain rename as "a multistep process that requires detailed understanding." It is a resource-intensive operation that will effect every DC in the forest, including those in the domains that aren't being renamed. Also, you cannot rename a domain in a forest where Exchange 2000 (or its successors) is in use. All clients and servers will need to be restarted, causing some service disruption. It is possible, but not trivial, to rename a domain.

Deactivation and Modification of Attributes and Classes

When object classes and attributes were added to previous versions of Active Directory, they could be deactivated if no longer required. However, they could not be redefined if they were incorrectly created. Now, classes and attributes can be redefined. This is particularly useful for developers in test environments. It also removes some of the risk associated with schema upgrades since changes are no longer permanent.

Conversions between User and InetOrgPerson Objects

As described earlier, many LDAP-enabled directory applications use InetOrgPerson objects to represent users. Active Directory uses User objects to represent users. The ability to convert Users to InetOrgPerson objects and vice versa allows for an easier transfer of user information between Active Directory and other directories.

12

Dynamic Auxiliary Classes

Auxiliary class objects are associated with other object classes to extend the attributes that are part of the class. In earlier versions of Active Directory these could be statically linked. When associated with a class of object, statically linked auxiliary class objects applied to all objects of that class. Now, auxiliary class objects can be linked to a single instance of an object rather than all instances of a class. This is known as dynamic linking of auxiliary classes.

Activity 12-5: Converting the Forest to Windows 2003

Time Required: 5 minutes

Objective: To convert your forest to a Windows 2003 functionality level.

Description: Your instructor will demonstrate how to convert a forest to the Windows 2003 functionality level, as this can only be done once per forest.

1. If necessary, turn on your computer and log on as the administrator from your own domain.

2. Attempt to rename your domain. Both partners may complete this step, as it will not be successful.

    a. Place the Windows Server 2003 CD-ROM in your server.

    b. Click **Start**, click **Run**, type **cmd**, then press **Enter**.

    c. Type **x:** (where *x* is the letter of your CD-ROM drive) and press **Enter**.

    d. Type **cd \valueadd\msft\mgmt\domren** and press **Enter**.

    e. Type **rendom /list** and press **Enter**. You will receive an error message indicating that the forest is not in the correct mode to perform a domain rename.

    f. Close the command prompt.

3. Attempt to upgrade the forest to 2003 functionality. Your instructor will demonstrate this step because it can only be done once in the forest.

    a. Click **Start**, point to **Administrative Tools**, then click **Active Directory Domains and Trusts**.

    b. Right-click **Active Directory Domains and Trusts** and click **Raise Forest Functional Level**.

    c. You will receive an error because the domain ad.multinatcorp.com is still in mixed mode. Click **OK** to acknowledge this error.

    d. Leave Active Directory Domains and Trusts open for the next step.

4. Upgrade the domain ad.multinatcorp.com to Windows 2003 native mode. Only the instructor will complete this step.

    a. Right-click **ad.multinatcorp.com** and click **Raise Domain Functional Level**.

    b. In the Select an available domain functional level box, click the down arrow, then select **Windows Server 2003**.

    c. Click **Raise**, click **OK**, then click **OK** again.

    d. Leave Active Directory Domains and Trusts open for the next step.

5. Raise the functionality level of the forest. This step is only to be completed by the instructor.

    a. Right-click **Active Directory Domains and Trusts** and click **Raise Forest Functional Level**.

    b. Click **Raise**.

    c. Click **OK** to confirm that this cannot be reversed.

    d. Click **OK** to close the successful message box.

    e. Close Active Directory Domains and Trusts.

6. View the functionality level of your domain and forest. All students can perform this step.

    a. Click **Start**, point to **Administrative Tools**, then click **Active Directory Domains and Trusts**.

    b. Right-click your domain and click **Properties**.

    c. The General tab in Properties shows both the domain functional level and the forest functional level. Your domain functional level will be Windows 2003 native, and your forest functional level will be Windows 2003.

    d. Click **Cancel** to close the Properties window.

    e. Close Active Directory Domains and Trusts.

7. If you are not proceeding immediately to the next activity, log off your computer.

UPGRADING WINDOWS NT DOMAINS

Windows NT domains are not organized in a tree structure like Active Directory domains. Windows NT domains are independent of one another. For users in one domain to be granted access to resources in another domain, a trust relationship must be established.

Windows NT trust relationships are one-way, non-transitive trusts. For two domains to trust each other, two one-way trusts must be created in opposite directions. The creation of trusts is never automatic in Windows NT.

Because trusts are not transitive in NT 4.0, many trusts must be created for interoperability between domains. In a network with four Windows NT domains, 12 trusts must be established for full interoperability. As the number of domains increases, the number of required trusts will continue to grow.

To calculate the number of trusts required, use the formula: $n(n-1)$ (where n is the number of domains).

Domain Structure

Active Directory uses sites to control replication within a domain and between domains. Conversely, Windows NT does not perform replication between domains, and replication within a domain is automatic. Windows NT networks were designed to use domain boundaries as replication boundaries, often with each physical location its own domain.

When migrating to Active Directory from Windows NT domains, you must decide whether the existing domain structure is adequate for your needs. If not, you should create a new design and migrate existing information from the Windows NT domains to the new Active Directory forest.

Active Directory does not require NetBIOS to function, but Windows NT domains do. Ensure that your Active Directory DCs are configured to use WINS when non-Active Directory-aware clients and servers (such as Windows NT or Windows 95/98) are still in use.

12

Keeping the Existing Domain Structure

If you choose to keep your existing domain structure, then the upgrade process is relatively simple. The first domain upgraded will become the forest root domain. Plan this very carefully, as it cannot be changed.

The first DC upgraded must be the PDC in the Windows NT 4.0 domain. This new Windows Server 2003 DC will take on the role of PDC emulator for the domain. As PDC emulator it will continue to provide directory updates to Windows BDCs.

When BDCs are upgraded to Windows Server 2003, the operating system upgrade is performed first. After the upgrade is complete, the server will reboot. During the boot process, the server will automatically log on using the local administrator account that was created during the operating system upgrade, and will present you with the option to keep the server as a member server or promote it to a DC. After choosing one of these options, the system will no longer automatically log on using the administrator account.

As you upgrade each domain after the forest root, you will choose to join the newly created forest. As each domain is upgraded, the two-way transitive trusts will automatically be made between the newly upgraded domain and its parent in the forest.

During an upgrade that involves many domains, you should raise the forest functionality level to Windows 2003 interim after completing the forest root domain. This will give you some of the advantages of the Windows 2003 functional level until the migration to Windows Server 2003 is complete.

Creating a New Domain Structure

Sometimes the existing Windows NT domain structure is not ideal. If you want a new domain structure, the easiest way to implement it is with entirely new hardware. Chances are good that if you are upgrading from Windows NT 4.0, it is time to upgrade the computers acting as DCs as well. This way, the new domain structure can be created without the logistical hassle of decommissioning your existing servers.

After the new servers are installed and the new domain structure is created, you can choose to either recreate all of the users and resources or migrate them to the new domains. For smaller organizations, recreating users and resources may be less complex than learning how to migrate the resources properly. For larger organizations, the benefits of a smooth migration are worth the time to learn, plan, and test.

Active Directory Migration Tool

The **Active Directory Migration Tool (ADMT)** migrates users, groups, and computer accounts from one domain to another. The objects can be migrated from Windows NT domains to Active Directory domains or between Active Directory domains.

The original version of ADMT was a graphical utility with wizards, trust migration, and testing option. The version that shipped with Windows Server 2003 has been enhanced and includes:

- Password migration
- A scripting interface for use with VBScripts
- An attribute exclusion list that allows you to define attributes not to migrate to the new domain
- A command line migration utility

The Active Directory Migration Tool is pictured in Figure 12-4.

The ADMT moves security principals from one domain to another. The source domain contains the original objects to be migrated. The target domain is where the new objects will be created. The target domain functional level must be a minimum of Windows 2000 native mode in order to proceed with the migration.

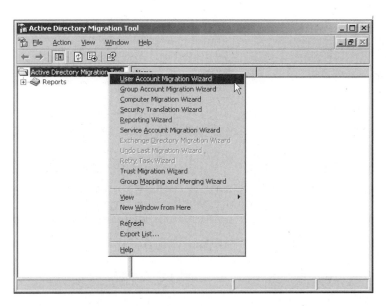

Figure 12-4   Active Directory Migration Tool

Other requirements for the migration include:

- Account auditing must be enabled in the source and target domain.

- A local group *sourcedomainname*$$$ (where *sourcedomainname* is the NetBIOS name of the source domain) must be created in the source domain.

- The local group *sourcedomainname*$$$ is used as part of the migration process and must have no members.

- The user performing the move must be a member of the Domain Admins Group in both domains.

- The source DC must be the PDC if migrating from Windows NT.

Objects with well-known SIDs or RIDs, such as the administrator account, will not be migrated.

Inter-forest Migration

The migration of objects from a Windows NT domain is referred to as an **inter-forest migration**. A Windows NT domain can never be part of a forest. Inter-forest migration also refers to migrating objects from one Active Directory forest to another.

During an inter-forest migration, user accounts are cloned from the source domain and copied to the target domain. You can configure ADMT to disable the original user account or to leave it untouched, allowing the administrator performing the migration to prepare the new Active Directory forest while the existing system is still in use. Once the new Active Directory forest is ready, the old system can be decommissioned.

Since the user account in the new domain will have a different SID than the original user account from the source domain, the new user account will be unable to access resources that the old account could. To avoid this, the old account's SID is placed in the new account's SIDhistory attribute. This is particularly helpful in a large organization when migrating users over slowly in groups.

When the new users log on to the network, they will receive an access token that contains the current SID of the user account, the SID from the user's SIDhistory attribute, the SIDs of any groups of which they are a member, and the SIDs from the SIDhistory attribute from any groups of which they are a member. These

SIDs will allow access to all of the resources that the original security principals had access to, as well as any resources which the migrated security principals have been granted assigned access.

PDC Overloading

If your original network is composed of Windows 2000/XP clients and Windows NT 4.0 DCs, there is a risk of overloading the PDC when it is upgraded to Windows Server 2003. When the PDC is upgraded, it will use dynamic DNS to create all of the appropriate service location records for itself as a DC in DNS.

Windows 2000/XP clients will first attempt to find DC information in DNS. If this fails, they will then attempt to find DC information using NetBIOS methods, such as a NetBIOS broadcast or a WINS lookup. In a large domain with only one Windows Server 2003 DC, all of the Windows 2000/XP clients will log on using only the Windows Server 2003 DC. In addition, as the PDC emulator, the Windows 2003 DC will also handle all password changes for non-Active Directory-aware clients, such as Windows 98 and Windows NT.

On a LAN, **PDC overloading** is an annoyance, but it is only critical if the server cannot handle the load. If this occurs during peak logon periods, for instance, it will result in slow logons. However, everything else will function properly.

On the other hand, if a domain spans WAN links, then the situation can overload them because of their relatively slow speed. Even if the domain is organized into separate sites, all of the Windows 2000/XP clients will use the Windows Server 2003 DC. When the WAN links become overloaded, network traffic may be excessively delayed and packets may even be dropped, causing errors in applications that require the WAN links. This can be a real problem if your company has many business-critical applications transferring data over WAN links.

To solve this problem, you can configure the first few Windows Server 2003 DCs to emulate Windows NT servers. This does limit the functionality that clients and member servers receive from the Windows 2003 DCs; however, if there are multiple Active Directory DCs, then the functionality they receive from each other is never limited.

When a Windows Server 2003 DC is emulating Windows NT, Windows 2000/XP clients and Windows 2000/2003 member servers will not use Kerberos authentication or Group Policy.

To enable Windows NT emulation on the server, use the registry editor to configure the registry key **KEY_LOCAL_MACHINE/System/CurrentControlSet/Services/Netlogon/Parameters/NT4Emulator** with the data type **REG_DWORD**, and a value of **1**.

 As a best practice, add this registry key before the DC is upgraded. If it is added after the DC has been upgraded to Windows Server 2003, then all Windows 2000 and Windows Server 2003 member servers will be forced to rejoin the domain.

This change is meant to be a temporary solution until there are enough upgraded DCs to handle authentication traffic from all of the Active Directory-aware clients and member servers. If some clients and member servers require access to Kerberbos authentication or Group Policy, then you can override the DC Windows NT emulation on selected member servers. This is required, for example, when BDCs are upgraded to Windows Server 2003 or when client computers use the administrative tools to manage Active Directory.

To force a client or member server to ignore Windows NT emulation on DCs, use the registry editor to configure the registry key **HKEY_LOCAL_MACHINE/System/CurrentControlSet/Services/Netlogon/Parameters/NeutralizeNT4Emulator** with the data type **REG_DWORD**, and a value of **1**.

UPGRADING WINDOWS 2000 DOMAINS

A forest with Windows 2000 domains will be at the Windows 2000 functionality level, with domains that are at Windows 2000 mixed or Windows 2000 native mode. Upgrading this type of forest is easy, because Active Directory has already been designed and implemented. There is no need to move user accounts, groups, or computer accounts.

 Before any Windows Server 2003 DCs are added to the forest, the schema of the forest must be updated. On the schema master for the forest, run **ADPREP.EXE /forestprep**. In each domain to be upgraded, run **ADPREP.EXE /domainprep** on the infrastructure operations master for that domain. This utility can be found in the \I386 folder on the Windows Server 2003 CD-ROM. To run ADPREP.EXE successfully, you must be a member of Schema Admins and Enterprise Admins groups.

Adding Windows Server 2003 Domain Controllers

When Windows Server 2003 DCs are added to the domain, you can upgrade an existing DC to Windows Server 2003, or install Windows Server 2003 as a member server and then promote it to a DC.

If a DC is to be upgraded, you must be sure that the server meets the upgrade requirements for Windows Server 2003. To find out if your hardware and software are capable of running Windows Server 2003, run **WINNT32.EXE /checkupgradeonly**. This utility can be found in the \I386 folder on the Windows Server 2003 CD-ROM.

Restructuring Existing Domains

When upgrading your DCs from Windows 2000 to Windows Server 2003, you may also decide to restructure your existing domains. Some Windows 2000 implementations are just simple upgrades of Windows NT domains, and are not structured for optimal use of Active Directory.

The ADMT can be used to migrate users, groups, and computer accounts from one domain to another within an Active Directory forest. This is referred to as **intra-forest migration**. Figure 12-5 shows an example the ADMT wizard being used to migrate users within the forest.

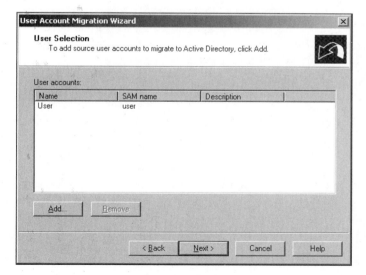

Figure 12-5   Migrating users within the forest

The requirements for using the ADMT for intra-forest migration are the same as those for inter-forest migration, with the following exceptions:

- A local group named *sourcedomainname*$$$ is not required.
- ADMT can be run on a DC in the source or target domain, or on a Windows XP Professional client.
- Administrative shares must exist on the DCs.

Accounts and groups that are moved during an intra-forest migration are not copied. This prevents two security principals in the same forest from having the same SID. Otherwise, a SID would exist on the original account and in the SIDhistory attribute of the new account.

When a user account is migrated in an intra-forest migration, all groups that user is a member of must also be migrated. When a group is migrated, all user accounts that are members of that group are also migrated. This is referred to as **closed sets**, and is done to ensure that existing permissions are retained for all migrated security principals.

Planning your intra-forest migration is critical if you do not intend to migrate all users and groups within a domain. Users may need to be added or removed from groups to prevent closed sets from unexpectedly migrating users.

To prevent global groups from migrating as a closed set, you can convert them into universal groups. Universal groups are stored GCs, rather than the domain database, and are not affected by domain migration.

CHAPTER SUMMARY

- ❏ Active Directory is capable of different functionality levels at the domain and forest levels.
- ❏ Windows 2003 interim domains can have Windows NT and Windows Server 2003 DCs. The domain functionality is the same as Windows 2000 mixed mode, but allows enhancements at the forest level.
- ❏ Windows 2003 native domains can only contain Windows Server 2003 DCs to gain additional functionality beyond Windows 2000 native mode.
- ❏ Windows 2000 forests are the default level of functionality for Active Directory.
- ❏ Windows 2003 interim forests can contain only Windows NT and Windows Server 2003 DCs. Windows 2003 forests can contain only Windows Server 2003 DCs.
- ❏ The first DC to be upgraded in a Windows NT domain must be the PDC. It will become the PDC emulator in the domain.
- ❏ ADMT migrates user accounts, groups, and computer accounts from one domain to another.
- ❏ When a user account or group is migrated, the new object will normally contain the SID of the old object in the SIDhistory attribute.
- ❏ PDC overloading occurs when all Active Directory-aware clients use the first available Active Directory DC to log on.
- ❏ In an existing forest, ADPREP.EXE must be used to prepare Active Directory before the first Windows Server 2003 DC is added.
- ❏ When ADMT is used for intra-forest migration, closed sets are used to maintain proper assignment of permissions. In addition, users and groups are moved rather than copied.

KEY TERMS

Active Directory Migration Tool (ADMT) — A tool that migrates user accounts, groups, and computer accounts from one domain to another.

ADPREP.EXE /domainprep — A command run on the infrastructure master of the domain to prepare Active Directory before installing the first Windows Server 2003 DC in the domain.

APREP.EXE /forestprep — A command run on the schema master of the forest to prepare Active Directory before installing the first Windows Server 2003 DC in the forest.

closed set — When intra-forest migration is performed, all groups of which a user is a member must be migrated when the user is migrated. In addition, when a group is migrated, all users that are members of that group must be migrated.

dynamic auxiliary classes — Objects that can be linked to a single instance of an object to add attributes, rather than all instances of a class.

InetOrgPerson — An object used by most LDAP applications to represent users.

inter-forest migration — The migration of objects between two domains in different forests. Migration from a Windows NT domain is also inter-forest migration.

intra-forest migration — The migration of objects from one domain to another domain in the same forest. Users and groups are moved in closed sets.

lastLogon — A user attribute used to track the last time a user logged on to a server. It is not replicated to other DCs. It is available in all levels of domain functionality.

lastLogonTimestamp — A user attribute used to track the last time a user logged on to the network. It is replicated to all DCs in the domain and is only available if the domain is in Windows 2003 mode.

Lightweight Directory Access Protocol (LDAP) — A standardized protocol used to query directories.

linked value replication — An enhanced replication mechanism that allows multivalued attributes to synchronize changes only, rather than the entire attribute. This is enabled for Windows 2003 interim domains and Windows 2003 domains.

NETDOM.EXE — A command-line utility used to rename DCs, create trusts, and join computers to a domain.

PDC overloading — This occurs when the first upgraded DC is overloaded with logon attempts from Active Directory-aware clients.

remote access policies — Policies that are implemented on remote access servers to control access. They require Windows 2000 native-mode domains or higher.

SIDhistory attribute — A user attribute that is enabled only in Windows 2000 native-mode domains or better. It is used to track the previous SIDs of migrated users and groups.

Windows 2000 forests — The default forest functional level that can contain Windows NT, Windows 2000, and Windows Server 2003 DCs.

Windows 2000 mixed-mode domains — The default domain functional level for Active Directory that can contain Windows NT, Windows 2000, and Windows Server 2003 DCs.

Windows 2000 native-mode domains — This domain functional level can be enabled when all DCs are Windows 2000 or Windows Server 2003. Enhancements include nesting groups, universal groups, and the SIDhistory attribute.

Windows 2003 interim domains — This domain functional level can contain only Windows NT and Windows Server 2003 DCs. The functionality is the same as Windows 2000 mixed-mode domains, but allows enhanced forest functionality.

Windows 2003 interim forests — This forest functional level can contain only Windows NT and Windows Server 2003 DCs. Enhancements include linked value replication and improved site replication.

Windows 2003 native domains — This domain functional level can contain only Windows Server 2003 DCs. Functional enhancements include lastLogonTimestamp, user passwords on InetOrgPerson objects, and DC renaming.

12

Windows 2003 native forests — This forest functional level can contain only Windows Server 2003 DCs. Enhancements include forest trusts, domain renaming, redefining schema attributes and classes, converting InetOrgPerson objects to user objects, and dynamic auxiliary classes

WINNT32.EXE /checkupgradeonly — A command run on an existing Windows server to determine upgrade compatibility.

REVIEW QUESTIONS

1. How many different functional levels are there for domains?

   a. One

   b. Two

   c. Three

   d. Four

   e. Five

2. Which is the lowest domain functional level that supports the installation of Active Directory from back-up media such as a CD-ROM?

   a. Windows 2000 mixed

   b. Windows 2000 native

   c. Windows 2003 interim

   d. Windows 2003 native

3. A Windows Server 2003 DC will be able to log on users, even if a GC server is unavailable. True or False?

4. Which DCs can hold an application partition? (Choose all that apply.)

   a. Windows NT

   b. Windows 2000

   c. Windows Server 2003 in a Windows 2000 native domain

   d. Windows Server 2003 in a Windows 2003 interim domain

   e. Windows Server 2003 in a Windows 2003 native domain

5. To avoid problems with closed sets when performing intra-forest migration of users and groups from one domain to another, what type of group can you use?

   a. Local

   b. Domain local

   c. Global

   d. Universal

6. Which functional levels can the target domain be set to when using ADMT? (Choose all that apply.)

   a. Windows 2000 mixed

   b. Windows 2000 native

   c. Windows 2003 interim

   d. Windows 2003 native

7. Which feature allows a global group to be a member of another global group?

   a. Universal groups

   b. Nesting groups

   c. Forest trusts

   d. SIDhistory

   e. InetOrgPerson

8. Which feature allows users to retain permissions to resources after they are migrated?

   a. Universal groups

   b. Nesting groups

   c. SIDhistory

   d. InetOrgPerson

   e. LastLogon

9. Which utility is used to rename DCs?

   a. Active Directory Users and Computers

   b. ADPREP.EXE

   c. Active Directory Domains and Trusts

   d. NETDOM.EXE

10. Which type of object is commonly used by LDAP applications to represent users?

    a. Alias

    b. InetOrgPerson

    c. User

    d. NetworkUser

11. Which domain functionality level allows the renaming of DCs?

    a. Windows 2000 mixed

    b. Windows 2000 native

    c. Windows 2003 interim

    d. Windows 2003 native

12. Which attribute tracks the last time a user logged on to the network and replicates between DCs?

    a. LastLogon

    b. SIDhistory

    c. LastLogonTimestamp

    d. LogonHistory

13. Which levels of forest functionality allow linked value replication? (Choose all that apply.)

    a. Windows 2000

    b. Windows 2003 interim

    c. Windows 2003

    d. Windows NT 4.0

14. Which features are enabled only in the Windows 2003 forest functional level? (Choose all that apply.)

    a. SIDhistory

    b. Renaming domains

    c. Renaming DCs

    d. Forest trusts

    e. Dynamic auxiliary classes

15. Which feature allows for easier migration and synchronization of user information with LDAP directories?

    a. Forest trusts

    b. Dynamic auxiliary classes

    c. Conversion of user objects to InetOrgPerson and vice versa

    d. Linked value replication

    e. Improved replication between sites

16. When a Windows NT domain is upgraded, which is the first DC upgraded?

    a. A member server

    b. A BDC

    c. The PDC

    d. Install Windows Server 2003 and promote it to a DC

17. The root domain can be changed now that domains can be renamed. True or False?

18. Which of the following are new features found in the version of ADMT shipped with Windows Server 2003? (Choose all that apply.)

    a. Password migration between forests

    b. Wizards

    c. Trust migration

    d. A scripting interface

    e. An attribute exclusion list

19. Which of the following are requirements for inter-forest migration, but not required for intra-forest migration? (Choose all that apply.)

    a. A local group *sourcedomainname*$$$ must be created

    b. The user performing the move must be a member of Domain Admins in both domains

    c. ADMT must be installed on a DC in the target domain

    d. Account auditing must be enabled

20. To build a parallel infrastructure while maintaining the existing domains, what type of migration would you use?

    a. Inter-forest migration

    b. Intra-forest migration

21. PDC overloading occurs only when the client computers are Windows NT or Windows 98. True or False?

SACRED HEART HOSPITAL CASE PROJECTS

Heartland Hospital has already implemented Active Directory and Windows Server 2003. Based on a glowing recommendation of your services from Mary Firth, Sacred Heart Hospital has engaged you to help with the upgrade of its Windows NT-based network.

Case Project 12-1: Domain and Forest Functional Levels

The network administrator at Sacred Heart Hospital has never worked with Windows 2000 or Windows Server 2003 before. As the first step in planning, you will choose the desired functional levels for the forest and domains. Write a short description of each domain and forest functional level that can be given to the network administrator. Include the features that are enabled at each level, as well as the types of DCs that can exist in each one.

Case Project 12-2: Migration Planning

Sacred Heart Hospital has three Windows NT domains. The diagnostic domain has three Windows NT DCs, five Windows NT member servers, and 65 client computers. The surgery domain has two Windows NT DCs, two Windows NT member servers, and 180 client computers. The general domain has three Windows NT DCs, four Windows NT member servers, four Windows 2000 member servers, and 625 client computers.

New servers will be ordered as part of the upgrade project. How do you propose to migrate to Active Directory?

Case Project 12-3: PDC Overloading

The network administrator at Sacred Heart Hospital heard that when a Windows NT domain is upgraded to Active Directory, there is a problem with PDC overloading. However, he does not understand what this is or why it happens. How would you explain this to the administrator, and how can this be prevented at Sacred Heart Hospital?

12

Glossary

A record — An address (A) resource record maps a hostname to an IP address.

access control entry (ACE) — An entry in a DACL or SACL that lists a security principal (by SID), a type of permission (such as read or write), and whether that SID is allowed or denied the permission.

access token — A binary structure that lists the identity, rights, and group membership of a user on the network. An access token contains, among other items, the user's SID and the SID of each group the user belongs to.

account policies — Configuration settings for passwords, account lockouts, and Kerberos. They must be linked to the domain to affect settings for the domain.

Active Directory (AD) — Microsoft's directory service for Windows networks. Active Directory is a Microsoft trademark.

Active Directory Connector (ADC) — A service that synchronizes information between Active Directory and the Exchange 5.5 directory.

Active Directory integrated zone — A DNS zone in which data is stored as objects in Active Directory. Available only on Microsoft DNS servers running on domain controllers.

Active Directory Migration Tool (ADMT) — A tool that migrates user accounts, groups, and computer accounts from one domain to another.

Active Directory Replication Monitor — A tool used to monitor, troubleshoot, and verify Active Directory replication.

Active Directory Services Interface (ADSI) — A programming interface that standardizes access to directories.

Active Directory Users and Computers — A Microsoft Management Console (MMC) snap-in for managing common Active Directory objects, including users, computers, groups, and some resources.

Active Directory-aware — A term used to describe application software that makes use of information stored in Active Directory.

administrative templates — Files containing settings used by the GPO Editor to define the registry key that should be changed, the options, and a description of the effects.

ADPREP.EXE /domainprep — A command run on the infrastructure master of a Windows 2000 domain to prepare Active Directory before installing the first Windows Server 2003 DC in the domain.

ADPREP.EXE /forestprep — A command run on the schema master of a Windows 2000 forest to prepare Active Directory before installing the first Windows Server 2003 DC in the forest.

ADSI Edit — An MMC snap-in that allows you to view detailed information about objects in Active Directory, as well as the structure of Active Directory.

ADsPATH — Describes the type of directory and the location of the object being queried through ADSI.

application partition — An optional Active Directory partition type that is replicated to chosen DCs in the forest.

assigned — An assigned application is advertised on the desktop and in the Start menu. When an application is assigned to a user it is installed on first use. When an application is assigned to a computer it is installed when the computer boots up.

asymmetric keys — *See* public/private key pair.

attribute — In an LDAP name, it is one discrete part of the name. Commas separate the attributes.

attributes — The schema contains a list of all possible properties or attributes that can be included in class definitions. When speaking of a class, its attributes are a collection of information (or properties) about each object instantiated from the class, which is stored in Active Directory. Collectively, an object's attributes define the object.

authenticate — Determination of which security principal is attempting to log on or access a resource. Most often, proving that a user is who they claim to be through the use of a name and password combination.

authoritative restore — An Active Directory restore that allows you to restore deleted or modified objects and have those changes replicated to other DCs in the domain.

authorization — Once the identity of a security principal has been determined (through authentication), it is necessary to determine whether that security principal is allowed to access a particular resource (authorization).

best practice — A preferred way of doing something, defined either by an authority or by common practice in well-run companies.

Block Policy Inheritance — A setting in the group policy configuration for an OU that prevents settings from GPOs higher in the tree from being inherited.

bridgehead server — A DC that is configured to perform replication to and from other sites.

child domain — A domain that is connected to another domain (its parent) in an Active Directory tree. The child domain uses a subdomain of the parent domain's DNS name in a contiguous DNS namespace. *Child.parent.company.com* is a child domain of *parent.company.com*. Parent and child domains are connected with a two-way, transitive trust.

closed set — When intra-forest migration is performed, all groups of which a user is a member must be migrated when the user is migrated. In addition, when a group is migrated, all users that are members of that group must be migrated.

common name (CN) — An attribute in an LDAP name that is not an OU or domain component.

configuration partition — The Active Directory partition that stores information about the forest's structure. This partition is replicated to all DCs in the forest.

connection agreement — Settings that control the replication of information across the Active Directory Connector.

connection object — A connection between two DCs used for replication.

container — Generically speaking, a container is an object in the directory that can contain a collection of other objects. Specifically, a class of objects called "container" is available in Active Directory. Two default containers created in an Active Directory installation are called Computers and Users.

convergence — The state when all replicas of a database have the same version of the data. (In Active Directory, this means that all DCs have the same set of information.)

country code TLD (ccTLD) — A top-level domain assigned by ISO country codes on a geo-political basis, such as *.ca* for Canada.

CSVDE.EXE — A utility used to import and export directory information from Active Directory using comma separated value text files.

data owner — A person or team responsible for managing the content of a part of the directory, not maintaining the directory service itself. Data owners will usually create objects and edit their attributes.

data table — The portion of NTDS.DIT that stores the attributes and properties for objects in Active Directory.

Dcgpofix — A command line utility that re-creates the Default Domain Policy and the Default Domain Controllers Policy.

dcpromo — The program that initiates the Active Directory Installation Wizard.

delegation — The process of distributing and decentralizing the administration of Active Directory by granting permissions to data owners.

delegation of control — Refers to assigning permissions on Active Directory objects so that data owners can manage their own objects. There is a Delegation of Control wizard to assist with setting permissions for common tasks.

Delegation of Control wizard — A wizard tool that facilitates granting permissions on OUs to allow non-administrators to perform certain functions.

Directory Access Protocol (DAP) — A protocol, defined as part of the X.500 standard, for querying directories.

directory owner — *See* service owner.

directory service (DS) — A central database that stores information about network-based objects such as computers, printers, users, and groups. Active Directory is a directory service.

disabled — an account is disabled or enabled by an administrator. Disabled accounts cannot be used. *See also* locked out.

discretionary access control list (DACL) — A list of ACEs used to control access to an object or resource.

distinguished name (DN) — An LDAP name that refers to the exact location of an object in the directory.

distribution group — A group that can be used to send e-mail to a group of users and contacts. It cannot be used to control security.

DNS namespace — The entire map of valid names in the domain name system.

document activation — The automatic installation of a published application when a user opens an associated file type.

domain — Computers, users, and resources using a joint security model, usually under common management.

Domain Admins — The group of users with complete administrative control over domain controllers, and by default, control over all machines in the domain.

domain component (DC) — An attribute in an LDAP name that corresponds with part of the DNS system.

domain controller (DC) — A Windows server, hosting the Active Directory database, which manages operations of a domain.

domain identifier — Three, 32-bit numbers that are statistically unique and identify a particular domain.

domain local group — A group that can be used within its own domain, but can include security principals from other trusted domains as members.

Domain Name System (DNS) — A highly available, scalable, and dispersed system that provides name resolution on the Internet or private networks.

domain naming master — The DC responsible for adding or removing domains from the forest. There is only one domain naming master per forest.

domain partition — The Active Directory partition that stores information about objects in the domain such as user accounts and groups. This partition is replicated to all DCs in the domain.

down-level client — A client that was not designed to work seamlessly with Active Directory, including Windows 3.1 and earlier, Windows 95, Windows 98, Windows Millennium Edition (Me), and Windows NT 4.0 and earlier.

dynamic auxiliary classes — Objects that can be linked to a single instance of an object to add attributes, rather than all instances of a class.

EDB.CHK — The checkpoint file that tracks which transactions in EDB.LOG have been written to the Active Directory database.

EDB.LOG — The transaction log used by Active Directory. It is always 10 MB.

EDBXXXXX.LOG — Old versions of the transaction log used by Active Directory.

Extensible Storage Engine (ESE) — A database design that uses log files to provide fault tolerance and improved performance.

File Allocation Table (FAT) — An older file format used by down-level clients and DOS. FAT disks do not support file-based permissions, auditing, or journaling.

file system — A security policy setting that defines permissions applied to the file system.

folder redirection — A user configuration setting that redirects folders from the local user profile to the server. Basic redirection redirects all users' folders to the same path (although variables such as %USERNAME% can be used). Advanced redirection allows completely different paths, based on security group memberships.

forest — A forest is the implementation of Active Directory. That is, one single forest really represents one single Active Directory installation. A forest consists of one or more domain partitions, a common schema partition, a configuration partition, and optional application partitions.

forest root domain — The first domain created in a forest. The forest root domain contains the security principals that can manage the forest.

fully qualified domain name (FQDN) — A host name that includes all parts necessary to resolve a name to an IP address from the host name to the root domain, including any subdomains or TLDs, such as *myhost.mysubdomain.mycompany.com*.

functional specification — The document created at the end of the planning stage that describes the Active Directory design.

garbage collection — The process of purging deleted objects from Active Directory.

generic TLD (gTLD) — A top-level DNS domain that is not assigned to a specific country, and is directly delegated by the root servers .aero, .biz, .com, .coop, .edu, .gov, .info, .int, .mil, .museum, .name, .net, .org, and .pro.

global address list (GAL) — A list of all e-mail addresses in a Microsoft Exchange organization.

Global Catalog server — A designated domain controller that holds a partial replica of every domain naming context in the forest as well as a complete copy of its own domain naming context. That is, it has key attributes of every object in the forest, available primarily for searching.

global group — A group that can contain only security principals from its own domain, but it can be used in other trusted domains.

globally unique identifier (GUID) — A 16-byte value generated by an algorithm that guarantees it will be different from every other GUID generated anywhere in the world. A GUID is used to uniquely identify a particular device, component, item, or object.

Gpresult — A command line utility that is equivalent to RSoP.

Gpupdate — A command line utility that forces the update of Group Policy on a workstation.

Group Policy — A technology enabled by Active Directory that allows administrators to define policy and rely on Active Directory and the operating system to ensure that policies are enforced. Group Policy is also used to automatically distribute software.

group policy container (GPC) — The collection of objects in Active Directory that hold GPOs and their settings.

group policy object (GPO) — Specific group policy settings applied in Active Directory.

group policy template (GPT) — A set of files and folders in the SYSVOL folder that hold settings and files for a GPO.

incremental zone transfer — A process whereby a secondary DNS Server can request changes made only to zone data, not the entire zone.

InetOrgPerson — An object used by most LDAP applications to represent users.

infrastructure master — The DC responsible for updating references in other domains to an object in the local domain. There is one infrastructure domain for each domain in the forest.

inheritance — The concept that a security setting on one object can be inherited by objects lower in the hierarchy. Examples include folders inheriting settings from other parent folders, or OUs inheriting settings from parent OUs.

inter-forest migration — The migration of objects between two domains in different forests. Migration from a Windows NT domain is also inter-forest migration.

inter-site replication — Replication occurring between sites.

International Organization for Standardization (ISO) — An organization devoted to defining standards for business processes. They have also created standards for computer networking.

Internet presence — In the context of DNS, the Internet presence refers to the DNS subdomain name used by the public to reach an organization's e-mail or Web servers. The term can also be used generically, as in "our company needs an Internet presence."

Intersite Topology Generator (ISTG) — Creates and manages the intersite replication of Active Directory naming partitions.

intra-forest migration — The migration of objects from one domain to another domain in the same forest. Users and groups are moved in closed sets.

intra-site replication — Replication occurring within a site.

IP security policies — Security policy settings relating to IPSec configuration.

joint security model — A means of organizing a computer network so that security principals (such as a user) can access resources hosted on all machines participating in the model. All users and resources share a common authentication scheme. A Windows domain is a joint security model.

Jscript (.js) — A scripting language that can be used to write logon, logoff, startup, and shutdown scripts. It is similar to JavaScript.

Kerberos — A network protocol first developed at MIT to allow for a wide-area, distributed method of securely authenticating users before they are allowed to access network resources.

Kerberos ticket — One of several types of binary constructs contained in Kerberos messages. Kerberos tickets are used in authentication and authorization.

key pair — *See* public/private key pair.

Knowledge Consistency Checker (KCC) — A process that runs on each DC to create the replication topology for the forest.

lastLogon — A user attribute used to track the last time a user logged on to a server. It is not replicated to other DCs. It is available in all levels of domain functionality.

lastLogonTimestamp — A user attribute used to track the last time a user logged on to the network. It is replicated to all DCs in the domain and is only available if the domain is in Windows 2003 mode.

latency — The delay or "lag time" between a change made in one replica being recognized in another.

LDAP name — The name used to refer to an object in an LDAP query. Commas separate the attributes.

LDAP server — Any directory server that supports LDAP queries.

LDAP URL — A uniform resource locator that defines the location of an object in the directory. The protocol used is LDAP://.

LDIFDE.EXE — A utility used to import and export directory information from Active Directory using LDIF files.

LDP.EXE — A utility included in the Windows Support Tools that queries directories using LDAP.

Lightweight Directory Access Protocol (LDAP) — A simplified version of DAP that is easier to implement and is designed for use on the Internet. This standard is managed by the IETF.

Lightweight Directory Interchange Format (LDIF) — A standardized text file format used to import and export directory information.

link — GPOs are assigned to a site, domain, or OU by linking them. A single GPO can be linked to multiple locations.

link table — The portion of NTDS.DIT that stores linked attributes that point to other objects in Active Directory.

linked value replication — An enhanced replication mechanism that allows multivalued attributes to synchronize changes only, rather than the entire attribute. This is enabled for Windows 2003 interim domains and Windows 2003 domains.

local computer policy — A GPO that is stored on the local computer, and is only available on the local computer. It is sometimes called the local GPO.

local group — A group that can be used only in the context of one computer, such as a workstation or member server. Sometimes called a **machine local group**. Local groups do not exist on domain controllers; DCs use a similar type of group called BUILTIN.

local policies — A wide variety of settings for auditing, user rights, and security options.

locked out — An account can be locked out automatically by the system after too many failed log-on attempts. A locked-out account cannot be used. *See also* disabled.

logoff script — A script that runs when a user logs off.

logon script — A script that runs when a user logs on.

Loopback Processing Mode — A computer configuration setting that changes the processing of user configuration settings. When in effect, a user's settings from the GPOs that apply to the computer will be used rather than the GPOs that apply to the user.

loose consistency — A state in which updates to Active Directory have not been replicated to other DCs.

machine local group — *See* local group.

mandatory upgrade — An upgrade that is performed automatically the next time a user runs the application.

Microsoft Metadirectory Services (MMS) — A program that aggregates data from and synchronizes data between multiple directories.

Microsoft Operations Framework (MOF) — A set of documents, guidelines, and models developed by Microsoft to help companies increase reliability, availability, and ease of management and support. MOF provides guidance for the operation of systems, particularly Microsoft infrastructure systems in large enterprises. Visit *http://www.microsoft.com/mof*.

Microsoft Solutions Framework (MSF) — A set of documents, guidelines, and models developed by Microsoft to help companies improve the effectiveness of software or infrastructure development projects. Visit *http://www.microsoft.com/msf*.

mixed mode — A domain is operating in mixed mode if it contains domain controllers running Windows NT 4.0 or earlier. Several options are not available in mixed mode. *See also* native mode.

Movetree — A tool to move objects from one domain to another within the same forest.

multi-master model — The replication model used by Active Directory. Changes to Active Directory objects can be performed on any DC in the domain. Changes are then replicated to other DCs.

multiple-master — A database that has many copies of the same information; each copy is writeable.

MX record — A mail exchanger (MX) resource record specifies the host that can receive SMTP mail for the subdomain.

naming context — A category or division of information within Active Directory. Each naming context is replicated separately.

native mode — A domain can be set to operate in native mode if it has no domain controllers that are running Windows NT 4.0 or earlier. *See also* mixed mode.

NETDOM.EXE — A command line utility used to rename DCs, create trusts, and join computers to a domain.

netlogon share — A default share that is available on all DCs. It is commonly used to hold logon scripts and policies. It is part of the SYSVOL.

No Override — A link setting that prevents policies linked at a lower level from having priority over the settings in the GPO.

non-authoritative restore — A restore of Active Directory used to restore a damaged database. Updates are replicated from other DCs in the domain.

nontransitive trust — A trust between two domains, realms, or forests that cannot be extended or used by other domains in the forest. *See* transitive trust.

Novell Directory Services (NDS) — A cross-platform directory service originally designed for NetWare 4 and up.

Novell NetWare Bindery Service — A security database used by NetWare Version 3 and earlier.

NS record — A name server (NS) resource record is used to delegate authority for a subdomain to another zone or server.

NT File System (NTFS) — Known almost exclusively by its initials, NTFS is the robust file system used by Windows NT, Windows 2000, Windows XP, and Windows 2003 Server. NTFS supports the ability to control and audit access, and uses a journaling system to minimize corruption.

NT LAN Manager (NTLM) — More commonly known by its initials, NTLM is the older network authentication protocol used by all Windows systems prior to Windows 2000. It is still used with Windows 2000, Windows XP, and Windows 2003 Server in certain circumstances.

NTDS.DIT — The Active Directory database.

object owner — Specifically, each object in the directory has an identified owner. More generically, sometimes used to mean data owner.

objectSID — The AD attribute that stores a security principal's security identifier (SID).

offline defragmentation — The process of compacting the Active Directory database to free up space.

one-way trust — A trust relationship where security principals in the trusted domain can use resources in the trusting domain, but not vice versa. Two one-way trusts are equivalent to a two-way trust.

online defragmentation — A process that runs every twelve hours to purge deleted objects from Active Directory.

operating system (OS) — The software that runs the computer itself, such as Windows, Linux, or DOS.

operations master roles — Roles assigned to specific DCs in the forest to prevent conflicts in Active Directory.

operations masters — DCs that manage specific changes to Active Directory that would be impractical to manage using a multiple-master replication model. (Also called Flexible Single Master Operations roles, or FSMO).

optional upgrade — An upgrade that users can run manually, at their discretion.

organizational unit (OU) — An Active Directory object used to contain or group other objects. An OU is a point at which group policy can be applied or permissions delegated.

originating update — A change to Active Directory made by an administrator on a local DC.

parent domain — The domain *parent.company.com* is a parent domain of *child.parent.company.com*. *See* child domain.

partition — *See* naming context.

patch (.msp) — An update to a Windows Installer package.

PDC emulator — A DC that emulates a Windows NT primary DC for domain synchronization and password changes for pre-Windows 2000 DCs. There is one PDC emulator for each domain in the forest.

PDC overloading — This occurs when the first upgraded DC is overloaded with logon attempts from Active Directory-aware clients.

policies — Collections of registry entries that are used to control Windows 9x and Windows NT workstations.

preferred bridgehead server (PBS) — A bridgehead server that has been selected by an administrator, not by an automatic process.

primary name server — The DNS Server where changes can be made to zone data.

printer — An object in Active Directory that represents a print queue (which in Windows NT, 2000, and 2003 is also referred to as a "printer").

propagation dampening — The process of preventing a DC from replicating with other DCs that have already been updated.

provider — An ADSI component that formats ADSI requests for a specific directory service.

Public Key Infrastructure (PKI) — An organized system that issues and manages certificates and key pairs to support the use of public-key cryptography in an organization.

public/private key pair — A set of two mathematically related keys used in public-key cryptographic (or asymmetric encryption). If a message is encrypted with one key, it can only be decrypted with the other. The public key is widely distributed; the private key is closely guarded.

published — A published application appears in Add or Remove Programs and must be installed manually by the user or through document activation.

recover — To repair a database; to return it to a consistent state; to fix corruption therein.

redeploy — Forces an application to redistribute the next time it is used. This is done after an .msi file has been patched.

registry — A security policy setting that defines security permission to be applied to registry entries.

registry hives — Major sections of the Windows registry. Originally, each hive was stored in its own file.

registry key — One or more related settings stored in the Windows registry. A key is similar to a folder in the file system; it can contain other keys or values.

relative distinguished name (RDN) — The part of an LDAP distinguished name that uniquely identifies the object within its parent container.

relative identifier (RID) — A 32-bit number, unique within the domain, that makes up part of a security principal's SID.

relative identifier (RID) master — The DC that is responsible for distributing a range of RID numbers to DCs in the domain. There is one RID master for each domain in the forest.

remote access policies — Policies that are implemented on remote access servers to control access. They require Windows 2000 native-mode domains or better.

Remote Procedure Call (RPC) — The default replication protocol within a site. An RPC connection requires permanent, high-speed connectivity between the sites.

replica — A copy of the Active Directory database stored on a domain controller.

replicated update — A change to Active Directory that was made through replication.

replication — The process by which Active Directory information is copied to multiple domain controllers and conflicts are resolved.

replication boundary — A set of data which is replicated to only specific replicas, or a barrier (physical or logical) that prevents replication. In the case of Active Directory, it is used to describe the fact that domain information is not replicated to other domains (except for attributes sent to the GCs).

replication partner — A DC that replicates with another DC.

replication topology — The set of physical connections used by DCs to replicate directory updates among DCs in both the same and different sites.

RES1.LOG and **RES2.LOG** — Files used for transaction logging if the disk runs out of space.

resources — Any shared piece of equipment or information made available to users on the network, such as file shares, e-mail systems, printers, and the like.

restore — To replace the current copy of a database (or part of it) with a back-up copy made previously.

restricted groups — A security policy setting that defines group membership.

Resultant Set of Policy (RSoP) — A tool used to show how settings are applied, and which GPO supplied a particular setting.

reverse lookup — The process of looking up a host's FQDN using its IP address, which is the reverse of the normal process.

RID master — The operations master for a domain that generates RIDs used by DCs when creating user, group, and computer objects.

roll forward (*or* rolling forward a transaction) — The process used by transactional database systems (including the ESE data engine used by Active Directory) in which a log file is used to ensure that partially completed transactions are fully recorded in the database files.

rollback (*or* rolling back a transaction) — The process used by transactional database systems (including the ESE data engine used by Active Directory) to remove partially completed transactions from the database files.

root domain (".")) — The top of the DNS hierarchy, which delegates authority for all TLDs.

sAMAccountName — A unique attribute of a user object that specifies the username used to log on to the domain. ACTIVE DIRECTORY domains can use the sAMAccountName or the userPrincipalName.

schema master — The DC designated as the schema master has the authority to make changes to the schema in the forest. There is only one schema master per forest.

schema partition — The Active Directory partition that stores definitions, attributes, and rules for all objects in Active Directory. This partition is replicated to all DCs in the forest.

schema table — The portion of NTDS.DIT that stores information on the types of objects that can be created in Active Directory.

scope (group scope) — Groups can have the following scopes: machine local, domain local, global, or universal. A group's scope determines where it can be used in the forest.

secondary name server — An authoritative DNS Server that has a read-only copy of zone data that has been transferred from a primary name server.

Security Configuration and Analysis snap-in — An MMC snap-in that compares a security template with the existing configuration on a computer, or applies a security template to a computer.

security descriptor — A package of binary information associated with an object or a resource, which contains the DACL, SACL, object owner, and related security information. For Active Directory objects, the security descriptor is an attribute of all objects and is called ntSecurityDescriptor.

Security Descriptor Definition Language (SDDL) — A format that efficiently describes SIDs, ACEs, DACLs, SACLs, and related constructs. SDDL is both reasonably compact and easily read by humans.

security group — A group that can be used as a distribution group and can also be included in SACLs and DACLs to control access and auditing.

security identifier (SID) — A binary number that uniquely represents a security principal. For most security principals, the two key components are a domain identifier and a RID that are unique within the domain.

security policy — The collection of user configuration and computer configuration settings located in Windows Settings, Security Settings. These can be updated using security templates.

security principal — An object in the directory to which resource permissions can be granted. In Active Directory, security principals are users, computers, and security groups.

security template — An .inf file that contains settings for some or all of the computer settings in a security policy.

Security Templates snap-in — An MMC snap-in that edits existing security templates or creates new ones.

service owner — A person or team responsible for maintaining and operating the directory service as a whole. The service owner will manage domain controllers and the site structure.

service ticket (ST) — A Kerberos ticket presented to a resource server, allowing it to authorize access.

shared folder — An object in Active Directory that represents a shared folder (a share folder) on the network.

shortcut trust — A manually created trust that improves the efficiency of interdomain authentications within a forest.

shutdown script — A script that runs when a computer is shut down.

SIDhistory attribute — A user attribute that is enabled only in Windows 2000 native-mode domains or better. It is used to track the previous SIDs of migrated users and groups.

Simple Mail Transfer Protocol (SMTP) — A store and forward replication protocol that is generally used when the connectivity between two sites is slow and unreliable.

single sign on — The concept that a user only has to identify himself or herself once (with a password or other security token) to access all resources that he or she has been authorized to use throughout the enterprise's network.

site — One or more well-connected (highly reliable and fast) TCP/IP subnets. A site allows an administrator to configure Active Directory access and replication topology to take advantage of the physical network.

site link — An object that exists in Active Directory to define the logical connection between two sites in a fully routed IP network. Site links are transitive by default.

site link bridge — An object that exists in Active Directory to define the logical connection between three or more sites in a non-routed IP network. A site link bridge may be formed from more than three sites and is manually created. Site link bridges are not transitive.

SOA record — A statement of authority (SOA) resource record provides information about the zone data.

soft recovery — The process of scanning log files to ensure that all transactions have been written to the Active Directory database.

special permission — A specific, granular permission available from the Advanced dialog box when setting permissions.

split administration model — The concept that service ownership and data ownership can be divided.

SRV record — The service locator (SRV) resource record provides a method to locate servers offering specific services in specific sites by using the DNS system.

standard permissions — Permissions shown on the main Security tab in an object's properties that represent the most common permissions granted to users. A standard permission represents several related special permissions.

startup script — A script that runs when a computer boots up.

Structured Query Language (SQL) — A standardized language used to query databases.

subdomain — A subdivision of a DNS.

symmetric keys — Encryption keys that can be used to encrypt or decrypt a message. The same key is used for both encryption and decryption.

system access control list (SACL) — A list of ACEs used to determine which actions are audited or logged for a particular resource.

system services — A security policy setting that defines which services will be started, stopped, or disabled.

system state — A collection of critical operating system files including the registry, Active Directory components, SYSVOL, and start-up files that can be backed up as a single unit on DCs.

SYSVOL share — A folder that is shared by default on DCs. It holds parts of the scripts, administrative templates, and registry files for GPOs.

tattooing the registry — The normally undesired effect of leaving permanent changes in the Windows registry, even after the policy no longer applies.

ticket granting ticket (TGT) — A Kerberos ticket used to request service tickets from a KDC.

tombstone — A marker in the Active Directory database that indicates an object has been deleted.

tombstone lifetime — The time period after which deleted objects are purged from Active Directory. The default is sixty days.

top-level domain (TLD) — A division of the DNS namespace that is divided directly off the root domain. It includes ccTLDs and gTLDs.

transaction — Any addition, deletion, or modification to Active Directory.

transform (.mst) — Customized settings for a Windows Installer package that are applied during installation.

tree — A group of one or more domains in a forest that have a contiguous namespace.

trust relationship (trust) — A link between two domains that allows security principals from one domain to be recognized by the other.

two-factor authentication — Authentication systems that require possession of a physical object (or present a biometric) and a password or PIN.

two-way, transitive trust — A trust relationship between two domains that can also be used by any other domain trusted by either of the domains. For example if *A* trusts *B*, and *B* trusts *C*, then *A* also trusts *C*.

type (group type) — Groups can be either security groups or distribution groups. Distribution groups cannot be included in SACLs or DACLs.

universal group — A group that contains security principals from any trusted domain and can be used in any trusted domain.

up-to-dateness-vector — A list of DC pairs and the last USN received from each pair.

Update Sequence Number (USN) — A unique number assigned to every object and attribute in Active Directory to track changes. Each DC maintains its own set of USNs.

user (user object) — An object in Active Directory that represents a user in your domain. A user is a security principal and may be a person or a network service.

user logon name (pre-Windows 2000) —The Active Directory Users and Computers property that maps to the sAMAccountName attribute.

user logon name — The Active Directory Users and Computers property that maps to the userPrincipalName attribute.

userPrincipalName (UPN) — A unique attribute of a user object that specifies the username that can be used to log on to the domain from clients that support Active Directory.

VBScript (.vbs) — A scripting language that can be used to write logon, logoff, startup, and shutdown scripts. It is based on Visual Basic and is sometimes called Visual Basic Scripting Edition.

Windows 2000 forests — The default forest functional level that can contain Windows NT, Windows 2000, and Windows Server 2003 DCs.

Windows 2000 mixed-mode domains — The default domain functional level for Active Directory that can contain Windows NT, Windows 2000, and Windows Server 2003 DCs.

Windows 2000 native-mode domains — This domain functional level can be enabled when all DCs are Windows 2000 or Windows Server 2003. Enhancements include nesting groups, universal groups, and the SIDhistory attribute.

Windows 2003 interim domains — This domain functional level can contain only Windows NT and Windows Server 2003 DCs. The functionality is the same as Windows 2000 mixed-mode domains, but allows enhanced forest functionality.

Windows 2003 interim forests — This forest functional level can contain only Windows NT and Windows Server 2003 DCs. Enhancements include linked value replication and improved site replication.

Windows 2003 native domains — This domain functional level can contain only Windows Server 2003 DCs. Functional enhancements include lastLogonTimestamp, user passwords on InetOrgPerson objects, and DC renaming.

Windows 2003 native forests — This forest functional level can contain only Windows Server 2003 DCs. Enhancements include forest trusts, domain renaming, redefining schema attributes and classes, converting InetOrgPerson objects to user objects, and dynamic auxiliary classes.

Windows Installer package (.msi) — A Windows application that is installed by the Windows Installer service.

Windows Installer service — A Windows service that is responsible for installing applications using the extensions .msi, .mst, and .msp.

Windows Management Instrumentation (WMI) — The Windows implementation of Web-Based Enterprise Management (WBEM) that uses a common set of interfaces to present information about a computer system in a consistent way across a variety of tools and platforms.

WINNT32.EXE /checkupgradeonly — A command run on an existing Windows server to determine upgrade compatibility.

wireless network (IEEE 802.11) policies — Security policy settings that configure settings for wireless access.

write-ahead log files — A database technology that ensures that any proposed changes to a database are written to a log file on disk before the transaction is confirmed to the originator, and before changes are actually made to the data. If the system fails, all confirmed transactions could be re-created from the log file(s).

X.500 — A standard for directory services created by the International Organization for Standardization (ISO).

X.509 digital certificate — A specially structured electronic document that describes the identity of a person or service. The certificate is digitally signed by its issuer.

.zap file — A text file that is used by Group Policy to install older applications that use a setup.exe file.

zone — A file or database containing DNS records for a subdomain.

zone transfer — The process by which a primary DNS Server sends copies of the zone data to secondary DNS Servers.

Index